4. REVISE

Read through your rough draft five times with *only one thing in mind each time.* Do not recopy the draft unless it becomes impossible to read.

a. Revise for IDEAS.
  __ for depth and honesty
  __ to clarify
  __ to make sure the thesis still fits the paper
  __ to cut irrelevant sections

b. Revise for DETAILS.
  __ add details for support
  __ sharpen details for vividness, concreteness

c. Revise for ORDER.
  __ is each paragraph about one idea
  __ do the paragraphs divide logically
  __ do you need transition words

d. Revise for WORD USE.
  __ conciseness
  __ vivid verbs
  __ metaphors
  __ precise word use
  __ variety in vocabulary

e. Revise for SPELLING, PUNCTUATION, SENTENCE STRUCTURE.
  __ search for errors you made in previous papers
  __ circle all words, punctuation, or sentences you're not 100
     percent sure of and look them up in a dictionary or Chapter 16

Refer to Chapters 7, 8, and 16.

WARNING: WRITING IS NOT THIS ORDERLY. The Sentence General has determined that the writing process is sloppy. A write-by-number approach may be dangerous to your best writing. You are normal if you do not follow this process exactly.

IDEAS AND DETAILS

"Tell as much of the truth
as one can bear, and
then a little more."
—JAMES BALDWIN

IDEAS AND DETAILS

A GUIDE TO COLLEGE WRITING

FOURTH EDITION

M. GARRETT BAUMAN

Monroe Community College

HARCOURT COLLEGE PUBLISHERS

Fort Worth Philadelphia San Diego New York, Orlando Austin San Antonio
Toronto Montreal London Sydney Tokyo

Publisher   **Earl McPeek**
Acquisitions Editor   **Julie McBurney**
Market Strategist   **John Meyers**
Developmental Editor   **Joseph W. Loftin III**
Project Editor   **CJ Jasieniecki**
Art Director   **Sue Hart**
Production Manager   **Cindy Young**

Cover Image: Tony Stone Images

Address for Domestic Orders: Harcourt College Publishers, 6277 Sea Harbor Drive, Orlando, FL 32887-6777. 800-782-4479

Address for International Orders: International Customer Service, Harcourt, Inc., 6277 Sea Harbor Drive, Orlando, FL 32887-6777. 407-345-3800, (fax) 407-345-4060, (e-mail) hbintl@harcourtbrace.com

Address for Editorial Correspondence: Harcourt College Publishers, 301 Commerce Street, Suite 3700, Fort Worth, TX 76102

Web Site Address: http://www.harcourtcollege.com

Harcourt College Publishers will provide complimentary supplements or supplement packages to those adopters qualified under our adoption policy. Please contact your sales representative to learn how you qualify. If as an adopter or potential user you receive supplements you do not need, please return them to your sales representative or send them to:

Attn: Returns Department
Troy Warehouse
465 South Lincoln Drive
Troy, MO 63379

Printed in the United States of America

2 3 4 5 6 7 8 9 016 9 8 7 6 5

Harcourt College Publishers

ISBN: 0-15-507477-6

Library of Congress Catalog Card Number: 00-101372

For Carol
Who lives as I would write

PREFACE

I read Rachel's essay aloud before handing back the papers. It described the night police took her from her abusive father and placed her in a teen group home. The authorities transported her in silence with no word about what was happening. At the home that night, another girl sliced her wrists and then attacked two teenagers. Rachel wished she were back with her father. When I finished reading the paper, the class murmured admiration. The dialogue was sharp, the description of the barren home and the faceless bureaucrats who extended society's impersonal charity was probing and precise, and her theme contrasting a father's abuse with society's legalized abuse was powerful. But the paper was not created by Rachel's attention to correctness or careful word choice. She had been paralyzed by focusing on these in earlier papers. What made this paper so good was Rachel's immersion in her subject—honest remembering, thinking, feeling.

People expect writing instructors to teach word manipulation; yet what makes writing sing—whether a narrative like Rachel's or a tough persuasive essay like Tim Dewart's in this book—are lively ideas and details. When a writer draws from a teeming mass of ideas and details, good words come easier. I believe the single most common cause of writer's block and of poor writing is trying to manipulate words when the writer has nothing much to say. Content is the primary issue of writing.

The goal of this book, therefore, is to help writers activate their brains to stir up more and better ideas and details. Its thesis is simple and straightforward: Good writing combines fresh ideas energized by vivid details. Within this principle, seemingly endless variation occurs. Chapters 1, 2, and 3 and major portions of most chapters are devoted to providing thinking options for writers.

In emphasizing the process of writing, this book takes a no-frills approach to theory; it reduces terminology and the number of steps so students are not intimidated and can see the essentials. Offering options instead of prescriptions empowers writers to try different techniques and liberates teachers from pedagogy. My style is personal in order to let students know there is always a voice behind writing.

Chapters 4 and 5 discuss options for paragraphing and organization. Chapter 6 discusses options for introductions, drafting, and overcoming writer's blocks. Chapters 7 and 8 deal with revision, including advice for peer review and conferences. (The Instructor's Manual discusses peer review strategies and philosophies.) Chapters 9–14 cover the most widely taught types of essays. Chapter 15 consists of a collection of student essays that range from good to excellent on a variety of writing tasks. Chapter 16 is a brief handbook that focuses on the essential rules. The premise of the handbook is that less is learnable; more is ignorable. The Instructor's Manual offers additional discussion ideas and in-class writing suggestions.

Ideas and Details focuses on student writing, including 26 complete student essays and dozens of shorter samples. Each chapter also contains several practice writing assignments that require immediate application of the ideas. These five- to ten-minute exercises encourage students to write, so the professor can spend less time going over the text and more time applying the concepts in hands-on participation. These exercises and the end-of-chapter suggestions often form sequences that lead to essays.

The fourth edition of *Ideas and Details* helps students be more self-reliant outside of class. Most chapters now conclude with a sample student essay and commentary showing how the essay hits and misses the chapter's principles. The commentary is formatted to match the peer review sheets at the end of the chapter, so it also serves as a model for how to write peer reviews. New sample brain teaser lists with commentary explain how to develop these notes into drafts. This edition offers more details on using logic and new peer group activities for persuasion. There are more student essays using argument, literary analysis, and Internet sources.

The biggest change this edition is the complete revision of the chapter on research to reflect the new century. Professor Christopher Otero-Piersante of Monroe Community College has co-authored this chapter with me. We have added suggestions for evaluating the credibility of Web sources, descriptions of computer indexes and reliable Web sites (with Web addresses) for college research. We have helpful hints for doing computerized research, including specific recommendations for finding reliable information through e-mail and newsgroups. The works cited section has, of course, been updated. Professor Otero-Piersante, who began teaching writing with an early edition of *Ideas and Details,* is as committed as I have always been to keeping the book compact, honest, fun to use and accessible to students. That focus has not changed.

I have been blessed by wonderful colleagues, editors, students, and friends during the writing of this book.

I would first like to thank the Monroe Community College Foundation for supporting the early booklet version used at MCC, and I want to especially thank two English Department Chairpersons—James Davis and Judith Hall—for their administrative support and editorial suggestions. Cheryl Desmond and Suzanne O'Brien deserve special thanks for meticulous manuscript preparation beyond the call of duty.

My colleagues Lee Adnepos, Nancy Bailey, Elizabeth Behr, Gail Bouk, Stasia Callan, Carol Cloos, Alan Glossner, William Goglia, Judy Hall, Erika Hartmann Hayes, Robert Herzog, Tony Leuzzi, Thom Metzger, Martin Napersteck, Christopher Otero-Piersante, Elaine S. Rich, Mark Spall, Ann Tippett, Holly Wheeler, and Carolyn Wendell provided detailed critiques and feedback. To my students and other professors' students who sent me letters responding to the book, I am deeply grateful. I want this book to be for students, and they help me see through their eyes.

In transforming *Ideas and Details* through four editions, I thank John Haakenson, Serena Manning, Cindy Young, Brian Salisbury, Sue Hart, Debbie Hardin, Robert H. Watrous, Camille Adkins, Marlane Miriello, Karen Allanson, Stephen T. Jordan, John Meyers, and Julie McBurney—editors at Harcourt—for their encouragement, wise and experienced suggestions, and clarity of intent. Joe Loftin, who guided this edition, epitomizes the spirit of Ideas and Details: when something goes wrong, have faith, be calm and think in a different way. CJ Jasieniecki and Anne Lesser, who scrutinized the production and copy-editing, did their best to whip me to virtue. I thank CJ especially for not believing perfection is impossible. I am deeply indebted as well to my colleagues at other colleges who honestly and meticulously reviewed the book and made it better, sometimes by demolishing walls, sometimes by realigning bricks. They are Therese Brychta, Truckee Meadows Community College; Christopher Gould, University of North Carolina; Tim McLaughlin, Bunker Hill Community College; Michael Miller, Longview Community College; Paula Ross, Gadsden Community College; Pat Kile, Richard Bland College of the College of William and Mary; Betty Bamburg, University of Southern California; Zita Ingham, Arkansas State University; and Paula Guetschow, University of Alaska; Susan A. Schiller, Central Michigan University; Lucinda Coombs, Central Maine Technical College; Jeanne Grinnan, SUNY Brockport; Paula Bennett, Seattle Central Community College; Mary Sottman, South Puget Sound Community College; Lynn McDonie, Antelope Valley Community College; Carolyn Mee, Beaver College; Amy J. Pawl, Washington University; Roxanna Pisiak, SUNY Morrisville; Ellen Tiedrich, Gloucester County College; Arthur Versluis, Michigan State University; and Jeb Wyman, Seattle Central Community College. I thank them all.

—M. Garrett Bauman

Contents

CHAPTER 4
Paragraphs: Ideas and Details in Miniature   63

CHAPTER 5
Order from Chaos: Thesis and Outline   71

CHAPTER 6
The Draft: That Frenzy Near Madness   87

CHAPTER 9

Description: Making Your Audience See   136

CHAPTER 10

Narration: Telling Your Audience a Story   150

CHAPTER 11

Informative Writing: Telling Your Audience What It Doesn't Know   169

CHAPTER 15
A Collection of Student Essays   285

CHAPTER 16
Handbook of English   330

CHAPTER 1

The Honest Writer

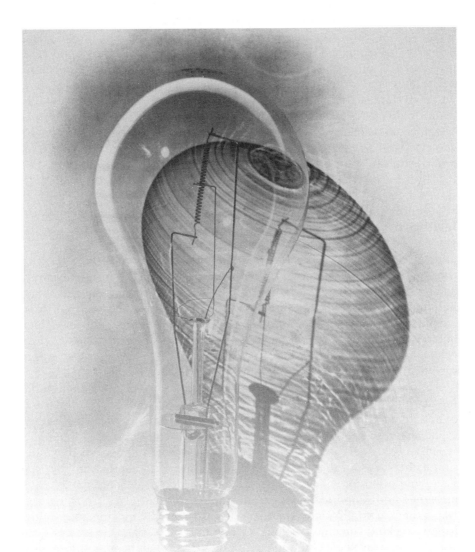

From the cowardice that dares not face new truths,
From the laziness that is content with half truths,
From the arrogance that thinks it knows all truth,
Good Lord, deliver me.

KENYAN PRAYER

Many students enroll for college writing courses with apprehension. Writing is hard work—and there's lots of it in such a course. You probably will have to expose your feelings. And some students say English teachers want to change their style—but isn't style something that's personal?

Let's look at these three issues a little closer. First, **writing *is* hard work,** even for professional writers. All writers have crumpled papers or made trips to the refrigerator when the words refused to cooperate. Sometimes, I seem to change ten words for every five I write. But writing can be made easier by practicing and by learning some shortcuts that this book and your professor will suggest. Compare learning to write to learning to play tennis or the guitar or learning to drive a car. How graceful were you the first time you tried these activities? And when you moved up to the next level of difficulty, didn't it seem almost as hard as starting over? Writing is at least this complicated; there are 750,000 words in the English language—750,000 choices. Your professor hopes to make you practice as hard and often as *both* of you can stand it. For research shows that the best predictor of success in college is effort. Not IQ, not the college you attend, not your SAT scores, age, sex, or race. Take comfort in that. *You* control your own effort.

Second, what about the papers in which you might have to **expose your feelings or ideas** that may sound strange to others? If you can open up, you'll learn one great truth about writing: *Telling the truth as you really see it is the only way a writer ever says something worth reading.* Alice Walker, the author of *The Color Purple,* writes openly about being blind in one eye and about growing up in a poor family. She says she was so embarrassed about her "crooked eye" that for six years she did not raise her head, for fear people might notice the "blob" on it. In life these things are embarrassing, but in writing, they make us feel and understand. A reader *wants* a writer to give of himself or herself—to know the writer's truth. As readers we respect such truth, since all of us have wounds that words may heal.

Almost all mediocre writers share two qualities—they're vague and they're half-hearted. This is not intentional, of course. Perhaps they want to be safe. Perhaps they fear making mistakes or saying something unacceptable and so choose a vague, comfortable half-truth. A writer should be sensitive to readers' reactions; however, the writer's first job is to create stimulating ideas for the reader to consider. You cannot do that timidly. Besides, your professor will be grading you on how forcefully your opinions are presented and supported—not on your opinions themselves. Your teacher wants the real you to emerge, and if you want to write moving, interesting papers, the kind you enjoy reading, trust your professor and classmates with your story. Zora Neale Hurston's mother, a poor black woman of the last century, told all her children, "Jump at the sun." Zora, who later became a great writer, commented, "We might not land on the sun, but at least we would get off the ground." Use this course to jump at the sun.

Third, will your professor try to **change your style?** Let's hope so! You had a writing style when you were 14. Would you like that same style to represent you on professional reports, letters, and college papers? Your style has changed as you've matured, for change accompanies all growth. Your professor will encourage further change and maturity by asking you to experiment with a variety of styles and techniques so you can find your best.

Your professor wants you to become the writer *you* want to be. And like all intellectual activity, writing should make a person feel more alive, growing. Consider that the great novelist Marcel Proust was still revising his work on his deathbed, hopeful, alive for the perfect word that would, as he said, "move the world." Near the end he revised a death scene because he saw more honestly how the character felt now that he was in the same predicament. Perhaps a writer ought to be an optimist, hoping that in the next words, the next sentence, the next idea, something will make a difference to a reader. If you don't stretch yourself to say something beyond what you already know, the writing will be flat. College should be a great stretching experience, whether you are 18 or 68. You really don't know how far you can stretch. Perhaps there is a novel or speech in your future; perhaps a letter to the newspaper that will change someone's life; perhaps a report that will get you promoted; or a letter that will calm a family feud. One thing is sure: Safe, predictable ideas won't change either you or your readers.

Trying different styles also prepares you to write for different audiences. Your tone must differ when writing to an angry customer, to an admissions officer you don't know, or to your favorite cousin. When you choose simpler words to speak to a child, technical terms to discuss a research project with a professor, or eliminate slang when speaking to your grandparents, you are adapting style to your audience. Which is the real you? *All* of them. In being sensitive to your audience, you stretch yourself into a person encompassing many different people.

As with learning any complicated skill, writing can paralyze you at first. I can't do all that at once, you think. You're right. That's why when people learn something new they sometimes seem to get worse for a while. Often this is only an illusion. You may simply start to set higher goals for yourself that you must work up to. If you hit the target every try, it's too close. Some assignments and techniques in this book may seem artificial at first, but with practice they will become part of your unconscious process. If I write for a while without giving an example—as I have been—a little twitch reminds me. At other times a subconscious detector tells me I'm stamping out the same bland verbs over and over. But every writer has to struggle *consciously* to learn these things before they become automatic. This book will focus on the essential concepts you need.

▲ **PRACTICE 1-1:** On the first page of your notebook, complete this sentence: "One hard aspect about writing that I'm going to work on this semester is . . ."

A PROFESSIONAL ATTITUDE

The writing you do in this course should be considered professional writing. It is real writing for a real purpose, not practice exercises. I say this because nothing you learn in college will be as important to your professional success as the ability to write well, no matter what career you choose. You may be able to land a first job after college without strong writing ability, but promotions and recognition will get harder at each level. Engineers, businesspeople, nurses, counselors, technicians, and teachers write far more than you might think—and always there is more writing as careers advance. The computer age has made writing more important than ever. The fax, e-mail, and the Internet are replacing the telephone and the personal visit.

Let me use as an example a friend of mine who is not a college graduate. Rick is a carpenter—a physical labor job, right? That was true as long as Rick worked for a boss. But he wanted to be independent, keep more of the profits, and do more creative carpentry. So he established a small, three-person building company—and found himself writing more and more and hammering less and less. He writes letters to inspectors *explaining* variations in housing codes; he writes *persuasive* complaint letters to customers and suppliers when he feels cheated; he writes accurate and vivid *descriptions* of additions or remodelings so customers can visualize them; he's become sensitive to audience, tone, and word choice, knowing they sell his houses as much as his reputation for craftsmanship. He's come to realize his business success has a lot to do with his success as a writer.

From a career standpoint, you owe it to yourself to learn to write effectively for these reasons:

- A boss may avoid asking you to do work that would otherwise enhance your career if you cannot write well. Although no one may ever say so, poor writing embarrasses both the writer and the company.
- Writing well makes you self-reliant; you don't have to depend on a secretary to fix your work. You can control your own destiny.
- A boss or client feels rapport when reading clear, organized writing, but alienated reading stuffy, disorganized, or vague reports and letters.
- Good writers create new ideas; think of the benefits this brings a career. In Chapters 2 and 3, you will learn to write on almost any topic thrown at you in college or at a job.

Robert Maynard, publisher of *The Oakland Tribune,* once said, "When we arm someone with the skill of written expression, we have given him or her a lifelong key to advancement." Almost any business or professional person today will put writing ability high on the list of what is desired in an employee. Many rank it above even courses in your career field.

Never underestimate the usefulness of good writing. I usually ask my students to do some real professional writing tasks for real audiences, and some have met with the kind of success that makes them realize the power the written word gives them. Rob was upset at the city law forbidding people to keep cars without license plates in their driveways. He'd gotten a ticket. For a class paper, he wrote a proposal to have the law changed so people who couldn't afford big garages could keep a rust-bucket car for the winter and a cleaner car for the summer without paying for two license plates and two insurance policies. The city council agreed and changed the law. Darlene, a single parent returning to college, had a male boss who made sexist remarks and discriminated against her in assigning tasks. She wrote a tactful letter of complaint to him (it's easy to blast someone and get fired). Her letter was so well explained and supported that the man not only treated her better, but admitted it opened his eyes to the way other working women were mistreated. These are examples of professional writing in its broadest sense.

Your college writing must show professional polish. This means not just the kind of grammar and spelling you'd want on your résumé, but also a professional attitude toward ideas, details, and honesty. Professionals revise (literally, re-see). Your professor may challenge you to look again at words, ideas, and details in an effort to help you think more professionally. This is natural; expect it.

Some college writing assignments in courses across the curriculum may seem boring or irrelevant to you. A paper on "Plato's Concept of Justice" in a philosophy course or "Prison Conditions in the Nineteenth Century" in Criminology may not excite you. But a person with a professional outlook will be able to get into almost any topic assigned. If you believe the world is interesting, you will find interesting things to think and say. If you expect boredom, you will probably find it. While I cannot promise this will always be true, most topics are made exciting by the concentration and curiosity the writer brings to them. A professional thinker takes this approach.

Why does college require so much writing? Because you learn more about a subject by writing about it. Studies have consistently shown that you will retain three to five times as much knowledge by writing about a topic than by simply reading or hearing about it. You make ideas part of you by actively describing them in your own words. If you really want to learn the material in your psychology or biology course, don't just highlight the book. Write out a few paragraphs after finishing your reading.

▲ **PRACTICE 1-2:** Think of a financial or job situation in your life now in which a strong letter might solve a problem or do you some good. Who would you write to and why?

◆ THE STRUGGLE AGAINST SILENCE

Personal reasons to write well are as important as professional reasons. You can write to touch someone you care about. You can write to discover who you are and what you believe. You can write to preserve important moments in your life. Writing for yourself also means you are taking control of events, making your life more your own. As Carlos Fuentes once said, "Writing is a struggle against silence." The writer does not just accept life, but works to understand and respond to it.

Chances are, in trying to stretch you, your professor will require both professional and personal writing. But most college writing will require a deeper honesty than you may have been asked for to this point. Not that people try to be dishonest. What I mean is that in college it may not be enough to just write what you *already know or already feel* about something; instead you must *discover more* about your subjects. It is dishonest to think that what you already know and believe about a subject is the entire truth. Sometimes you will discover new ideas through research, but many times they can come through looking closer at your own experiences and feelings—probing deeper into what you may have accepted too easily in the past.

I recall a student who was in a wheelchair. Tom, in his late 30s, had been shot three times in the lower spine, shattering two vertebrae and leaving him unable to walk. This happened in 1973 during the Vietnam War. Tom had spent many years in veterans' hospitals. He decided to attend college, even though he had been a high school dropout. He sat in the front corner of the classroom—isolated—wearing purple and silver mirror sunglasses that hid his eyes. The few things he said were sarcastic snaps, and the other students shrank away from him. He was in the class but not part of it. His papers were poor in grammar, but even worse to me, they were bland. "Nothing ever happened to me in my whole life but one thing," he said after I returned a D-minus paper to him. "I don't care about this stuff."

"So write about that one thing that did happen to you," I said.

"No way!" Tom said. "I don't want to. If I do, a lot will come out I don't want out again. It's no good. You don't know what I might do if I get upset." During the semester Tom had trouble with the police regularly. Once he showed me a bruised knee he said the police had given him during a brawl when he refused to leave a buddy's room in the spinal ward of the hospital.

"You're kind of proud of that, aren't you?" I asked.

He admitted he was. "I guess I like fighting cops."

"Do you know why?" I asked.

It was then that Tom reached up and slid off his mirror sunglasses, slowly, reluctantly. I suppose he wanted to see me better, but I saw his eyes for the first time. They were old, exhausted eyes. "Yeah," he answered, "I know why."

After this, Tom slowly began exploring his inner landscape—his own heart. It is the most wonderful and terrifying subject any of us have. Tom wrote several papers that erupted, that gripped his readers. He read one to the class, and people sat near him to be in his workshop group so they could find out more. His writing made him real to them, and they wanted to know what he'd been through. They didn't pity him; they simply hungered for his experience, because real writing makes a reader live more too. He explored the day he was wounded, what Vietnam meant to him, the father who deserted him, his own son he hadn't seen since becoming disabled, a girl he loved. He made us laugh when he described how scared walking people are of those in wheelchairs, how when he noticed the look of fear on them he'd pretend he was going to run them over. Tom's life poured out on paper, and the class read it and cared. Tom taught them they could write for real, and some people who had previously hidden behind safe topics took a chance too.

Tom turned his pain into power and freed himself. He'd feared going over these events because they hurt, but he learned that holding them inside hurt him again and again, while they lost terror and control of him as he shaped them into words. Tom still had a long way to go at semester's end, but he told me, "At least my mind's started walking again."

Tom's is an exceptional story of self-discovery, but most writing teachers can tell stories about how writing has freed writers from self-imposed handicaps.

▲ **PRACTICE 1-3:** In half a page, tell about a time when your own habits, fear, or laziness held back your growth as a person. Remember Tom.

HONESTY

Let me reinforce this point another way. In college most of your papers will be essays. The word *essay* comes from the French *essai*, which means *to try* or *to attempt*. Michel de Montaigne, a French writer who in the sixteenth century invented the term to describe what he wrote, saw the essay as a trial of an idea, an attempt to express something as clearly and honestly as possible. He was reacting to the fake, predictable, and overidealistic writing of his peers. For de Montaigne writing was liberation—a way of freeing himself from what he was supposed to think. Not only society, but our own habits, fears, and laziness prevent us from seeing and thinking freshly and honestly. For instance, when we become accustomed to seeing work as duty and drudgery, we may block out the pleasures work gives us. We may forget that we work because we love someone or that work makes us stronger, more capable people and makes us proud.

When de Montaigne tried an idea, he wasn't satisfied until he turned it upside down, cross-examined it mercilessly, wrung every last possible drop of truth from it, and exposed every possible half-truth or lie hidden in it. He even cast a medallion that he wore on a cord around his neck. It read *"Que sais-je?"* or "What do I know?" This curious phrase changes meaning as you emphasize "I," "what" and "know." See if you can discover those different meanings.

De Montaigne's unrelenting honesty comforts me. He makes me believe humans can find truth, can write it, and perhaps can even live by it. Use this book and your writing course to free yourself of old ways and dead notions and to find ones you can live by today.

Here are some examples of things we think we know but don't question carefully. Let's start with a cold scientific fact: Water boils at 212 degrees

Fahrenheit. It's one of those things you memorize in elementary school. But water does not boil at 212 degrees on a mountaintop or below sea level. Nor if it's salt water or carries dissolved minerals. Nor in a vacuum. The truth is more complicated than the simple fact I'd like to believe. Besides, how do I know it's 212 degrees? I've never tested it.

Next, consider this story. In 1969, I watched live television pictures of the first man stepping on the moon. I saw Neil Armstrong's boots kick up gray lunar dust as he planted a flag there. I went outside and stared at the pale moon and wondered if I'd ever walk there. The next day I went to my summer job at the warehouse and asked people what they thought about the moon landing.

They laughed. "You really believe a man's on the moon?" one guy said. "It's all made up in Hollywood."

"Sure," another said. "You go to college to believe *that?*" I sputtered and argued feebly for a few minutes, then gave up. Did I *know* men were on the moon? No. And I didn't know enough to prove it to these people, most of whom had not graduated from high school. In fact, how did I know it wasn't a Hollywood trick? I do *believe* men landed there in 1969, but back then I was basically taking the government and the media's word for it.

My point is simply that a lot of what we think of as factual truth is based on blind trust of authority and our own prejudices and preconceptions without firsthand observation, hard logic, or research. We hear and we believe.

▲ **PRACTICE 1-4:** What are two ideas or facts you accept only because you have been told to believe them? Try for one from your personal life (something family or friends have told you) and one from social, historical, or scientific areas. Raise questions about them.

Let me end this chapter with a few ideas that are, I hope, as honest and direct as I can be about writing. First, in your personal and professional life there will be times when you will be asked to use language to comfort sleeping minds—to reassure and soothe your listeners with predictable statements. This is civilized dishonesty. We all do this. But it is not the best that is in us. Use this course to strive for a deeper honesty, one that does more than avoid the obvious lie—one that tries to touch the heart of a topic. In the long run, these will be the only things you write that will matter to you or anyone else. **The enemy in college (and life) is not other people or our duties, but our own passivity.** To listen without speaking, to follow the feet ahead of us instead of peeking behind the blackberry bushes—that is our enemy. Each half-truth we accept or repeat without really putting it on trial shrinks our intellect. Intensity expands our intellect—and our well-being. Psychologists like M. Scott Peck say that an intense, sometimes painful, pursuit of truth leads to happiness and mental health, while unhappiness and mental illness are more likely to come to those who passively accept things as they *seem* to be.

Second, talent in writing is overrated. Ninety-nine percent of all writing tasks do not require natural genius, just a reasonable intelligence and a willingness to work. You *can* do that. *Will* you? Annie Dillard, a Pulitzer Prize winner, goes so far as to say, "There is no such thing as talent. . . . We all start out dull and weary and uninspired. . . . Genius is the product of education." She says people want to believe in genius because they can blame their genes instead of working to improve themselves. So don't begin with excuses. Your professor will not ask you to write Pulitzer Prize–winning books. But if you work hard, you will write better than you think you can. Teaching yourself to write or speak well or to do any task well is often teaching yourself to find what is interesting in the job at hand. **The effort to revise also separates good writers from the pack.** The funny thing is, anybody can revise a paper one grade better with an hour's work. Few do. And revision separates the really honest writer—the one who will put his first thoughts on trial—from the writer who chooses a lesser honesty.

Third, **write for a real purpose to a real audience.** When your writing course allows, write your papers about topics that matter to you and imagine sending them to a particular person. Write your paper on alcoholism to your friend's alcoholic father; write your paper on energy taxes to your senator or to the owner of a local trucking company or even to the pollution-sensitive owl in your backyard; write your paper on prenatal care to your sister and her new husband. If you cannot think of an audience, imagine that listening carefully as you write is someone who is not judging you but rather who needs help visualizing your ideas, asks questions, wants to learn something from your paper.

Most students want simple formulas for writing. I'd like to give them to you, but they don't exist. Good writing balances rules and creative freedom. This book will strive for clear guidelines, but remember that rules often rule out great possibilities.

Highlights of Chapter 1

- Writing courses create three major apprehensions: That it will be hard work; that you may have to expose your feelings; and that your style may change.
- All of these can be positive if you see them properly. Learning a difficult skill makes you a valuable person; exposing feelings may give you more control over the events of your life and may touch other people; and being open to new styles helps your writing mature and reach new audiences.
- This course is an introduction to a professional attitude toward writing that will advance your career for years to come.
- The personal writing you do will stretch you and give you the intellectual independence de Montaigne advocated.
- Both types of writing require de Montaigne's energetic engagement in the trial of an idea. What do you know?

Writing Suggestions and Class Discussions

1. In your opinion, what makes a piece of writing outstanding? List four or five qualities and star the most important. Bring in a short, published example to read to the class, pointing out specific sections you believe are particularly good.

2. *Try,* in de Montaigne's sense of the word, any current issue (the Mideast, abortion, or genetic engineering, for examples). Suspend judgment and biases. Instead, focus on honest questions and ask "what do I know?" after each comment you make. Play around, and take all sides.

3. Write several paragraphs describing your relationship with a past teacher of writing. Which guidelines for writing do you remember best? What did you like or not like about that teacher's approach to writing?

4. Honesty Assignment: Briefly describe an embarrassing moment and one thing it taught you that you may not have realized at the time. (One of mine was during my first lecture to a large college class. I leaned forward on the lectern—to show how relaxed I was—and the entire table and lectern collapsed with a crash, my notes floating down amid the class's roaring. It knocked some of the stuffiness out of me and made me realize how tentative my position in front of the class was.)

5. Honesty Assignment: Think about one weird idea you have—something not socially acceptable today, something even your friends would think strange. Explain it in one paragraph.

6. Write a "personals" ad for yourself—but be 100 percent honest about who you are and whom you seek.

7. Honest writing often balances two realities—our inner, private one and an outer, public one. Write a paragraph or two about an intensely important moment of your life as honestly as you can. Then write, again as honestly as you can, how someone else might have seen your experience differently.

8. How will you use writing in your future? List all the kinds of professional writing you may face in your career. Be specific about whom you will be writing to and why.

9. Make a list of ten things you really care about, that are important in your life. They may be people, ideas, beliefs, objects, goals, or whatever else matters. Write one or two sentences about each. Your teacher may ask you to share these with the class or a small group and help you develop them into topics for future papers.

10. Think about a person who died or passed permanently out of your life. In freewriting style, not worrying about grammar or sentence structure, record what you remember of that person. Don't stop until you have several insights that you didn't know before you started. Stretch your knowledge and feelings.

11. How will you use writing in college? List five writing tasks you will have to do in your major field and in other courses while in college.

12. Read pages 286–290 on the journal and write a journal entry.

13. Read pages 311–320 on the professional letter and write a brief professional letter to a business, government, or college official.

14. In peer groups, take one of the following clichés and test it for honesty. First, decide what the quotation means by paraphrasing it in your own words. Then give an example of how it might be true. Then explain why it might be an incomplete truth. Remember, your job is to discover how much truth is in the saying, not to simply label it true or false.

    "What goes around, comes around"
    "Every cloud has a silver lining"
    "You can't teach an old dog new tricks"
    "You can't tell a book by its cover"

15. Read the following essay that was written by a student in response to writing suggestion 3.

CHICKEN AT WEGMAN'S

Jennifer M. Horton

She always arrived after the bell rang. Of course we chattered and shuffled our papers and sat on our desks, but when she appeared in the doorway we all settled.

"Oh, you are so good to me," she would purr in her Lithuanian accent, for she knew she was the only teacher to whom we granted such respect.

To look at her, one might expect to see her buying grapes or yellow daffodils at a fruit stand. She was a big woman with a round, wise face. Her almond-shaped eyes were sharp, icy blue. They were eyes that had seen much of life--her family had escaped the Soviet Union during World War II, but her father and brother had been killed along with millions of other refugees. She had high cheek-bones and straight, short gray hair. When she spoke, her consonants were sharp but not harsh. They gently clicked and ticked across her teeth. Her vowels were slow and smooth, and she rolled her r's when she got excited. She had no use for an extravagant wardrobe. Simple skirts and sweaters suited her best, but they were always warm pinks, bright blues, or mustard yellows.

Mrs. Litvinas was our Advanced Placement English teacher during our senior year of high school. Most of us had come to the course on recommendation from previous teachers. Most of us had understood the intricate books we had read. Most of us could write a well-developed essay explaining the political symbolism of Madame DeFarge's crocheting. We joined the A.P. elite, but few of us expected what was to come.

We learned to be alert in her class, never knowing what morsels we might find in her lectures. She challenged us every day to work harder, learn more, and be better than we had been the day before. "Today you will write for me," she would say as she passed out the assignments. "You will tell me how Faulkner uses time as a structuring device in the first half of his book." Some of us cringed silently; others moaned audibly. "Thank you, Mrs. Litvinas," she prompted us. "Thank you for helping me to become a better person."

"Thank you, Mrs. Litvinas," we all mumbled in singsong, then laughed at ourselves.

I can still hear her. Each day she passed out an in-class writing assignment, she would plod up and down the aisles, saying, "If you have not read, you will write on your paper, 'My character needs improvement.' When you finish that, you may sit quietly and contemplate your immortal soul. Do not philosophize! I do not care to read your little philosophies. I want to know if you have read the book. You must read the books in order to pass my class. If you do not read, you will never survive me. I will break you!" Her voice still rings in my mind.

Sometimes she'd mock our papers by reading in a nasal tone, "And so therefore I believe that I think that in conclusion . . ." and pound her fist on the podium. "No! Don't insult me with that garbage. We both know you can do better. All of you."

When our papers were returned, more often than not they were covered with red markings: a "NO!" beside one passage, a triumphant "YES!" beside another, or perhaps an "I know where you stopped reading."

In class she would say, "Be glad there is still room for improvement. Life would be so dull if you were already perfect." When we discussed the "lock theory" in <u>Darkness at Noon</u> or Faulkner's southern code of honor or Ionesco's social criticism, she would slice the air and say things like this: "Nothing is a throw-away. Only a small writer would put that sentence there for no reason. You must drink every word in. You must read it over and over until it becomes part of you." And so we drank and drank until we overflowed with Shakespeare and Conrad and Chekhov and Forster. We became, as Mrs. Litvinas would say, "masters of the craft."

Strangers might think Mrs. Litvinas mean, maybe crazy, but those of us who knew her loved her. We waited for her philosophical wanderings. "You must be with people who make you more," she insisted with a broad sweep of arm. "None of this drinking beer at parties. Get a bottle of wine and take your mother on a picnic. You have got to realize, ladies and gentlemen, that there is more to life than chicken at Wegman's" [a local supermarket].

This was her favorite line and we all knew what she meant about what was important in life. Those of us whom she touched with her strength, knowledge, wisdom, and love went out into the world perhaps a little better prepared to face the challenges that life offers.

Discussion/Writing

1. What makes this essay honest and not fake praise of a teacher?
2. How do you react to Mrs. Litvinas's teaching methods? Honestly look for both good and bad aspects.
3. Describe a teacher you had whose strong personality left you with mixed feelings. Balance your honest gut feelings with an honest, objective evaluation.

CHAPTER 2

The Two-Part Secret
of Good Writing

Ideas and Details

Eternity is in love with the productions of time.

WILLIAM BLAKE

You probably didn't expect the best kept secret of writing to be given away so soon, but here it is. All successful writers—whether businesspeople or professionals—have this ability, and many writers who have serious flaws in other aspects of their writing can get by with just this one skill: **the ability to combine ideas and details.** Another way of saying this is that the successful writer must continually move between the general and the specific.

Ideas and details are the heart of your writing. They alone cause readers to say, "This is great!" or "Let's take this to the board of directors." No one I know ever received an award, a job offer, a kiss, or a promotion for perfect spelling or punctuation. Readers of magazine essays, love letters, and business reports care about interesting ideas brought to life with vivid details, and that is what your reader will pay attention to unless distracted by poor spelling and organization.

Let's look at what *ideas* and *details* mean, why they're both necessary, and how you can work with them comfortably.

 ## IDEAS

An idea summarizes; it concludes, highlights, or generalizes. It's usually abstract. Here's an example to study. Thomas Paine, who wrote many books and pamphlets in support of democracy at the time of the American Revolution, once said:

> Where there is bread, there is one's fatherland.

If your first reaction to this sentence was like mine, you found it vague or confusing. Most ideas take time to unravel. I would loosely interpret Paine's sentence to mean that people's patriotism and loyalty are given to those who satisfy their material needs. Let me share some other thoughts that occurred to me while thinking about this. If a government stops supplying our needs, do we become less loyal? Is our love of country really disguised self-interest? I wonder if the loudest patriots are the wealthiest? Would Americans trade their precious freedoms and Bill of Rights for bread if times were tougher? Is company loyalty no more than fear of losing a paycheck? I don't *think* I'd care less for my own family and friends if they didn't do things for me, but would I? Are people that self-centered?

I'm not sure if I agree with Paine's idea, but notice what's happening. *My comments are already moving away from the general to the specific.* Paine's idea stands above specifics. It can apply to many possible situations and leaves room for readers to supply their own examples. But without moving to specifics, its meaning is vague. In the original essay this quotation was tied to specific details—Paine used it to summarize some of his reasons why a people should have the right to revolt against a king and be free—when the king did not feed, clothe, educate, or protect them—as happened in 1776. Like any good idea, the details gave it vitality.

▲ **PRACTICE 2-1:** Below are four more idea sentences. Any could be the seed from which an entire essay grows. Examine them carefully to see what *expectations* a reader would have after reading them. What kind of details does the writer need to explain them?

- Robin Williams may be the funniest person alive.
- Technology today is humanity's greatest hope and greatest threat.
- Growing up on a farm prepared me for life.
- The Internet is not just a communication tool; it changes our work, families, and values.

 ## DETAILS

Let's look at *details:*

A young man strolls a sandy beach at dawn, picking his way along the line of discarded shells, seaweed, and crab legs brought by high tide. He picks up several souvenirs. He plans to display them on his bookshelf when he returns from vacation. A fisherman casts in the surf a few yards off, and nearby is a pool of water left by the retreating tide. The young man notices a fish in the tidal pool.

"It's a bottlenose skate," the fisherman says. "A lot of them get trapped by the tide."

The fish is flat like a flounder, white on the bottom, brown on top with a long, whip-like tail. It thrashes the water.

"Skates are garbage fish," the fisherman says. "They compete with the game fish." The young man looks closer.

The pool is sinking into the sand and the skate gasps. It thrashes, searching for deeper water, then settles into a three-inch deep puddle. "A half-dozen get stranded every day," the fisherman says. "People don't eat them. Look—" he gestures down the beach where gulls are pecking at another skate, which is still alive.

The young man bends, touches the skate. It's slimy. He tries to grasp it, but his hand slips off.

"All right," the fisherman says, setting his pole in its holder. "Get the other side." Between them, the men drag the skate down to the surf. The skate jerks free as it hits water. It surges, tail splashing. The young man's souvenirs jangle into the frothy water and are lost.

The skate disappears.

Notice that this little story is a collection of sights, sounds, and touches. It is easier to visualize the first time through than Thomas Paine's sentence because it is concrete and specific. We're not talking about dozens of possibilities here, but of one day at one beach with one fish. **Details can be facts, descriptions, stories, examples.** They give us life close up, one piece at a time. Ideas give us life from the mountain top, in grand scale. Details make a reader visualize, so what you write seems present and real. **An**

idea does something else for a reader—it gives a sense of purpose and more significance to the details than first meets the eye. You might consider details and ideas to be sight and insight—the physical presence and the mental meaning. Readers need both to feel satisfied with a piece of writing.

The story about the skate might end as it is, leaving the reader to figure out what insight is behind these details. Fiction usually does not tell, while narrative essays often make the meaning clearer by climaxing the story with a generalization. Let me suggest some. One thing seems clear—the young man understands better the life that inhabits his souvenirs. In a sense both men have been fishing. Has the older man been resensitized to the lives he takes for sport, or is he just being polite? The loss of the shells in the frothy sea and the fact that gulls eat many skates each day suggest it is futile to save one life. Is it?

Notice that we had to move to details with Thomas Paine's idea to clarify and develop it. The story about the skate was a collection of details; to clarify and develop it, we must move toward ideas that give meaning and purpose to the details. Alone, neither is enough.

Read the following, and try to figure out what each paragraph needs to satisfy a reader.

1. Is it fair for a woman who gets raped and pregnant to have to deliver her rapist's baby? Then there's the possibility she may be in danger of dying herself. But there are lots of women who use abortion like birth control and don't give a damn that a little life is involved. And I personally know of at least one anti-abortion protester who had an abortion herself! On the other hand, if we say a woman has total rights over her own body, doesn't that also give her the right to use drugs, be a prostitute, or commit suicide?

2. Education today needs to be more personal. Too much that goes on in schools is theoretical and professional; students and teachers both forget they're dealing with people because they focus too much on the *job.*

The overall affect of 1 is confusing; it has interesting examples, but it's difficult to figure out what the writer's main point is. The writer needs to help pull details together with *a unifying idea.* Example 2 is just the opposite. It has a clear, forceful idea, but hasn't come to life with details to illustrate it. See if you can complete paragraph 2 with vivid details from your experience and provide an idea that would tie 1 together. As you write, don't hesitate to *add details or change the idea a bit.* That is how writing gets better!

Aside from the specific facts and skills college teaches, it also aims to move you smoothly into a professional mode of thinking. The amateur thinker thinks only when inspired. It makes that person unreliable. Wouldn't you be shocked if a doctor, teacher, or accountant said, "Sorry, I'm uninspired today." We expect professionals to be able to think as part of their jobs.

This is especially true of writing tasks. You may not be able to write a poetic masterpiece every day, but you should be able to put together a clear, interesting piece of writing almost any day you're asked. We'll be discussing other techniques for doing this throughout the book, but the first and most important is *learning to think in both general ideas and specific details in each writing task*. Ideas and details enhance each other, build each other up. They create inspirations.

The professional thinker (and you should see yourself this way) tests ideas against details and draws ideas from details. If your employer asks, "Do you think we ought to start a day-care center for company employees?" you've been given an idea to work with. Your first step is to test it against some details—how many employees would bring their children to the center, how much will it cost, is there room, and a dozen other specific questions. This should help develop the original idea.

If your boss says, "We get 40 percent more damaged merchandise returned from our shipments of widgets to New England than anywhere else in the country," you've been given a fact (a detail) in search of an idea to explain it. Could it be transport (bad New England roads); personnel (a truck driver on that route who throws boxes); manufacturing (widget psychopaths on the assembly line); or something else?

▲ **PRACTICE 2-2:** For each of the following concrete details, create an idea that draws a conclusion or generalizes:

- In 1971, 62 percent of new college freshmen said they thought an important part of college was to "develop a philosophy of life." In 1999, 28 percent agreed.
- There are many more cells in each human body than there are known stars in the universe.
- Only accidents kill more college students than suicides.
- 2+2=4 (Hint: The most obvious details often lead to the most profound conclusions.)

WHAT MAKES A GOOD IDEA

What makes a good idea? The best ideas are original, but since true originality is rare, your teachers will probably be happy if you present an **unusual or fresh idea** and avoid clichés and commonplace ideas. Fine, but how do you get unusual ideas? It's easy to grab the first idea that comes to mind. The problem is, those ideas come to everybody else's mind first too. Chances are, if you take the first idea off the top of your head, you'll be saying something trite and dull. Look at your facts or story more closely— what truth might be lurking there that isn't obvious? Here's an example. When asked to tell a story about themselves, many students write about being in car crashes. Ninety percent of the time the professor can predict the theme or idea—bad news for a writer. After the wounded are put in the ambulance and the tow truck hauls the once-sparkling car to the dump, the writer will say that he or she has learned how serious driving is and will drive more carefully in the future.

That may be true, but the essays you remember say things like this: "Being in an accident made me realize how close I am to death *all* the time and not really aware of it. A loose bolt, a piece of glass, a flying rock, one drink too many, and I'm gone forever." If the writer then goes on to speculate how people block this out of their minds and still drive, the writer is brewing a good idea.

▲ **PRACTICE 2-3:** Think of one or two additional meanings to be drawn from car accidents.

Being **brutally honest** helps make good ideas. Social pressure to say the acceptable thing and fear of embarrassment or of being different hold back fresh ideas more than a lack of brain power. No one deliberately tries to come up with boring ideas, but too often we censor ourselves. There will be more on this in the next chapter, which is devoted to getting ideas. But for now ask if your idea has an unusual twist or slant to it. If not, dig deeper.

A second aspect to a good idea is **complexity,** because the truth is usually complicated. One way to make your ideas deeper is to **develop several competing ideas.** Writing seems shallow if the writer implies there's only one way of seeing the topic. If you believe in simple explanations, I'd like to discuss selling my old car to you. To develop the habit of deeper honesty, force yourself to look for ideas that compete with your first ones. Put them on trial. This means you must dig up ideas that potentially contradict your first idea or offer alternatives to it. For example, if I believe young teenagers try drugs because of peer pressure, I should look for competing explanations before I plunge into a blind defense of that idea. Less parental supervision, films emphasizing risk taking and pleasure seeking, and despair about getting a job in an era of business downsizing are ideas that compete with peer pressure to draw teens to drug use. Can you think of one more competing explanation?

Why should you challenge your own idea? First, you will impress your reader with your openness and insight. Second, you will write a more honest paper. Third, you will anticipate objections your reader may consider and you can answer them. You can write, perhaps, that peer pressure is involved in other causes of teen drug use. Peers fill the void left by missing parents and employers who'd rather fire than hire people.

There will also be more on this in the next chapter, but let me take some time here on competing ideas because it's so important. Students frequently tell me they've been working hard on their next paper, pull out a sheaf of scribbled notes, and then say they're frustrated because since they've been thinking so honestly, they can no longer figure out which side to take in an argument. They say they've become confused and can't recognize the truth now that they're searching for it.

One student had decided to write about television advertising. "Everybody hates TV ads," Carrie told me. "They try to get you to buy things you don't need or even things harmful to you. They lie and deceive. But everybody knows that," Carrie said. "I can't write a paper telling people what they already know."

"So what do you think ought to be done about commercials?" I asked.

"Well, first I thought we could just not allow them anymore. But who'd pay for the shows on TV? Maybe we could charge people to watch, like with cable TV. Then I thought, well, what about poor people? And legally, don't the advertisers have a right to say what they want?" She sighed. "But what about *my* right not to hear the same dumb ads over and over? I'm so sick of dogs selling beer! Well, then I thought, why not just turn off the TV set? Maybe enough people not watching would make them create better commercials. Suppose a lot of us wrote letters. . . ."

"How about that?" I said.

"Oh, no! People are too lazy. I don't know if *I'd* even bother. The other night I caught myself laughing at a new ad. And I hum the jingles sometimes. I don't know what to write. It's just a mess. I need another topic."

"What? And waste all this good thinking?" I told Carrie to be glad, not upset. Her conflicting emotions and ideas had made her better informed, even though the only research she'd done—the most important kind—was in her internal library.

The temptation for a writer in Carrie's position is to glance at her watch and say, "I've got to get this paper done by Friday. I'm just going to pick a side, call it 'Just Say No to Commercials,' and state that the answer to bad advertising is to twist that little dial to the off position." Then the real idea she's come so close to shrivels and dies. But don't kid yourself. The paper will still be hard to write because it's tough work to tell only half the truth.

The honest response to confusion is to accept it. Don't worry. Most people are confused when they think. All research into creativity and idea getting shows that you must tolerate chaos for a time until the confusion rearranges itself into a good idea. You have time to sort out the contradictions later in the last three stages of writing: Organizing (Chapters 4–5), Drafting (Chapter 6), and Revising (Chapters 7, 8, and 16). In the thinking stage of writing, don't pick *one* side but gladly choose two or three sides before deciding what the truth is. If one fixed idea comes to you at the start of your paper and never changes, red lights and buzzers should rattle your head to warn you that you're not really thinking.

Work patiently through competing ideas, testing each with details to see if it is supportable. If one answer doesn't emerge during the thinking or outlining stage, perhaps it will in drafting or revision. If *the* answer doesn't come by then, the worst you have is a paper that says, "There's no simple answer to television advertising—the sellers, the station owners, and even the viewers are all to blame. No one solution can satisfy the rights of everyone involved." This is essentially what Carrie wrote.

Despite what I've just said, here's a warning: Deliberately trying to be complex *just to be complex* usually leads to confusing writing. Complexity should be the *result* of honestly exploring an idea—of opening yourself to see as many possibilities in it as you can. It's not something you add to a paper like a pinch of salt.

▲ **PRACTICE 2-4:** Which of the following ideas promise the most originality? Which could you expand into an essay? Do any go too far?

- Suicide *is* a reasonable response to misery.
- It's tough to be a teenage parent.
- Racial discrimination continues to make this society unfair.
- Discrimination hurts the haters as much as those who are hated.
- We love innocence in others, but not in ourselves.

WHAT MAKES A GOOD DETAIL

What makes a good detail? **Vividness! Details must be specific, dramatic if possible, and direct, not secondhand.** Suppose you wanted details to bring the following idea to life: "College athletics do more harm to the student than the supposed benefits of character building we hear about so often." Which of the following gives the most vivid details to support the idea?

A. College athletes spend so much time practicing they have very little time left for studies and they're too tired to do a good job anyway. What does playing basketball, tennis, or football teach them about their field of study? Yes, they're taught competition, winning at any cost, but will that get them a good job when they graduate? Most athletes take easy courses and do poor work. They miss the real meaning of college. A lot of them never even graduate, and when the coaches get four years' effort out of them, they couldn't care less what happens to them.

B. Bill Peterson has just limped back to his dorm from football practice, where he has spent two hours slamming his body into a metal sled. The coach has yelled at him, "Hit harder, Peterson! Drive into his guts!" He's limping because the all-star fullback stepped on his ankle. "Pull those legs in when you go down, Peterson," the coach said. "You could trip the runner."

Peterson is a starter this year but has no hope whatsoever of playing pro ball or of making the big money. At the dorm, he picks up his history notebook and heads for his night class—scheduled around football practice. He sighs. The professor has been talking about Thomas Jefferson and the American Constitution as the first institutionalized statement on the dignity and nobility of man. "What a crock!" Peterson says. "Maybe I'll sit in the back and catch a few 'Z's.'"

Is there any doubt that **B** involves readers more, makes us think more? **A** is general and **B** is specific. **A** relies on abstract terms like "the real meaning of college"; **B** makes those ideas concrete by talking about Jefferson's concept of "the dignity and nobility of man." **A** is bland (athletes are "too tired" or "have very little time"); **B** is vivid, *showing* us how tired Bill is, not just *telling* us.

Finding the powerful detail can be just as creative as developing an interesting idea. Our eye, as well as our intellect, must be trained to see better. One of my students who wrote of hugging an old woman said, "her chest was as hard and flat as a weatherbeaten plank." The story of years of living was in that comparison. Another student, writing about working in a nursing home, gave intimate, honest details: "I have put diapers on a 100-year-old woman, helped quiet an old man after a bad dream when he called on his long dead wife, and put countless people on bedpans only to have them miss and urinate on me instead."

Good detail may look a bit different in informative writing, but it follows the same principles. If I announced that you will probably earn more money after finishing your associate or bachelor's degree, you might not even bother to yawn. But if I gave you the details, told you that college graduates' starting salaries for 1998 average $29,000 per year to high school graduates' $15,000, I've given you something specific to visualize (you can visualize $14,000, can't you?).

The chapters on descriptive, narrative, informative, and persuasive writing will suggest specific ways of creating vivid details for specific writing assignments. But for now, remember that details plant the reader's feet on the ground. Support each of your ideas with at least a couple of examples, description, or facts. Only then will the reader be able to see your idea clearly.

▲ **PRACTICE 2-5:** Rate the vividness and specificity of each of the following details as good, fair, or poor. Then rewrite two of the weaker ones for more specificity:

- Nurse O'Hare is a real witch.
- Many homeless people are mentally disturbed.
- Many General Motors trucks from the 1980s have gasoline tanks that explode easily in accidents.
- In the 1990s more women and minorities than ever before attended college.
- Today 27 percent of men and 24 percent of women have college degrees. Twenty-six percent of whites, 14 percent of blacks, and 12 percent of Hispanics have college degrees.
- The price of food has shot up in the past five years.

THE DIFFERENCE BETWEEN A TOPIC AND AN IDEA

Students often ask, "What's the difference between a topic and an idea?" and "How can I tell if my details are detailed enough?" Good questions. Let me respond through an example.

Suppose you decide to write a paper for your English class on growing old. Perhaps you've been noticing your grandmother slow down and remember bicycling and swimming with her. Your topic is "growing old." But it's not an idea yet. **An idea must make a point about the topic.** An idea generalizes or summarizes. And there are hundreds of possible points one *could* make about growing old:

- Growing old stinks.
- Growing old is the high point of life.
- Growing old teaches us about the youth we rushed through.
- Society treats growing old as if it were a disease.
- Growing old comes as a surprise to most people.

These are all complete ideas—they generalize and require supporting details. The first two—first off the top of my head—are superficial. They show a simplistic lack of depth because I haven't subjected them to competing ideas. But all have moved beyond the vague topic stage.

If I decide to write on "Growing old comes as a surprise to most people," I might start by scratching down some supporting details:

"Suddenly, you can't do what you always did, and other people just assume they ought to help you."

Is this detailed enough? No! I'd call it **fuzzy detail.** It does support my main idea and it sets up the transition to real details, but it's just not vivid. **You will know you're specific enough when your details do some or all of the following:**

- You name names.
- You refer to a *single* instance, not a group.
- You use exact statistics or numbers.
- You quote people directly.

For example, sharper details for my growing-old idea would be: "At 72, Evita Perez's knee began swelling up after grocery shopping, and her daughter began raking leaves and cleaning out gutters when she visited. Evita laughs about shrinking two inches so that she can no longer reach the top shelf in the kitchen. 'I woke up one day, and the floor had dropped!'"

▲ **PRACTICE 2-6:** Write down a *topic* (like "growing old" or "patriotism") that you care about. First, list three preliminary *ideas* you have about the topic. Now pick one and write three hard details to support it. Bonus: Honestly question your idea by stating a competing idea and a detail that supports the competing idea.

SHOULD YOU START WITH IDEAS OR DETAILS?

Should you start with an abstract idea and then add details to liven it up? Or should you start thinking about papers with details and develop the overall idea from them? Both sides have their advocates and **either method will work as long as you move back and forth between ideas and**

details during the thinking process. Remember: The thinking process is not neat; neatness is for the final draft. But let's consider the pros and cons of each method as a starting point.

In life outside school we usually learn things by starting with details and drawing conclusions. As children, we first touch hot stoves or we slobber out half words, and later theories about heat and language emerge. The idea of death was not real to me until, at age 13, I saw my Uncle Samuel looking like wax in a casket. Divorce was an empty abstraction until I lived through one. As we experience things one by one, our brains work to develop ideas that explain our experiences. Most of our self-learned ideas grow this way over years.

On the other hand, most teaching starts with ideas and asks you to apply them to specifics. Moral guidance from religion or family begins with abstract ideas like "Thou shalt not kill," rather than letting you kill to see how it feels and discover what punishment follows. Biology professors give you the abstract plan behind a frog's internal muscle and digestive systems and then ask you to dissect a specimen, rather than handing you a frog and scalpel to let you figure out the principles by trial and error.

For a writer, sometimes details offer the best place to start—when you're doing personal writing, for instance, where recalling specific places, people, and incidents will lead you to ideas. William Faulkner was fond of saying that he started his great novel *The Sound and the Fury* because he had a picture in his mind of a little girl with dirty underwear. She had climbed a tree to peer into the second-story window of a house. Faulkner claims he wrote the book to figure out how and why that little girl came to be there.

Your professional writing tasks may more often start with an idea given to you. Your employer may ask you to come up with a plan to reduce employee absenteeism or to persuade a client to stay with your firm. Your job is to supply details. This might also be true with informative essays or reports in which the topic is assigned to you.

Details are easier to get than ideas. They tend to come to us whole. Ideas, however, rarely, if ever, emerge complete—like a light bulb flashing on. We need to play around with an idea, rub it up against details before we can say clearly what it is.

Think about how you might create ideas and details when you consider topics for papers. Examine the following as potential essay topics. What will be hard or easy in each?

- Democracy
- Your favorite vacation spot
- Airport terminals
- Artificial intelligence

Democracy is the most abstract and general topic. Therefore, an idea will be easy to get and details harder because the topic does not help you visualize it. But much has been said about democracy, so even though *an* idea will be easy to get, saying something fresh will be harder. However, that means competing ideas will be readily available. Your favorite vacation spot and airport terminals are both visual, so you'll have an easy time with details, but a harder time creating an abstraction about them. The vacation is one of the most common topics ever assigned, so a fresh idea will be even harder. Beware the topic that looks familiar or easy at first glance! The airport topic is more unusual, so as long as you stay away from the obvious approaches (hijacking problems and delays), almost anything you say will be fresh. Artificial intelligence (or computer intelligence) is less abstract than democracy but not nearly as specific as the other two. Visualizing will be a problem. Since it's a technical topic, details will be hard to get unless you're well read on computers or do some research.

▲ **PRACTICE 2-7:** Think through the following topics as I've done with the previous four for ideas and details:

- Earrings
- Pet food commercials
- What conservatives stand for
- One of your family legends

One last point: There's a classic formula for details and ideas. It says about 75 percent of your writing should be details, 25 percent ideas. There's nothing sacred about this formula, but it's a handy guideline. Many college students think abstractions sound more intellectual, more important than homely details. Your professor is likely to tell you, however, that most papers suffer from too few details rather than from too few abstractions. Almost every professor wants more and livelier detail.

In this way writing is like life itself. We need principles or ideas to guide us, but we spend most of our time dealing with little details of eating, working, and loving. We could ponder the meaning of love forever, but eating M&Ms and holding hands in a park gives substance to our abstract idea of love. Likewise, we don't continually ponder the direction of our career but do concrete tasks in front of us: answer the phone, plan the next meeting, and collect our paycheck. Once in a while, we need to step back, to see if the details of our job or love life match our ideas, make one life. It's the same with writing.

Highlights of Chapter 2

- Good writing combines ideas and details, and the writer who hopes to be in touch with a reader must continually move back and forth from abstract ideas to concrete details.
- Ideas give meaning and purpose to writing. They tie things together. Details help readers visualize ideas. They are memorable and touchable.
- Honest ideas should be both fresh and complex. Strive to develop competing ideas in the thinking stage of writing.
- Good details should be specific and vivid. The more nitty-gritty they are, the better.

- You can start with either details or ideas in developing topics to write about, but both are necessary and usually writers have several supporting details for each idea they present.

Writing Suggestions and Class Discussions

1. "If this were my last day alive, I would . . ." Make a list of ten specific things you might do. Then pick two or three and list specific details about them in note form. Be vivid, concrete, and honest. Don't write to impress people.

   Now, create a single unifying idea that best summarizes the philosophy of your last day. Write a short paper based on these notes.

2. What follows are some famous generalizations—ideas that need details. Pick one and use it for your core idea. Illustrate the idea with three or four concrete details and build it into a coherent paragraph. To sharpen your honesty skills, try to find an exception to the idea and work that in too.

   "Heaven is under our feet as well as over our heads."—HENRY DAVID THOREAU

   "Imitation is Suicide."—RALPH WALDO EMERSON

   "Fear not that your life shall end, but rather fear that it shall never begin." —CARDINAL HENRY NEWMAN

   "Most folks are about as happy as they make up their minds to be." —ABRAHAM LINCOLN

   "Failure is impossible."—SUSAN B. ANTHONY

   "We see things not as they are; we see them as we are."—ANAÏS NIN

   "The man who sees the world at 50 the same as he did at 20 has wasted 30 years."—MUHAMMAD ALI

3. The following generalizations are all about love. Pick two to work into a coherent paragraph. You'll need to supply details—examples, facts, stories, or descriptions—to make them more concrete. Some of the quotes go together easily, but you may find it more interesting to put contradictory quotations together. You may agree or disagree with the statements.

   "Love is perhaps the only glimpse we are permitted of eternity." —HELEN HAYES

   "Love is the delusion that one woman differs from another." —H. L. MENCKEN

   "It is impossible to repent of love. The sin of love does not exist." —MURIEL SPARK

   "A broken heart is wonderful five years later, when you see the guy in an elevator and he is fat and smoking a cigar."—PHYLLIS BATTELLI

   "Love is an act of endless forgiveness."—PETER USTINOV

   "Love is what you go through with somebody."—JAMES THURBER

   "The face of a lover is unknown—because it is invested with so much of oneself."—JAMES BALDWIN

4. What follows are collections of details about AIDS in search of an idea. Create two ideas that the details suggest.

   - AIDS may be transmitted from mother to fetus.

- AIDS may lie dormant in a person for as long as ten years, while the person infects other people.
- Three-quarters of North Americans say they run "no risk" of getting AIDS.
- AIDS is now the leading cause of death for women aged 25–39 and children aged 1–4 in New York City.
- Most Americans say they have "little or no sympathy" for those who get AIDS from homosexual activity. Twenty-five percent of these say God is punishing them through AIDS.
- In 1997–98, cases of AIDS declined about 10 percent, but deaths due to AIDS declined about one-third.
- People between the ages of 13 and 24 accounted for 15 percent of all HIV cases and 4 percent of AIDS cases in 1998.
- Twenty-four percent of all people with AIDS in 1997 were intravenous drug users.
- Sixty percent of AIDS cases are caused by heterosexual intercourse.
- Many people in developing countries resist using condoms.

5. For one of these topics, generate a list of details that can be used in a paper: quotes, stories, facts, descriptions. But also list ideas as they occur to you. Try for three ideas and nine or ten details on the topic you choose. Mark each item on your list as an "I" or a "D."
   - Teaching morals to today's children
   - Physical education classes
   - Your favorite vacation spot
   - War movies
   - Abuse of the elderly
   - Choose a topic yourself

6. Follow the instructions for 5. This time consciously start with ideas first, freely moving to details.
   - An ethnic group to which you do *not* belong
   - United States–Russian relations
   - Personality of the last person you dated
   - Dentists
   - Thick pan pizza
   - Choose a topic yourself

7. Write down three *competing* ideas to explain one of the following:
   - Men under 25 cause far more automobile accidents than women under 25.
   - Why do bad things happen to good people?
   - If teenagers today know more about sex than other generations ever did, why are there more teenage pregnancies than ever before?

8. Idea to details writing. Express in one sentence one of your guidelines for living: how to be happy, what is important in life, what is right, what is real, how individuals relate to society, family, nature, or God. Now illustrate your sentence with specific details. To be more fully honest, also consider a competing idea or objection someone might have to your philosophy.

9. Details to idea writing. Describe a powerful dream you've had. Start with vivid details: who's in the dream, where it occurs, objects, events, how you feel, odd or unrealistic aspects. Then interpret the dream—look for symbols, how the dream relates to your awake life. Suggest *several* possible ideas before concluding.

10. Write a list of ideas and details for a personal topic that interests you. Label each item as an "I" or "D."

11. Write a list of ideas and details for a professional writing task you might have someday. Imagine, for instance, that you have been asked to deliver a speech to your local business group or library or church group, or to write a press release or a memo on hiring procedures.

12. Write a list of ideas and details for a college paper due in another course. Label each item as an "I" or "D."

13. What is one idea you have mixed feelings about and would like to explore more deeply? Explain why you have mixed feelings and give a few details. (One of mine is how much freedom a teacher ought to allow students in writing assignments. One side of me says students should develop their own topics completely from scratch. It's democratic. The other side of me says students need to be shown they *can* write on anything and that in their careers they will most often be assigned topics. It's less democratic, but more practical.)

14. Write a two- or three-page essay based on any one of the previous writing suggestions. Aim for a fresh idea with some complexity and plenty of vivid details.

15. Evaluate the following list as potential paper topics. How hard would it be to come up with a fresh, complex idea and vivid, specific details for each? Also consider how these topics match your experiences, knowledge, and biases: What are your *personal* strengths and weaknesses in each?
    - The national budget
    - Concepts of beauty and ugliness
    - Stereotypes of grandparents
    - City parks
    - Lesbian parents
    - Your first encounter with violence

16. Write a letter to your boss asking for a promotion or raise. Present several reasons (ideas) why you deserve this reward and support each idea with specific details.

17. Write a brief summary of a key concept you're learning about in another course. Write out the main idea so it's accurate and clear, then illustrate the idea with several examples. Imagine your audience is a student in the class who doesn't understand the concept.

18. Write a brief criticism of an afternoon talk show. Make an overall point about what you don't like, then support it with at least three specific examples.

19. Read the following student essay. As you read, pay attention to how it moves between general ideas and specific details.

NOSY PEOPLE
Melissa Waheibi

Most people are nosy. We enjoy peeking over the neighbor's fence. We want to know what's cooking in the kitchen. We want to know what's on television tonight. We ask for a mirror while getting our hair cut, just to see how it's coming along. While having dinner at our favorite restaurant, we want to know where that amazing aroma is coming from, and why our dinner doesn't smell like that. We watch the news to see if the war in the Balkans has ended yet, how our stocks are doing, and to check out tomorrow's weather. This basic nosiness is fine. It doesn't interfere with anyone and keeps us informed.

Then there is unhealthy nosiness. Do we really have to know why Larry got fired? Do we really have to know where the big boss went on his vacation? Do we really have to search through the closets to find Santa's bag of goodies? And do we really have to know who hosted that huge party everyone attended but us?

Some nosiness gets us in trouble. Let me confess. I was baby-sitting at a neighbor's house, and after I put the kids to bed, I sat next to the wooden crate that held their photo albums. I peeked. At the bottom of the crate, I noticed a fat manila envelope. As I opened it, my uneasy stomach told me I shouldn't be touching it. Inside, I found about 30 letters the father had sent the mother while they were at college. Of course I shouldn't have read them. But I did. And I found out that . . . (you would be disappointed if I didn't tell, right?) . . . they got engaged because she was pregnant! I shouldn't know that! That's personal stuff! I think they even suspect I looked because I haven't been asked back. My stupid, nosy nature got me in trouble, and I'm out 20 bucks a week.

Some people say they're not nosy, just concerned. Like when we pace the halls of a hospital, constantly wondering what is going on in the nearby operating room. But is it out of deep concern that we slow our car to gaze at a nasty accident? Is it out of deep concern that we make our friend promise to come out of the dressing room in her new corduroys? I'm sure some good Samaritans pull over to assist at accidents. And I'm sure some true friends really are concerned that those corduroys don't make her look fat. But mostly, that's not why we look.

I was watching Ricki Lake one night, and I was horrified--not at what I saw--but at myself. I found myself screaming at the screen, "You're so stupid! Why did you sleep with him? You knew he was married!" One third of television shows between 9 a.m. and 6 p.m. on the big networks are talk shows. We have Sally Jesse, Regis and Kathie Lee, Maury Povich, Vicki Lawrence, Jenny Jones, The View, Leeza, Oprah, Rosie, Montel, and Ricki Lake. Why do we care what other people are doing with their lives? How did that become our business? Is it because we're concerned, or does watching them make us feel good because our lives aren't as screwed up as theirs are?

Nosiness is a human trait. It may grow from concern for others, but often causes problems and shows us in an unfavorable light. Society would run a lot smoother if we learned to mind our own business.

Commentary

Ideas: This is a wonderful topic for originality and there's an intimate honesty about it that appeals to me. She also has several competing ideas to explain types of nosiness. But I feel let down at the end; I really want a strong main idea to tie it together. She is excellent at showing people *are* nosy, but the paper needs to go deeper into *why*. Why is being nosy "unhealthy"? Why do we look at horrible things and pry into secrets even when we know it's wrong?

Think of how *you* might answer these questions.

Details: Melissa does a fine job here. There are plenty of details for each idea. Many are vivid and honest. She uses hypothetical situations, actual examples and facts for nice variety. Can you add two or three new details to hers?

Structure: This essay is organized as a classification essay. Each new paragraph focuses on a different type of nosiness.

Style: I'm not sure about using the "we" and "us" approach. I like the way it includes the reader with the writer as co-spies, but many examples might not apply to some readers. But there's probably enough so we find ourselves saying, "Uh-oh, she caught me!"

CHAPTER 3

Getting Ideas

Brain Teasers to Help You Write on Almost Anything

Writing is thinking.

ANNE MORROW LINDBERGH

There are no limits set to thought.

EDITH HAMILTON

Not all those who wander are lost.

J. R. R. TOLKIEN

A former editor-in-chief of *Ladies' Home Journal* once said that she learned to be an idea person when she first started working as a young assistant editor. Each Monday, she and every other staff member had to bring to a meeting a list of 25 great ideas for articles. This gave her boss hundreds of ideas from which to choose for the dozen or so needed each month. It also gave the young assistant editor a headache. For the first few weeks she felt as though each idea was an elephant being born.

Then the ideas began to come easier. Some weeks she began having 30 or 40 ideas—better ones her boss could use. The important trick she learned was to let her subconscious mind work on the problem all during the week and not sit down at 3 o'clock on Friday afternoon to create 25 ideas. All week long she'd jot an idea or two down as it came to her—stimulated by all sorts of things—a taxi ride, a meal in a Hungarian restaurant, an unusual garden she saw, a newspaper article. Soon she realized that almost anything could become an idea for a magazine article. "Just knowing I had such an assignment made me remember things I'd otherwise have forgotten," she said. One of the side benefits of becoming an idea-creating person was that she lived at a more intense pace, appreciated life more.

This is *incubation.* You plant a seed of an idea, and your subconscious brain—which has far more brain power than your conscious brain—will work on the problem. The solution that suddenly comes to you does nothing of the sort. It has been planted in the subconscious, which thinks about it while you go about your normal life, unaware of its activity except in flashes here and there. When the idea has ripened, it rises to the conscious level. My point is this: You don't have to wait helplessly for a magic moment to strike in order to write. You can arrange your own inspiration. In fact, it might be most accurate to say that working with ideas creates inspirations. Inspiration comes to those who sniff around a lot for hidden bones. It isn't luck when they dig up a great idea.

There are two things to remember about using your subconscious brain power. The first is that better ideas come if you **make a conscious assignment to your subconscious.** If you ignore the task, your subconscious will work instead on your bowling form or try to recall the telephone number of that great-looking person you met last week. The subconscious likes to be tickled once or twice a day with reminders if it's to keep going.

The second thing to remember about incubation is that **ideas often don't come out fully formed** like a newborn baby. They usually emerge in misshapen bits and pieces—the arm or leg of an idea. I'm using this grotesque image to describe ideas because most people don't want to accept such fragments as the offspring of their minds. Have faith. Be prepared to write down the idea fragments as they're delivered. You don't need 3 × 5 cards or a computer—although they work for some people. I'm a bit sloppy myself. I use any handy paper, and as I sit to write my first draft, it looks as though I've spread out the trash in front of me. The novelist H. G. Wells had an unusual system to keep new ideas organized as they emerged in bits and pieces. He kept a dozen big barrels around his home, one for each book he planned to write. When fragments of an idea or details came to him, he'd jot them on a slip of paper that he tossed into the appropriate barrel. When a barrel filled, Wells knew he had enough material to write a book.

There's no need to buy barrels. Two pages of notes are plenty to create a two- or three-page paper for a college course.

"Two pages of *notes?*" I imagine some students protesting. "Why not just write the essay? I thought you were going to save us work in this book?"

This whole chapter will address this question, but a few comments are in order now. First, I want to help you do a *good* job, an honest, deep piece of writing. Writing a draft without notes is easy if you want to do poor work, but it's the most agonizing way I know to create a good final essay because the revisions go on forever, trying to make up for the thinking that should have been done first. **A little sweat in the notes saves bleeding in the revision.** Notes nail down details, connect ideas, and help us concentrate. Researchers into creativity in many fields have shown that this is how the best idea people operate. They've proved it's dependable, saves time, produces more interesting ideas, and helps blocked writers get going again. Why shouldn't it help you? And remember this—all these notes are *easy writing* because you pay no attention to spelling, word choice, or complete sentences.

So when your boss or professor assigns a writing task, start *that day.* Suppose your anthropology professor tells you to write on "Cultural Differences within the United States." In your next class, listen to the roll call. Do Mozzamil and Mustapha want to be called "Mo" and "Steve"? Does a woman with the French name "Lemieux" pronounce it "Leemo" instead of "Laymeoo?" Does the woman of Indian background touch other women while talking? Perhaps that afternoon you go to the dentist and get a shot of Novocaine. As the needle punctures your gum and the pain shoots through your cheek, you recall that the Chinese use acupuncture, which is painless. Perhaps you run into a woman in a bicultural marriage. Ask her a few questions. Talk to the Japanese fellow on your volleyball team. Eat at a Thai or Mexican restaurant. Read the "World News" in the city paper. AND WRITE DOWN ANYTHING RELEVANT. These activities will be fuel for your subconscious, and when you write your paper, deeper, more original ideas are more likely to arise as well. Inspiration results from *many* good ideas banging into each other.

Now, let me tell you how I got the ideas for the previous paragraph, because I wasn't doing it for a college paper. I knew I needed an example to illustrate my idea on incubation so you could visualize it, so I went to a sheet I keep marked "Examples." I made this up when I began the book. It's about 40 to 50 items long most of the time, and I add and subtract from it continually. I picked "Cultural Differences" more or less at random after considering "Grandmothers" (too easy and sentimental) and "Lasers" (too narrow). Nothing much came immediately. The next day when I took attendance in my class, I noticed the names from so many cultures. Later that afternoon I saw my wife talking with an Indian woman in the parking lot—she touched my wife's arm and hair as they spoke, a cultural difference with westerners. That night our daughter Amy brought a friend to dinner, an exchange student from South Africa. We had a heated discussion of apartheid with Despo, who offered some unusual comments about American racism. That never appeared in my paragraph, for I couldn't see how to make such an encounter seem like an average occurrence in most people's lives. As I wrote these details into the paragraph, they brought to mind an American woman married to an Arab man and the incident of the Novocaine. (I didn't really go to the dentist, but recalled a lecture I'd heard a year earlier in which the speaker talked about why Americans never invented painless anesthesia while the Chinese never invented chloroform.) From this messy, haphazard material, the paragraph emerged. I rewrote it as a student might see the assignment, but the incubation process was exactly the same for me—and cost me little brain-squeezing pain.

▲ **PRACTICE 3-1:** Take five minutes maximum to recall some specific cultural differences you've noticed where you live. Write in list form and do not worry about spelling or sentence structure. Tomorrow, add new things that occur to you from school, your job, travel, or television. Add to the list throughout the day until class time.

 ## IMPROVING YOUR IDEAS

It's easy to come up with dull ideas—they're the first ones off the top of our heads. The tops of our heads are notoriously dull—clichés, television jingles, routine responses, and pass-the-salt ideas live there. The Greek writer Euripides once said, "Among mortals, second thoughts are best." Believe him! Second, third, and fourth thoughts create the unusual angles and viewpoints that make ideas creative. Put ideas on trial, as de Montaigne said; call them into question, as Edith Hamilton said. This is what the successful people who compete against you are doing.

So *how* do you go deeper, draw out your more original ideas? You can order yourself to be profound. Richard Wilbur tells the story of a poet who dove under water and held his breath until he thought up a line of poetry and sputtered verse as he gasped to the surface. It kept him in great shape, but really didn't lead to great poetry. Or, like most professional writers you can *make a habit of creativity* through regular note taking and incubation; you can get yourself into the groove of having ideas just as ball players groove a batting swing. Columnist Ellen Goodman says she goes "through life like a vacuum cleaner, inhaling the interesting tidbits in my path, everything I observe or read." Other long-term ways of being and staying creative are keeping a journal and reading stimulating books. They will reward you in many ways. But these methods won't help you get next Friday's paper done.

For an immediate improvement in your ideas, **use brain teasers— systematic ways of stimulating and exploring regions of your mind to find out what ideas lurk there subconsciously.** These are the ways people think. At first, these brain teasers may seem artificial and awkward to use, but when you practice with them for a semester or two, they will become a part of the way you think, will help you create ideas quicker and with less agony. They will make it possible for you to think or write on almost anything. Brain teasers also help you to be more honest, for they draw out complex, conflicting ideas you may be holding back.

Brain teasers go beyond what you tried in the last chapter. There you *randomly* bounced between ideas and details—a kind of free brainstorming. It's a great technique to get started and may be enough to bring some papers to the Order and Draft stages. But there will be times when simple brainstorming doesn't evoke fresh enough ideas, times when you want more focus. Brain teasers will get you going again, and some even organize papers. If you feel blocked or empty, try one or two brain teasers to reenergize yourself. You can use several or all to get started on any topic.

All the brain teasers follow the same overall process. First, **make long lists.** Since your brain contains thousands of ideas, you must never settle for the first few that appear. Write down the obvious stuff, but keep going, for the longer the list you create, the more you'll have to choose among and the more likely that better ideas and details will turn up. Sure, you'll throw away much of these lists, but we're only talking about a rough list anyway. I recommend a half-page minimum for a brain teaser list. One page is better. It takes time to wake our deepest brain. Why a list and not freewriting? Items on a list are easier to organize than a paragraph. Also, freewriting tends to focus you on one idea; a list leads you to many alternatives.

Part of the problem any writer has is translating a nonverbal concept into words. How many times have you thought, "I know what I want to say, but I can't put it into words." Second, then, to eliminate this problem, **make a list of ideas in rough form—not worrying about wording or grammar.** Turning the ideas into words becomes a separate step. A little sloppiness is good compost: Don't rewrite brain teasers for neatness. If you use a computer for brain teasers, be sure to turn off the spell checker and grammar checker, which will distract you. In the early stages of writing, concentrate on *what* you want to say (the ideas and details), not on the structure (which comes next), the words (which come during the draft and revision), or the mechanics (which come last). Brain teasers are *not* word association but a list of ideas. One-word items are too vague to help a lot. Phrases of three-to-ten words or occasional sentences will tweak your brain more.

Third, **you must not prejudge ideas or details as you compose an idea list.** Write everything down, no matter how dumb some items sound. Judge later when you choose which ones will appear in the paper. If you judge at the list-making stage, you may shut off the flow of ideas. Good ideas have a way of hiding underneath weaker ideas. Research into the creativity of scientists, businesspeople, artists, writers, and many others proves that self-criticism kills creativity if done too early—save criticism until later. To summarize:

- Make a long list (half to one page).
- Concentrate on ideas/details, not words.
- Move quickly, and do not prejudge items.

 ## TEN BRAIN TEASERS

1. Use Your Senses

List sense details about your topic—smell, taste, touch, and sound, as well as sight. This will help you get into the topic and supply you with vivid details for the draft. Our senses connect our mind to the world around us, so by recalling sense impressions you recreate the subject for yourself, engaging brain and feelings, stirring subconscious memories. Drenching yourself in sense impressions is enjoyable once you catch on—one of the secret pleasures of most professional writers.

Let's try an example. List all the sense details you can about your mother (or another relative). Start visually—describe her face, the way she walks, favorite gestures, the way she looks when angry, sad, or laughing. Then become more specific—try her teeth, hair style and color, her favorite clothes. Bring up other things.

Now move to touch sensations—the way she felt your forehead for a fever, a time she struck you in anger, the temperature and texture of her skin, what it feels like to kiss her cheek.

Now sounds—the tone of her voice, the noise of her steps, peculiar expressions she uses when she speaks, unusual sighs or other noises like snores, wheezes, or gurgles. (Yes, mothers do these things. Be honest.)

Now smells—smell her perfume or kitchen or work odors, the unique odor of her room.

You can't just read my words to understand; try it. Write down as much as you can about your mother, letting your mind go. Probe deeply for the forgotten or unusual detail. Think sensuously. Recall key scenes. For me, my earliest memory is of my mother pushing my baby brother in a carriage across a busy street and me wondering where my father was; another key scene was the first time she learned to drive a car with a stick shift and made the car jerk up and down the street like a bucking bronco; a third was the night in a darkened hallway when she leaned against me and told me my father was dying of cancer.

Not only does a sense brain teaser prepare details and get you into a topic, but it also leads inevitably to ideas. Write any *ideas* that occur to you as well as details. For example, I noticed in my three key incidents that my mother always comes to my mind with my father, and it makes me recall that he so dominated her life that she really had little life of her own at times. This is an abstract idea, not a sense detail, and could become the main idea of an essay. This is exactly how brain teasers move writers from notes to a paper idea.

Using senses doesn't just apply to personal topics like mothers. Suppose you're writing about public smoking laws. Use your senses to visualize scenes of smoke-filled cafeterias or restaurants. If you're a nonsmoker, get down all the smell and breathing sensations you've experienced in a smoke-filled room—your burning eyes, your raw throat, the film on the windows, the stale odor of your sweater afterward. If you *are* a smoker, use your senses to describe the personal agony you suffer wanting a light—your dry throat, your nervous hands, your eyes involuntarily glancing at the door. The sense brain teaser is an excellent way to start almost any topic. It draws you into your topic and provides sharp details. It will not help you organize papers.

▲ **PRACTICE 3-2:** Make a half-page list of sense details about bus or air-plane travel. Move quickly; pay no attention to spelling or writing complete sentences. Be as specific as possible. In class your teacher may ask you to read your list and discuss how to develop it into a paper.

▲ **PRACTICE 3-3:** Write a half-page list of sense details about a topic of your choice. Other brain teasers in this chapter will develop the same topic in different ways.

2. See the Topic from Alternative Viewpoints

This brain teaser gives you *perspective* by making you see the topic from out-side your own narrow viewpoint. This is another secret of honest writing. When using alternative viewpoints, you must try to see the topic as some-one else would, to inhabit another's mind and eyes for a little while and not impose your views on others. It helps open our own eyes.

For example, if you want to write on a personal relationship that has soured, first list all the people whose viewpoint might be different from yours:

- Igor (your ex-boyfriend)
- Igor's mother
- Igor's friends
- Your parents
- Your friends
- Igor's new girlfriend, Bertha
- Your new companion, Lars
- Your children (if any)

Now spend time with each viewpoint, trying to see the break up as each of them would; what would they think in their secret hearts about it; how would they explain its causes or place blame? Remember that each of them will have a different focus. Lars may care less about the past than future;

friends may think Igor was tied down to you; your mother might take your side, but underneath her sympathy perhaps she hopes the experience teaches you a lesson about jumping too quickly into relationships. Ask yourself as you proceed how much truth is in these ideas.

If you still don't feel as though you have enough ideas, you can create a list of *character types* who always have viewpoints on any topic. This is a kind of cross section of human opinions. How would the following view your topic:

- An accountant
- A socialist
- A lawyer
- Your religious leader
- Your favorite singer
- Someone in the year 2050
- An ecologist
- A psychologist
- A child
- A politician

You are doing a little bit of stereotyping here, but just imagine what a lawyer might say about the break up. He or she would consider it a legal/contract problem. What new facets would that bring up? Your religious leader might relate the break up to your moral and spiritual beliefs. Obviously some of these character types may not be very helpful on this topic: the ecologist and socialist perhaps. The person from the future may simply say, "It won't matter by then," and suggest not worrying about it. Give each one a few minutes. If nothing comes, move to another. We all have little bits of all these perspectives inside us. To cultivate your deep, honest ideas, give each perspective a chance to speak. See who speaks loudest and clearest to you and listen for new ideas. Alternative viewpoints help free you from your usual self so you can probe your deeper, more unusual self.

Here are three examples of people thinking from alternate viewpoints. Loren Eiseley, the great nature scholar, said, "In the world of the spider, I do not exist." The aging actress Shelley Winters once said, "I think onstage nudity is disgusting, shameful and damaging to all things American. But if I were 22 with a great body, it would be artistic, tasteful and patriotic." Last, there's a story anthropologist Bronislaw Malinowski tells. While working with cannibals, he informed an old chief that the millions of dead in European wars were not eaten by the victors, but buried. The old cannibal shook his head. "How barbaric!" he said. All three make us think by shifting our perspective.

The competition among the different viewpoints will lead to more honest and sophisticated ideas. Good ideas toughen up under pressure from other ideas; poor ones crumble. Alternative viewpoints also help you relate better to your audience because you will think of things your reader may want discussed. As the English novelist W. Somerset Maugham once said, "The measure of a writer is the number of selves he encompasses." Can you, for instance, visualize the world your parents saw when they were your age? How did they feel then about music, war, computers, jobs, and college? What hopes and fears filled their thoughts?

Suppose you're writing on a less personal topic for a communication course, like how television affects our view of marriage. You can start by listing some alternative viewpoints:

- Young children
- Advertisers
- Teenage couples
- Program writers
- Actors/actresses
- Lesbian and gay people
- Marriage counselors
- Religious leaders
- Senior citizens
- People in troubled marriages
- People in wonderful marriages

Go over each one, writing down the viewpoint of each and giving a specific detail. For example, senior citizens might complain that older married couples are often portrayed as grouchy and unloving. Remember, no matter how you feel about this conflict, each person or group will feel it is doing what's right and will justify these feelings. When you finish, you can begin sorting through the viewpoints to decide which to use. If you decide on your message before honestly exploring all sides, you'll be a little bit like the Queen in *Alice in Wonderland* who wants to have the punishment first and then the trial.

Examining alternative viewpoints is best for honesty, for widening your perspectives, and for audience awareness. It may help you organize but may tend to pull a draft in different directions.

▲ **PRACTICE 3-4:** Your college is suffering budget problems and is considering reducing costs by eliminating the required writing course. List five people or groups who would have different perspectives on this plan. Explain each of their viewpoints in a half-page list.

▲ **PRACTICE 3-5:** Imagine the perspectives four or five different people might have on the topic you chose in Practice 3-3. Fill a half page with their viewpoints.

3. Break Stereotypes, Break Unquestioned Ideas, and Break Slogans

Stereotypes, unquestioned ideas, and slogans are enemies of creativity—blocks that prevent honest, imaginative thinking. All three encourage us to think in accepted, common patterns—which as you know is not really thinking.

STEREOTYPES place people or ideas in closed-minded categories:

"Poor people don't want to work."
"A woman can't build a house."
"They're white; they're probably racists."
"Fat people are so jolly."

Sentences like these portray a writer who does *not* look carefully at life, a writer who sees groups and generalities, not individuals. Stereotypes are comfortable lies that make the world seem more simple and predictable than it really is. They're hard to break because they make thinking easy. But when you break them, your writing leaps to life. Do poor people really not want to work? The fact is that 40 percent of poor people do work, 45 percent are children, and 12 percent are disabled.

Leo Buscaglia, the famous "love doctor" psychologist, said he liked to touch students so they knew he was real—a human and not a faceless professor. He told students when they came to his office, "I'm gonna hug you!" and it terrified some, he said, because it broke the safe stereotype.

UNQUESTIONED IDEAS A creative thinker must peek behind unquestioned ideas once in a while to keep from being closed-minded. Doing this has led to some of humankind's most creative concepts. The Declaration of Independence challenged the divine right of kings—the unquestioned belief that a king received his right to rule from God. Thomas Jefferson questioned this by stating that "all men are created equal" and that a king should rule, not by God's authority, but by "the consent of the governed." What changes so few words have made in the world!

For centuries the dissection of the human body was forbidden. Until this unquestioned idea was challenged and the body dissected, people believed our emotions came from our hearts (not our minds) and even thought a man's erection came from air in his lungs!

Unquestioned ideas are invisible to us because almost everyone takes them for granted, like eyesight or the ability to walk. When I mentioned Thomas Jefferson's famous phrases, did you go one step further and ask if "all men are created equal" and "consent of the governed" have also become unquestioned *today?* If challenging these ideas is upsetting, it's because our belief in them is deeply ingrained.

SLOGANS are stereotyped use of words. If you find yourself concluding, "Man does not live by bread alone," or "Just Say No" watch out! You're not thinking; you're repeating something off the top of your head. While stereotypes are comfortable and unquestioned ideas are invisible, slogans come to us with a sense of discovery: "Ah, I've got it!" But it usually means just as we had the chance to move into new territory, we found our way back to the worn, common road of thought. Students sometimes protest, "But this slogan is true! I've seen it!" Perhaps. But if it's true, put it into your own words at least to make it your truth.

I've lumped stereotypes, unquestioned ideas, and slogans together because the same brain teaser applies to each. To get fresher, more honest ideas, imagine yourself as a puncturer of balloons. ***Become a cynic who suspects all commonly held ideas and sayings to have little lies in them that need exposing.*** Think like the philosopher Nietzsche, who said, "Joyous distrust is a sign of health."

To break these three idea killers, first list all the stereotypes, unquestioned ideas, and slogans you can about your topic, all the "common" truths. These are the things you'd write in your paper if you wanted to create a below-average paper. Next, find *exceptions* to items in this list. Think of people, cases, incidents that may contradict the common belief. Write as long a list as you can. After you've attacked the stereotypes, unquestioned ideas, and slogans, you can honestly decide what you really think and will have plenty of material for an outline/draft.

For example, let's assume your sociology professor assigns a paper on "Women in the Workplace." Here are some stereotypes, unquestioned ideas, and slogans I've heard about this topic:

- Women can't do the heavy work a man can. (stereotype)
- A woman's place is in the home. (slogan)
- Working mothers hurt kids by not being home. (unquestioned idea)
- Men will not go to a woman doctor. (unquestioned idea)
- Keep women barefoot and pregnant. (slogan)
- Equal pay for equal work. (slogan)
- Would you want women shot if they were allowed in combat? (unquestioned idea)
- Women are too emotional to be president. (stereotype)
- All male bosses are chauvinists. (stereotype)
- Women bosses aren't feminine. (stereotype)

Notice that these stereotypes, unquestioned ideas, and slogans come from *both* sides of this controversial topic. Now, the creative task is to puncture these balloons.

Some, like "a woman's place is in the home," are easy to pop. Suppose Queen Elizabeth I, Venus Williams, Catherine the Great, Marie Curie, Jane Goodall, and Oprah Winfrey had stayed home? My list could go on for pages. What a drab world we'd have without these perspectives and personalities. See if you can poke other holes in this slogan. Notice that the "pop" is more powerful if you use specific examples.

Other statements are harder to attack. I do think it's awful to shoot women in battle. I've been brought up to believe women should be treated with a gentler touch than men. Maybe, however, I need to get behind the "manners" I've been taught. Are those manners sexist? Maybe the real issue is that it's awful to shoot men in battle too.

I found "equal pay for equal work" to be the hardest slogan to criticize. I agree with this. But my job in this brain teaser is to question what I believe on the surface. So here's how I might puncture that slogan: How do we ever know work done is equal? Doctors may earn as much in two hours as a truck driver does in a week. People with seniority often earn far more for the same job as newer employees. What about quality of work? Many mediocre workers get the same pay as outstanding workers.

My conclusion: Equal pay for equal work sounds good in theory, but I discovered that variables not related to the worker's gender make such an idea hard to define, to put into effect, or to enforce. I'm not happy with this conclusion because I want to believe in the possibility of gender fairness, but until I think some more about it, I'll be forced to qualify that generalization. Can you find some exceptions to *my* conclusion?

You can research facts to break stereotypes, unquestioned ideas, or slogans too. It is commonly thought, for instance, that American workers are overpaid, underworked, and inefficient compared to workers in Japan and Germany. But in a few minutes I dug these facts from a brochure of the U.S. Bureau of Labor Statistics: German workers were paid an average of $22 per hour, U.S. workers an average of $15, and Japanese workers an average of $13. American workers labor 100 fewer hours than the Japanese, but 400 more than the Germans. And U.S. worker productivity is 22 percent higher than the Germans and 24 percent higher than the Japanese. These put a few dents in the stereotypes at least.

This brain teaser shows us some of the walls we or our upbringing have built around our inner world. Tearing down these walls, or at least peeking around them, is one way people think. Loren Eiseley, the great nature and science writer, once warned any thinking person "not to love anything *official* too fondly . . . otherwise one is easily destroyed." Breaking stereotypes is good for creativity and challenging established ideas and a great approach to most college papers. It may irritate traditional audiences.

▲ **PRACTICE 3-6:**

- List five stereotypes about men and **break** two of them with examples, facts, or logic.
- Treat "all men are created equal" as an unquestioned idea and poke two holes in it with specific cases in which this is not or should not be so.
- List five common slogans used to debate public policy (for example, "Guns don't kill people; people kill people") and pop holes in two of them.

▲ **PRACTICE 3-7:** List three stereotypes, unquestioned ideas, or slogans about the topic you chose in Practice 3-3 and **break** them.

4. Classify Your Topic

To classify is another way to think. Classifying breaks a subject into categories and places individuals in each category. For example, biology divides all living creatures into two main classifications: plants and animals. It further classifies types of animals according to whether they are mammals, fish, or insects. The thinking you do here is to figure out sensible, inventive categories that show underlying qualities among members of the same group that may not be obvious at first glance. People classified whales as fish, for instance, until realizing that some not-so-obvious qualities, such as lungs and feeding offspring with milk, made whales closer to land-inhabiting mammals than to fish.

In a classification brain teaser, break your subject down into categories *several times* until you come up with a creative pattern. For example, suppose your topic is "Dreams." You could break dreams down into daydreams and night dreams. Too general and obvious? Yes. Suppose I classify night dreams as follows:

- Dreams in which you're chased
- Sexual dreams
- Falling dreams
- Replay-of-the-day dreams
- Dreams in which you can't run or speak

To finish this brain teaser, I'd list examples and descriptions of each. Suppose your topic is "Education." Off the top of my head:

- Elementary school
- High school
- College

I hope this classification bores you. It bores me. But it *is* a starting point. So I try working just on high school. How about:

- Good high schools
- Bad high schools
- Average high schools

Again not fresh enough because the categories are too vague. How about this:

- Preppie high school
- Learn nothing high school
- Vo-tech high school
- Parochial high school

This is getting better. I can think of people and facts to put under each. I might get even more specific by classifying types of parochial schools.

Let's go back to our main topic, "Education." I could have taken a different route. Instead of schools, I could have classified students, courses, or teachers. Take a minute or two to imagine several classifications for each.

The more specific your subject, the more you can do with it. This seems like a contradiction, since you might think the broader the topic, the easier it is to think up things to write. Not true. It's easier to think up common thoughts on big topics, but harder to say something fresh. Suppose you start with "Technology" as a topic. The possibilities are too overwhelming. Narrow it to medical technology and you can classify it more vividly. Narrow medical technology further to "Types of Gynecologists" or "Types of Sports Doctors," for instance, and the paper almost begs to be written.

You might have one objection to classifying—it seems to create stereotypes! It puts individuals in categories. Isn't that what we were fighting in the last brain teaser? Yes, it was. However, our main objective in this chapter is increasing the ways we have of thinking. Breaking classifications that have become stereotypes is one way people think; creating classifications is another. Classification need not be stereotyping—if you keep in mind and remind your reader that individuals do not all fit their categories perfectly. Classification helps us see patterns; it is only dishonest if it's applied too strictly. Classifying works well for scientific and technical writing and many college assignments. It is a strong organizer.

▲ **PRACTICE 3-8:** Classify types of television comedies, poems, art works, or heavy metal music. Have at least five categories. Now pick one of these types and classify it into at least three subcategories. Give a specific example of each.

▲ **PRACTICE 3-9:** Classify the topic you chose for Practice 3-3. Break it into at least three categories and list examples for each category.

5. Compare and Contrast Your Topic

You can get more ideas by comparing your topic with something else. This is another basic way people think. We contrast socialism with capitalism, murder with manslaughter, retailing with wholesaling, the Yankees with the Mets. To understand our world, we stretch one thing to meet another, creating meaning. If you must write a paper on John Steinbeck's novel *The Grapes of Wrath,* you might discover ideas by comparing it to another novel. Steinbeck's novel is about poor people struggling to survive tough economic times, so it might go well with Alice Walker's *The Color Purple.* Start listing differences:

STEINBECK	WALKER
People are Okies, white midwesterners	People are black southerners
The antagonist is the capitalist system (banks, sheriffs, the rich)	The antagonist is the heroine's chauvinist husband
Characters travel across country	Character makes an inner journey
Pessimistic ending	Heroine succeeds in the end

This list should continue for half a page. What do I do next with this list? Well, I might create my main essay idea by combining a number of these contrasts, or I might go into one difference in depth: say to figure out why Steinbeck's characters fail and why Walker's heroine overcomes oppression.

Sometimes comparison or contrast is implied in the question given to you—"Contrast the Democratic and Totalitarian View of the Press," or "What Similar Techniques Do the French Painters Monet and Renoir Use?" Other times you may be given a topic and can discover a useful comparison to bring it to life. If you must write a paper on modern nursing ethics, think of several possible comparisons:

- Two nurses whose ethics are different
- Two situations that require different ethics
- Nursing ethics of the last century compared with today's ethics
- The contrast in ethics between doctors and nurses
- Similarities between nursing ethics and those of another profession

You would then explore *one* of these in depth, listing as many comparisons and contrasts as possible.

A list of similarities and differences takes the pressure off; you can say, "I'm only listing things." But when done, you'll have some ideas and details and the basis for organizing your paper as well. Comparison or contrast can open up almost any topic in any situation. Its drawback may be that you must work hard to get beyond superficial comparisons.

▲ **PRACTICE 3-10:** Think of three possible comparison and contrast approaches to *one* of these topics: manners, e-mail, or Christmas shopping. Pick your best and create a half-page list of specific points to support your idea.

▲ **PRACTICE 3-11:** Think of a comparison or contrast approach to your topic from Practice 3-3, and list a half page of specific details to support it.

6. Create Metaphors

A metaphor is a special comparison, not between things in the same category (two novels, for example), but between things in different categories (a novel and a beverage):

- "Reading her book is like drinking a cool, clear glass of water."
- "Her party was like an insane asylum."
- "Rap music is a sermon delivered with hammer blows."
- "Love must be made fresh every day—like bread."
- "Old-age homes are like warehouses."
- "The city is wearing a veil of fog this morning."

Why make such comparisons? Because it's fun, and it stirs a reader's imagination and visualization. The metaphor brain teaser helps *you* because it suggests many ideas.

Let's return to the topic of "Education" again to show how you could use a metaphor brain teaser to come up with new topics that did not appear in the classification brain teaser. Start by listing all the comparisons you can think of, not worrying if some sound silly.

Let's try "College":

College is like: a factory

the army

a farm or garden

a beehive or ant nest

the ocean

a circus

a meal

a tree

No apologies—this is my rough list. Now I glance over the list, adding a few details to each item to see which ones have the most potential. In trying to compare college to a factory, I think of college courses in which the same work is done in mass-production lecture halls, or how class recess resembles a shift change. The *idea* behind this metaphor suggests that college is routine, uncreative, time serving. Someone who felt this way may have the concept for a paper here.

I liked the circus metaphor, especially thinking about the last week of classes when everyone's a bit wild—people dress outrageously and "clowns" try out their routines in class. As an instructor, I feel like a ringmaster trying to keep the show going. Some students give beautiful performances, while that tiger in the front row snarls over his last paper. To explore this concept further, I'd want to make a list of all the circus things I can think of and try to find equivalents in college life. See if you can add to the following list and if you can find college equivalents for these items:

- Three rings
- Buying a ticket
- High wire act
- The elephants bellowing
- The sideshow
- Monkeys
- Peanuts, popcorn, and cotton candy
- The bleachers
- The cages
- The freak show
- Cleaning up the elephants' mess
- The whip and chair

The overall mood a piece like this would create is light, a kind of gentle, sarcastic humor that doesn't take college too seriously, but as an entertaining game—much different from the grim metaphor of a factory.

Recently I asked a composition class to help a student with her paper on teenage suicide by suggesting metaphors. Let me recreate the discussion to show you how ideas emerged.

ME: What can you compare suicide to?

STUDENT A: An ending.

ME: Okay, what kinds of endings are there? Let's think of endings, and then see if we can come back to suicide.

STUDENT B: A rear end.

STUDENT C: A cliff edge.

STUDENT D: A book ending.

STUDENT A: Yeah, like a book with the last pages ripped out—that's suicide.

STUDENT B: How about a dead-end road?

STUDENT A: Or a road that leads nowhere.

STUDENT E: Suicide's more an escape.

ME: From what? Metaphors ought to be visual.

STUDENT F: An escape from prison. Life's like a jail to some people. They want to be free.

STUDENT E: Suicides like to control what happens to them. They feel like victims until they plan to kill themselves. Then they're in charge.

ME: So what's *that* like?

STUDENT G: Like—writing a play. They make everything happen as they want—for once.

A metaphor brain teaser can lead to a main idea and be the backbone of your essay, but it can also be used simply to create a few sparkling details. It's good for creativity, visual detail, and humor. In college and business writing, you may want to keep metaphors on a short leash.

▲ **PRACTICE 3-12:** Pick one of the metaphors for college (or invent one of your own) and make a half-page list of specific equivalents.

▲ **PRACTICE 3-13:** Create one or more metaphors for your topic from Practice 3-3 and give a half-page of details.

7. List Examples

This brain teaser provides you with *details.* Simply list all the specific examples about the topic you can think of. If you're writing about abortion, list all the cases you've ever known: ones from the news, people you know, stories mentioned by friends or teachers. **An example must be a single concrete instance, never a generality.** This brain teaser tells you quickly which topics you don't know enough about before it's too late. If it's an assigned topic, it'll tell you what research you need to do.

If I were going to write a paper on alcoholism, for instance, these examples occur to me:

- Matt—A gentle young man who was attending AA during a course he took from me. Several times his writing and class comments were incoherent. He was quiet and lonely.
- Rico—An older man who declared he was a recovering alcoholic. He told me about the hell of shakes and fits he used to go through and how desperate he was to make up for the time he was "dead" for his four children.
- Jeanette—The mother of a teenage alcoholic. Her son had ruined her family, bringing her almost to divorce. She threw him out of the house.
- Ed—A 50-year-old man who stole money from his daughter for booze.

Once I started this list, I realized I knew far more alcohol-related stories than I thought—another ten or so besides these. Catching one example often hooks more. To develop this list into a paper, I might narrow it to teenage alcoholism or the effect of alcohol on families.

Examples are essential to support or visualize most writing. This brain teaser is a good one to use early in writing a paper, but will not help you organize.

▲ **PRACTICE 3-14:** List a half page of your own examples for a paper on alcoholism or drug abuse. Fill out some of the examples with details. To move you toward an idea, state a *point* the examples seem to suggest.

▲ **PRACTICE 3-15:** List a half page of examples for the topic you chose for Practice 3-3.

8. Make a Bug List

One way to approach any topic is to criticize or complain about it. You begin this brain teaser by saying, "What really bugs me about _____ is _____." Then you list all the complaints you can think of. A bug list helps you formulate a problem, and solving a problem is a great topic for many college papers. One tested method to impress your boss is to solve a chronic work problem. In both cases, you start with a bug list and move to solutions.

In preparing to write this book, I made a bug list about texts. Some are too filled with terminology, some too complicated, some too theoretical, and some too impersonal. The bug list told me what I wanted to avoid.

One of my recent students worked at a nursing home, and I suggested for one paper that she use a bug list to decide what she could write on. Christine listed dozens of complaints: about the elderly residents themselves, about the way the home was managed, about the families of the residents, and, most creatively, about her own flaws as an employee. She decided there was no easy way to make the home more humane and caring. She wasn't aware of this until she went through an exhaustive list of complaints. Old Mr. Fitzwater was just a miserable grouch, whose bad humor couldn't be blamed on family or staff. And there was that gloppy un-food served each day—she'd spit it out too if someone tried to feed it to her. And while she understood why an orderly might feel irritated by continual messes, she didn't like employees handling the old people as if they were machines to be oiled. She even found complaints about the building's design that encouraged isolation; it was more tomb than home. Now Christine could not cure all these ills in her paper, but by listing the problems, she saw how some things could be fixed, and she even brought them to her supervisor. And she found a new bug: He was afraid to do anything about her bugs.

Dissatisfaction has solved many problems, so put yourself in a sharp, critical mood for this brain teaser. Mention little things as well as large, abstract things so you have both details and ideas. Be honest. In reviewing your brain teaser list later, you may decide to tackle a lot, as Christine did, or you may focus on just one interesting or creative criticism and seek a solution for it. Bug lists are excellent for career problem solving and argumentative papers. If not used with other brain teasers, however they can lead to excessively negative writing.

▲ **PRACTICE 3-16:** Make a half-page bug list about public transportation, the World Wide Web, or a fast-food restaurant.

▲ **PRACTICE 3-17:** Write a half-page bug list about the topic you chose for Practice 3-3.

9. Use Humor and Fantasy

Go wacky and wild. Think of all kinds of fantasy situations about your topic or the humorous side to it. This form of thinking is often downgraded because it sounds unintellectual or silly, but fantasy and humor have solved many personal and world problems. The German poet Goethe once said, "The intelligent man finds almost everything ridiculous." Dorothy Parker, the great humorist, said, "Wit has truth in it." And psychotherapist Sheldon Kopp said, "Laughter is the sound of freedom." Think how a grin or joke can often end arguments. Think of all the comic movies, plays, and books that have changed people's ways of thinking. One of the greatest antiwar plays ever written was *Lysistrata*, a story about the women of two warring armies who go on a sex strike until their husbands agree to stop fighting. No sex for any man, the women on both sides vow. It's a hilarious fantasy that makes a serious point about the stupidity of war—that killing and love-making don't go together—and Aristophanes wrote it 2,400 years ago.

Some people will find this brain teaser hard. But anyone can develop this part of his or her thinking repertoire. Being able to let go, without prejudging dumb ideas, is the key. Included in this book—in Chapter 14—is an essay by a student on "Pigs as Pets" that grew from such a fantasy. It's funny, but it also makes serious points about the human attitude toward animals.

Here are a few ways to help loosen your imagination:

1. **Reverse expectations of the normal rules of reality.** Gary Larson, who created "The Far Side" cartoon, does this with deer who hunt people, salmon who wear tourist caps and ride a boat upstream to the spawning grounds, and ants in lab coats trying to figure out how to get rid of their pests—humans.
2. **Break a social, scientific, or mathematical law** related to your topic and imagine the results. Did you hate the federal 55 MPH speed limit? Imagine the results of having no speed limit. Do you hate high taxes? Imagine a world without them, or a world of 100 percent taxation, or a world without money.
3. **Create a new rule or law and imagine its effects.** Suppose libraries could be recorded on microchips that could be implanted in each human brain at the age of 10. What would happen? If you're interested in world harmony, you might imagine a world government or the outlawing of foreign travel.

Humor or fantasy can spark personal writing, fiction, and satire, and occasional flashes enliven professional writing. It's creative, but risky. Know your audience first.

▲ **PRACTICE 3-18:** Think of a fantastic or humorous way of ending war, preventing divorce, or reducing traffic deaths. Fill out your idea with a half-page list of details.

▲ **PRACTICE 3-19:** Think of a fantasy or humorous approach to your topic from Practice 3-3. Fill a half page with details.

10. Anticipate Your Audience

This brain teaser makes you think about how your reader may react to your topic. Answering these questions suggests strategy as well as new ideas and details:

- Who is my audience? Describe its concerns or features.
- What does my audience already *know* about the topic?
- What does my audience already *believe* about the topic?
- How might my audience respond to my opinion? Be specific, especially about objections they'd have.
- What does my audience want (need) to learn?
- What might my audience resist hearing? How can I overcome this bias?

For example, suppose I'm thinking about writing about garbage. Perhaps I spent a summer working at a landfill, took a course in the environment, and think it's an unusual topic. Here's how I might anticipate audience.

My audience is my English professor and a peer group in class. I'd bet they don't *know* much about garbage. Most people leave full bags at roadside each week without worrying where it goes. But one woman in class made a few comments about nuclear waste. My professor's hard to read;

she said she enjoys nature but hasn't said anything specific about pollution. I'll assume she's more interested in good writing than my environmental views. Probably most people in class *believe* we have too much garbage, but they don't know the details. I'd guess most would like to stop unnecessary garbage but won't put much time into it. About half would *resist* my pet idea of having lots more mandatory recycling, especially the Republican guy in the front who speaks out against government rules. Maybe I could say something about how rules are necessary until people get more responsible. To convince them, I'll have to motivate them. Plain numbers—tons of aluminum thrown away—won't grab them. They may be more impressed by the loss of trees and ugly strip mining pits. They'll be most influenced by threats to their health by incinerators burning garbage and poisons leaking into our drinking water or even the rising cost of garbage collection. I'd like to get them to change their personal buying habits, but I'll have to do it in a way that doesn't sound like I'm accusing them.

Doing this audience analysis clarified my topic, created some ideas, and uncovered objections I must answer in the paper. Because it stresses strategy, it's effective with argumentative writing. The downside: This brain teaser may draw you away from your beliefs and into saying what you think your audience wants to hear.

▲ **PRACTICE 3-20:** Suppose you're writing a letter to your classmates about changing a government policy. After stating your point, describe your audience's beliefs, knowledge, and possible reactions to your idea. You may also ask a peer group to give a "live" reaction.

▲ **PRACTICE 3-21:** Describe a potential audience's reaction to your topic from Practice 3-3.

If you can only remember one thing from this chapter, remember this: The more brain teasers you devote to a topic, the wiser you'll be writing the paper. Your idea will be tougher, more resistant to attack if you scrutinize it from many perspectives. Another way of saying this is that you have to kiss a lot of frogs before you find your prince or princess idea. People's typical response to a problem like writing a paper is to get *rid* of it; brain teasers help you learn to embrace a problem and make something positive out of it.

Brain teasers should be fun—you are playing the mind's video game, punching all the buttons and switching electricity through the cobwebs of the skull. Enjoy it, relax, watch the show. There is no perfection, no rule for neatness or order.

Brain teasers give you control over your thinking. You can passively accept whatever ideas come to you, not knowing if they're the best or most honest you have, or you can reject intellectual helplessness. Active use of your brain's capabilities leads to self-reliance and confidence. **You edge a few inches closer to mental freedom when you can challenge an idea you find appealing.**

Writing is about interesting ideas brought to life with vivid details. All the structure, word manipulation, and grammar in the world won't breathe life into an idea-dead paper. Spend time creating lots of ideas, because good ideas make structure, word choice, and grammar easier. Content creates form.

OTHER BRAIN TEASERS IN THIS BOOK

Journals (Ch. 15)   Good for personal writing, but can develop professional or college writing if focused. Uses incubation to stir the brain. Weak for tightly directed assignments.

Freewriting (Ch. 1)   Good for getting the flow started, working toward a focus. For people who don't like lists. Very hard to revise.

Bouncing between ideas and details (Ch. 2)   Good for all types of writing. Helps focus and support writing.

Looping (Ch. 5)   Good for shaping freewriting toward a draft. Lacks overview of the whole paper.

Clustering (Ch. 5)   Good for visually oriented people, shows relationships among items so outlining is easier.

Thesis development (Ch. 5)   Good especially for research, college papers, and persuasion. Focuses your purpose before drafting. Weak for narrative and descriptive papers.

Iceberging and other eye-training brain teasers (Ch. 9)   Good for creating sharp detail and symbolism.

Six brain teasers for introductions (Ch. 6)   Good for focusing your idea as well as getting started.

People-describing brain teaser (Ch. 10)   Good for narratives, but also for career writing when analysis of people is required.

Informative brain teasers (Ch. 11)   Process, cause, effect, and essentials. Good to organize and focus college and business writing.

Persuasive brain teasers (Ch. 12)   Facts, values, logic, Maslow's hierarchy, and refutation. Good for arguments.

Literary essay brain teasers (Ch. 13)   Gut reactions, critical perspectives, and explication. Good for any topic analyzing a text.

Using sources (Ch. 14)   Good to fill in missing material and to surprise readers with facts. Can control the paper or downgrade your own ideas if overused.

Two Sample Brain Teasers and Commentary

BUG LIST--GROCERY STORES

  —Long express lines/people with 20 items

  —People with checks, coupons, food stamps, and unscannable items in express lanes

  —Trashy newspapers:

    "Aliens in Congress!"

    "Lawyer Eats Baby!"

    "Liz's Face Falls Off"

  —Too much plastic packaging

  —Plastic bags--tear, dump groceries in car

  —After your hands are full, the cashier tries to hand you the little receipt slip

  —Carts in the parking lot. Wind blows them. Scratch cars.

  —People, especially kids with colds, grab bulk cookies with their bare hands.

  —Big Ruth!

  —Not enough cashiers

  —Carts with stuck wheels

HUMOR--FUNERALS

  —"Doesn't he look good!" He's dead!

  —Telling strangers how sorry you are.

  —Praising the dead one, even when he was a rat and everyone in his family is glad he's dead

  —Soft pillows for the dead

> —Old men carrying the coffin
>
> —Justin saw a casket dropped and the corpse rolled into the church aisle. Half the crowd screamed. The rest laughed.

Commentary

Format: Both brain teasers are good starts. They're in list form so the ideas can be extracted. Both are specific without being wordy. The length of each item is good, although "Big Ruth" and "Old men carrying the coffin" are too vague to mean much to me. The funeral list is too short. There's just not enough there yet.

How the authors might focus their brain teasers for a paper: The funeral notes emphasize ironies—contrasts between appearances and reality. This would make a good theme. But it needs more details. The author might try Breaking Unquestioned Ideas and Slogans ("he's gone to a better world" or "her suffering's over"), Examples, Alternate Viewpoints, and Anticipating your Audience to get more ideas. The bug list on grocery stores is an easier topic and may be too broad, but it has some sparkling details to work with. To be a successful paper, it will have to be narrowed down. Two focuses I see in it deal with customer behavior and improving the environment of the store. She has avoided the obvious path of attacking the check-out people. If the author wants more to think about, she could try Using Senses, Breaking Unquestioned Ideas, and Contrast (between two stores). What else would you suggest?

 ## ROADBLOCKS TO GOOD IDEAS AND DETAILS

Despite all these brain teasers, there will be times you will find yourself staring at a blank piece of paper at 2 A.M. or at a few sentences that are so bland and empty you can't build a thing on them. All writers have these awful moments, so nothing is wrong with you as a writer if you have blue dry spells.

Fear of Risk

Despite the desire to do well, many people are just afraid to put anything on paper that is daring or a bit odd. They're afraid of being judged as weird or of revealing something secret about themselves. When they sit down to write, the flow of ideas is blocked by this internal censor. Sometimes the mind will let safe ideas through and you can manage to write something. Other times, the hold-back message shuts down the flow of *all* ideas. You want to write, but nothing comes.

SOLUTIONS: Tell yourself to write down the most outrageous things about your topic—the wildest, grossest, most absurd things. You reduce the fear of risk by telling yourself this is a throwaway list that no one else will see.

If I'm writing about pollution control, for instance, and I'm blocked, I can let loose the little demon in me to say irresponsible, risky things:

- Let's pollute faster so we kill off humanity—the world may be better off without us.
- There ought to be pollution hit squads. Instead of taking polluters to court, these action groups could break polluters' windows or dump garbage, oil-killed animals, or chemical wastes on the lawns of the company's president. We could picket their houses, churches, and clubs.
- To cut down on garbage, we could forbid all wrappers on things that don't need to be sanitary, such as clothes.
- Use big machines to crush garbage into blocks and build houses with them.

Next, I evaluate my absurd, secret list. Bullet 1 is just nastiness talking; 2 is illegal and mean, but modified a bit, it might be usable. Perhaps we could pass laws to hold individual employees responsible for company pollution and prosecute, fine, and jail them as individuals. Bullet 3 may also have merit if I tame it down a bit; 4 sounds like a technological problem (to make odor-free garbage houses), but turning junk into treasure is a concept I might be able to use with other items—such as automobile tires or bottles.

Insecurity about Your Ability to Think

People with this block are amazed that anything at all appears on paper. When *any* idea appears, they are so thrilled they don't dare put it aside or try for another option. They feel compelled to accept any idea as a gift of the gods. These writers do not see writing as *a skill to be learned because they think of it as a onetime miracle.*

SOLUTIONS: Writing is a learnable skill to be relied on, and a wealth of ideas exists in everyone's brain. In his book about human intelligence, *The Dragons of Eden,* Carl Sagan calculated that the human eye can absorb 5,000 bits of information per second and that all this data is stored in the brain, which recombines each bit many times with others, forming ideas and adding to them second by second. The average human brain contains an unimaginably large number of pieces of information and ideas—2×10^{13}— which is *far* greater than the total number of all electrons, protons, and neutrons in the universe! Be impressed with your own brain power. Rely on it.

If you're a thank-God-I-have-an-idea person, you're too humble. Use brain teasers regularly for several months until you build up your confidence that you do have many ideas to choose from. You must demystify creating ideas. Having ideas is human nature; it comes with our genetic code.

Highlights of Chapter 3

- Brain teasers are ways people think. They are learnable and can be used to teach yourself to think clearer, more creatively, more quickly.
- Use your subconscious brain for incubation unless you enjoy frustrating yourself. Think early and often and take notes painlessly. Remember: Ideas create inspirations, not the other way around.
- Continue with a particular brain teaser until you hit a dead end or until you catch fire. When you catch fire, follow the ideas and details until the heat dies down.
- Trust yourself—you *do* have ideas.
- Coming up with ideas regularly is a part of most jobs for college graduates. You won't even be asked to write a report for the boss until you come up with good ideas first.
- Use these brain teasers *any* time you get stuck for ideas or details. They can help you choose a topic, develop a topic, or jump-start a stalled draft.
- Brain teasers improve honesty. They are not formulas because each person uses them differently. They help you probe deeper into your unique experiences and views. Risk letting your mind free.

Writing Suggestions and Class Discussions

1. Incubation Exercise: Your teacher will assign a paper. At each class meeting bring in a half-page list of new ideas and details for that paper.
(Note for numbers 2–11: All brain teasers should be in *list* form and *note* form, not in paragraph style.)
2. Sense Brain Teaser:
   a. Fill one page listing sense details about your first home. Try for all five senses, being as specific as possible. Allow these details to bounce into ideas, but keep returning to the senses.
   b. Same as a, except list sense details about the first time you ever saw death. Recall hidden details.
   c. Same as b on any topic of your choice.
3. Alternative Viewpoint Brain Teaser:
   a. In a sentence or two describe one failure you have had. Then list your feelings about its significance, causes, and effects. Now write out how two other people close to you saw your failure differently. Try to think as they would. Now make a fourth and fifth list choosing two of the types of people on p. 39 for your alternative viewpoints.

b. Take any controversial issue today and write half-page lists for the viewpoints of each of the parties involved. Concentrate on honestly seeing the issue as they do.

c. Do an alternative viewpoint list for any topic you choose.

4. Break Stereotypes, Unquestioned Ideas, and Slogans Brain Teaser:

a. Take some unquestioned idea (playing the national anthem at sporting events, for instance)—and see if you can expose some unreasonableness about it.

b. In a paragraph describe a situation in which someone stereotyped you because of your age, sex, race, physical appearance, or other reason. Then list all the exceptions to this stereotype that you can think of—in yourself or others.

c. Pick a popular slogan that bothers you and list five to six objections to it.

5. Classification Brain Teaser:

a. Classify a type of film into subclassifications. For example, classify three types of space films or four types of war films. List an example for each type.

b. Classify reasons why people succeed in their careers; what different qualities does success require? Give details for each.

c. Classify any topic of your choice. Give details for each category.

6. Comparison/Contrast Brain Teaser:

a. You are assigned to write on war. Develop some ideas by comparing/ contrasting two wars. Fill a page with points of comparison.

b. Compare or contrast two magazines of the same type (*Cosmopolitan* vs. *Self* or *Time* vs. *Newsweek,* for instance).

c. Write a comparison or contrast brain teaser for any topic of your choice.

7. Metaphor Brain Teaser:

a. Life is like _____. List ten possible metaphors to finish the sentence. Then pick one and fill the rest of the page with details that could develop it. No clichés.

b. A teen's first sexual encounter is like _____. List ten possible metaphors. Then pick one and fill the rest of the page with details that could develop it.

c. Create a metaphor list on any topic of your choice.

8. List Examples Brain Teaser:

a. You are assigned the topic "Computers and the Average Person" in your introduction to computers course. List at least ten specific, concrete examples you could use in this paper. Allow your mind to produce ideas as the examples come. Circle any ideas that seem to tie the examples together.

b. List ten examples of teenage crime. As you review your list, add explanations for its causes or ideas on how to stop it.

c. List ten examples on any topic that interests you.

9. Bug List Brain Teaser:

a. Make a 15-item bug list on one of the following topics:

- Illegal immigration
- Evangelists
- Television advertisements
- Your job
- One flaw in your personality

Now circle the two or three items that have the most potential for a paper and try to probe deeper into them by providing details and more explanation.

b. Write a bug list on a topic of your choice.

10. Humor/Fantasy Brain Teaser:
    a. List all the humorous things you can about one of these topics:
       - Blind dates
       - Family holidays
       - Funerals
    b. List a page of humorous or fantasy ideas about any topic of your choice.

11. Anticipate Your Audience Brain Teaser:
    a. In one sentence summarize a paper assignment you've been given for a college course. Then explain what you believe the professor expects in an "A," a "C," and an "F" paper.
    b. List a page of audience analysis about any topic of your choice.

12. Peer Review: Bring to class a brain teaser you're thinking about expanding into a paper. Read it to your group, explaining as you go. Write down the group's suggestions and circle important items. Finally, write one sentence that explains your paper's tentative main idea. Share it with the group.

13. Which two brain teasers do you think would dig up the strongest ideas or details for the following topics? Without actually doing the brain teasers, describe what each will provide for your paper:
    - A report to your boss about which software program the company should purchase
    - A letter to a girlfriend/boyfriend breaking off the relationship
    - A research paper for sociology on the minimum wage
    - A cover letter for a job application
    - Your own home page to put on the Internet

14. Using any *three* brain teasers, develop two pages of ideas/details on one of these topics:
    - Retirement
    - Pornography
    - City life
    - A book you read recently
    - Country life
    - A first job

15. Using any *three* brain teasers, develop two pages of ideas/details on any topic of your choice. This can be a personal, college, or career topic. Try to choose something you care about or must write anyway.

16. Develop a rough outline from one of the brain teasers in 2–11 and write the rough draft of a two- or three-page paper from it.
17. You wake up one morning and discover one of three changes in your life:
    - You have aged 25 years. If you're over 50, you lose 25 years!
    - Your sex has changed.
    - Your species has changed.

    Thinking from alternative viewpoints, describe the next 20 minutes of your life accurately. These may be read aloud to peer groups and debated.
18. Your peer group's job is to write a bug list of what's wrong with high school, then solve two or three of the problems.
19. Your peer group's job is to break television stereotypes of cowboys, businesspeople, one ethnic minority, teenagers, or police officers. Choose one, state the stereotype, then break it.
20. This is your fantasy: You are director of community relations for a successful corporation. The company wants to donate $1 million to your community for goodwill. You are to advise them how best to donate the money. List various possibilities, then give reasons for your choices. A peer group may debate these lists.

Student Essay

The following essay began from a sense brain teaser list. Read the essay and then the notes and comments.

SPRING BREAK: MAZATLAN, MEXICO

Tinamarie Ciccarone

Waiting for the train, I felt like a young child going to the circus. This was my first vacation alone-- destination: Mazatlán, Mexico. Like the other hundreds of students, my mind filled with visions: the sun setting into the ocean, the serene beach at night. I was going to have the best time of my life. The Mexican train was scheduled to arrive at 3 o'clock, but that hour came and went. The train station was falling apart: chipped paint, holes in the wall, and the unspeakable rest room. Hyper students and baggage crammed the lobby.

As the hours crept by, I encouraged myself by flipping through the brochures of our hotel. The Riviera was

---

the best beachfront in Mazatlán. I dreamed of crystal water and hours of undisturbed tanning on white sand. My excitement rebubbled, and when the train finally arrived in the darkness like a wobbly earthworm, our eyes widened and faces glowed. We chose seats in the dark and fumbled baggage into the racks above. My aching backside was thankful for a padded seat and we slept.

I opened my eyes at 7 a.m. and scanned the car for the first time in the light. The vinyl orange seats were layered with grime, and my white sweatshirt had become gray overnight. Some seats were loose and shook their occupants. The floor--the original color of which could not be determined--was black, sticky, and wet from spilled beer. Food wrappers, empty beer bottles, and cigarette butts collected under the seats. Someone three seats down dropped a powdered sugar doughnut. An army of ants seized it.

Pretty soon a guy with a bunch of keys hanging from his belt came through, yelling, "Cerveza! Cerveza!"

I limped stiffly down the aisle. The bathroom knob resisted turning, and the door hesitated before giving in to my push. A wretched smell rushed my unprepared nostrils, and I gagged. I took a deep breath and entered. What else could I do?

The bathroom walls were gray with dirt and slime, the floor wet with either vomit or urine or a putrid combination. The tiny window was closed, trapping the deadly smell. The toilet was black and unusable. The sink was filled with solid human waste. Before I could add to the vile mess on the floor, I jumped out and slammed the door behind me. I stumbled to the booth connecting the cars and sucked in breath after breath of fresh air. Unbelievable! I could not use the bathroom, wash my hands, or change my clothes for another twenty hours.

As I gazed at the countryside, I saw the Mexican people for the first time. We were snaking through a small village. Dozens of identical-looking children, barely clothed, sat in front of houses no bigger than my father's utility shed. Holes in the brick walls served for windows and door. Clotheslines draped across the front yards. The passing train excited them. They

shouted, waved, and ran alongside. I waved back and they
shrieked joyfully, like puppies behind a fence at
my attention. As they vanished in the distance, I walked
back to my seat, angry, disgusted, and confused about how
I felt. A tear collected--for who?

By the time we arrived, I knew a little bit what life
was like for unwealthy, ordinary Mexicans. I had not
used a bathroom for 27 unbearable hours. I ate and drank
tiny portions, making sure not to run out of food. My
body, like everyone else's, smelled like a gym locker.
My hair was ragged and tangled and my clothes were now
brown. I never thought I'd reach Mazatlán, but of course
we did.

Being young, somehow I managed to do some of the wild,
fun things I'd planned. I spent hours on the sandy beach,
the sun's warmth penetrating and soothing me. The sparkling ocean was filled with sailboats, water skiers, and
swimmers. Fancy, modern hotels and sophisticated night-
clubs strung along the beach let us in.

But I could see now what else infested Mazatlán.
Locals scavenged like rats. Children begged money or
food. Sometimes they trailed behind an old, hunched
woman, but mostly they hunted alone. By the end of the
week I no longer could see the beach's beauty. The hotels
were no longer brilliant towers. The ocean lost its
gleam, and the sun became plain hot. The happy, care-
free college students seemed like mere shadows. What I
saw were human beings who did not live like human beings,
did not look like human beings. Finally all I could see
were the children. Like stray cats, they sniffed through
every garbage can in the back alleys, hoping for something, anything. None of them had return tickets in
their purses.

Discussion

This is a vivid, honest essay with strong details. Tinamarie used the Sense
Brain Teaser to help prepare herself to write the previous paper. This is how
her notes looked. I've omitted the scratchouts, fixed the spelling, and rearranged her entries to make it readable, but it was a *healthy* jumble in the
original.

```
Brain Teaser for Spring Break 1989

SIGHTS--Train--shabby, dirty, old, worn down, broken win-
dows, opaque with grime and dirt.
   Original color gone; the floor was sticky, black, wet in
spots.
   Food wrappers and garbage under seats.
   Spiders, bugs crawled on windows and floor.
   The bathroom!!! Filthy, stinky, no toilet seat.
   Toilet was black not gray or brown--BLACK--The sink was
gray with a large hunk of human waste.
   Flies gathered for a hearty meal.
   Mazatlán--the beautiful ocean and beach.
   Nice restaurants and nightclubs on one side vs. the
poor, hungry, dirty people begging for food and money.
   Their broken-down buildings, streets, and sidewalks.
SOUNDS--the train was obnoxious, frightening like it was
forcing its motion, like it was going to fall apart.
   Constant banging from the connecting doors between cars.
   Loud, rock-n-roll.
   Rowdy laughter, drunken shouts on the train.
   The guy who walked up and down the aisles selling beer
had a bunch of keys hanging down. You could hear those keys
jangle from the other end of the car. He yelled out
"Cerveza!" in a scratchy, harsh voice over and over.
SMELLS--the BATHROOM was unbearable! stench of human waste.
   Air stale and uncirculating.
   B.O., spilled beer, rotten food.
```

Commentary

Notice that Tinamarie did not use all her brain teaser sense details—some good ones like the flies in the bathroom and the noise of her peers never made the essay. She might have forgotten them or she might simply have found her theme didn't need them. Don't worry about using everything on your brain teaser lists. Notice that other things she barely mentions in her list become much more important in the finished essay—especially the children. A brain-teasing list is valuable not only for what you write down, but for how it helps incubate new ideas when you begin the draft or outline.

Finally, she mixes sentences, phrases, and sometimes single words, allowing ideas to flow as they want. Using the five senses as headings kept her on track when one sense ran dry.

CHAPTER 4

Paragraphs
Ideas and Details in Miniature

. . . If design govern in a thing so small.

ROBERT FROST

So far this book has tried to open up your thinking process to create more and better ideas and details through the controlled chaos of brain teasers. In Chapters 4 and 5 we will begin shaping these creative lists into more finished writing. Paragraphs are good places to begin thinking about order, for like essays, paragraphs combine ideas and details. In an essay the key idea is traditionally called a "thesis"; in a paragraph, the key idea is traditionally called a "topic sentence." The rest of an essay or paragraph consists of details that enliven or support the key idea. In theory, everything in an essay or paragraph must *relate* to the key idea.

In actual writing, of course, paragraphing isn't so neat. What fits together and what doesn't involves interpretation, and it may be tough to realize you are repeating yourself. It's also true that many paragraphs by reputable authors lack topic sentences, contain two ideas, or use repetition for effect. It's simply the nature of writing to break rules. *As long as your reader can follow you,* you'll get away with breaking rules. But it's also fair to say that most good writers *do* follow two guidelines most of the time:

- **Each paragraph should combine one idea with as much vivid detail as you can pack into it.**
- **Each paragraph should stick to one key idea.**

 ## THREE WAYS TO BUILD PARAGRAPHS

Here's an example from a student's essay on being a waitress:

```
When you wait on tables, remember that people are unpredictable.
With this in mind you won't get flustered, annoyed, or irritable
when customers ask for margarine instead of butter, whole wheat
instead of white, cottage cheese instead of coleslaw, and French
fries instead of salad with their linguini alfredo. Nor will
you think anything of it when a person orders pumpkin pie topped
with chocolate ice cream or scrambled egg beaters (cholesterol-
free powdered eggs) with greasy home fries and bacon.
```

—Lisa M. Agban

This paragraph states its **key idea in the first sentence** and then enlivens it with six compact examples of diners' unpredictability. This common paragraph pattern can be visualized like this:

The "broadest" part of this paragraph, its topic sentence, comes first, at the heavy end of the inverted triangle. The "smaller" or narrower details represent the narrow end of the triangle. But a sentence about how waitressing hurts your feet or about salary would simply not fit in this paragraph. A sentence about the unpredictability of customer tips *would* fit. The topic sentence-to-details paragraph is common because it makes sense; it's clear from the beginning where you're going, to both you and the reader. Here's another example of the same pattern from an essay about the destruction of rain forests:

Rain forests contain nearly half of all the plants and animals] *Topic Sentence*
in the world--many of which have unique medical properties that]
humans must save from extinction. Some rain forest plants are _*Details*
used to treat Hodgkin's disease, multiple sclerosis, and _*Detail*
Parkinson's disease. A delicate, tiny blue periwinkle flower
found only in Madagascar, for example, is the key element in a _*Detail*
drug used to treat leukemia. Ecologist Norman Myers estimates
there are five million rain forest species found nowhere else
in the world, and many are becoming extinct before we ever discover what wonder drugs they contain.

—Sally Lujetic

While topic sentence-to-details paragraphs are most common, good writers occasionally **start with details and build to their key idea,** as in this student essay about working in an insurance agency:

The face of the clock, reflecting the cool, gray wall, reads
8:55. Outside the office, a face presses against the glass door--
its nostrils flared, accusing like some grimacing, tribal mask.
Do I look intimidating sitting amid disordered files, vagrant
pens, computers, and fax machines, and muttering words like
"subrogation" or "earned premium"? Inside the bright but still
inaccessible office, I almost feel guilt for allowing this person to stand outside while I sit inside. Like a near-realized
sneeze, the feeling passes, and I pretend nobody's waiting to
get in. When the indifferent clock reads 5:05, similar masks
reappear at the door, along with pummeling fists. Sorry! The office is closed. "C-l-o-s-e-d," I mouth to the irate face outside.
The clock's indifference has completely become mine.

—Irene Kuzel

This intimate, honest paragraph gains power from the delayed message; the sharp details of the author's thoughts and description of the customer, office, and clock make us *want* a conclusion in the last sentence. If we were to visualize this paragraph, it would look like this:

Details –

Topic Sentence –

This paragraph shape works well to build up suspense in narrative paragraphs. Here's another example of the same pattern:

My first day of school, I wore a frilly pink dress with lacy crinoline puckering out around my bottom. The night before, Mom had to hide it so I wouldn't wear it to bed. I felt so pretty that day, as if I could stand on tippy toes forever like a ballerina. Mom held my hand, smiling. When the school bell rang, I thought everything was going to be okay, but Mom fainted with one of "her things." I tried to catch her, but she slipped through my small, helpless hands to the pavement. A trickle of blood ran down her sleepy face. Epilepsy, we'd been told. I knew she didn't <u>want</u> these things, but why did she have to have one <u>now</u>? A girl with pretty, carrot-colored hair stared with sympathetic, mocking eyes and asked, "Is that <u>your</u> mommy?" So badly did I want to be accepted by the other children, I lied as I walked away. "Oh, no," I said, "That's not <u>my</u> mommy," words that haunted me for years afterward.

—Christine Bailey

This paragraph starts simply, complicating and expanding to larger issues. As an introductory paragraph to an essay, it tempts us to read on for more detail.

Informative or persuasive paragraphs can also use the details-to-topic sentence format, as in this one on the issue of gun control:

narrative detail

Carol Kolen, a Chicago psychologist, was attacked several years ago at the University of Illinois Medical Center by two men, one carrying a gun. She fought off the rape but was severely beaten. Then one Saturday morning last year, she was attacked outside a neighborhood church. She bought a gun, and practices regularly at indoor shooting ranges. Many people install costly

FACT details

security systems in their homes, double-check their locks, won't walk to the store after dark, and panic if they lose sight of their child in a mall. But does it make a difference if your

Descriptive detail

assailant aims a gun into your back, swings a steel bat at your head, or pokes a knife in your chest? No. The threat lies in

Topic sentence

the assailant--not the weapon. In a society as violent as ours, the law should not take away our right to protect ourselves

from criminals. Recent bills like the Metzenbaum/Stark bill before the Congress jeopardize our safety, security, and freedom
as citizens.

More specific restatement of topic sentence

                                        —Barbara Collins

This paragraph plants the reader visually with a specific incident, then
gives four other examples before widening to the key idea—that a gun control bill before Congress was unsound. The details-first paragraph makes
sense because readers are more easily interested by stories and examples
than by abstractions.

Later in the same essay Barbara relies on a third type of paragraph
construction—one in which **the topic sentence is surrounded by details:**

Defenders of gun control say there are too many killings not
to outlaw guns. But many killers today are on drugs. According
to my sociology professor, 75 percent of all murders last year
were committed by people under the influence of drugs. The person high on cocaine or in need of a fix won't stop to wonder if
his victim will fight back or is armed. His lowered inhibitions
make for haste—and you can't scare him away with threats or a
stick. You have to shoot because when a drug addict needs
drugs, that is the <u>only</u> thing that matters. When I worked at a
drug rehabilitation center in Scotia, NY one summer, a polite,
sensitive 16-year-old boy sobbed to me his story of cocaine addiction. One day his friends bought from a local Brooklyn
dealer and after discovering the cocaine was actually cleans-
ing detergent, they hunted the dealer down in a park where they
beat and kicked him. Then one of the boy's friends handed the
boy a gun and said to shoot the dealer. In his rage and frustration, he did.

This paragraph begins with a statistic and hypothetical examples, makes
its main point in the middle, and then concludes with a specific example. It
could be diagrammed like this:

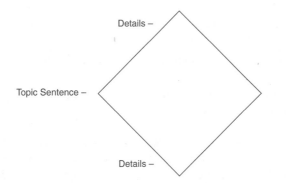

Details —

Topic Sentence —

Details —

Some paragraphs may not need a definite topic sentence, and the three patterns only suggest options for arranging details and an idea. Most writers do not say to themselves, "Aha, now I'm going to write a details-to-topic sentence paragraph." But writers *do* sense the placement of details and idea. You must always move your reader between the general and the specific. You want to avoid paragraphs that simply state and restate the main idea as the author tries to clarify one thought and never gets to details.

Start a new paragraph when you change the subject, change the speaker, change the place, or change the time.

 ## TRANSITIONS

Most sentences and paragraphs naturally flow smoothly. But if you find the jump between two sentences or paragraphs difficult or awkward, try using transitions to connect them.

Repeat key words. Pick up a key word from the previous sentence. Such a word (in this sentence, it is "word") helps writers sew sentences together.

A common way of doing this without being wordy is to use pronouns that recall the previous sentence:

"*This* is why we must . . ."

"Because of *this* man . . ."

"*It* is a problem . . ."

Or use specific transition words:

Time Transitions: now, then, meanwhile, before this happened, afterward

Space Transitions: on the other side of the room, farther down the trail, nearby

Contrast Transitions (to highlight opposition): however, despite this, although the police say, on the other hand

Example Transitions (when giving evidence): for example, in fact, for instance, one case involves

Addition Transitions (amplifying a point): in addition to, besides, on top of this, also

Concluding Transitions (to end a section or essay): thus, therefore, or finally

Place Marker Transitions (to move the reader from point to point): second, next, lastly

These are key trail markers for readers. By numbering your points clearly, you prevent readers from thinking you only have one mixed-up argument; transitions help readers see how things fit with each other. Transitions are invisible—like punctuation. Don't fear boring a reader with them. Many times you will use transitions naturally. However, if people seem confused about how your paragraphs or sentences connect, consciously include more transitional expressions. As an example, read the last three sentences of this paragraph without my two transitions, "however" and "as an example."

Highlights of Chapter 4

- Each paragraph should combine one idea with vivid details.
- If your paragraphs are skimpy—one or two sentences long—consider adding more detail.
- If your paragraphs sprawl over a page or two, see if you have mixed two or more key ideas into one paragraph.
- In revision, add transitions to show how the parts of paragraphs are related.
- Vary your paragraph patterns by occasionally starting with details and building to the key idea.

Writing Suggestions and Class Discussions

1. Write a topic sentence-to-details paragraph on one of these topics. Do a half-page brain teaser first and include at least four details in the paragraph. Be creative with the topics:

   - Oil
   - Your favorite television program
   - Zoos
   - Presidential politics
   - High school dances/balls

2. Write a details-to-topic sentence paragraph on one of these topics. Do a half-page brain teaser first and include at least four details in the paragraph. Be interesting:

   - Bridges
   - Math teachers
   - A scar or flaw in your body
   - One bigot you've met
   - Thanksgiving rituals

3. Write a topic sentence-surrounded-by-details paragraph on one of these. Do a half-page brain teaser first and include at least four details in the paragraph. Be creative:

   - Halloween
   - Litter
   - Laundromats

- Something in school that's hard to learn
- The human hand

4. Bring your best paragraph to class for a peer review, revise it, and turn in a finished copy.

5. Write a "paragraph anthology" paper of three paragraphs on unrelated topics. Give each a title. Each paragraph should be about half a page in length. Underline your key idea.

✓ **PARAGRAPH PEER REVIEW CHECKLIST**

1. Underline the topic sentence. Does the rest of the paragraph stick to it? If not, suggest changes.
2. What is the most interesting part of the paragraph?
3. How well supported is the topic sentence? Suggest one more detail the author could include.
4. How could one of the details be made more vivid?
5. What is the "shape" of the paragraph?
6. Mark all transitions used. Where might others be used?

CHAPTER 5

Order from Chaos
Thesis and Outline

A place for everything, everything in its place.

BEN FRANKLIN

A system-grinder hates the truth.

RALPH WALDO EMERSON

In the quotes on page 71, Franklin and Emerson summarize the debate about organizing. On one hand, writing needs order. Ideas presented randomly as they flow from brains—or brain teaser lists—are often chaotic. On the other hand, overorganization can kill the very truth writers hope to convey, for truth has a nasty habit of resisting preplanned schemes. This chapter seeks a reasonable middle ground between these extremes: the minimum organization needed to focus your topic. Why "minimum"? Because except in rare cases, no one ever exclaims, "Your organization really grabbed me." Fresh ideas and vivid detail do that.

That's why brain teasers are crucial. Nothing makes organizing a paper easier than creative, vivid brain teasers; nothing makes organization harder than a vague, skimpy list of preliminary ideas.

Let's start with an attitude. Organization must come from you. Don't cram your ideas into somebody else's box. Nor can you ignore organization, for it rarely occurs magically without conscious effort. The writer who plans how the essay will be structured and who studies a draft's structure will discover the holes in ideas ("I never did say *why* Tom Cruise was so powerful as an actor"), unbalanced emphasis ("Oh, no! I spent four paragraphs on one movie and only one paragraph on the other") and redundancy ("I'm saying the same thing about Leonardo DiCaprio in the second and fifth paragraphs—I ought to combine them"). The writer who plans will discover these things—before the reader does! In other words, developing a thesis and outlining should not only refine existing ideas, but should create new ideas and details: *Structure is a brain teaser too.*

A WORKING THESIS

A thesis is the key point your essay makes—the assertion, message, core idea, or purpose the rest of the essay illustrates or proves. This is where conscious organizing usually begins because a thesis creates the relationship between a paper's parts. Here are sample thesis sentences:

- Fathers and mothers who try to fulfill their lost chances through their children often crush the children's personalities.
- The end of communism has pressured the United States to prove its sincerity about peace.
- The abstract painting exhibit on campus is awful.
- Bill Clinton was a better president and worse man than most leaders.
- My roommate models her life on a TV soap opera.

Some of these are personal, some informative, some argumentative, but as theses, they share two qualities. First, they give the essay a flag to rally around. They lead a reader and writer to anticipate and visualize the essay to come. Second, they are assertions—complete statements.

▲ **PRACTICE 5-1:** What do the five theses promise a reader?

▲ **PRACTICE 5-2:** Make up two trial thesis sentences, then say what each promises your reader.

Statements such as "My essay is about welfare" or "Welfare is an important topic of concern today" fail as theses. What *about* it? There's no flag. Is the writer really going to tell us welfare is important? That's obvious. The real message hasn't emerged yet. A thesis asserts a viewpoint: "Two solutions look more promising than others to solve our welfare mess: Workfare and Entrepreneurism."

Not all essays need a working thesis. Narratives usually *imply* their messages, and simple reports don't need formal theses. In "How to Repair Your Bike," or "A Summary of the Minutes of the Student Senate Meeting," the thesis is obvious. However, almost all analytical, persuasive, and informative writing does require a thesis.

Try to develop a working thesis sentence during or after your brain teasers, but before beginning your first draft. You will probably modify it several times during the writing. This is a good sign that your thinking is not too rigid; until final revisions, you should still be learning about the ideas.

A thesis develops in two stages:

1. **Narrow the original topic** until it is vivid and small enough to handle in your allotted space.
2. **Make an assertion or express a viewpoint** about this narrowed topic.

Sample: A Working Thesis

Suppose the professor for your psychology course assigns a paper on love. The topic makes you—and me—panic. Thousands of books, poems, and articles have been written on the subject. How can you say anything significant in four or five pages? Well, you can, and here's how.

First, *narrow* the topic before doing brain teasers. Love? What kind? Sexual? Brotherly? Love of country? Can you list three other kinds? Your brain teaser will be hopelessly vague unless you're more specific than "love." To narrow, think a bit about the *circumstances* of the paper:

- For whom am I writing? (audience)
- Why am I writing this? (purpose)
- What obvious topics should I avoid? (freshness)

These three questions apply to most writing tasks and will save you wasted work on doomed topics. In this case, your psychology professor is the audience. You may grab an uninformed audience with a general topic, but not her. Your purpose is to show you've learned something; you can't just throw back her lectures. To be fresh, avoid topics and approaches common to other students. With this in mind, I hear this message: Avoid the topic of sexual love. Many psychology classes dwell on it, and I'd guess most students will choose it or parent–child love. I would pick the less-travelled topic. "Love of Country" cries out. Honestly, I'm skeptical that I can write something decent about this, but let's try.

To narrow it more for vividness, I do some brainteasing—*asking questions:*

Is love of C. different in socialist countries than in democracies?

How is L. of C. different in monarchies?

In Hitler's Germany?

Should I deal with how governments encourage patriotic love?

Should I deal with the people's *need* to love?

Should I contrast L. of C. in different countries?

Should I deal with L. of C. in different races or cultures?

Would people today really say "I regret I have but one life to give for my country" like Nathan Hale?

This brain teaser helps me understand what's involved in this topic; I'm *learning* more. At this point I'm going to try an example brain teaser on Love of Country:

U.S. purple mountains/fruited plains—L. of C. based on beauty.

What do the Soviet, French, or Nazi Germany patriotic anthems say? Research?

The frenzy of Hitler's speeches—the spell and regimentation. The goose step parades, the *sieg heil* salutes. What was behind that frenzy?

The shame of Germany after WWI—a broken country.

The Soviet May Day parades with missiles, tanks, and blocks of soldiers. The gray mass of people—somber—dull.

U.S. parades on Memorial Day—dancing, fun, music, entertainment. A sprinkling of soldiers. More loose and individualistic.

The tomb of the unknown soldier—all countries.

The editorial in my local paper critical of the U.S. on July 4th.

State-controlled press for Nazis and Chinese.

Japan: highest L. of C. was *Kamikaze* pilots.

U.S.: draft resisters say they love the U.S.

I learned or reminded myself of much while doing this and think I'll narrow my topic further to "a comparison of the psychology of love of country in Nazi Germany to America today." My brain teasers kept returning to this, and I'm reasonably sure no one else in class will have such a topic. If I'm not sure the professor will accept it, I'll ask her for approval.

Now I'm ready for the second step in creating a thesis: *to make an assertion.* Since I've decided to write a contrast paper, I should do a contrast brain teaser for more detail. Here's a start on it:

Nazi Germany	*U.S. Today*
Poverty-stricken	Prosperous
Ambition to be on top	Already on top
Chaos, emotional insecurity	Orderly society, more secure
Resents outside intrusion	U.S. intrudes in other lands
Fervent, frenzied L. of C.	Cool, cynical L. of C.
L. of C. meant obedience	L. of C. means . . . who knows?

In psychology class perhaps you've studied Abraham Maslow's hierarchy of needs,[1] and you recognize that some of these contrasts fit his categories. The Germans may have been patriotic because they were broken by World War I and poor; they had strong safety and esteem needs that Hitler appealed to by promising prosperity and a powerful empire. The United States already has considerable material and national security, so its love of country can afford more open-minded cynicism. So here's my **trial working thesis:** "Nazi German and modern American love of country differ because the needs of the citizens differ."

This section you've just read is pretty much as it came from my head so I could demonstrate how the process works. It *is* sloppy, and I had no idea what thesis was coming. If I'd taken different paths (for instance, developing the contrast in Soviet and U.S. parades that I found tempting), the thesis might be radically different. I've tried to reveal the connections between topic choice, brain teasers, and thesis formulations, but I know at each stage there are unseen jumps of thought. You must make these on your own; they are what make ideas truly your own. To develop a good idea, you must play back and forth between thesis and brain teasing.

Here's another suggestion to narrow a topic and conjure up the thesis lurking in your early thoughts. Write the following sentences, and finish the incomplete idea.

"What I really want to say is . . ."
"Reader, what I really want to tell you is . . ."
"What interests me most about my topic is . . ."

If you're still stuck, back up. Make a short list of key words from your brain-teaser lists and formulate a thesis sentence from them. Or first create a trial title for your paper—a phrase of three or four words—and build a thesis sentence from it. Imagine you have 15 seconds to convey your main idea. If you use a computer to create a thesis sentence, I recommend not

---

[1] Maslow believed there is a hierarchy of human needs: moving from the basic biological needs (hunger, thirst, and safety) to the more complex psychological needs (self-fulfillment, appreciation of art).

trying to edit your first attempts. Just hit return and start over. After you write four or five versions, edit the best one.

▲ **PRACTICE 5-3:** Choose a topic for your next paper and suggest three ways of narrowing it. Then write a possible thesis sentence.

 ## LOOPING

Some students skip a working thesis, saying, "I'll just write a draft and fix it later." A few people can do this—but if you question them closely, virtually all really have done brain teasing and thesis work in their heads beforehand. Most writers who skip thesis preparation start confidently for a sentence or two. Then the next paragraphs fumble into new ideas or repetition. Somewhere halfway through the paper, the writer realizes what the thesis might be, and the paper smooths out a bit near the end. Revision of this tangled stuff is torture; the ideas smear together and the details are skimpy. It's almost a sure route to a poor grade. In effect, the writer is using the draft to generate ideas, organize them, and find the right words to express them. It's too much to ask of one sitting.

You *can* freewrite to generate ideas and structure, however, by **looping.** To loop, write freely for ten minutes, without censoring ideas, much as you do during a brain teaser, except that instead of listing, write full sentences, letting one flow to the next. Then *extract* the key sentence or concept from this freewriting and copy it on another sheet of paper. Write for another ten minutes using the extracted sentence as a guide, then extract the best key sentence from *that* freewriting until you formulate a thesis. Looping works well for people who like writing connected sentences rather than the helter-skelter of brain teasers.

Rethink your thesis at all stages of writing a paper, except when revising mechanics and grammar. A perfectly formulated thesis that never changes during draft and revision is a red flag. You may be grinding down the truth for the sake of the system. Slop around in the topic before settling on a working thesis. Find out what's there, pile up some building blocks, and—with a *working* thesis—have a rough plan before constructing the essay. As Shakespeare's King Lear said, "Nothing will come of nothing." All this work on theses has *not* led to just one sentence! It spades up new ideas and makes the glue that will hold everything together.

▲ **PRACTICE 5-4:** Create a working thesis sentence for one of these topics. First list three to five potential narrow topics within the general one, and choose the one you think will be the freshest. Then do a half-page brain teaser. Finally, write a working thesis. Show your work on paper.

Or, try looping; write three free-form paragraphs, extracting a key sentence from the first to start the second, and from the second to start the third. Your thesis must still be narrow and stated as an assertion.

- Freedom of the press
- Tourism
- Underwear ads in newspapers and magazines
- Single mothers
- Choose your own topic

 ## OUTLINES

   Like theses, outlines create a Ben Franklin–Ralph Emerson debate. I've heard students say of former high school teachers, "My God! She said we had to have fifty 3 × 5 index cards and a two-page outline. The outline had to have five divisions and each division had to have at least two subheads and *they* had to have two subheads and they . . ." However, I've heard other voices: "My teacher said not to worry about an outline: Just write what we feel and it'll be true. Just be loose. Well I'm real loose—I'm totally disorganized. I need help." I advocate a middle ground. Here's why.

The detailed outline on multiple levels looks like this in the abstract:

       I.
      II.
          A.
              1.
              2.
          B.
              1.
                  a.
                  b.
              2.
     III.
          A.
          B.
              1.
                  a.
                  b.
                  c.
              2.

Its relentless order seems as inevitable as fate. It gives a writer who molds ideas and details to it a false sense of security—just because you are organized doesn't mean you've said anything worthwhile. It may also paralyze many writers who assume their ideas are bad because they don't easily adapt to the outline.

Third, it may kill spontaneity in the draft. Advocates of this system *want* to eliminate the dangers of spontaneity—disorganization, uncertainty about what to say in the next sentence, redundancy. But they kill spontaneity's virtues too—coherence of mood, surprise, discovery. Overoutlining often creates dead, lifeless drafts. The writer simply colors inside lines already drawn.

Finally, ruthlessly detailed outlines create unnecessary labor because they're seldom used in practice. As philosopher Søren Kierkegaard once commented, "Most systematizers are like a man who builds an enormous castle but lives in a shack nearby." Most advocates of intricate outlines don't use them themselves. They instead write from humbler shack outlines. We get hung up on detailed outlines because humans like abstract order and want to believe that creativity can be planned perfectly. It can't. Actual writing based on a minutely detailed outline usually is dull. Most good writing by scientists, businesspeople, and essayists fails to meet the standards of a multidivision outline.

The other extreme, starting without any outline, may work for some people, but it too is flawed. Without any plan, you *are* going to stumble, wander around, repeat yourself. If you want to do a good job, you will do heavy rewriting to separate the brilliant tidbits from the garbage and simply to see what you've said. This path, of course, is the one writers must take when composing at the last minute. This approach gives the writer the illusion that a draft is being produced because pages fill up.

THE SCRATCH OUTLINE

The scratch outline is a single-level outline that only shows main headings (only the "I," "II" and "III" in the example). For a two- or three-page paper, three or four headings will do. For a four- or five-page paper, five headings will do. An essay entitled "Dangers of Seatbelts" might be outlined this way:

- Introduction
- Pregnant women
- Fire during an accident
- Drowning during an accident
- Back problems

The writer then assigns details from brain-teaser lists to the appropriate heading and starts drafting. The scratch outline *does* offer direction but *does not* stifle creativity. Within each section, *details are fluid* so you have some spontaneous creation and still know where you're going next. A scratch outline can be seen as a whole; headings can be easily added or rearranged. Most professional writers use this kind of bare-bones outline.

To turn your brain teasers or other notes into a scratch outline, I'm going to suggest three options professional writers use. Let's assume that my topic is "death" and that I've already narrowed it down to deathbed moments.

1. Use Brain Teasers with Built-in Outlines

Classification, Comparison or Contrast, and Alternate Viewpoints create structure by their nature. You may have to consolidate or rearrange a bit, but they point you toward a narrow thesis and an outline. For example, if you do a classification brain teaser on "Death," you may classify different ways people behave while dying.

- Calm—death is natural, a part of life
- Begging forgiveness—to make up for wrongs
- Humor—playing a joke
- Philosophical—the "deep thoughts" death
- Religious—death leads to afterlife

This is already an outline. You only need to make a thesis assertion and find examples to illustrate each heading, and you're ready to write. As examples, you might use stories from deaths you've witnessed or from famous people. For humor, I recall that the comedian W. C. Fields—a lifelong atheist—was found on his deathbed reading a Bible. "What are you doing?" a friend asked Fields.

"Looking for loopholes," Fields answered.

Distribute your examples to the headings. If you have headings with no examples, you drop them. If you have interesting examples with no heading, try to invent a new one. For instance, I just recalled that Revolutionary War hero Ethan Allen was lying on his deathbed when someone whispered to him, "Sir, the angels are waiting for you."

General Allen snarled, "Goddammit, let them wait!" I might add a new category called "Defiance."

Your thesis might assert which approach to death makes the most sense and defend it. ("Of all the ways people die, going with a joke makes the most sense.") Or it might explain the motivation behind each type of death. ("The way you die tells the world how you lived.")

A scratch outline for an alternate viewpoints brain teaser uses competing views as outline headings. In comparison or contrast the major comparisons are headings.

One danger of using brain teasers with built-in outlines is falling into a cookie cutter approach: stamping out outlines without thinking of your message first. *Never let a pattern interfere with what you think is true.*

▲ **PRACTICE 5-5:** Make a scratch outline on "Interracial Dating" or "Athletes as Role Models," using any of the organizing brain teasers as a pattern.

▲ **PRACTICE 5-6:** Make a scratch outline for your topic in Practice 5-3, based on one of the organizing brain teasers. Note: You may have to rewrite your thesis to fit the brain-teaser format.

2. Make a Bullet Summary from Your Brain Teasers or Freewriting

A "bullet" is a little dash, star, or box like the ones that mark lists in this book. Read through your brain teasers or freewriting, and on a separate sheet of paper, write the highlights in list form, starting each one with a bullet. Imagine that your notes are a lecture from which you're trying to pick out the key points for a test. These should be ideas, not details—for they are your potential outline headings and should summarize other items. If you end up with more than four or five headings for a short paper, try combining some. Fewer than three headings means you may need another idea or two. For the topic of deathbed behavior, I might end up with something like this:

- Defiance
- Humor
- Religious
- Philosophical

To get my bullet outline ready for a draft, I have two options. First, I can use my four headings as labels and **label each item on my original brain teaser list.** I circle labels so they stand out on a messy brain teaser. On a computer, insert the heading, capitalized, before each item. An examples brain teaser listing famous deaths might be labeled like this:

(DEFIANCE)

Beethoven shaking his fist at the sky a moment before death.

(RELIGION)

John Donne lying in his coffin to have his picture painted.

(HUMOR)

Dylan Thomas's last words: "I've just drunk 18 straight whiskies—that's a new record."

(PHILOSOPHICAL)

Gertrude Stein's last words: "What's the Question?"

(PHILOSOPHICAL)

Thoreau—when somebody asked if he'd made his peace with God, he answered, "I wasn't aware we'd quarreled."

(HUMOR)

W. C. Fields, looking for loopholes.

(DEFIANCE)

Ethan Allen telling the angels to wait.

(??)

Houdini (escape artist) saying, "I think this thing's got me."

(HUMOR - RELIGION)

Ramon Narvez (espionage agent) was told by his priest to forgive his enemies. "I have no enemies, Father," he said. "I have shot them all."

When you sit down to write your draft, compose a sentence or two that describes what you want to say about the defiant death, for example, and then scan your notes for each defiance label and add them as details.

A second option to finish a bullet summary outline is to **rewrite the brain teaser details under the headings.** Read through your brain teasers and rewrite each item under one heading. This is easy on a word processor. Just cut and paste the brain-teaser material under the headings. If you're hand writing, leave enough room between headings, or give each heading a separate sheet of paper. Here's how this method would look:

Defiance
  Beethoven
  Ethan Allen

Humor
  Dylan Thomas
  W. C. Fields

Religion
  John Donne
  Narvez(??)

Philosophical
  Gertrude Stein
  Thoreau

When you compose your draft, everything is in place, but you have to do more rewriting of notes beforehand. With both options, if you find details that don't fit the headings, you must cut them or create a new heading. You can also begin to scratch out the dumb stuff you encouraged during the brain teaser.

3. Use Clustering, a Visual Diagram

Write your general topic in the center of a clean page and then draw lines out, like radiating spokes from a wheel hub, to related ideas. It stimulates ideas (as a brain teaser does) yet keeps the key topic at the center of focus. Each item must connect to another by a line—either to the central topic or to any radiating headings. Go through your brain-teaser lists and assign each item a place on the cluster sheet. Try connecting each item to headings first. If it doesn't belong, connect it with a line to the main topic. When done, you'll have a visual representation of your ideas—where you have the most ideas, what fits with what.

An outline developed from **clustering** would look like this:

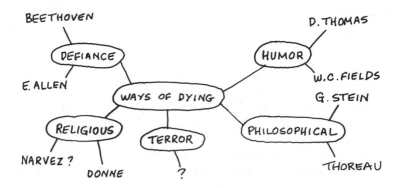

Your last step is to decide what order the outline headings should follow. Don't worry about the order of details. Rearrange the headings a few times to see how they'll flow when you write the draft. Most writers save their most creative idea for last.

▲ **PRACTICE 5-7:** Suppose your research for the classification of deaths topic uncovered these examples:

- John Greenleaf Whittier's last breath: "My love to the world."
- Mark Twain's last written note: "Death, the only immortal who treats us all alike, whose pity, peace and refuge are for all—the soiled, the pure, the rich and the poor, the loved and the unloved."
- Emily Dickinson's last words were disputed: either she said "Oh, is *that* all?" or "I must go in; the fog is rising."

- Theodore Dreiser prepared these last words, but did not say them: "Shakespeare, here I come!"
- O. Henry's last words: "Turn up the lights. I don't want to go home in the dark."
- Thomas Jefferson died on July 4, 1826. His last words: "Is it the fourth?"
- Wilson Mizener to a priest: "Why should I talk to you? I've just been talking to your boss."
- J. J. Rodale, organic health food advocate, uttered these words on a national TV interview just before he dropped dead: "I'm so healthy that I expect to live on and on."
- James Thurber's last words: "God bless . . . God damn!"

Incorporate these examples into a scratch outline. You may use some categories developed in the chapter, but create at least two new ones.

▲ **PRACTICE 5-8:** Do a page of brain teasers for your topic from Practice 5-3 and distribute the material to your scratch outline from Practice 5-6.

 ## SAMPLE DRAFT FROM OUTLINE

THE FINE ART OF DYING

How will we spend our last breath when facing the brink of eternity? As the soul shakes free, will we defy death? Will we reach into philosophical depths for the meaning of life? Will we pass silently away? Will we congratulate death with a sporting handshake and a joke? Or will we go with faith in a new life?

I suspect the few people who think about dying imagine approaching the grave with dignity, summoning up spirited words or actions that will reveal their true hearts. The notorious atheist W. C. Fields was found reading the Bible on his deathbed by a friend who had come to pay his last respects. The religious friend smugly asked what Fields was doing with the Holy Book. "Looking for loopholes," the comedian replied. Death himself must have grinned at such pluck and integrity.

Perhaps the simplest dignified response to death has been defiance. On the brink of reckoning, people dare the cosmos to take them. Beethoven sat bolt upright when he spotted a flash of lightning. Long cursed with deafness by the Powers-that-Be, he shook his fist at the heavens, sank back, and expired. There was music in this gesture, one last measure beating valiantly against the silent tomb. Told to confess his sins, 15th-century Italian painter Perugino refused because he didn't believe in an after-life. Were demons gleefully stoking a fiery pit for the unrepentant? Good! He would find out, he vowed.

For those of a philosophical mind, Gertrude Stein's death. . . .

Commentary

Because you went through the notes and predraft writing with me, you can see them behind this draft. Notice how the introductory paragraph sets up the classifications to come. Instead of simply saying, "I will discuss five types of deaths in this essay: defiant, philosophical, silent, humorous, and religious," the writer poses questions to get readers to think about which option they would choose. These questions set up the categories. W. C. Fields is used to visualize a specific example early but also to create the thesis, that our death shows how much integrity we have in the way we have lived. This point needs to be made in each of the categories. Notice that each of the next paragraphs focuses on one of the outline headings, and examples illustrate each.

CONCLUDING COMMENTS: Outlines are like bones. Nobody sees them, but a person would sag into a baggy lump without them. You need some skeleton to help your essay stand up. Your thesis is also almost invisible—like a brain—but it makes your essay walk straight instead of reeling and wobbling. How do you know if you're organizing too much or too little? If you feel lost during drafts, try more organization. If you feel bored and confined, try more brain teasers and maybe looser organization. The one thing you cannot do is simply write the way you always have if it's not working. The writer who really wants to improve can do so at *every* stage of writing: thinking up fresher ideas and details, making theses and outlines, writing the draft, and revising.

Highlights of Chapter 5

- Organization balances spontaneity and control. You can kill thinking with a stranglehold outline and you can become hopelessly lost without some plan.
- Writing brain teasers with plenty of ideas and details will do more to solve your organizational problems than any organizing formula I can offer.

- Developing a thesis is the first step to organizing many papers. This sentence states your paper's key idea. Consider your audience, your paper's purpose, and freshness when you shape this sentence. After you have a trial thesis, read over your brain-teaser notes to make sure it fits what you have. This sentence may be the most revised sentence in your paper.
- I advocate a scratch outline, but you have to be comfortable with your method. Try a variety of methods during this course. You may have been using the wrong method for yourself. Persuasion and research require more outlining than narration and description. Try looping, clustering, labeling, and drawing lines if you never have before. Give yourself a lot of options.

Writing Suggestions and Class Discussions

1. Narrow three of these topics into ones you can handle in two or three pages. Concentrate on freshness—anticipate the obvious things others might say. Some topics may seem "boring"; you must *make* them interesting. Prepare brain teasers for each as you work along. *Or* try looping to narrow two of these topics.
    - Road construction
    - Disaster films
    - Courage that's overlooked
    - A book you've read
    - Prejudice you've suffered
    - High school versus college
    - Open topic
2. Now, write a working thesis for each of your narrowed topics. Be sure it's a complete sentence and makes an assertion the rest of the essay can relate to. If you "looped" in 1, you're done!
3. For your best thesis sentence in 2, write a scratch outline. Aim for three or four main headings and assign your best brain-teaser material to them. Use any outlining method discussed, but tell which kind. Bring all work to class.
4. Write a draft for the outline.
5. Evaluate the following as potential theses. What strengths and weaknesses do each have? Imagine what you'd have to do as a writer to fulfill reader expectations for each.
    - Pets bring out the worst in their owners.
    - Japanese products have been extremely successful in the United States.
    - Noise pollution is bad.
    - Statistics on teenage pregnancy don't tell how it hurts one young woman at a time.
    - Chevrolets are better than Fords.
    - I'm going to write about my first love and my latest love.
    - The New York Yankees and the Boston Red Soxs are rivals.
    - San Francisco is the Paris of the United States.
    - We ought to extend mandatory recycling to tires.

6. Write a brief, *tactful* letter of complaint to a company or organization that has mistreated you. Make a half-page list of ideas and details, formulate a thesis that specifies what you want from the organization, then outline your letter. Consider your reader's viewpoint.

7. Write a three-year review of your life. Your object is to *evaluate* your last three years, not simply to tell what happened. Although the topic is already narrowed, you need to create a thesis and an outline with details for each heading.

✓ **PEER REVIEW CHECKLIST FOR THESIS/OUTLINES**

AUTHOR: _____

REVIEWER: _____

Paraphrase the author's thesis in your own words to give him or her a new option.

1. Is the thesis as narrow and clear as the samples in this chapter? If not, suggest other angles.

2. Does the thesis have spark? Freshness? Suggest how to improve it.

3. What promises does the thesis make for the coming essay?

4. Does the outline make sense? Try rearranging the main headings. Try adding or combining headings. Even if it looks perfect, suggest one change the author can chew on.

5. Are there enough details for a vivid essay? Add some and sharpen some by asking the author to explain orally what will be said about a heading or two.

CHAPTER 6

The Draft

That Frenzy Near Madness

There was a world in my eye.

ALICE WALKER

Planning to write is not writing. . . . Writing is writing.

E. L. DOCTOROW

"Why is it that I can never get a paper going! I thought I was into the topic— I did some brain teasers and made an outline. Yet my pen just wants to doodle when I sit down to write the draft. Everything I start to write looks awful— if anything comes at all." I've heard this many times over the years, and I've often felt exactly the same way myself. Most writers sometimes experience choking uncertainty when starting a draft. It may be fear of commitment to one idea or switching from the note-taking method of thinking to thinking in sentences. Whatever the reasons, here are a few ideas to make the draft go easier.

THE CONCRETE INTRODUCTION

Warm-ups Are for Leftovers

The introduction can be particularly hard because most people don't put much prewriting thought into it. A typical outline just says "intro." Yet we instinctively know that our introduction will set the tone for the whole paper, will grab or sedate a reader, and will either point us in the right direction or bog us down in swampy confusion. So as our first task in the draft we must write a key paragraph without the prewriting help the rest of the paper has. No wonder writers hesitate at that first sentence. I do. I've already thrown out two introductions to this chapter.

Many introductions are "warm-ups" as the writer gropes for the right tone, the properly phrased thesis, and an interesting lead-in. When I tell students their introductions are too long or vague and that they should get to the point quicker, they sometimes respond that the reader has to get used to them. But what's really happening is that the *writer* is getting used to the topic. Nothing gets a reader used to you faster than a sharp opening; nothing makes a reader feel uneasy sooner than an introduction that mushes around a topic. How does this one make you feel?

> Homelessness is a very important topic today. The future of our society depends on solving this problem. So many people are suffering, and homelessness is different than it was ten years ago. It's time we did something to cure this blot on society.

This introduction evaporates if you try to squeeze a specific idea out of it and does not give a clear picture of what's ahead.

To avoid introduction paralysis, start your paper not by warming up but by being already hot. Warming up is for leftovers; an introduction should set a fresh appetizer before your reader.

One strategy is simply **don't write the introduction first.** Start by drafting the first main heading in your scratch outline, and write the introduction after the rest of the draft is done. As your draft evolves, the introduction you do write later will fit the paper better. The weakness of this approach is that you may miss the self-guidance the introduction provides. You can compromise by starting the paper with this simple working sentence: "The purpose of this paper is . . ." Obviously, you'll have to improve this bland opening during revision.

Many professional writers try another method for the first paragraph. Their first few sentences attract and stimulate the reader's *interest.* Once interested, a reader is ready for your thesis, so a good introduction frequently starts with several concrete, perhaps puzzling details, then presents the paper's main idea in the last sentence of the opening paragraph. All six of the introduction types below share this principle.

One specific technique is to start with an **anecdote**—a short story related to your main idea. It can be a personal, researched, or fictional story. Here's an example that could substitute for the vague introduction on homelessness.

> Hattie McBride's dress was torn and dirty. She pushed her shopping cart into an alleyway, pulled out the folded cardboard from the lower rack and spread it under a fire escape. She rummaged among the wadded clothes and utensils on top until she pulled out a bottle of cheap wine. After settling down on the cardboard, she sighed. She was a grandmother and once owned her own home. Now, like thousands of other street people she's become a social problem. Let's look at one solution for people like Hattie.

These details should make a reader hungry for the idea that would explain them—the thesis sentence, which comes next.

Another opening starts by asking **a good question.** That's the trick—a *good* question. Obvious questions or those needing only "yes" or "no" responses don't arouse our interest. Examples of bad questions: "Would you like to be a street person?" or "Are most homeless people happy?" There's mild interest in these, but they don't push the reader toward a theme, just a yes or no response. A better question is one with open-ended answers, such as this:

> Everytime I walk downtown and see men, women, and children shuffling around in rags and scavenging like stray dogs, I wonder why. Why would a person *choose* to grub in garbage dumpsters, sleep in abandoned cars, and huddle around wine bottles? What can be done to help reclaim these people into society? After talking to some of these people and reading about the topic, I think there are three main reasons why people end up on the street, and that there *is* hope for some of them.

These questions are specific and involve readers by *asking them to account for a situation, not simply respond to a question like a test.* Whether readers do think of an explanation or are simply puzzled, your audience will be primed to listen to what you have to offer, and that's the introduction's job. Notice also how concrete details hold our eye as these questions develop.

A third technique is to start with a **striking fact or facts:**

> Nearly two thirds of all homeless people once held responsible jobs and 25 percent *are* employed; one tenth hold college degrees; over half have families, most of whom know about their present condition. Homeless people should

bother us not because they've degraded themselves, but because they point out how industry, education, and family have failed.

The same pattern holds here: vivid details followed by the author's thesis. A striking fact must be something unexpected. The following doesn't qualify: "Many automobiles produced in our high-tech society continue to be unsafe." But this does: "Twenty percent of the cars we drive today have life-threatening flaws in their construction." Always remember the power of the specific.

A fourth technique is to start with **a quotation** that leads to your thesis:

> "For God's sake, get them off the beach!" said one of the contest organizers. "Get the security people—now!" It seems during a publicity session at the 1989 Miss America Contest in Atlantic City that several homeless men crawled out from under a lifeboat the gorgeous women were using as a photo prop. The men had slept all night under the boat. Police officers escorted them off so the photos of sea, casinos, and American beauties could continue to maintain the image of America the beautiful, home of the brave and free. Cruel as the organizer's words sound, they may reflect a typical American attitude toward the homeless: We don't want to think about you.

Strong quotations dramatize an idea—interest readers by creating conflict or mystery. You read on to find out why the person said it or what the author of the paper will say about the quotation. That leads to your thesis.

Fifth, **open with a problem or dilemma**—viewpoints that contradict each other. Present several sides of a controversial situation before working toward your solution in the thesis:

> Being homeless means being powerless. No money, no stake in your society, no knowledge of how to escape. Most citizens are ashamed of homelessness, especially of homeless children. Yet without an address you can't vote, receive welfare and, often, attend school—things that give you power. However, there is good reason to require addresses. Society must protect itself from being cheated by fake voters, welfare frauds, and parents sneaking children into better schools outside their towns. In a conference in Washington, D.C., advocates of the homeless think they have found a way around the address dilemma: social security numbers assigned on birth certificates.

Problem/dilemma introductions clarify issues and entice your audience.

Sixth, ask yourself, "what will people first think of this topic?" and **speak directly to the reader's concerns.** This is how I began this chapter, imagining negative thoughts some students have starting a draft. First, vividly identify with your readers' viewpoint, then lead them toward considering a new idea. Addressing the reader as "you" may help:

> Perhaps you've seen the wino curl on the grate by the post office, the plastic sheet "tents" spread over bushes outside an office building at night for homeless people, the man who emerges from a doorway to ask for a dollar you're too afraid not to give him. Perhaps in disgust you want to shout at them, "You shouldn't live this way! No human being has to accept this!" I felt this way too, until I met Robert Cole, the philosopher of the homeless.

Three final points. **One,** avoid the dictionary definition introduction: "*Webster's Dictionary* defines homelessness as 'the state or condition of being without a domicile; indigent.'" This does not move the paper anywhere; it's superficial and corny. The two cases for which it might work would be if you were really going to pick apart the definition in your paper (Is it really a condition or is it an attitude? What is a domicile?) or if the definition had things in it most people wouldn't know. Writers who start with dictionary definitions, however, usually ignore them and move on. So will the reader.

Two, your introduction hooks the reader, but it also *promises* the reader what will come. As in the striking fact example, you may even list the main points to be covered. But be careful not to promise what you can't deliver—the essay will be like a flashy car that gets repossessed during a big date.

Three, be brief. A play reviewer once estimated he spent a year and a half of his life waiting for curtains to rise. Don't do that to a reader.

WHAT TO FOCUS ON DURING COMPOSITION

Once you get past the introduction, you may be fortunate enough to experience that frenzy near madness—a compelling rush of energy and insightful concentration that carries writers along. You may need only to refer briefly to your notes to start another cascade of sentences. If this happens and the draft still sparkles in the cold light of the next morning, consider yourself lucky.

But the frenzy of inspiration has a finicky way of not showing up or of teasing a writer with a two- or three-sentence burst and then vanishing. The writer who depends on inspiration will have some lucky effortless compositions but much more despair and frustration. The fact is that most writing—just like most living—is done at an ordinary pitch of mental excitement and must be done in a professional manner. Fine frenzies are memorable and cherished because they are not everyday happenings. All writers must learn to write without them. Ironically, it's when I'm plugging away at an ordinary pitch of concentration that inspiration sneaks into my fingers and brain. While I cannot promise this fickle muse will carry you off, you can improve the odds of an inspiration through concentrated prewriting and focus during the writing of your draft. Here are four suggestions:

1. Most importantly, concentrate on the logical, smooth flow of ideas and details. Think visually as you bounce between ideas and details. As you clarify a generalization, supply details to visualize it. As you give examples, think of the conclusion you can draw to round out the paragraph.

2. Use your outline intelligently. Your scratch outline headings should become topic sentences for paragraphs most of the time, and the listed details will fill out your paragraphs. But don't think of this as a coloring book in which you're simply filling in spaces. You should think up new examples and recast ideas as you write. Don't let an outline chain you. But also don't run off in totally new directions for long sections without referring back to the outline—you could end up confused or with what should be two papers. If you really see a whole new direction for the paper as you draft, take a few minutes to throw together another scratch outline, scrap the old draft, and chase after your new thoughts.

3. Move fairly quickly as you write the draft. It helps things stick together. If your mood changes between writing parts of the draft, the tone may change. Ideas that you mean to bring up later (but that aren't written down) tend to be forgotten during interruptions. Ernest Hemingway believed that the best time to interrupt the draft for the day was at a spot where he knew exactly what the next sentence would say. That way, the following day, it would be easy to start up again. Other writers tend to stop at a tough spot, hoping incubation will solve the problem for them overnight.

There are some writers who work slowly. The French writer Gustave Flaubert was known for drafting only one paragraph per day during the composition of *Madame Bovary*. But for almost all writers I'd recommend a fast pace—a two- to three-page paper should be drafted in one sitting if you've done good prewriting work, and a four- to six-page paper should be no more than a two-sitting effort. It takes a certain sustained effort to engage your mind in the topic. The speed record may be held by Isaac Asimov, who claimed he could draft a nonfiction book in 70 hours. That's hot!

4. To ease the flow of words, imagine speaking your draft to someone as you compose. If it's a personal essay, imagine the person to be a friend. If it's an argumentative or informative essay, imagine speaking to your intended audience. If you don't remind yourself this way that you're writing for people, you may treat writing as a mechanical process, and the sparkle of a human voice will evaporate from the draft. Visualizing your audience helps you fill in gaps, keep a consistent tone, and suggest new ideas as you compose. Some writers say their sentences aloud and then type them. Others compose aloud from the outline into a tape recorder and then transcribe to paper, just to get this effect of audience. As I "talk" to my reader, I imagine her saying things like "What's that word mean?" . . . "Get to your point!" . . . "How does all this relate to me?" . . . "Keep my interest—give me a story or a wild fact." . . . "Where did you get that fact?"

What Not to Focus on in the Draft

- Do not think about mechanics, spelling, or sentence structure.
- Do not work hard at word use and style.

Why not? Because secondary matters bog down a writer during the draft and interrupt the smooth flow of ideas and details. If a great metaphor or vivid verb comes to you, fine. Take it. But don't spend five minutes during the draft searching for one. Save this effort for revision.

Drafting on a Computer

To keep you focused, I recommend turning off your beeping spell-checker or grammar-write. They're just interruptions now. Likewise, don't dawdle over font sizes or title page graphics. You really haven't started writing until you write words. Right now it's ideas and details that count. The big advantages of the computer in drafting are that it saves everything in clean type and you don't have to worry about line or page endings. If you want to start with a proper format, pull down the layout menu and set your margins at 1 1/4 inches, lines at double space, font at something plain in size 12. Left-justify and use black ink.

DO SAVE YOUR WORK ON A DISK! And double-check that it's saved before you exit. The computer now eats more papers than dogs do, but most teachers are as hard-hearted as ever about deadlines. If your computer has an automatic save feature, activate it. One summer a three-second power outage from a lightning storm caused eight pages of hot new work to vanish before my eyes. I'd like to spare you that. If a paper seems to have been eaten, it might only be hiding under other windows. Reduce whatever is on your screen to see what's behind it or check your file menu.

When You Get Stuck

Notice, it's not "if" you get stuck. All writers spin their wheels in the mud of a draft occasionally. You can continue to gun the engine and splatter goo hoping you will wiggle loose, or you can try alternative strategies to get you to the dry land of the next sentence. **Here are some specific tips I use when I get stuck.**

1. *Use brain teasers* discussed in Chapters 2 and 3.
   - Move from ideas to details or from details to ideas.
   - Think with your senses to visualize the topic.
   - Imagine an alternative viewpoint to your last sentence.
   - Classify or compare the last point you made.
   - Think of a metaphor for your last or next point.
   - Break stereotypes you've just stated.
   - Try a humorous or fantastical touch.
   - Give an example.
   - Think about what bugs you about what you're saying.
2. *Study your scratch outline* and think up a transition phrase to move you to the next point:
   - "On the other hand . . ."
   - "The next reason to support this proposal is . . ."
   - "Secondly . . ."
   - "However . . ."
   - "Despite this fact . . ."
   - "The next morning . . ."
   - "When I saw Bill again . . ."

3. *Reread the last page you wrote.* When you reach the blank space, you may build up enough momentum to leap across it.
4. *Reread your thesis* and ask how the next point should relate back to it.
5. *Ask what your reader would want to know at this point.* Would she have a question to ask? Would he be confused or want to protest? Use the responses as a cue.
6. *Skip the tough section and move to the next.* Fill it in later. You may discover that it's illogical or doesn't belong in the paper.
7. *Write several alternative sentences* to see which sounds best.

 ## BLOCKS DURING DRAFTING

As I mentioned in Chapter 3, fear of risk and insecurity about your ability to think can disable a writer. These can also occur during the draft. You suddenly fear you're going to say something really dumb or embarrassing, and your pen quivers in hesitation. You think, what will my professor think if I say I've used cocaine? Or that my uncle abused his children? Is my idea juvenile? Maybe I should be safer, hide more. Maybe I should just scrap it all and start over.

These are common fears. You must risk sounding silly to get anything drafted. The fact is, no first draft sounds polished. And dealing with embarrassing facts forces you to be more honest about the topic. In any case, there's time to reconsider these things in revision. At the draft stage, trust yourself and keep moving.

Some delay is good for incubation, but inability to start can be a lack of commitment. If you sigh a lot and say to yourself, "I just don't want to do this," remember the story of Cortez. The Spanish explorer landed his soldiers in Mexico in the 1500s, then burned all the ships. He told his men there was no alternative to fighting for their goals, no escape. They fought hard! You too must burn your ships to be really committed to college. You *are* going to graduate. Not writing this paper is *not* an option. Behind you lies only empty water. Ahead, on the other side of this paper, lies your fortune. Write!

Unfortunately, additional blocks may emerge during drafts

Fear of Messiness

We've heard it so often: "Neatness counts." And neatness does count in writing, but *only in the final draft.* Many people want to write drafts logically, grammatically, progressing word by word to a perfect conclusion. They're doomed. Within a few sentences they see the imperfections, the ideas that contradict each other, the detail that doesn't fit exactly, the awkward sentence. "All right," they say to themselves, "I'll write slower, more carefully." Before long they're up to their hips in quicksand and the writing stops. Why? Because they're asking too much of themselves. Even an average genius cannot think, organize, draft sentences, and consider words and grammar at the same time. Shakespeare and Mozart *may* have churned out masterpieces with little revision, but the history of literature by writers as great as James Baldwin, E. B. White, and Mark Twain is a history of messy cross-outs, redrafts, thrown-away pieces, and ink spots. Bob Dylan said, "Chaos is a friend of mine," and Thomas Wolfe claimed he cut 100,000 words from one novel (that's about 150 papers of the length you might write in this course). If ideas, details, honesty, organization, brilliant word choices, and grammar could come at once, we'd all be best-selling authors.

SOLUTIONS: Go play in the mud. Relax and enjoy the surprises and messiness of thinking. The fact is that most ideas creep out of dark and sometimes dirty places. If you demand perfection, when these misshaped creatures peek out they'll be driven back inside your brain, and new ones will be slow to emerge. Accept the fact that writing emerges incomplete. Write your sentences down in their sloppy condition with inserts written sideways on the page and arrows to the back of the paper, and your brain will send others after them—ones that may be better or that may transform the frog into a prince.

Poor Work Environment

Your sister plays loud head-banger music. Your desk is too low and makes your back ache. The room is stifling hot. You just ate and feel sleepy. Your paper's going nowhere. Anything relating to your physical environment can affect your ability to write. Some people like to be comfortable and cozy. That makes me fall asleep; I like a hard chair in a cool room. Some people must turn on music or the television. Others can't concentrate through such distractions. Some people require absolute silence and privacy. Others like to sense people moving around them because utter silence is intimidating. Some people are morning people, some evening people. And so on.

SOLUTIONS: Control the things you *can* control. Manipulate your environment so it helps instead of hinders you. Put books under your desk legs (or saw them down an inch) so you're comfortable. Work at the time of day you are at your best. Don't kid yourself—maybe you really *are* watching the television. Try writing in silence. A few years ago one of my students had a mother who interrupted him just as he sat down to write. She'd want to talk or make him do chores or complain about some aspect of his behavior. Mike began to suspect she saved these things until he opened his books. I suggested Mike finish his work at school. He did, and his writing improved one grade almost immediately.

People serious about thinking and writing give their minds the best environment they can, instead of letting a poor environment control them. If you really want to write, you will get it done. Cesare Cantio wrote a novel in prison using a toothpick for a pen and candle smoke for ink.

CONCLUSIONS

Don't dawdle. A murky, wordy ending hides your message. You want a sharp, crystal sentence or two that highlights your key idea. I'll give you specific suggestions for conclusions to narrative, persuasive, and research papers in later chapters, but one all-purpose conclusion simply **returns to a concrete example, fact, anecdote, question, or dilemma from your introduction.** An essay on the homeless might conclude this way:

> Hattie McBride died of malnutrition on her cardboard mat under the fire escape. If the work-for-shelter program and tenement rehabilitation plan I proposed were enacted, we might not find more Hatties dead in alleys.

Highlights of Chapter 6

- Introductions should interest a reader with details, then present the thesis that leads a reader to the main body. You can do this by telling a story, asking a good question, presenting a striking fact, quoting someone else, opening with a problem, or addressing your reader's concerns.
- While drafting, focus on the logical, smooth flow of ideas and details, moving quickly without being bogged down in minor matters, and addressing your intended audience.
- While drafting, do *not* focus on style, words, mechanics, or spelling.
- When you're stuck, use the brain teasers from Chapter 3, refer to your outline and thesis, reread the last page you wrote, ask what your reader would want to know next, or search for a transition word to the next point.
- Two common drafting blocks are fear of messiness and poor work environment. Tell yourself not to be afraid of a little dirt; and change your work environment if it hurts your work.

Sample Introduction

TOUGHER PUNISHMENT FOR SEX OFFENDERS

Silver, a 30-year-old executive, was raped and beaten in her home by an ex-boyfriend and another friend. During the assault she sustained a black eye, busted lip, and bruises to her arms and thighs. She was choked, leaving welts around her neck. Caramel, a student, was raped by an acquaintance in the front seat of her car after he asked for a ride. During the attack, she sustained bruises on her left breast, along with aches all over her body. Both women were subjected to this ordeal at the hands of men they had once trusted.

Since sex offenders disregard the physical and psychological pain they inflict, here is a way of dealing with them. I propose that sex offenders be punished to fit the crimes they commit. A convicted first offender might be sentenced to ten years in prison without chance of parole and should receive a penile electric shock once daily during that time. Repeat offenders should be incarcerated for twenty years and given two shocks daily.

—Pamela Fleming

Commentary

The opening two examples vividly *grab our attention,* and the proposal is equally vivid. It's (pardon the pun) shocking and should be controversial reading. It uses the classic introductory *pattern of details moving to thesis.* But it's spread over two paragraphs. In a short paper (two to three pages), I'd like the introduction in one paragraph. It promises to convince us to agree with her punishment scheme—a tough sell perhaps. *Issues she might cover* are the 8th Amendment to the U.S. Constitution, which prohibits "cruel and inhumane punishment." Another is the possibility that a rapist would be more likely to kill a woman rather than risk her testifying against him under Fleming's plan. She addressed these in her paper. The *length* could be reduced by cutting the last sentence of the first paragraph. It's not really part of her point. Suggestions for *wording:* "Sustained" is used twice and is vague. The beginning of the second paragraph could be cut to start "Here is how I propose dealing with rapists." The first part of that sentence argues the point before saying what it is. Overall this is a powerful introduction that will require strong support to sustain it.

Writing Suggestions and Class Discussions

1. Evaluate the following introductions. The peer review checklist on p. 100 will help guide you.

As Sir Walter Raleigh stepped up to the executioner's block, he ran his finger along the ax blade. "This is sharp medicine," he said, "But a sound cure for all diseases." Raleigh, most historians now agree, was innocent of treason, but capital punishment prevented him from being discovered innocent. I think we ought to have capital punishment today, but I think there ought to be a two-year delay to allow other evidence to turn up.

There are an estimated 50,000 Amerasian children in Ho Chi Minh City and other Vietnam towns where American servicemen congregated. Many have been abandoned not only by their fathers but by their mothers who couldn't handle the social pressure from having an American's baby. The children often scavenge in the streets where they are called <u>buidoi</u>--the dust of life. Nine of ten Amerasian children live in slums, usually a collection of shanties perched along a polluted canal. Most have no medical care, suffer untreated ear infections, eye disorders and parasites, and as social outcasts, they are harassed and beaten (Long 19). The Vietnamese deny them education, jobs, and even food rations. Many Amerasian boys are sold as servant-slaves because they can sustain more hard labor than Thai or Vietnamese boys. Hundreds of Amerasian girls are sold into prostitution by relatives: pimps can make $500 a night for American-looking girls (Yates 3). These children are casualties of the Vietnam War and deserve to be brought to the United States and rehabilitated.

—Molly McGuidwin (student essay)

Imagine the police pounding on your door one fall day. You answer and your stomach knots. A red-haired officer softly tells you your daughter who had been running in the park has been raped and beaten with jagged rocks and a pipe by a pack of school-age boys. This nightmare became reality to the parents of a 28-year-old jogger in New York City last year. What runs shivers down my spine is that one of the kids involved said, "It was fun." Our efforts to rehabilitate teens like this have been futile. We need to take a new approach to teen crimes of violence.

—Lisa Neal (student essay)

The program <u>20/20</u> showed a four-year-old boy who'd been abused by his mother's boyfriend. Beatings with a heavy object caused permanent brain damage. His back had inch-and-a-half deep whip marks from a leather belt. And the abuser carved his initials into the boy's backside. This boy will never ride a bike, walk, or even talk. He is fed intravenously and must urinate through a tube in his penis. He received a lifetime of retardation and pain. Yet the abuser received 15 to 20 years in prison, and the mother who let this happen received five years. Another baby burned to death after kerosene had been poured over him. The only two adults in the house were never even put on trial. Beyond how they could do this and what we can do to help, the question we must ask is: What is wrong with our judicial system?

—Tara Geska (student essay)

This is addressed to heterosexuals. Twenty years after lesbians and gay men threw coins, bottles, and parking meters at the cops who attempted to arrest them for being queer, many of you still see no reason to fight for our rights. Most of you are not by our side. Yet homophobia hurts you almost as much as it hurts us.

—Allan Richards (student essay)

2. Bring to class two magazine articles that strike you as having strong introductions and explain why they work well.
3. List three environmental conditions that encourage *your* thinking/writing. List two things that hinder your thinking/writing. Discuss how to change the poor conditions and create or maintain the good ones.
4. For your next paper bring to class two alternative opening paragraphs, using two of the six methods suggested. Both introductions should be on the same topic but use different approaches.
5. Suppose you had to write a paper on family stress for a sociology class. Write three trial introductions, using a different technique in each. For the last sentence of the paragraph, invent a thesis or main idea that leads from the details to the paper.
6. Write introductions for two of these topics. Try to hook the reader's interest, then lead toward a thesis the paper will develop:
   - Men's or women's hairstyles
   - 2 A.M.
   - Animal experimentation
   - Dates who drink
   - Birthdays

✓ | **PEER REVIEW CHECKLIST FOR INTRODUCTIONS**

Author of Introduction: _____

List three possible titles for your paper:

_____

_____

_____

Reviewer: _____

1. Which title do you find most intriguing and why?

2. Does the introduction grab your attention and set up the paper? Why or why not?

3. What promises or expectations does this introduction give a reader for the essay? Suggest issues or questions the author should cover.

4. Make a suggestion to improve the wording of the introduction. Mark your suggestions on the draft itself.

5. What is the sharpest detail that draws your eye into the introduction? If you think the introduction needs better detail, suggest what might be done.

6. Is it too long or too short?

CHAPTER 7

Revising Drafts
Writing Is Revising

The manuscript revealed the usual signs of struggle—bloodstains, teethmarks, gashes, and burns.

ANNIE DILLARD

My pencils outlast their erasers.

VLADIMIR NABOKOV

Many people assume a writer's job is 95 percent done when the first draft is complete. Now, they think, we'll correct spelling and typos, read it over to see how it flows, and then crank out a clean copy.

I wish writers could operate that way. But experienced writers—whether they publish essays, write business reports, or compose senior theses—know that "revision" means "re-seeing." A writer is simply not doing the job if re-seeing is limited to fussing over spelling and a few surface blemishes. That's amateurish. You must re-see and re-feel the entire paper, back down to its roots. Ralph Ellison revised *Invisible Man* for ten years, and Boris Pasternak said of his first draft of *Doctor Zhivago*, "Everything is corroded. . . . It is disgusting." The person who writes a company's annual report or the committee that writes your college catalogue may revise for months. The inspired genius who whisks out immortal masterpieces on the first draft is 99.99 percent myth.

For virtually all writers, including Nobel Prize winners like Pasternak, revision means a total, word-by-word re-seeing of the draft. Revision means rewriting good parts as well as bad. Only during revision does most writing move from poor to acceptable or from acceptable to good or outstanding. Your professor does not expect from you the fanatical dedication of published writers like Ernest Hemingway, who revised the last paragraph of his great World War I novel, *A Farewell to Arms,* 39 times. But your professor *does* want you to revise more than just the surface, to take the manuscript through at least one complete revision. Your writing *will improve* through honest, close revision, and only then will you know how good you are as a writer.

REVISION MYTHS AND REALITIES

Revision draws from a different part of your brain than brainteasing or drafting. Creating is self-centered, accepting, and sloppy; revising is reader centered, judgmental, and orderly. Although most people find one easier, we're all capable of both.

The lonely writer tapping away in solitary confinement is largely myth. Most writers in professional situations depend on advice and criticism from others during the revision process. They give us perspective on what we are too close to notice; they remind us what we forget to mention or point out what might confuse a reader. Even Shakespeare had help. His acting company commonly deleted scenes and suggested changes during rehearsal for such classics as *Hamlet* and *Romeo and Juliet.* Most bosses ask to see drafts of proposals, reports, or significant letters their employees write—and will suggest changes. Or they may ask *you* for suggestions on *their* drafts. Grant writers, legislators, and scholars all ask peers for criticism before the public sees the written document. The word "criticize" in this sense does not mean to rip the writing apart but to highlight weaknesses *and* strengths and to make *positive* suggestions.

Let me illustrate how a writer combines personal revision and outside criticism by using this book as an example. In sixteen years of college teaching,

I'd written hundreds of assignments, course outlines, and instructions. Some bombed! In one research assignment, my directions for using the microfilm machine were vague enough that one student ended up shooting a reel of film from the viewer like a spider gone berserk. Each semester I revised flaws and pursued new ideas, finally expanding these into a short "Guide to Writing" used only at my college. Teachers and students told me what worked and what didn't. One class sent me twenty-four letters! More revision.

When I mailed sample chapters for an expanded book to publishers, my future publisher sent these to teachers at other colleges for their reactions and criticism. The reviews broadened my limited viewpoint. More revision. New chapters had to be written; others combined, relocated, or eliminated. One chapter expanded from 10 to 40 pages and helped me discover exactly what process of writing I believed worked best. More reviews (nearly 50 pages in all) and more new voices in my ear helped me. For this fourth edition, more new voices and ideas helped me revise. Over 30 professors and editors and hundreds of students have their fingerprints on this book, and they have helped me write better than I can alone.

I was happy to have new things to think about, because with each draft of a piece of writing, I exhausted myself. Do you know this feeling? After working for hours on a draft, do you feel wrung out, as though you have said everything you possibly can about the topic? Well, peer criticism jump-starts a writer's dead battery if it's the right mix of honest encouragement, suggestion, and flaw finding.

An important part of your college education is to learn how to handle both kinds of revision—revision on your own and revision with the help of others. Let me suggest some things to look for and a process to follow when revising first drafts.

 ## ON YOUR OWN

I recommend a five-step revision process, but keep in mind this is an *ideal process that rarely if ever can be followed exactly.* Like thinking, revising is a sloppy process. That said, you'll find a revision checklist on the inside front cover of the book. Consider this another brain teaser to remind you to think in all the ways you should during revision.

Basically, I believe you should **revise major things first**—the ideas and details—and then work on secondary items like organization and word use. Correct punctuation and spelling last. Why? So you don't waste time correcting spelling if you later decide you need a better word or waste time thinking up a great adjective if the entire sentence gets thrown out. Imagine a draft essay as a building to be rehabilitated. There's no point painting until the room walls are in place, and that shouldn't begin until the supporting girders are square and plumb. Occasionally, changing a word or phrase can clarify your main ideas, and if it seems important, go ahead. But don't spend your early revision time tinkering.

You may want to read your draft over for general flow, but if you **read through for one focused thing at a time,** you'll do more real thinking and less falling in love with what's already there. Writers often get "sick" of drafts because they're following the draft, instead of demanding specific things of it. If you keep rereading and waiting for a "bump" to jolt you, you will fall asleep. I recommend reading through and revising the draft once for each of the following aspects.

- Ideas
- Details
- Order
- Words
- Mechanics

A two- to three-page paper can be revised for all of these in an hour, and careful revision is almost sure to raise your grade one level.

▲ **PRACTICE 7-1:** Try the five-step process that follows in class or at home with the draft of a paper. Stop and do each step separately before reading on.

1. REVISE IDEAS

Honesty, Freshness, Coherence

Clarify the _main_ idea. First, read through your draft quickly. Now, without referring back to the essay, try to state your main point or purpose. Write it out in one sentence. You may be surprised that you'll be able to say it sharper after reading the paper. Compare it to the existing thesis sentence and substitute the new one if it's better or revise the old, if necessary. If you had trouble writing a statement of purpose, your paper may ooze in several directions.

If your paper lacks sharp focus, try this technique: Read through the paper again, copying down sentences that seem to state purpose. Try to combine these sentences into one statement. If this works, great. Replace the existing wobbly thesis. If you can't combine the purpose sentences, you'll have to accept the fact that you mixed two or three paper ideas together. You must then divide the essay into parts, some of which will become your paper and the rest of which will leave the house in a brown bag.

Second, when revising for ideas, **test your main idea for _honesty_ and _freshness._** I read through once uncompromisingly, ruthlessly honest to see if I've slipped into superficial thinking or oversimplification. Qualify or moderate extreme sentences. Be particularly alert for contradictions or potential rebuttals to your arguments. Don't ignore them. Your paper will be stronger and more honest if you confront and respond to them (see "refutation" in Chapter 12). For example, as I reread this section, I worry that I'm simplifying revision by making it seem too mechanical, too much like a write-by-number activity. No techniques substitute for your intense concentration or involvement in your ideas. A checklist is only a reminder of things to look for.

Third, **read through the draft as your reader will.** If you have a particular reader in mind, *be* that person. What will confuse him? What points will she deny or contradict? What have you left out that will be important to her? This is a wonderful brain teaser for revision.

▲ **PRACTICE 7-2:** Reread your last paper and (1) underline key sentences that reveal purpose; (2) combine these into a one-sentence statement of purpose; (3) find two places in which you could have raised an objection or modified an idea for more honesty or freshness. Make the revision.

2. REVISE DETAILS

Visualize and Support

Read the draft again, just for details. Are they vivid and convincing? Support each major generalization by adding examples, sense details, descriptions, and facts. Suppose you had written the following in a draft of a paper on Tennessee Williams's play, *The Glass Menagerie:*

> Laura lives in a fantasy world in this play. For instance, there's her glass menagerie, the old phonograph records she plays, and her visits to the greenhouse. She can't even attend business college.

The right information is here, but it's not vivid enough to make us see Laura's fantasy world. Let's expand just *one* of the details:

> Laura lives in a fantasy world. The greenhouse she visits is full of exotic flowers—tropical plants that can't exist in the cold world of St. Louis where she lives. Their fantasy world is protected from reality by artificial heat and fragile glass, just as Laura can go on living only because her mother and brother protect her from the cold reality of the Depression.

In revising for detail, remind yourself that a reader is hungry for facts, quotes, pictures, and examples. Feed him details.

▲ **PRACTICE 7-3:** Find three places in your last paper that could use more details and add them.

3. REVISE ORGANIZATION

Make It Easy on the Reader

Check the essay's *overall organization.* You don't even really have to read in the normal sense—just skim the main sentences. If it's more than five pages, I usually take notes on a separate page by jotting down a heading for each paragraph or section. This helps me see more clearly what my main points are, if I'm repeating myself, or if I should combine two sections. Now's the time to cut redundant paragraphs or draw arrows to move things around.

Next, **check that each *paragraph* sticks to one idea.** Are the *transitions* smooth between them? (If not smooth, add key markers like "On the other hand," "Another reason to support this proposal is. . ." or "Once outside, Fergusen saw . . ."). If you see a lot of skimpy one- and two-sentence paragraphs or one paragraph runs over a page, a red signal light should buzz. You may be able to join the bitty paragraphs or insert paragraph breaks into the elephant-sized ones, but it may be a sign that as you motored through the first draft, your thinking became scattered. Make sure every sentence points at the same target.

Finally, flip directly from your introduction to your conclusion. Is your main point consistent? If not, scream, and then revise.

▲ **PRACTICE 7-4:** Revise your last paper just for organization. Outline the paper, check paragraph unity, and add transitions where needed.

 ## 4. REVISE WORD USE

Waxed Words Sparkle

At this point you should know which sentences and paragraphs will be in the final paper. Now focus on polishing words. Look small. Tinker. Wax and polish. Do you repeat the same words, or challenge the reader with a few exotic *palabras?* Be ruthless to clichés—they are corpses in your living essay. Did you define key terms? Be more concise. Punch up bland verbs. Substitute slashing, red-eyed adjectives for dull ones. Create a metaphor to make a boring paragraph crack with lightning. New words can improve ideas. Consider sentence variety. Unlike the previous sentence, which was a short, imperative sentence, this complex one delays the main subject and verb with an introductory phrase. Both kinds snap the reader to attention. Chapter 8 is devoted to word polishing.

▲ **PRACTICE 7-5:** Pick any paragraph from a previous paper and improve three word choices and perk up a vague or dull spot with a metaphor.

 ## 5. REVISE MECHANICS

My grandmother told me always to wear clean underwear. She wanted to be sure that if I was hit by a car and taken to the hospital they'd know I was from a decent family. I think of my grandmother when I revise for mechanics. I do it for decency's sake.

Reading through the paper lightly for mechanics will only catch the errors you *don't* normally make. The deadly errors are the ones you make regularly and don't see. Go through the paper once searching just for the errors teachers repeatedly mark on your papers. This must be a conscious effort, or you won't improve. If your vices are sentence fragments and apostrophes, go through the draft once, searching only for the little vermin. Work with the handbook section of this book; don't guess. If you're a weak speller, check any word you wouldn't risk in a $1,000 bet. After two or three papers, they won't be *your* errors.

▲ **PRACTICE 7-6:** List your three most common grammar, punctuation, or other small errors. If you don't *know* what they are, examine your last few papers. Use this as your own individual checklist. Write it in your notebook.

 # HELP FROM OTHERS: PEER EDITING AND TEACHER CONFERENCES

By this time, you should have exhausted your own resources. Your draft should be scratched up with improvements. Now your professor may mark your paper, ask you to give it to other students to read (peer editing), or talk it over with you (conferencing). These can be your most valuable opportunities to really learn to write. Peer editing and conferencing do more than help with one paper. They teach skills that will serve you a lifetime: Giving and receiving positive criticism leads to renewed enthusiasm and ideas in marriage, career, sports, and friendship as well as writing. You'll write for a real reader, not a cardboard one; you'll see how others write; and you'll learn from them.

How to Give Peer Criticism

When called on to critique another student's paper, your goal should be to help the writer create better ideas, sharper details, smoother organization, and more vivid word choices. You may also repair punctuation and spelling.

The reviewer/editor must be honest. The person who writes on your paper, "I love it!" or "I wouldn't change a thing!" may flatter you momentarily, but doesn't help you one bit. You may be shy about fooling with someone's ideas or feel unqualified to criticize, but making an honest effort to help someone else improve a paper will teach you to revise better yourself. You'll learn to see some of the hidden possibilities behind existing words, to see your own drafts more objectively. Teachers who encourage peer editing expect *both* parties to learn.

You must be tactful, of course. The person who scrawls changes all over the paper and says, in effect, "revise everything" is just as dishonest as the person who wants to award the Nobel Prize. Help the writer to his or her destination.

Because most writers need help recognizing what they have written and help understanding how a live audience reacts, it's probably best to start your comments simply by mirroring back to the writer the message or feeling the essay gave you.

You can do this with one or two of these lines: "What I remember best about your essay is. . ." or "The main point I get from this is. . ." or "The most visual part of your essay is. . ."

Or you might make a bullet summary of the main point as you read. After the author lets you know you're aboard the same spaceship, you can move to suggestions for ideas, details, organization, and wording. Work together. If you were confused at a certain point, for instance, brainstorm with the author for several possible clarifications. Whatever you react to strongly in any way should be discussed with the writer. Try to *enjoy* peer editing; allow yourself the pleasure of inhabiting someone else's mind for a while.

How to Receive Peer Criticism

Remember, your peer editors try to be honest. If they feel confused, you may point out things that you think clarify the point, but you can't tell them they're not confused. What peer editors tell you is something you can never see for yourself: how another person receives your communication. You can never be your own reader.

Strike a balance between total acceptance and total rejection. If you're too pliable, you may accept changes you shouldn't. It's *your* paper; don't let a strong peer dominate your idea. On the other hand, some closed-minded writers seem to say, "It's written this way because that's the way I wanted it. It's my paper, isn't it?" This person supposes the paper is perfect because it came out exactly as intended. I'm skeptical. More importantly, papers *shouldn't* come out exactly as intended; to me that's a sign that I haven't *learned* as I moved through the stages of writing. Your paper is not a monument to what you thought at one moment, but an attempt to communicate an idea as freshly and vividly as possible to someone else. Listen to what your readers say. Before rejecting changes, first ask the reviewer, "Why do you say that?" You don't have to follow each suggestion slavishly, but do welcome new possibilities as potential friends.

Bring questions to a peer editing session. Ask about things you've wrestled with or wondered about. For example, "Is this a corny sentence?" or "It seems too long. What should I cut?" or "I'm worried I sound too harsh. What do you think?" Only by showing yourself eager to find weak spots will reviewers really open up to you.

 SAMPLE REVISION

Here is the opening paragraph from a letter written as a class paper by Tina C. Maenza. First is the rough draft as brought to a peer review session:

Dean H. Freericks
Assistant Vice President for Facilities Management
John Beane Center
SUNY AB
Buffalo, NY 14261

Dear Mr. Fredericks,
    As you probably are already aware of there is a major prob-
lem with student parking at our school. At the end of every
class one can be sure to find a line of students in their cars
waiting for people to leave so they can park. Not only is this
an inconvenience, but it causes arguments among students racing for empty spots, and it makes us late for class. You should
consider building parking garages or consider some other possible solutions to this problem.

The reviewer thought the thesis was clear, but suggested that the author
"put in a story, more details" to catch the reader's eye. She also pointed out
a few flaws in the letter format, the choppiness of the first sentence, and
exaggeration in lines 2 and 3 ("every" and "be sure"). Here is the same text
with the author's revisions penned in:

July 14, 1999

Dean H. Fre*de*ricks

Assistant Vice President for Facilities Management

John Beane Center   *Looking at their watches every 30 sec.,*
                     they wonder just how late they will be to
SUNY (AB)   *class today. Teachers are not sympathetic*
Buffalo, NY 14261   *+ some threaten to penalize tardy students*
                     by reducing their grades.

←Dear Mr. Fredericks,   *What can we students do?*

                                       exists
←As you probably are already aware of there ~~is~~ a major prob-
                                            almost
lem with student parking at our school. At the end of ˄every
      almost
class one can˄be sure to find a line of students in their cars
         ˄
waiting for people to leave so they can park. Not only is this
an inconvenience, but it causes arguments among students rac-
                        making
ing for empty spots (and ~~it makes~~ us late for class.) You should
consider building parking garages or consider some other possible solutions to this problem.

    Notice that the author revised additional items beyond the ones sug-
gested. Next is the final draft with more improvements. The new visual

details certainly help, as do the ironed-out sentences and "little" corrections, including the reader's name!

                                              July 14, 1999

Dean H. Fredericks
Assistant Vice President for Facilities Management
John Beane Center
Suny at Buffalo
Buffalo, New York 14261

Dear Mr. Fredericks:

As you probably already are aware, a major problem exists with
student parking at our school. Following most classes, one can
almost be sure to find a line of students in cars waiting for
people to leave so they can park. Looking at their watches
every thirty seconds, they wonder just how late they will be
today. Most teachers are not sympathetic, and some threaten to
penalize tardy students with reduced grades. What can students
do to make class on time when we drive? Besides being an in-
convenience and making us late, it causes arguments among stu-
dents racing for an empty spot. Please consider building
parking garages to solve this problem.

Teacher Comments

Your teacher will probably be the most attentive reader you will ever have. If you write a boring or confusing letter to customers or supervisors, they will stop paying attention. Your professor will persevere and mark the rough, confusing, or vague spots. *Improvement* is the point of this effort. Therefore, the most important marks on your papers are not the grades but the comments. Each one is a guide for future papers. Study each comment on returned papers carefully. If you don't see where you went wrong or how you could improve a section marked "awkward" or "vague" or why a teacher wrote "good" somewhere, find out. Ask. Be hungry for feedback; that's how you move forward. If you think of comments as simple test scoring, you've thrown away a road map. If you don't understand, look the problem up in this text, talk to your professor, or go to your college's writing center. Take the time to figure out the symbols and abbreviations your teacher uses. Here are some common ones.

Abbreviated Comments on Your Papers

Agree or Ag—Agreement. Nouns, verbs, or pronouns don't match each other. See pp. 350–351.

AWK—Awkward. Something is clumsy, and your professor doesn't have a category for it.

C—Comma error. See pp. 333–339.

CAP—Capitalization. See pp. 343–346.

G—Good work here.

MM—(1) Mixed metaphor. See Ch. 8.
      (2) Misplaced modifier. See pp. 348–350.

Org—Organization. Two points mixed together or one point split apart. See Ch. 5.

¶—Paragraph needed. See Ch. 4.

?—Confusing section. Look for missing words awkward sentences, illogical idea, or misused words.

Red—Redundant. Needs cutting. See Ch. 8

R.O. or **C.S.**—Run-on or comma-spliced sentence. Needs a period or semicolon. See pp. 347–348.

Ref—Reference. Usually unclear pronoun reference. See p. 351.

SF—Sentence fragment. See pp. 346–347.

SS—Sentence structure. May be awkward or nonparallel construction. See pp. 346–350.

Tense—Verb tenses don't match. See p. 350.

Thesis—Thesis needed or unclear. See Ch. 5.

Trans—Transition needs improvement. See Ch. 4.

Vague—Need clarification or more detail. See Ch. 2.

Wordy—Be more concise. See Ch. 8.

WW—Wrong word used. See Dictionary of Usage, pp. 352–355.

If your teacher has conferences about rough drafts, think of them as opportunities. Come with prepared questions. "Why does my opening sound flat?" or "Did I overdo the facts on the dangers of nuclear waste?" *Take notes* and mark sections your teacher discusses so you remember. As with peer editors, be open to suggestions and try to re-see your work objectively through your professor's eyes. However, if the professor seems to have the wrong idea about where you want to go with the essay, make clear what you really want to accomplish and ask for suggestions on how to get there.

 ## THE FINAL DRAFT

1. **Title** the paper and make the title work for you. The best titles convey information and also a concrete image to hold the eye. Which of the following titles promise boredom and which promise an experience?
   - English Paper #2
   - Air Pollution

- Whose Poison Gas Is It
- Death Stalks Your Home

   Good titles often come from phrases near the end of your paper, from metaphors you use, or dialogue you quote. Why waste time thinking up a bunch of titles? Well, Margaret Mitchell's first titles for *Gone with the Wind* were duds: *Ba! Ba! Black Sheep* and *Tote the Weary Load.* The title symbolizes the whole work.

2. **Format** the paper.
   - Write your name and class in a corner.
   - Center the title one quarter of the way down the page.
   - The title should be capitalized but not underlined or in quotation marks.
   - Number the pages.
   - Double-space and use only one side of the page.
   - Leave one-inch margins.
   - Staple or paper-clip your essay.
3. **Proofread** after typing or printing and make corrections—that's what professionals do. If you have a lot of mistakes, print a corrected copy. Here are some sample proofreader's correction marks:

   ¶   New paragraph
   No ¶ No paragraph
   ⊔⌐⌐   Reverse order of items enclosed
   ∧   Insert mark (write new items above line)
   ℐ   Delete mark (can be used for one letter or one line)
   ≡   Capitalize letter
   lc   Lowercase letter
   #   Space needed
   Stet   Ignore the changes

Revising on a Word Processor

You are a writer, not a typist. Word processors are wonderful for small changes and for inserting new material.

   But there are some drawbacks. First, because small changes are easy, you'll be tempted to focus on small items. You may be deceived by a neat surface appearance into not really studying the logic and sentences. You've got to dig up a draft, no matter how polished the work *appears.* Second, word processors with spell-checkers may give you the illusion that your spelling is fixed. However, if you type "affect" where "effect" belongs or "kiss" instead of "kill," the machine recognizes a legitimate word and won't alert you to your error. Rely on your own knowledge—and on dictionaries.

   Since you can do so much revision with a computer with such little pain, you should experiment: Combine paragraphs, separate them, move them around, add details, rephrase. You can ask most computers to count the number of times you used "I" or "was" if you're afraid of monotony. You can usually reformat with different fonts—but please!—only one font per paper, and avoid the script fonts that are hard to read. This is one place

I advise you to be bland. To keep this rich activity safe, print a copy of each draft or use "save as" instead of "save" when storing a revised draft on disk. This tells the computer to set up a new file, so you can still whistle up the old draft in case you feel you've revised away a good sentence you want back. Early drafts also document how much revision you've done.

Highlights of Chapter 7

- Welcome revision. Your essay will survive being picked apart and glued up. That is how ideas are made better and how professional writers—whether they write memos or publish books—operate.
- Peer criticism requires both honesty and tact. *Use* the specific suggestions in this chapter to get started.
- Revise with specific things in mind, not just for general flow. Revise your papers one time each for ideas, details, order, words, and mechanics. Use the specifics in this chapter as a checklist. But remember: No checklist or process for revision can substitute for your intense concentration and involvement in your subject.

Writing Suggestions and Class Discussions

1. Make up three questions about the draft of an essay you're working on. Leave room for responses and attach them to your rough draft for your peer editor or professor. Try for a mix of broad questions on thesis or organization and specific questions about particular words or sentences.
2. To have a sample to practice revision, write a half-page paragraph on one of these topics:
   - Adult toys
   - Children and toys
   - Wise elders
   - What I don't like about my present job
   - "_____" is a great song because . . .
   - Open topic
3. Revise the paragraph from Number 2 on your own:
   - Rewrite the main idea/topic sentence without looking at the original and compare it to the original. Use the clearest one or make changes.
   - Sharpen the details—make at least two points more specific.
   - Circle all transitions and improve if necessary.
   - Improve three word choices and rewrite any clichés. Then find two or three needless words and cut them.
   - Check all spelling and grammar.
4. Bring your revised, retyped paragraph to class for a peer editing session. Attach two questions about the paragraph for the reviewers. Using peer suggestions, revise and submit a finished paragraph.
5. If you have an electronic classroom, write a home page for yourself for the World Wide Web and collaborate in revising it via e-mail.

6. Your peer group will write an ad for a commercial product. Your client wants one picture and about 100 words to appear in the Sunday newspaper.
7. Read the following student essay. How would you advise the writer to revise it?

BASTARD

Miguel Martinez

I have always been awed by the strange bonds fathers are supposed to have with their sons. Literature, television, and film have shown these relationships to be complex and intense. Even my friends in school would relate stories of massive power struggles. The part about love they left out but I knew it was there.

I grew up believing my father to be dead. At least that's what my mother told me when I asked her. I know the only reason I did ask was I had just entered kindergarden and my classmates were always talking about this strange being, a sort of god, they called Daddy. Contrary to popular belief, those of us having only one parent do not feel that anything is missing. At least I didn't until I found out I was an oddity. There is no biological instinct inside us saying that there should be someone else. There was just me and my mother. Period.

Off I went through school. My mother was involved with other men, and we lived with two of them. They were never 'Dad,' just 'Uncle.' These relationships didn't work out, and when I was six, my mother gave up on men entirely. We moved to the east side of the city, and she started working. For the next ten years, my mother and I didn't see much of each other. She was a waitress, keeping odd hours, and I was in school or playing. She did make a big point of eating together, even if it was in the greasy spoons she worked in.

When she was able to spend more time with me, I was sixteen, and pretty set in my ways. I suppose I should have let her have her way, but the arrogance of youth took hold again. I left. I didn't have anywhere to go, I just wanted to travel. I spent the next 8 months traveling the country. I did return eventually, only to find my mother filled with a sense of failure. It hurt knowing I

had caused someone such hard feelings. She begged me
to enter the Navy, and while I wasn't a big fan of the
military, I went. The night before I was to leave for
boot camp, my mother sat me down and asked if I ever
wondered who my father was. I told her, quite honestly,
that I didn't, that she had said he was dead. Well, she
gave me his name and told me he was living in South Carolina. She told me he didn't care about me, as he had
always known who I was, but never made any attempt to
contact me.

   The news didn't faze me. Friends will ask if I have
any urge to find him. I get satisfaction from their expressions when I tell them I have his address and phone
number. But just as they can't understand my apathy toward him, I can't understand their reliance on fathers.

Here are comments on the draft by the writer, peer editors, and professor.

THE WRITER'S CONCERNS ABOUT THIS DRAFT

1. I didn't explore the aspect I wanted to--it seemed too general and jumpy in what I was trying to get at.

2. One sentence that drove me crazy was 'Off I went through
   school' (third paragraph). It just didn't flow.

PEER EDITOR COMMENTS MADE BY STUDENTS READING THE DRAFT

1. The only 'jumpy' part was the fourth paragraph. Time seemed
   too compressed. You were six and then entered the Navy.

2. You need more detail on growing up without a father. The most
   vivid detail was your <u>not</u> asking about your father. The least
   was why your mother wanted you to join the navy. I'd like to
   see more about why you didn't miss or need a father.

3. Paragraph 3--for <u>ten years</u> you didn't see much of your mom???

4. First paragraph needs more detail.

TEACHER'S COMMENTS

1. It's strong in honesty. Daring. Potentially a powerful paper.

2. But it doesn't follow its nose to the end of the idea. Your
   purpose is unclear, as you suspect. Are you dealing with (1)
   the mother-son relationship; (2) the life of a single mother;

(3) the social problems of bastards; (4) your lack of need for a father, or...? All these are here, but you need to decide what main point the others will support. Conclusion is inconclusive.

3. Paragraphs 1 and 2 are good--a snappy start.
4. #4 needs more detail--it's abrupt, seems to start a new idea.
5. #4 Last sentence is awkward.

You will find a revised, final draft of this essay in the back of the book. Although the student followed some reader suggestions, notice how he found new areas to explore simply as a result of talking about the essay and hearing what other people saw there.

✓ **PEER REVIEW CHECKLIST FOR REVISION**

Author of Paper:_____

Reviewer:_____

Instructions:
1. Read the paper slowly and carefully.
2. Mark parts that were confusing or problems with a "?".
3. Mark strong sections with a "G" or "*".
4. Check the appropriate boxes and write out comments.
5. Return this sheet to the author and discuss your reaction.
6. Do not mark small things like spelling yet.
7. This sheet should be attached to the final draft.

	STRONG	AVERAGE	WEAK
IDEAS: Originality/Freshness			
Depth/Complexity			
Audience: Well Targeted			
DETAILS: Number of Details			
Vividness			
ORGANIZATION: Main Point Is Clear			
Smooth Flow Between Ideas			
WORD USE: Concise and Vivid			
MECHANICS			

The strongest part of this paper to me is:

I'd like to know more about:

Here are two suggestions I have:
1.

2.

✓ **PEER REVIEW CHECKLIST QUESTIONS FOR REVISION**

Author:_____

One question or problem the author wants the reviewer to help
with:

One sentence the author is not satisfied with (mark it and explain
why it bothers you):

Reviewer:_____

My response to the author's first concern is . . . (discuss and
brainstorm with author):

Here's a possible rewriting of the weak sentence:

I feel the purpose (thesis) of your essay is:

One area that could use more detail or support is:

What idea could be added or cut to enhance the paper's purpose?

Find a paragraph needing smoother transition and suggest it.
(No, it's not perfect!)

Suggest at least three word or sentence structure changes.

CHAPTER 8

Writing with Style

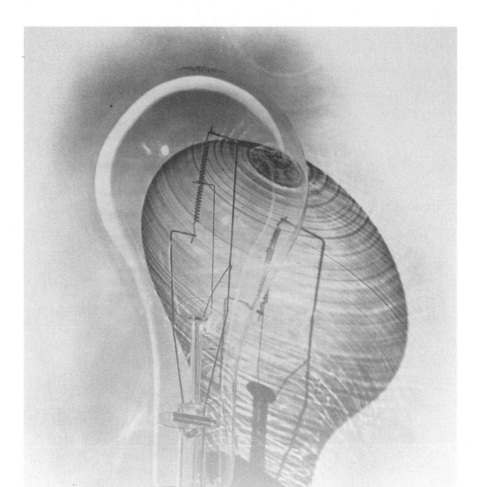

To improve one's style means to improve one's thoughts.

FRIEDRICH NIETZSCHE

The language must be careful and appear effortless.
It must not sweat.

TONI MORRISON

She would write 8–10 words, then draw her gun and
shoot them all down.

E. B. WHITE on KATHARINE WHITE'S writing

After revising your draft for ideas, details, and organization, comb through your words. Words make ideas croak or sing, convey an authoritative or awkward tone, and arouse or sedate readers. A smooth, clean style proves a writer sweats the words. It isn't luck.

Nietzsche's words heading this chapter remind us that glittering words cannot somehow brush fancy makeup over a bad idea or no idea. Revising words means revising ideas, for words and ideas are inseparable and together create "style." Katharine White reminds us that we must struggle to find the right word. And Morrison reminds us we must sweep away the signs of our struggle.

 # HONESTY

Vocabulary

Some writers think big words sound more sophisticated or intellectual. They click the thesaurus icon on their computer for fancy synonyms and might revise this sentence this way: "They inaugurate a scrutinization of a thesaurus in diligent quest for ostentatious synonyms." I hear readers snoozing. An expanded vocabulary does create options, but the big word approach usually doesn't work. First, if the writer doesn't *really* know her words, they tend to be used off-center: sometimes confusing a reader or showing the writer's *un*sophistication. Second, big words rarely impress good readers, who want a smooth journey, not a sojourn over gargantuan, albeit splendiferous, boulders. Usually the simplest, most direct word possible is best. The fanciest draws attention to itself. Use the occasional fancy word or technical term when you need to; don't sprinkle them like salt over the entire paper. Write within yourself.

This does not mean you can get away with dull or monotonous words. Your vocabulary should be colorful and vivid, but that rarely requires big words.

▲ **PRACTICE 8-1:** Revise the following for clear vocabulary:

- The industrial unit will downsize operations to maximize return on investment.
- My antagonist inaugurated a campaign to terminate my presidency of the Ostentatious Vocabulary Association.

Accuracy

Honest writing demands accuracy, and this means **revising the sloppy word choices** we *all* make in rapid draft composition. If you don't find three or four inaccurate word choices in each paragraph of a draft, you're either a genius or not searching hard. Ask if each word presents exactly the tone or picture you want. It's obviously wrong to misstate a fact or statistic, but **it's also dishonest to exaggerate or use absolutes:**

- Al *always* arrives late.
- Marcie's *never* had a sick day in her life.
- You'll *love* the new Ford carburetors.
- Drug dealers are murderers, *pure and simple.*

Absolutes are words like "always," "never," "all," "every" or "none." Leaving no room for exceptions, they sound dramatic and make writers feel forceful, but they are often dishonest. Notice, I did not say "always dishonest." Some absolutes are true: *All* humans die. Ask yourself in revision if an "often" or "usually" might better describe Al's lateness or if a "hardly ever" or "as long as I've known her" might more accurately describe Marcie's health.

To say someone will "love" a carburetor will probably be an exaggeration for all but the most fanatical car owner. It might be more accurate to simply describe its outstanding features. Why is it exaggeration to say drug dealing is murder, pure and simple? Because it's neither pure nor simple but requires distinctions—drug dealing differs from, say, strangling someone, or from selling automobiles that may also end up killing the user—and you must show *how.*

Being tough with words will make your ideas tougher too. Question key words ruthlessly. **Hunt for "weasels":** words that seem to say something but weasel out of it. (For example, "Computers *may* help you write one to two grades better." Bananas *may* help you write two grades better too.) Inaccurate language makes you appear an unreliable and sloppy thinker.

▲ **PRACTICE 8-2:** Revise these sentences for accuracy:

- The antiabortionists never consider the lives of pregnant teenagers.
- The United States has been completely humiliated by its ineffective immigration laws.

Euphemisms and Crude Language

Euphemisms are expressions that make things sound nicer or grander than they are. When a used car is called "pre-owned" or "pre-enjoyed," a trucker a "commodity relocation engineer," or a garbage collector a "sanitary engineer," the writer is prettying up the truth. During the Vietnam War, American generals denied they invaded Cambodia, a neutral country; they announced they had "launched a protective reaction strike," suggesting self-defense.

Notice that many euphemisms hide behind crooked use of big words. In a famous letter released during the Vietnam War, orders were given to assassinate a secret agent, but the words "assassinate" and "kill" never appeared. The agent was to be "terminated with extreme prejudice."

Euphemisms have their place in conversation. If your friend Bob is fired, you may choose to say he "lost" his job, "was laid off," or "furloughed" to spare his feelings. But unless you need to spare your *audience's* feelings, writing demands a stricter standard of honesty. If Bob was fired, say he was fired. Consider whether it's more accurate to describe an agent as "shot," "murdered," "assassinated," "blown away," "offed," or "eliminated." How do these each have different implications? At a funeral, the dead person may be euphemistically referred to as "the dearly departed" or "the late Bertha Smith," certainly not as "the stiff" or "the corpse." The dead are "conveyed to their final resting places," not "hauled to the worm farm."

Notice that some alternatives to the euphemisms here are unnecessarily brutal. **Crude expressions,** like euphemisms, give you power or distance over unpleasant facts; euphemisms deny them; crude words exaggerate them so they can be laughed at. **In revising for honest words, ask if your choices are *appropriate to the subject***—not sickeningly sweet, not unnecessarily crude. The honest writer can't be so polite the message is wimpy or so impolite the message is forgotten. Obscenities, therefore, should only be used if necessary to duplicate the way a person speaks; the drama they create is usually dishonest—a cheap way to shock the reader. They are inappropriate in all professional communication.

▲ **PRACTICE 8-3:** Revise these sentences for euphemisms or crude language:

- When buying a reconditioned car, delve into the mechanical functioning as well as the amenities or you may own a less than wonderful vehicle.
- The judge thinks a surrogate mother is just a uterus with legs. (Taken from an actual television news broadcast.)

Clichés

Clichés are dead places in your essay. Like all inaccurate word choices, they come easier than the perfect word and have a way of nesting in rough drafts. Revision must root them out and plant live words in the empty holes. Some writers may defend clichés by saying, "Everyone knows what a cliché means." I disagree. For example, is the expression "toe the line" or "tow the line?" Visualize it and you'll see different images for each spelling. A student who described a nasty woman as "an old batilacks," had no idea the original expression referred to a weapon, a "battle axe." Nor do readers pay close attention to clichés. They know there's no new idea, no new, interesting word use that requires attention. Do you really want your readers to drift away? Complete these images:

Hungry as a _____

Gentle as a _____

Quiet as a _____

Eats like a _____

Busy as a _____

Slippery as _____

Most people will complete these images with the same one or two words; the expressions are that predictable. Clichés slide easily in *and out* of readers' minds. If you want to show how slippery a political issue is, for instance, don't compare it to a "greased pig" or an "eel." Compare it to a wet gangplank, a slimy creek bed, an icy wheelchair ramp, or a salesman asked for a refund. As Hollywood producer Sam Goldwyn used to say, "We have to get some fresh platitudes." Start by picturing what you're describing. Feel, see, hear, taste, or smell it as a *thing,* not as a word.

New clichés are born each year, sounding exciting and creative. Lately you may hear someone say, "Give him props. His music's butters. It's mad phat. And that girl's a dime." Translation: "Give him credit. His music's great. It's very cool. And the girl's outstanding (a ten)." I like "butters" and "mad phat." For today, it's creative. But if these expressions last they'll sound as stale and corny as "souped-up car," "pinko," "sexpot," "mod," and "D.A." do today. (Ask your professor what they meant—if he or she was around then!)

▲ **PRACTICE 8-4:** Invent two creative alternatives for each of the clichéd expressions listed above. Be visual and fresh.

▲ **PRACTICE 8-5:** Revise these clichés to be more fresh and visual:

- Don't put all your eggs in one basket.
- Curiosity killed the cat.
- Fight fire with fire.

Sexist Language

Aside from the ethical argument that sexist language is wrong and that by using it you personally contribute to bias against women, sexist language can alienate readers (both male and female) who find it offensive. You may also create a picture of yourself as a sloppy thinker who stereotypes and generalizes without much thought. If you always refer to lawyers or scientists as "he," for instance, you should know that nearly 50 percent of all current law students and 40 percent of all advanced degree science students are women. Here are three options for dealing with the "she-he" problem:

- When the sex of an example is irrelevant, use "he or she" or a pronoun without sex reference. "A student should prepare his schedule . . ." could be "students should prepare their schedules . . ." or a "student should prepare his or her schedule . . ."
- You may sometimes use "he" and sometimes "she" for examples, as this book does occasionally. Just remember, some nurses are male, some mechanics are women.

- Use a gender-neutral term instead. "Salesman" can be "salesperson;" "postman" can be "postal worker" or "mail carrier."

Do these little variations matter? Some people might claim we know "mankind" includes both males and females, as do jobs that end in "man." But even though we "know" it, hearing "man" used thousands of times in our lives to describe the species, respected positions, and important activities probably has hammered values into all of us. Many researchers believe these small messages affect our self-image, confidence, and the dreams and goals we set for ourselves. Whether you agree with this or not, it's undeniable that most educated people, most businesses, and most public institutions are sensitive to sexist language. The penalties far outweigh the rewards for using such language today.

▲ **PRACTICE 8-6:** Revise these sentences to make them less sexist.

- An athlete must accept his responsibility to be a role model.
- The chairman must control his audience.

VIVIDNESS

Someone might ask, "If I weed out big words, extreme words, clichés, and sexist and crude language, won't my style be dull?" No. You're cleaning away the debris to make room for real style. Honesty and vividness come from concreteness and from improving key words—especially verbs, modifiers, and metaphors.

Concreteness

During revision, replace general or vague words with concrete words that are specific or appeal to the reader's senses. This is the difference between pretend meaning and real meaning. If you can't pin a sentence down to specifics, cross it off. You haven't lost a sentence but *gained* clarity. Notice how wimpy the following sentences are:

- The Saturn is a *good* car.
- We had an *exciting* time!
- Abused children suffer *mentally* as well as *physically.*

The vague words needing pep are so general that a reader has no specific image from them. In revision, choose words that relate to specific details:

- The Saturn is a sporty, economical, reliable car.
- Our blood pressure blasted off, and we screamed ourselves hoarse.
- We see the scars and burn marks on abused children, but a mother screaming, "I wish you were never born!" scars them too.

Here's a brief list of vague words to watch out for:

good	bad	great
nice	fantastic	beautiful
ugly	cute	sad
happy	success	awesome
awful	terrible	big/little

Their hazy generality poisons vividness. If you try to improve these words with a thesaurus, you may substitute "salubrious" or "benevolent" for "good," or substitute "deplorable" or "grievous" for "sad." Though slightly more specific than the originals, these still don't *define* or *visualize*. In revising for concreteness, resee the thing described; **think in pictures, not in words.** Replacing vague words with specific ones will do more than any other technique to make your writing more tangible and clear.

▲ **PRACTICE 8-7:** Rewrite the following sentences for more concreteness. This requires you to interpret the writer's purpose, because the sentences are vague:

- American foreign policy in Latin America is messed up.
- What an ugly sight a garbage dump is.
- He is really a great friend.

Verbs

One key word to examine is the verb, the strongest word in any sentence because it conveys action. Yet when I ask my students to underline all verbs in their papers, 80 percent turn out to be forms of "to be": was, were, are, is, am. "To be" is the dullest English verb. Other colorless, bland verbs include "go," "have," "get," "do," and "become." Some vivid, action verbs are "hack," "spring," "peel," "plow," "flick," "gobble," or "rip." Study this sample sentence from a student draft:

EXAMPLE: "As the rush of people walk through the downtown area, the clanking and shaking of the old train is heard."

This sentence buries its vivid words "clanking" and "shaking." Make them the main verbs and scratch out the weak "is heard" at the end. Also "walk" is a weak verb when the writer has the word "rush." Here's how the writer's peers revised it:

EXAMPLE: "As the people rush downtown, the old train clanks and shakes past."

In the next sentence "is" saps potentially stronger verbs:

EXAMPLE: To many people a college education is a burning desire.

BETTER: Many people burn for college educations.

▲ **PRACTICE 8-8:** In the next two sentences, first locate the strong words and then restructure the sentence around a stronger verb.

- The question often asked by apartment dwellers is, "How am I going to furnish this place?"
- There was a clashing of negative events that helped me find myself.

Some verbs like "look" or "walk" are so general, I almost always substitute more specific ones. "She looked at me." Boring. Did she stare, leer, examine, peek, glance, or glare? Notice how the substitutes are more specific and visual than "look." Each adds tone and attitude. Many flat sentences spring off the page with new verbs.

▲ **PRACTICE 8-9:** List ten substitute words for "walk" that are more visual and more specific.

Adjectives and Adverbs

Many writers have been told adjectives and adverbs describe. True. But adverbs (which modify or describe verbs) and adjectives (which modify or describe nouns) are *helpers*. Rely on better nouns and verbs first. Which of these pairs is the sharpest:

- Janet walked very, very slowly.
  Janet dawdled.
- The car moved quickly away.
  The car sped away.
- Jack was an extremely big man.
  Jack was a Goliath.

In each case the second is more precise and visual because a weak adjective-noun or adverb-verb gave way to a strong noun or verb.

One particularly flat type of adjective or adverb is the **intensifier,** a word that says, "yeah, well, even more than the next word." These are the most common ones:

very	extremely
so	definitely
too	excessively
really	least
-est (ending)	most

Here are a few in inaction:

- He was the happiest man alive.
- It was a really easy assignment.
- The oil spill was extremely bad.
- Laws for handicapped rights are so very hard to pass.

Intensifiers remind me a little bit of shouting arguments I used to have with my brother: the louder the better. This sentence beats its chest: "It was an extremely, definitely, extra-important, most so very needed event." The problem is, there's no chest to beat, no concrete noun or strong verb to accentuate. Replace intensifiers with more concrete nouns or verbs. For example:

- He was ecstatic.
- The oil spill covered 300 square miles.

▲ **PRACTICE 8-10:** Revise the other two examples.

Metaphors

Vivid writing often relies on metaphors. Albert Einstein used the metaphor of riding a light beam to help explain his theory of relativity, and scientists F. H. Crick and J. D. Watson used the metaphor of two snakes wrapped around each other to describe the structure of the DNA molecule. In Chapter 3 you learned to use metaphor as a thinking strategy. In revision, sharpen metaphors for *compactness, coherence,* and *concreteness.*

Metaphors should be compact. Metaphor power comes partly from suggesting a lot in a small space. Don't explain yourself away:

> Cameron was very tall and very thin and has often been compared to Ichabod Crane. His most distinguishing feature would be his long fingers. If you've ever been to a costume shop and put on a pair of phony fingers, you'll know what his look like. Well, maybe not that long, but they are bigger than yours and mine.

This writer had an interesting, vivid comparison, but he diluted it into a thin tea.

> **REVISED:** Tall, thin Cameron has been compared to Ichabod Crane. His fingers are like the scrawny, phony fingers in a costume shop.

You can suggest metaphors sometimes with just one word—the ultimate in compactness. Here are some from student papers:

- Sandy chirped a reply.
- This popcorn kernel of a man was a marine?
- Bill's cabbage brain couldn't understand.

▲ **PRACTICE 8-11:** Write out a one- or two-sentence metaphor and then rewrite it compactly with one star verb or adjective. For example, "Our economics course is like a maze in which you cannot find your way out, like experimental rats in a psychology experiment" could be reduced to: "We groped through the maze of economics all semester."

Metaphors should be coherent—everything in the picture should fit together. The following metaphors pull the reader in several directions:

EXAMPLE: Our household was emotionally *barren,* much like the *deserts* of loneliness people create to save themselves from being *bruised* or *hurt* by someone else. (The writer creates an effective desert image but then stirs in a new metaphor with "bruised." He needed to continue his desert image, perhaps with a reference to being lost, thirsty, or victimized by sun or desert predators.)

EXAMPLE: Even though James Brown possessed extraordinary potential as a musician, his motivation was like an *abrupt red light* that *faded* in and *slithered* out periodically. (Another good metaphor derailed. The word "slithered" switches images. Red lights can fade but they can't slither. The writer should have stuck with the traffic light imagery.)

▲ **PRACTICE 8-12:** Revise the two examples listed above.

Finally, **metaphors must be concrete.** They should appeal to our senses with sharp sights, smells, sounds, tastes or touches. Notice how the following improves with more specific visualizing:

EXAMPLE: Her dreams were ruined by fear, like the presence of an ugly pollutant in a clean body of water.

REVISED: Her dreams were ruined by fear, like chemicals seeping into a pristine pond.

▲ **PRACTICE 8-13:** Rewrite these sentences for sharper metaphors:

- General Colin Powell was a tower of strength.
- We are at a crossroads where we must sink or swim.
- His voice was like a lion's. It made a lot of noise and it felt like it was coming after you down a hallway if you tried to get away.
- Peace comes like rain.

 # STYLISH SENTENCE STRUCTURE
Variety

Glance at your sentences. Do they all follow a subject—verb—modifier format? Are most stubby or are they long, twisted snakes? Readers like variety. Reading many short, choppy sentences is like picking up a handful of beads; help the reader string them together. A page of continuous long sentences is like a jungle to hack through—you want more air and light. Break up a series of straight statements with an occasional question. Mix simple, compound, and complex sentences (see Chapter 16).

▲ **PRACTICE 8-14:** Find a place in your last paper in which three sentences in a row are nearly the same length or use almost the same structure. (*Hint:* Look for ones using a subject—verb—modifier pattern.) Change the length or pattern for variety.

▲ **PRACTICE 8-15:** Just to see what your sentence lengths are, count the number of words in each sentence of your last paper. What is the shortest? What is the longest? What is the average length? In class compare with your classmates.

Parallel Structure

Parallel structure means matching words or groups of words in a series or on each side of a conjunction:

> **EXAMPLE:** The president ordered troops, ships, and planes overseas. (*Troops, ships,* and *planes* are all nouns.)

> **EXAMPLE:** She wanted to stop the civil war, unite the American people, and open the harbors for oil tankers. (Three verbs with modifiers.)

> **WRONG:** The president ordered troops, ships, and bombed the airfield. (The last item is a mismatch.)

> **WRONG:** She wanted to stop the civil war, the votes of Americans, and open the harbors for oil tankers. (The second item, a noun, mismatches.)

You might consider one other aspect of parallel structure when working on a particularly important sentence: the items should build to a climax.

> **EXAMPLE:** His childhood days were filled with fear, cruelty, and a concealed love. (Because the student contrasted love with negative things, it springs up at the end like a surprise blossom; in the middle of the list, it would lack emphasis.)

> **WEAK:** The congressional plan backfired; 2,000 soldiers were killed unnecessarily, Congress was recalled for an extra session, and the plan cost $100,000 more than expected. (The soldiers' deaths is most important and therefore belongs last.)

▲ **PRACTICE 8-16:** Write two sentences that list parallel items in a series. Each item must be a phrase or clause of at least three words.

 ## CONCISENESS

Essayist and children's book author E. B. White recalled his former writing professor, William Strunk, leaning on the lectern in class, peering over his wire-rimmed spectacles, and barking, "Avoid unnecessary words! Avoid unnecessary words! Avoid unnecessary words!"

I'd like to leave it at that, but we need to make a distinction. I receive a number of papers each semester that are *brief*, say half the length asked for. They're usually not *concise*, however. Concise writing says *as much as possible in as few words as possible*. This means keeping a reader interested, supplying vivid supporting detail, and emphasizing key points. Many brief papers simply state a thesis without bringing it to life. They may be wordy or vague or simply cover less than a concise longer paper.

Few people could top President Calvin Coolidge for brevity. Once asked by his wife what the Sunday sermon was about, Silent Cal replied, "Sin."

"Well, what did the preacher say about it?" his exasperated wife asked.

"He was against it," Coolidge replied.

This brevity says nothing. However, most great writing is concise. The Lord's Prayer is fifty-six words; Lincoln's Gettysburg Address is about 200; the Ten Commandments is under 300; and the Declaration of Independence is about 1,500. (Freshman papers run 500 to 1,000 words.) On the other hand, a U.S. Department of Agriculture memo on how to price cabbage weighed in at over 25,000 words!

We all talk around our ideas most of the time. But in revision, average writers can trim 20 to 30 percent of their draft. Much small-scale wordiness takes up space but contributes nothing:

Wordy	*Better*
"He went on to say . . ."	"He added . . ."
"The hat was red in color . . ."	"The red hat . . ."
"We proceeded to depart."	"We departed."
"In my opinion it seems to me . . ."	"I believe . . ."
"Ken was slugged by Joe."	"Joe slugged Ken."
"Due to the fact that . . ."	"Because . . ."

Here's an introduction that spins nothing into empty cotton candy:

> **EXAMPLE:** It is very interesting to compare what different essay writers have to say about writing essays. In our book we have different essays on writing by E. B. White, Alice Walker, and Joan Didion, who are all famous twentieth-century authors today.

Notice the repetition and lack of a clear thesis; the writer may think she's started, but the reader knows she's still clearing her throat.

> **IMPROVED:** E. B. White, Alice Walker, and Joan Didion present three different views on writing essays.

Nothing important is lost; the sentence is improved for being direct. Like watery wine, low-test gasoline, or air-puffed bread, wordy writing doesn't offer enough pop per ounce. Readers expect a certain density of information per paragraph. A high-octane effort means not only using high-intensity concrete words and vivid verbs, but removing the water.

Redundancy: A hat that is "red in color" says it twice; red cannot be a shape or a smell, only a color. Is the "honest truth" more true than just "the truth"? Chop redundancy to strengthen the following sentences:

- The Constitution was totally demolished.
- He is a completely unique artist.
- The railroad was extended a distance of 60 miles.
- I plan to enter the field of nursing.
- In the fall of the year school once again reopens.
- At that point in time, we faced a serious job crisis.

All writers puff up first drafts; good writers condense final drafts. Concentration and practice, not talent, will make your writing concise.

Connecting words such as prepositions, "that" or "which," or anything not carrying the main weight of a sentence may be fluff. Cutting two verbs to one strengthens sentences, especially if you exterminate a "to be" verb:

WORDY: The bureaucrats avoided some *of the* work *they were* assigned.

CONCISE: The bureaucrats avoided some assigned work.

WORDY: The catalytic converter *is used for the purpose of* reducing air pollution.

CONCISE: The catalytic converter reduces air pollution.

▲ **PRACTICE 8-17:** Make each of these sentences more concise. Save vivid words, and convert hidden strong verbs into active ones.

- At that point in time Lee attacked north for the purpose of scaring the Yankees.
- The Capitol was entirely destroyed by fire.
- He had a long gray beard that had not been trimmed very recently.
- Ike brought tears of laughter to a great number of people with his jokes.
- Those who commit murder are not deserving of the state's mercy.

 ## USING A COMPUTER TO REVISE WORDS

Computers are great for word revision. Although software varies, a thesaurus feature can find synonyms for poor word choices and a word search will tell if you overused one word. You may be able to instruct your computer to beep at suspect words: absolutes like "always," intensifiers like "very," clichés you want to put a lid on (beep!), vague words like "good," or "to be" verbs like "was." Then you scroll through your draft and consider changing each. You don't have to change all of them, but the computer is ruthlessly honest about telling you exactly what's there—if you want to know.

▲ **PRACTICE 8-18:** Create a hot list of style words and instruct your computer to alert you when your draft uses absolutes (p. 120), intensifiers (p. 125), vague words (p. 124) and forms of the verb "to be" (p. 124).

Highlights of Chapter 8

- Revise your draft for words and style by going over it once for *each* aspect listed. A focused reading is more likely to pinpoint problems than just riding the flow to find a bump.

- Revising for *honest word use* means using a vocabulary you control, testing the accuracy of your words, avoiding weasels and absolutes, and getting rid of euphemisms, crude language, and clichés.

- To make your style more *vivid,* revise for more concrete words that visualize, replace "to be" and other dull verbs with action verbs, replace some weak modifier–subject combinations with stronger nouns and verbs, eliminate intensifiers, and flash an occasional metaphor.

- Revising *sentence structure* can improve style too. Vary your sentence lengths and format and revise for tight, climactic parallel construction.

- *Concise writing* has more impact. Ruthlessly cut wordiness.

- As you read over your draft, anytime you find yourself daydreaming or skimming, stop! Go back. Read the last few sentences with microscope eyes. A reader's attention will be twice as fragile as yours. Sharpen a verb, eliminate a wordy phrase, or be more concrete to keep that reader with you for the rest of the ride.

Writing Suggestions and Class Discussions

Revise the following for honest word use, vividness, parallel structure, and conciseness.

1. It was a blistering June day; the heat could be seen radiating from the pavement.
2. Pete is definitely one of a kind.
3. We must grab the bull by the tail and face the situation.
4. The first time I encountered José, it was in a foreign country.
5. The Pursian Gulf War was filled with a great many human atrocities.
6. Dr. Baikman is a short, dark man who looks as if he's beginning to get old.
7. She has a way of making people feel very special.
8. Alan's superficialities were especially on my bug list.

9. Queen Morena dumped on the count. She declined his matrimonial proposal.
10. A garden is in her face where roses and white lilies grow.
11. Americans must give up drugs if they want to escape the prison of this filthy crutch they use to bury their weaknesses.
12. After returning from the little girl's room, I proceeded to expostulate on the numerous beneficial phenomena of mixed-gender lavatories.
13. When I was at the age of 12, my mom started to become a little better, treating us more like human beings, although the discipline was still there.
14. Upon my arrival, I quickly apprehended the culture change and beheld the New Hampshire accent and idioms embellished by the McCormack family.
15. After the whistle, Sam attacks his opponent with a killer instinct, driving him to the mat and gratifying what he sets out to accomplish.
16. There was a fear of anyone approaching him.
17. His right eye was dangling out of its socket, his lower lip was stretched under his chin, his nose was almost completely torn from his face and hanging facial skin.
18. Her medication was putting weight on her that was visibly noticeable within a few days after it was prescribed.
19. Carolyn's life was like water, moving and shifting with no anchor.
20. It's always too late to straighten a kid out after he's been in jail.
21. There are many different variations in color.
22. Janet lacked a confidence factor.
23. Negotiations will either grind to a halt or be hammered out.
24. At 7 A.M. in the morning, the weatherman predicted major thunderstorm activity.
25. Make a chart listing "male" and "female" at the top and write the qualities brought out with each reference to gender in these 24 sentences (e.g., fear, purposeful). Then evaluate the *overall* sexist slant to the first twenty-four sentences.

Three Ways to Revise Style

1. Exchange rough drafts with another student in class. Do all you can to help each other with honest word choices, vividness, sharp sentences, and conciseness.
2. Your professor will mark one paragraph in your draft or paper needing stylistic pruning and pep. Revise it thoroughly.
3. Find an example for 10 of the following in the draft of a paper you're preparing. Then revise. Most people can find at least two of the starred items in drafts:

   - Overly fancy vocabulary
   - *Absolutes
   - *Exaggeration

- Weasels
- Euphemism
- Crude language
- Clichés
- Sexist language
- *Areas needing more concreteness
- *Dull verbs
- *Weak adjectives or adverbs
- *Intensifiers
- Weak metaphors
- Monotonous sentence structure
- Nonparallel sentence structure
- *Redundancy
- *General wordiness

Sample Revision for Style

Here is a rough draft of part of a student essay, with suggestions made for style. The author is Mary Updaw and the comments were made by her and others. Ignore the comments as you read, then go over each of them.

GOOD INTENTIONS

WORDY
and weak verb

I (was in urgent need of) a tracheotomy operation a year

VAGUE
not
concrete

ago. (Since then, some difficult situations have occurred.)

So this is for the strangers (whom) I meet daily and their

unnecessary

good intentions.

weak verb- ride? enter?

When you (get on) an elevator with me, do not suggest I

weak verb

(go see) my doctor if I cough. I do not have enough time

between floors to explain to a perfect stranger my condi-

tion. Please do not stare at me with sympathetic eyes if

you notice my trach bib. I am not some poor little lamb

Absolute

you should feel sorry for, and I resent (any) indication

that I am. Please do not ask foolish questions if you see

> me using my inhaler. I am not a drug addict, and (I feel)   *wordy*
> it should be (quite) obvious I am taking medication (for my   *cut intensifier*
> health). I do not (go up to) people I see popping aspirin   *redundant*   *weak verb*
> and (ask) if they have a headache.   *better verb*
>
> If your child happens to (look) in my (direction), (please   *stare?*   *used twice— cut one*
> do not whisper in his ear and steer him in another (direc-
> tion). I am not (some kind of) freak he should (be afraid of).   *a*   *wordy*
> To the strangers who want to swap medical war stories, I
> say forget it. I have not been graced with a Purple Heart
> for my condition; they are only for the men who deserve
> them, (and, frankly, it's none of your #*!% business). For   *too crude! harsh + unnecessary*
> the well-wishers who secretly are glad it is me and not
> you, you are more transparent than you realize, (and I
> don't care to be around you). *redundant — this is obvious*

Commentary

Reviewers knew this draft based on a bug list had strong potential. Honest and direct, it hit the reader hard. They also liked the style of the sentences, which are balanced and parallel to make Mary's structure clear. The notes focus on cutting wordiness, replacing vague words, weak verbs, and sharpening the existing sentence structure. The final draft is 20 percent shorter but more lively in style.

Final Draft

GOOD INTENTIONS

> I urgently needed a tracheotomy operation a year ago. But the real shock came later--dealing with strangers and their good intentions.

When you ride an elevator with me, do not suggest I rush to my doctor if I cough. I do not have enough time between floors to explain my condition to a perfect stranger. Please do not stare at me with sympathetic eyes if you notice my trach bib. I am not some poor little lamb you should feel sorry for, and I resent indications that I am. Please do not ask foolish questions if you see me using my inhaler. I am not a drug addict; it should be obvious I am taking medication. I do not ask people popping aspirin if they have a headache.

If your child glances at me, please do not whisper in his ear and steer him in another direction. I am not a freak he should fear. To strangers who want to swap medical war stories, forget it. I have not been graced with a Purple Heart for my condition; they are only for the men who deserve them. For the well-wishers who secretly are glad it is me and not you, you are more transparent than you realize.

✓ **PEER REVIEW CHECKLIST FOR STYLE**

Author:_____

Reviewer:_____

The reviewer should read through the rough draft **only** for style. Make suggested changes on the rough draft itself, but please leave the original legible for the author.

1. Find two weak verbs (is, are, has, or get) and suggest more visual action verbs to replace them.
2. Accuracy/honesty: Find an exaggeration or absolute that ought to be modified. Suggest a revision.
3. Concreteness: Find a cliché that needs a fresher image or an unsupported generalization that needs more detail. Suggest a revision.
4. Find an intensifier and suggest a stronger noun or verb to replace the weak one the intensifier tried to build up.
5. Look for an example of sexist language or stereotyping and suggest a revision.
6. Conciseness: Pick one paragraph of the essay and make at least three suggestions to eliminate redundant or empty words.

CHAPTER 9
Description
Making Your Audience See

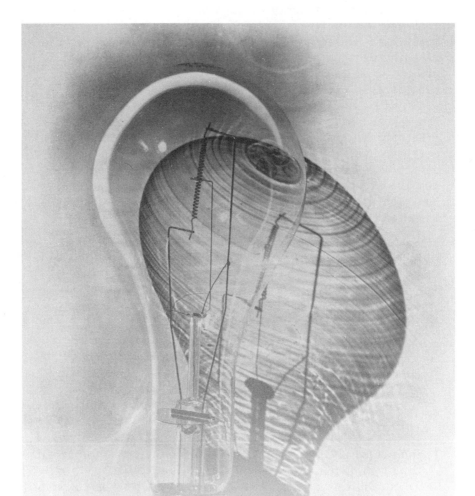

The question is not what you look at, but what you see. . . .
A man has not seen a thing unless he has felt it.

HENRY DAVID THOREAU

To see takes time—like to have a friend takes time.

GEORGIA O'KEEFFE

Look! Look!

COLETTE (her last words)

Which of these statements are true?

- Description is flowery and poetic.
- Description bogs down writing.
- Description belongs in creative essays, not persuasive or informative writing.

None. They all distort the real nature of description. Fancy, gooey descriptive passages can smother ideas and is unacceptable as professional communication. Such passages give description a bad reputation. **Good description doesn't need to be gooey or fancy.** For example, the following passage describes a seizure a student's infant daughter suffered as a result of a DPT vaccine for pertussis:

> Lying in a puddle of vomit, Katelyn's head tilted to her shoulder, her eyes fixated left, looking like quarter moons. When I picked her up, I realized her head was locked to her shoulder. "Katie!" I yelled. She didn't hear me. Once in her father's arms, her legs locked straight out. Her tiny arms pulled tight against her chest, and her head shot back. My husband held down her tongue just as her jaw locked shut. Her eyes rolled upward, then they were gone.

At the hospital, the child's condition is stabilized, and the author goes on to describe her condition:

> There, lying in a crib resembling a cage, clad only in her diaper, was our baby daughter. Her chest was covered with leads monitoring her heart. Her arms, braced with tongue depressors, were violated with tubes and needles. Inches from her body was a "crash kit" equipped with electric paddles should they be needed.
>
> *—Alana J. Lockwood*

This vivid, factual description draws readers into the author's informative critique of the DPT vaccine, which each year causes seizures in thousands of normal children.

Description breathes life into writing—transforms typed words into pictures, sounds, and ideas. *Good* description makes the writer's idea dance in readers' heads, so they forget they're reading words. *Bad* description, by trying to impress readers with lush words, distracts from the idea.

Good description is essential for *all* writing, from business reports to personal letters to poems to persuasive essays. **Description commits writers to honesty by pinning down vague statements with concrete details.** Honest description shows the world as it is with all its warts, pimples, and secret beauties. It challenges safe stereotypes and preconceptions by getting down on its knees to scrutinize the world closer, to find and report what's really there. This tough attitude resists gooey description, making writing lean and hard, as in this student example:

> It takes 938 steps to walk from one end of the beat to the other. The air is cold and crisp, the kind that fills my lungs with crystals—like a dagger in my chest. Only an hour and a half left until I'm done. The night is clear, almost too clear. The sound of my boots pounding the frozen turf is the only real

thing. Our Air Force bombed Libya two days ago—an act of war. Tonight the lieutenant issued live ammunition. Boring guard duty became relevant.

Step 452, almost to the mid-point, 17 steps away. I can see where I marked the center with a line scratched in the path. The center is an insecure place, where the distance between start and finish is the same. I just hope that the powers that run things have enough sense to go back to the start.

—*Scott Nairy*

This passage makes us *see* as well as understand, which is description's great virtue.

In persuasive or research papers, powerful description can support a thesis in combination with statistics and other facts. In a paper arguing for strong penalties for pregnant women who use drugs, a student's research describes the effects of cocaine on newborns:

Because cocaine causes fetus malnutrition, when the baby is born, its dry, cracked skin resembles the cover of an old, leather-bound book (Fulroth 70). Cocaine babies are almost always underweight. Their heads are 20 percent smaller than average. Their limbs jerk and jitter constantly, and their hands fly periodically to the sides of their heads, eyes startled wide in terror. Cocaine babies' heartbeats soar, and their lungs pump like hyperactive bellows. They cry inconsolably, a creepy, catlike wail that can last hours and which indicates severe neurological damage (Knight 71).

—*Heidi Daniels*

 ## A WRITER'S EYE: SIX WAYS TO VISUALIZE IDEAS

Experience the Subject: Don't Think in Words

When I ask students to describe a place, I often receive an essay that begins: "My room is 10 feet 6 inches by 11 feet and painted blue. I have a bed, a dresser, a stereo, a chair. . . ." This dead thing wants to be buried. Some students who realize it's flat "enliven" it with so-called descriptive words: "My room is robin-egg blue with beige accents. I have an antique maple dresser, an enormous bed, a four-speaker Dolby-sound stereo cassette player. . . ." Bury this one in a fancy casket; it's just as dead as the first. Both examples fail because of mistaken goals.

- Description is *not* a catalog of everything present.
- Description is *not* created by thinking up picturesque words.

Description *is* created by mentally reexperiencing what you hope to describe. Thoreau and O'Keeffe must have had this in mind when they wrote the sentences heading this chapter. A catalog may help as a brain teaser, but it won't create *quality* description. For that you must create an *idea* on which the description hangs, and you must concentrate on seeing and feeling your subject, not on choosing descriptive words. Evoke it inside yourself, and only *then* describe it in words. Reexperiencing often leads to vivid words naturally *and* ties description together.

Suppose I was writing about access for the disabled in public buildings. My first brain-teaser list of descriptive details might include the following:

- wide stalls in rest-rooms
- interpreters for the deaf in college
- low water fountains with large handles
- wheelchair lifts on buses
- disabled people I've known

I could use this list to compose a paper, perhaps on "Improvements in Public Access in Recent Years," but these descriptive details aren't sharp enough to write a strong paper. I haven't reexperienced them vividly.

Let's take the bathroom stall example. I started to skip this for decency, but I realized that decency allows people to hide many facts about the disabled. Imagine yourself entering that stall in a wheelchair. Experience the bodily movements you need to accomplish this simple act. Go slow: See or feel each moment clearly before going on. Could you do it during ten minutes between class? I picture myself rolling amid the waists of walking people, bumping open the rest-room door and scraping past, rocking and turning several times to shut and lock the stall door, spilling books and papers off my wheelchair tray when I hoist myself with the cold bar, my chair sliding nearly out of reach, contorting to flush the knob behind my back and speeding to class late, bumping cluttered chairs to make a space, and wondering if the professor thinks I'm using my disability to get away with something.

I try to experience Carmen—a wheelchaired student in my literature class one summer. A wonderfully smiling young woman, she loved romantic stories. I experience being her—four feet tall, round-faced, back-bent wrists gripping the chair control knob. I imagine someone dressing me, cramming shoes onto my unresponsive feet, straightening my clothes so they feel right. During those hot classes, did she wish she could shift in her seat like others? Using a pen cost her agony during quizzes. Yet she made no complaints, no special requests, no mention of her disability. She seemed to fly, not to roll.

Thinking of Carmen reminds me of Eva, the old blind woman who lived with my family when I was a boy. Eva never bumped walls or furniture as she walked. From memory, she taught me to read, and she taught herself to read Braille and do leather work for pocket money. She sewed and did all the housework my mother or grandmother did, and when she eventually went to a nursing home, she learned its paths within months. Eva "saw" more than any of the seeing people who lived in our house. Her disability gave her special power and authority.

That makes me recall Tom, a disabled student who scoffed angrily when he was named a hospital's "Patient of the Year" for scoring a 4.0 GPA while working full time. "I'm not a patient," he sputtered. "I'm a man."

I've presented my train of thought roughly as it came out. It's a brain-teaser in paragraph form, not finished writing, but it shows more life, more intense description than my first list. Most important, it stimulated my mind. I can advocate disabled rights now with vivid detail. If I advocate a hands-off policy, I have three examples of tough, independent people. If I want to inform people about barriers the disabled face, I have better information.

Although it may seem like I thought in words, I really thought in pictures, touches, and sounds, for that's how we experience things. Experience the subject from *inside*, not from outside. Allow yourself to become your subject, let it speak through you; don't treat it as an object. At its extreme, this is the mystical experience of poets and fiction writers, when they swear something "wrote itself." But even a restaurant menu writer must see, taste, and smell dishes to describe them well. Business reports and college papers require it too. The more you refeel or visualize your topic, the easier vivid description will be.

Some writers can type or write *as* they reexperience, but many writers can't. If words block experiencing, try this: Sit back, *pen out of reach*, and picture your subject, imagining new details as you expand into it. Relax. Let the topic talk. Release your subconscious. Censor nothing. Accept everything. Concentrate on seeing ever more sharply as you go on. Push your memory, recall facts, use *all* your senses, daydream. Most people stop when the first shadowy pictures appear. You should continue. Go slower, deeper. After a vivid experience gels, record your sensations on paper, still not paying attention to words. Simply record vivid images, allowing new description to flow too. *Later* you will take control and fine-tune the picture. As W.E.B. Du Bois said, "Produce beautiful things, but stress the things rather than the beauty."

▲ **PRACTICE 9-1:** Experience two of these, and only afterward record your descriptions. No catalogs, no fancy words.

- Your room
- A machine or tool
- Teenage alcoholism
- Senior citizens
- An experience with the police

▲ **PRACTICE 9-2:** Freewrite a page for a descriptive topic you're considering for a paper.

Use Brain Teasers to Train Your Eye

Experiencing concentrates on unrestricted seeing. Brain teasers prod your eye in a more organized way. The two most important descriptive brain teasers from Chapter 3 are **Senses** and **Listing Examples.** If as you reexperience your topic, you only see obvious things, switch senses. Concentrate on hearing your topic or smelling or touching it. Or consciously list examples for your topic. Then experience it.

Suppose you're describing to your boss flaws in the design of the store you work in. Be a customer. Walk through the door. Wait! How does the door open? Is it a pull door people always push because it has a horizontal, long handle, not a small grabber? *Feel* yourself jolt as the door bounces—loose from many bumps, shabby. It angers people. How about the entranceway—cluttered with gumball machines and a kiddie ride? The *sound* of the whirring, whumpy-whump of the horse ride and kids begging mothers for quarters. Angry mothers, worn-down mothers. Nickle–dime robbery. Now into the store. The first *sight* is the line of people and cash registers, instead of a pretty dress, glittering jewelry, or the *scent* of sweet perfumes. Walk through other stores with your senses for *comparison.* Now you're ready to write.

For fresher description, push past the obvious with a **Break Stereotypes** brain teaser. Describe the obvious, then puncture it. Suppose you're describing the wonderful vacation cottage your family rented last year. There's the breathtaking view of lake and mountain, the Fourth of July fireworks display reflected in the water, the fish that beg to be caught, the clean, wholesome country air. Stop! Look closer! Listen harder; didn't you see trash in the stream leading to the lake? Weren't trucks hauling building supplies up that pristine mountain? Didn't motorboats roar past midnight?

Comparisons, alternate viewpoints, and **drawing analogies** can also stimulate your descriptive eye. If you're describing a local park, for instance, think of alternative viewpoints. Some people might only see broken glass, litter, missing basketball nets, and a rusted fence. Others might never notice the missing net, but just see dunks, layups, spins, passes, the thunk-thunk of dribbling, laughter, and sweaty drama. Yet others might see the park as it was years ago—a bandstand, people in straw hats, and a popcorn wagon. Allowing yourself to *experience* these other viewpoints makes you see more. We are what we see, so the more you see, the more you become, and the more powerful and alive your description will be.

▲ **PRACTICE 9-3:** Do a Senses brain teaser and one other brain teaser to gather sharp description for the following topics. *Experience* them for five minutes before you focus on words.

- A childhood place
- An eyesore local authorities should fix or remove
- A commercial product about which you have strong feelings
- Student housing

▲ **PRACTICE 9-4:** Use a Senses brain teaser and one other to dig up more descriptive detail for your topic from Practice 9-2.

Use the Iceberg Principle

Ernest Hemingway explained his descriptive technique as "the iceberg principle." He said powerful writing only shows the tip of the iceberg, nine tenths of which rides under water. In essence, he meant that less description is sometimes more because it can suggest more than is visible. When faced with describing a complex or huge topic, *don't feel obligated to cover everything!* You may end up with a shapeless catalog. Instead, **search for small, key details that capture the essence of the larger picture—like a camera close-up.**

In describing a new word processing program, for instance, you'd probably confuse and bore readers by detailing all its features. Anyone who has resolutely begun to read the manual that accompanies a computer knows what I mean. You might illustrate the computer's accessibility by describing how one or two functions operate, such as moving a sentence from one spot to another and reformatting.

The iceberg principle draws readers in close. That perspective creates surprise and drama. It also requires you to *trust your reader.* By relying on a small, intimate detail, you hope the reader will *infer* the larger picture by actively imagining along with you. (If someone writes, "Ralph set fire to the child's kite," there's no need to add, "I think it was cruel.")

Describing a red-veined, bulby nose and a sleek, powdered nose suggest quite different things about the noses' owners. Such description can carry the idea of an essay by symbolism or by representation. To describe a group, you don't have to describe every member of the group. Pick *typical* representatives. This applies to describing "Japanese Cars," "Presidential Dirty Tactics," "Robert Frost's Poetry," or "Modern Dances."

If I wrote about women in their thirties, forties, and fifties returning to college, here are two examples of "iceberg tips." Bernie, a little volcano of a woman, erupted into life after being bottled up for years. She had raised her children and, at fifty-plus, wanted to go into real estate and politics. College started her lava flowing again. She laughs at her mistakes, loves combat in class discussion, and relishes risks. Then there's Alecia, early thirties, petite, and shy under her long hair. She's afraid she'll fail, but is even more afraid of never trying. She knows something creative lives in her, but the world has squashed her before, and she hesitates to risk herself in front of 30 people. She's taking two courses, just dipping a toe into the water to see if sharks will bite.

These two examples don't capture all the problems and feelings of being an "older" woman in college, but as the tip of the iceberg, they stimulate a reader's imagination and memory. Icebergs strike more ships than watery generalities.

▲ **PRACTICE 9-5:** Take an iceberg approach to two of these topics to describe the group to which they belong:

- "Older" men in college
- Suburban houses *or* city apartments
- Local election campaigns
- Local weather

▲ **PRACTICE 9-6:** Take an iceberg approach to your topic from Practice 9-2.

Try Other Eye-Training Tricks

- **Describe your topic as if to an audience unfamiliar with it.** A colleague of mine often asks his students to describe a ballpoint pen and its use (or any other object of modern civilization) to a hermit Tibetan monk. If you imagine your audience knows nothing, you must see freshly.

- **Think of your topic as part of a *process***—not as a thing. A static thing invites dullness, but few things are truly static. The entire earth rockets through space a million miles per day, rotates at 1,000 miles per hour, and its crust rises and falls two feet under us each day. Everything has an origin and an end, and is recycled into new life. Open your mind to see your topic as a process in time and space. A simple description of your room, then, connects to all the people who lived there before, how it came to be, and what will happen to it after you're gone. If you're writing about handling customer complaints at work, make your audience picture the process all parties go through before and after confrontations.
- **Describe what's *not* there.** A person who doesn't smile, cry, or become embarrassed may be interesting for that. The fact that my first word processor could not combine single and double spacing was a major drawback. The lack of dorms shapes atmosphere at many community colleges.

▲ **PRACTICE 9-7:** Look closely at a small natural object, like a moth's antennae, an ant's face, or a few grains of soil. Try two of the "other" techniques to think descriptively. Pull your details together with an idea. Do the same for some overlooked part of your anatomy.

▲ **PRACTICE 9-8:** Use one of the "other" techniques to dig up more description for your topic from Practice 9-2.

 ## REVISING FOR VIVID DESCRIPTION

To this point I've suggested ways to *think* descriptively. Now, here are a few tips to sharpen description when you revise *wording*. Be open to change. *All* words describe; we want your description to move from shadowy first-draft description to the kind you can rap your knuckles against.

The Sense Test

Ask if your descriptive passages pass the sense test—can you see, smell, taste, touch, or hear something in every passage?

> **EXAMPLE:** The accounting procedure is awkward to use.

> **REVISED:** The procedure requires flipping back and forth among three pages.

"Awkward" is an abstract word we understand intellectually, but it cannot be experienced by readers' senses. "Flipping back and forth" suggests awkwardness and helps readers experience the procedure more fully, with sound, sight, and touch.

> **EXAMPLE:** The tenement smelled dirty and rotten.

> **REVISED:** The tenement smelled like mildewed shoes.
> *or* The tenement smelled of urine and stale beer.

The revisions create different images, but both are sharp. "Dirty" and "rotten" are not sense oriented.

The Specificity Test

In revising, ask if existing description can be more specific. Test your honesty—how concrete and exact can you be? The broader a description is, the vaguer it reads; the narrower it is, the sharper. Try *several* options for unspecific words before deciding.

> **EXAMPLE:** Heather walked into the room.

Specify the word "room" as "lecture hall," "kitchen," or "men's room" and the sentence focuses instantly. Also specify "walk" as "strutted," "dashed," or "limped" and the sentence leaps at readers.

> **EXAMPLE:** Ordinary household lawn chemicals cause harmful side effects on a human being's health, including respiratory, skin, and neurological problems. They also can seriously pollute and deteriorate the quality of nearby watersheds.

Here's how a student made this topic more specific and tangible:

> Lawn chemicals cause headaches, runny noses, rashes, and nausea. Other symptoms may include vomiting, heavy sweating, dizziness, and disorientation. Their nitrogen seeps into groundwater, ending up in streams and ponds. This causes algae buildup, reduction of oxygen, and eventually, dead water.
> —*Jeanette Crouse*

Specificity names names. Change "car" to "Lexus" or "Taurus" and change "candy" to "M & M's" or "Peppermint Patty" to help your writing jump into a reader's eyes.

Specificity enhances your meaning as well as visual appeal. Scan these two phrases:

- A beggar with a cup.
- A beggar with a Burger King cup.

Why describe the cup? It visualizes, but also pinches us with the contrast of "king" and "beggar." Try new descriptive adjectives, but slash those that don't carry meaning as well as visual appeal. Don't describe just for more words.

▲ **PRACTICE 9-9:** In the following sentences, first mark words that could be more specific or appeal to our senses and then suggest three alternatives for each. *Don't* limit yourself to one-word replacements.

- Bill ate his lunch noisily.
- The union leadership called for a protest.
- The summer breeze off the water is lovely at night.

▲ **PRACTICE 9-10:** Revise one of your practice writings on your own topic by applying the senses or specificity test.

The Freshness Test

For fresher description:

- Replace clichés with original expressions. (See Chapter 8 for more.)

    CLICHE: The 100-foot canyon walls stood over us.

    FRESHER: The canyon thrust out its 100-foot chest.

- Create a metaphor for dull description.

    EXAMPLE: He had scary eyes.

    REVISED: He had eyes like half-peeled grapes.
        or His eyes tightened around my neck.

- Cut flat details. If you can't improve a dull spot, leave it out—see if anything's really lost. If you wanted to sell a head of lettuce, would you leave on the brown, wilted leaves?
- Do a mini-brain teaser for weak descriptions. Freewrite until something vivid emerges. Select the best for the revised description.

Highlights of Chapter 9

- Vivid description is appropriate for *all* writing—whether a business report, technical manual, paper on global poverty, or letter telling Uncle Moneybags about the poverty of modern students. Description breathes life into your words.
- A sharp descriptive eye helps writers appreciate and understand life more intensely, for description is the art of experiencing the world honestly. It is *not* fancy word painting.
- The most important part of writing good description is to experience your subject.
- You can also use brain teasers to stimulate concrete thinking or use the iceberg principle to find the representative detail.
- Other eye-training tricks are to describe the topic to a naive audience, see your topic as a process, or describe what's missing.

Writing Suggestions and Class Discussions

1. Write one long descriptive sentence about the greatest meal you ever ate or your favorite piece of clothing. Use as many senses as you can. Pack in details without writing a general inventory.
2. Write your own abstract, dictionary-like definition of love, hate, or madness. In a separate paragraph, *show* the definition in action. Experience an incident or example. Use picture words, no abstractions.
3. Describe the youngest person you know who is pregnant, homeless, on drugs, in college, dead, or rich.
4. Describe a hospital room. Find *four* overlooked details that, like the tip of an iceberg, represent the hospital experience.

5. Bring a music recording, photograph, or reproduction of an art work to class. Before playing or showing it, read aloud a one-paragraph description you wrote of it. Use experiencing, brain teasers, and the iceberg theory to write your description.

6. Blind writers like Homer, Jose Luis Borges, John Milton, and Helen Keller rely on other senses. Sit in an unfamiliar setting like a bus stop or mall, close your eyes, and *experience* only through your other senses. Spend 15 to 20 minutes. Then write a vivid description.

7. Describe a technical process you know better than most people (developing photographs, tuning a car, or doing a company payroll, for example). Describe this process clearly and vividly for a reader with average knowledge. Use experiencing, brain teasers, and the iceberg theory to start.

8. Describe a common object like a button, key, scar, or can opener. Discover details others might overlook. Write one paragraph.

9. I SPY Assignment: To develop your descriptive eye, *discreetly* observe a stranger for 10 minutes, learning all you can. Study clothes, habits, quirks, speech patterns, as well as physical features. Write several paragraphs. **Warnings:** Don't intrude on the person, and do this in a public place. One student of a colleague of mine got carried away (literally!) when he hotly followed his subject for an hour, and the man turned out to be a detective who arrested him and phoned the professor to verify the "weird alibi."

10. Write a descriptive paper on a place. Vivid detail should support a theme or idea. Write two to three pages. Use experiencing, brain teasers, and the iceberg theory to start.

11. Describe a group you belong to—a company, church, club, team, or clique. Describe it vividly and develop a theme. Use experiencing, brain teasers, and the iceberg theory to start.

12. Peer groups will reexperience areas of the college you're familiar with: bookstore, library, or cafeteria, for examples. Dig up creative, vivid descriptions, not through fancy words but by discovering sharp details. The groups will spend part of the period observing and writing, then reassemble to share their notes. Strive to find overlooked details.

13. Expand any practice exercise that turned out well into a two- to three-page paper.

Sample Analysis

```
                    THE MOWER
                  J. Andrew Lee
    I must have been six. My neighbor, Howard, was mowing
his lawn. It was noon and, as usual, I was devouring my
```

Lee 2

Oscar Mayer bologna and Miracle Whip on white bread sand-   *names*
                                                                names
wich and drinking grape Kool-Aid. Mom had poured it into   *sight*
                                                                and
a Fred Flintstone Dixie Cup, my favorite!   *taste*

   After washing down my lunch with cartoon ecstasy, I   *fresh*
                                                                expressions
wandered around our backyard. Howard's mower was shirring

away with the same intensity as the Blue Angels jet show I   *sounds*

saw that summer. The stench of cut grass and cheap gaso-   *smell*

line pulled me behind the garage onto Howard's lawn. I

could see the front half of the old mower idling for the   *iceberg*
                                                                detail
next row of grass. As I snuck closer, I spotted Howard

lying behind it. He was as still as when he napped on the

old hammock on his front porch. But his skin was the shade

of my grape Kool-Aid. As I stared the world around me   *fresh*
                                                                metaphor
turned black and tunnel shaped, and the tunnel ended at

Howard. My six-year-old mind pushed me closer. I reached

my hand to him to let him know this joke wasn't funny.

When I touched his neck, my fingers froze. I'm not sure   *touch*

why, but the roaring mower made my mind race in place   *sound*

through all the possible things I could do. I did nothing.

   His forehead bulged with a vein that reminded

me of what the moles did to our lawn this spring. Big   *fresh*
                                                                metaphor
purple blotches covered his legs. The blood that seeped

from his nose was just like the fake blood my sister and   *iceberg*
                                                                detail
I made with leftover cranberry sauce at Thanksgiving.

Sweat still dripped from his forehead.

   I must have stood there five minutes before my mother's   *sound*

screaming blew away the tunnel and the Blue Angels'

roaring. It was mid-July and hot as hell, but when she   *cliché*

dragged me into the house, I was freezing.   *touch*

Sound

sight

"That's no place for you to be," my mother panted, her words cut off by sirens out front.

I said absolutely nothing. I watched the paramedics roll Howard onto a bed with wheels and stack him into the ambulance. My mother came behind me. "Are you OK, Andrew?" she whispered.

I looked at her--through her--and asked, "Is Dad OK?" As she held me crying, I felt nothing. I felt her holding me, but my mind felt nothing. I was inside, but I smelled gasoline and cut grass.

smells
iceberg
details

Commentary Based on Peer Review Sheet

What point does the essay make? It deals with the collision between a child's fantasy world and real life. The author is describing the moment when death became real for him and not just a game played with cranberry sauce. But the exact impact is vague.

Are there any symbolic messages here? Yes. The author uses the iceberg principle to reveal the child's mind. Just think of all the irrelevant, childish thoughts he left out from the half hour the essay covers. The ones he chose have symbolic meaning. The Blue Angels jets defy death as they roar overhead. But old Howard just keeled behind his roaring mower. The cut grass is suggestive of life being cut down. Asking about his father suggests a sudden awareness that death can come to others too.

Organization? The first paragraph starts with his innocence. The next two paragraphs deal with his one-on-one confrontation with the dead man. In the final section, his mother faces the death with him, but from inside the house, at a little distance. The order is clear. But I'm left with unanswered questions. I want to know why he specifically asked if his *father* was OK. I also am curious about the emphasis on "nothing"—doing nothing, feeling nothing. I think he's getting at that empty feeling, that helpless feeling we have when we must face big, cruel things we can barely imagine, but I'm not sure.

Give the essay the sense test. This essay was picked for *Ideas and Details* because it does well in all descriptive details. As noted in the margins, the author uses sounds, sights, tastes, touches, and especially smells to make a reader feel the scene.

Where can it be more specific? Not many places. Naming the food zeros us right in. But I'd ask the author to consider doing a bit more with the black tunnel—describe it more for us.

Where can the description be fresher? The only cliché used was "hot as hell." He's playing around with hot and cold, as in alive and dead, but it could be fresher. But the description of the swollen vein the stroke victim suffered is wonderful, as are some other expressions marked above. This essay accomplished a lot in a short space; it is economical, vivid, symbolic. He avoids the catalog approach to describing the dead man and selects details with symbolic value. The language is simple and direct, not strained by picturesque words. I like the word "shirring" to describe the lawn mower, even though he made it up.

✓   **PEER REVIEW CHECKLIST FOR DESCRIPTION**

Author: _____

Reviewer: _____

Answer the questions as specifically as possible and discuss the essay with the author.

IDEAS: What point do you think the essay makes?

Are there any symbolic messages here? Explain.

ORGANIZATION: Describe this essay's organization. Highlight the main pattern, don't evaluate.

Would the essay be improved by rearranging, combining, or cutting some sections? Which? Why? Is anything important missing?

DESCRIPTIVE DETAILS: Give this essay The Sense Test. Where does it do the best, where poorly?

Which section(s) could be more specific? What are the most specific details?

Find a place where the description could be fresher.

CHAPTER 10

Narration

Telling Your Audience a Story

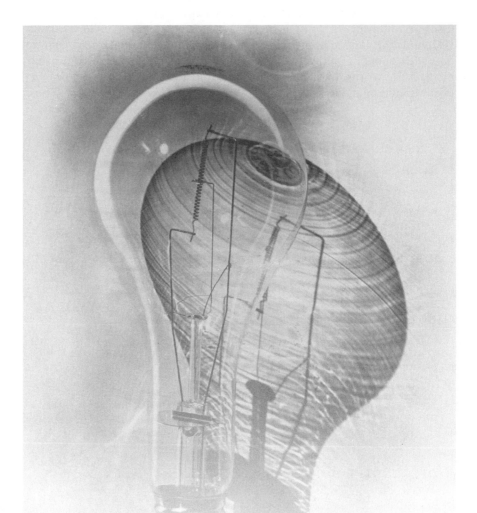

God made man because He loves stories.

ELIE WIESEL

Real suspense comes from moral dilemma and the courage to make and act upon choices

JOHN GARDNER

The earliest writers in every civilization have told stories to convey their messages. Homer's tales of Cyclops, the one-eyed monster, and Circe, whose spells transformed humans into animals, not only entertained but informed and persuaded the ancient Greeks about geography, the gods, humanity's place in the universe, and other things as Homer knew them. The ancient myth of Sisyphus, for example, tells of a greedy king who is condemned in hell to roll a huge boulder to the top of a hill. Just before Sisyphus reaches the peak, the gods make the boulder roll back down, and Sisyphus must start all over again. Up and down the hill he chases the rock for all time. Over the centuries the story has been a parable about greed and also appealed to people as a memorable expression of the futility of much human effort.

Jesus frequently told stories to make his message stronger. "The Good Samaritan" and "The Prodigal Son" seem to stick in our minds much better than, say, a typical sermon on charity. When Jesus told a crowd, "Love thy neighbor," a lawyer asked, "Who is my neighbor?" Jesus, realizing the man wanted to put a limit on who he was required to love, did not directly define the word "neighbor." Instead he told the story of a man beaten and robbed by thieves in his own country. The victim's neighbors, a priest and local official, walked by without helping. Then a Samaritan, a stranger in the victim's country, stopped, washed the man's wounds, took him to an inn, and paid for his lodging. When Jesus finished, the lawyer knew the meaning of the word "neighbor," not from definition, but from the actions in the story.

Why have these stories lasted so long? Because stories are more visual, more easily remembered than abstractions. When we recall Sisyphus groaning behind his boulder or the supposedly "good" men passing the injured man before the Samaritan stops to help, the writer's abstract message flows along with the story.

Successful speakers from corporation executives to U.S. presidents know that telling a vivid story can be more effective than facts alone. People view a storyteller as creative and smart, as one who commands attention with powerful images.

 CONFLICT

The heart of a good story is conflict: forces in tension with each other. The four common types are: person vs. person, person vs. society, person vs. nature, and person vs. self. A person struggling against an employer who cheats clients is person vs. person; someone battling the city to hire more disabled people is person vs. society; someone struggling to find the ski lodge after a sudden squall separates him from the group is person vs. nature; a woman trying to decide whether she should have an abortion is person vs. self.

▲ **PRACTICE 10-1:** Take a moment now to recall examples from your own life to illustrate each of these conflicts. One of them may become your next paper. I will refer to this "practice" during the rest of this chapter. Write a few lines for each.

- You vs. another person
- You vs. society
- You vs. nature
- You vs. yourself

Let's look closer at what makes a good conflict and why it helps your story absorb readers' attention. First, only real sparks make real fires. **Conflicts that don't deeply affect us won't make strong stories.** A story about a mother forbidding her daughter to date a certain boy does not sound very promising, no matter how it upset the writer. However, if the daughter learns that her mother has deeper motives—if, for instance, the boy reminds the mother of a boy who jilted her or of one she always wished she married instead of the daughter's father—then we have more hope for this conflict. Or perhaps we will discover the mother is envious of the daughter's social success. Or perhaps the daughter is dating a wild boy because she doesn't like the relationship her parents have. Here we have something more meaningful. The best conflicts draw out some **deeper significance in the characters or the action.** Readers want conflict so they can care about the outcome, so they can cheer and fear and doubt with the narrator. They also want **conflicts *difficult* to solve.** Wrong vs. right or strong vs. weak doesn't grip readers as much as conflicts in which wrong and right are murky or in which the forces opposed are equal.

Our lives are full of both inner and outer conflicts, but sometimes we don't recognize them. Here are three almost sure ways to find a strong conflict to write about.

Think about the most intense turning points in your life. These have changed not only the *outer* course of your life but the *inner* course as well by developing your philosophy or identity. Readers want a story to matter to the writer, or it won't matter to them. For this reason it is sometimes harder to write about a personal triumph—winning the big race or election—than about a defeat or a tragedy. Winning tends to keep our beliefs intact; often we learn more in losing. However, I can recall an excellent story a student wrote about winning a state wrestling match, because in his moment of triumph he stared into the eyes of the slumped man he'd defeated. Nor do big tragedies necessarily mean a person has grown. As Isaac Bashevis Singer said, "A wise man gets wiser by suffering. A person without wisdom may suffer 100 years and die a fool." The moments that make us grow, that tear away the predictable boundaries of our lives, are the ones that make good papers.

One of my students, a woman who worked at a chemical dependency center, wrote about her conflict with her brother, who was a cocaine addict. Despite what she knew from dealing with addicts, she allowed him to "violate" her with a "merry-go-round of anger, shame, guilt, and fear." Her turning point occurred when she realized that she was "addicted to an addict," that she was "a codependent" even though she never used drugs, because she supported and cared for her brother. Her emotional investment was destroying her, and she learned to let go—to stop feeling responsible for where he was at night, who he was with, what was happening to his body and mind. She still took him for treatment, but she learned she had to break her own emotional addiction.

▲ **PRACTICE 10-2:** List three turning points that changed your outlook on life.

Look for good conflicts by thinking about an interesting person you've known: the resident rebel in family or town, the eccentric uncle, the homeless woman who hangs around campus, the "respectable" neighbor who abuses his children. You may be personally involved if you take sides with or against the rebel. You may debate whether to notify the authorities to help the homeless woman. Or, as an honest, intense observer, you may simply report the conflict you see. People who climb outside norms have built-in conflict. Your own rebellions may make good stories too.

▲ **PRACTICE 10-3:** Describe one of the most interesting people you've known and sketch out a conflict that focuses on this person.

Brain teasers can suggest strong conflicts for narrative essays. A bug list will surely turn up areas of conflict in your life. You can do a general one first and then pursue the one that most intrigues you. Dig out the depth of your dissatisfaction. The alternate viewpoints brain teaser will help you tell an honest story. Look at the story you're considering from the viewpoint of the other people involved to discover your weaknesses and their strengths. This allows you to make *real* opponents in the story, not just cardboard cutouts. Because a major aspect of storytelling is making readers visualize the story, sense brain teasers will help your final draft. Remembering with senses will stimulate your imagination too.

▲ **PRACTICE 10-4:** Use a bug list, alternate veiwpoints, or sense brain teaser to create more notes for one of the stories you sketched in Practice 10-1 or 10-3.

 ## COMPLICATION

After finding a powerful conflict, you must make it grow more complicated as the story continues. The novelist E. M. Forster said he always imagined one of his readers to be a person who only cared about what happened next, who wanted to be surprised by new twists, new angles, new insights in each paragraph. If the story stagnates, it's usually because it has ceased to convey *new information*. This does not mean you must have continuous action as many television shows do. Moving forward can be a matter of mental twists and insights as well:

The new doctor doesn't seem to care about my infected ear. He makes me do all the talking, stares at me when he thinks I'm not looking. Is he nervous? His hand seems to shake a lot. Is that booze I smell on his breath? Or just medicines? He leaves the room and returns after a long time. Maybe I have some horrible sickness and he's afraid to tell me. He even sends the nurse in to tell me I can go.

When I pay the receptionist and get my prescription, I notice a photograph of the doctor and a girl who looks like me—we could be sisters. "His daughter died last month," the receptionist whispers.

What gives this little story some life is not the surprise ending—that's always too late to interest the reader. What gets it going is the initial conflict—the doctor doesn't like the narrator (person vs. person)—and what keeps it going are the **competing explanations** for this thought that flash through the narrator's mind. Each sentence searches for facts and ideas to explain this behavior; each complicates the story. Without *them*, the ending would have been flat.

Creating complex conflict often means discovering competing ideas in yourself; at each turn in your essay ask if you really felt 100 percent as you wrote. The spots where you waver or doubt need to be in the essay to lead the reader through your honest decision making. Making choices creates conflict and reveals your character and theme. Stories in which things happen *to* a passive narrator lack this element. We *are* often victims of fate, accidents, and bad luck, but the key moments in our lives are the ones we can do something about, the ones in which we **choose our destiny.** This is what John Gardner meant in the opening quote to this chapter.

I once had a student, Bill, who was in his late forties. He wrote a gruesome narrative about what happened to his wife when they decided to commit her temporarily to a mental hospital. Once Bill's wife was signed in, the authorities could keep her there until *they* thought she was cured. They began chemical and electric shock treatments that hurt and scared Bill's wife. She begged to be released. Bill began to doubt her and believe the medical authorities that she was far gone, because each time he visited her she was wilder, more rumpled, more "crazy looking." Some friends and family even told Bill to "detach" himself from his wife. But something deeper in the relationship drew him back. He believed the authorities were more disturbed than his wife, and he eventually fought in court to release her.

This powerful conflict has a number of twists that keep a reader involved. The most interesting is the inner conflict in Bill—whether to believe "sane experts" or the "crazy" wife he loves. The only major flaw in Bill's rough draft was his portrayal of the orderlies and nurses as snarling sadists with dripping fangs. It's easy to see why Bill felt this way, but he portrayed them in descriptions and dialogue that were too exaggerated. He projected his feelings for them instead of seeing them as they were. We worked together using alternate viewpoints and discovered the "enemy" was not cruelty, but indifference. Most employees simply wanted to slide through tough workdays a little easier. People like Bill and his poor wife who asked questions were "troublemakers." The workers were not devils, but people who'd grown calluses over their feelings. Bill didn't release them from their responsibility for his wife's pain, but in looking closer at the orderlies and nurses, Bill discovered the real problem in his wife's mental health care. He believed the employees inflicted pain on patients like his wife to make them act more deranged and therefore less human. If they could feel they were dealing with crazy people, it made their disturbing job easier. It's a powerful, honest insight because it's not oversimplified. The lesson: **be skeptical of any angels or devils you create.**

▲ **PRACTICE 10-5:** Using one of your practice notes in this chapter, list some complications in the conflict.

◆ HOW TO RUIN A STORY

Teachers and textbooks don't often advise students how to mess up; but if you're interested in ruining a story, here are three ways to do it. First, **give a lot of background in the opening.** If you're going to tell the story of your great fishing adventure, start the story with getting ready the night before, your restless sleep, waking, breakfast, packing the car, driving to the dock, and casting off. This is boring in one sentence. Imagine how boring it can be stretched out to a full page! If you want an exciting start, begin the essay like this: "I was rebaiting my hook when I realized that a squall had just blocked off the sun and was heading straight for our boat." Or start when your buddy spills the lantern fuel into the campfire. If the story is about meeting a wonderful person during a vacation, start with the moment the wonderful person bumps into you with his cotton candy and tangles it in your hair. *Don't* start with packing, travel, unpacking, and setting up on the beach.

The Greeks used the expression *en medias res* (begin in the middle) to describe starting where real conflict begins. Have your characters begin *in motion,* not preparing to move. Do this and you'll be surprised how busy you'll be telling the real story and how little time you need spend on that story killer—background.

Here are some openings from student papers that hook a reader:

> I was hunched over my crying baby brother when I heard Joe's footsteps behind me. "He fell," I tried to explain, "he was on the bed but he rolled and I . . . I . . ." Pain shot through my spine like a freight train had burst through the floor straight into my rear end. As he cocked his boot again, my mother dashed into the room and screamed.
> —*Raquel E. Torres*

> Night falls by the time we reach the inn. The crisp, country air, ten degrees colder than the city, makes us shiver. Moths flutter around the lanterns that light our passage, and the only sound is the crunching of gravel beneath our feet. Sumie hurries ahead, sliding open the heavy wooden door.
> —*Bernadette Verrone*

She was gone—again. I watched her red Trans Am disappear up the grad-
ual grade, then turned to see my bus round the corner, creeping toward me
like a bug in the cool, moist dawn. The breeze was cold, and faraway thunder
drummed summer out of service. The bus groaned to a halt in a diesel haze.
The driver opened the door, and I was sucked off the street.

—*James Babcock*

A second way to ruin a story is to give away the ending. If the following sentence began a story, you wouldn't want to read the rest: "Little
did I know the first time Bob approached me after class to borrow a pen that
in seven months we'd be married." It's dramatic but kills the rest of the story.
Compare that to this opening: "There was absolutely nothing special about
Bob that first day he approached me after class to borrow a pen. I would
have completely forgotten him except the next day he handed me a dozen
pens with a bow around them. Now I've got a nerd after me, I thought." The
second version lets us know something is going to happen, but not what.

Giving away the ending applies not only to events, but to the theme.
Good readers enjoy figuring out the significance of the events, and an opening sentence like the following can ruin that: "I don't know if I'll ever marry
again, but if I do I'll put my wife ahead of my friends." The writer of narratives must tease readers a bit, give them new events and ideas and also leave
them a bit unsatisfied so they'll keep reading.

Tease them until the climax, that is. The third story killer is to **draw out
the climax too long,** explaining too much. The climax should hit hard
and then end.

▲ **PRACTICE 10-6:** Pick two potential places where you could begin one of
the narrative conflicts you developed earlier in this chapter. Which place
seems best and why?

◈ DESCRIBING PEOPLE

If conflict is the heart of a narrative, its body is the characters—
the physical presence that moves the conflict. This is where your description must be sharpest, to make the people in your story jump off the page.
We tend to make people in our stories reflect our own ideas, habits, and
values instead of presenting them as *they* are. Using an alternate viewpoint
brain teaser is the best way to overcome this. Give each main character—
especially those with whom you disagree—a few minutes of rough notes. Think
as they do. See as they see. What motivates them? What do they care
about? This is essential for *honest, vivid conflict.* If you've been cheated by a
salesperson, you must try to convey what she believes, perhaps her anx-
iousness to succeed, or you will create her as a fake cardboard figure.

Besides understanding how your characters think, you must help the
reader *see* them. Here are some of the things that create a picture of a person in words:

- Physical description
- Habits
- The way they talk
- Their possessions
- What others say about them
- Gestures

The man who empties an ashtray three times during an evening communicates character through this habit. If he also picks threads from his sleeve and rearranges the couch pillow continually, his character will be dominated by neatness in a reader's eyes. Gestures—like poking a listener with a forefinger while speaking, or wrapping a sweaty arm around your shoulder—also create character. In preparing to write about people, **use the preceding list as a brain teaser,** making a list of details for each item.

How do you know which details to actually include in the draft? Let's take **physical description** as an example. Simple, factual description adds detail, but will rarely light up a page. The following is accurate and specific: "Gregory Bates has brown hair and brown eyes and is 5'10" tall and weighs 165 pounds." But these words do not bring the unknown Mr. Bates to life; they should stay on the brain-teaser page. A reader *assumes* a person is of average build unless told otherwise. Brown hair and eyes are so common they only narrow Bates down to several billion people. Instead, search for and choose **unique, distinguishing details:** Bates's mohawk haircut, the wart on his chin, his gangly arms. The reader will automatically fill in the rest as "average."

Here's another trick to describe people: You want not just the unique features of the person but also those details that convey *more* than simple description. When choosing details from your brain-teaser lists, pick ones that suggest deeper aspects of the person, **ones that capture personality or beliefs.**

Take eyes as an example. No other part of the human body is described so often. Yet "the windows of the soul" attract more flies than fresh air, more clichés than fresh description. Soft, brown eyes, sky blue eyes, and sparkling eyes are dead eyes. A writer needs to find a twist: cow-brown eyes, winter-blue eyes, eyes sparkling like razors. Or are those eyes dung brown, chocolate brown, peanut-butter brown, sooty, muddy, or walnut? Make a list of all the kinds of brown you can think of and then choose the best one for your person's eyes. This will give the reader something specific for *better visualization*. It will *also convey more of the person's character*. Muddy eyes, for example, suggest vagueness, confusion, or even dirtiness of the personality. All of these browns are equally suggestive.

▲ **PRACTICE 10-7:** What do these descriptors say about the person?

- lizard-green eyes
- moss-green eyes
- faded-green eyes
- cash-green eyes

▲ **PRACTICE 10-8:** Take a moment to list several vivid substitutes for these bland descriptions:

- sparkling teeth
- rosy cheeks
- dark hair

Possessions reveal character because they represent choices we make. True, most of us own many things unthinkingly—toothbrushes, pens, underwear. But our unique possessions represent conscious choice—the 20 boxes full of baseball cards or chest of grandmother's lace doilies, the pink flamingo or religious shrine in our front yard, the Harley or Honda in our driveway. Gestures, habits, and what others say about someone also reveal character. A one-page brain teaser listing details should result in plenty to bring a person to life in words. If you can't fill a page of notes, you don't know enough about the person to write him or her into the story.

▲ **PRACTICE 10-9:** Write a descriptive brain teaser for one person in the story you've been developing during this chapter.

▲ **PRACTICE 10-10:** Here's part of a student's narrative essay that describes a person. As you read, mark the six descriptive techniques and look for unique details that also symbolize Lish's personality or beliefs.

THE RED HEART

Lisa Neal

I first saw Lish the first day of classes my freshman year at Fredonia. Her parents dumped her at the back door of the brick dormitory like a bag of garbage and then roared off in a black Cadillac.

I was shocked that the left side of her head was shaved and displayed a small tattoo of a black heart. Her hair on the other side was carrot colored and braided like an Indian squaw's. With her head held high, she sauntered in with two leopard skin bags.

Her arrival sent shock waves throughout the dorm. I'm not sure if Lish felt the rocky movement or just ignored it, for minutes after arriving she invaded the bathroom with an old green toothbrush with yellowed bristles and a worn box of Arm and Hammer Baking Soda. I was dismayed she was living in the single room across the hall from me. She left her door wide open as she unpacked her sparse belongings, which included posters of puppies and a Paddington Bear with matted fur and a tattered blue coat. Her night table and dresser were left empty except for a glass incense candle and a fluorescent pink tape recorder.

As the days passed, I deliberately ignored Lish, but her presence oozed under my closed door, and I soon watched her with the curiosity of a child at the circus. At first, though, I only noticed her hair changing from carrot to watermelon pink, the way she dragged hard on her Virginia Slims cigarettes, and the addition of an earring in her nose.

Her parents whizzed in once more that semester, this time in a gray Rolls Royce, to bring her winter clothes. For the fifteen minutes they stayed, the entire hall was pierced by yelling. I heard a few snatches of her father's growled words, calling Lish a "humiliation" and a "disgrace to the family." Her mother whined how Lish should be more like her older sister who was going to become a "respectable and wealthy lawyer" instead of a social worker. The barrage of voices ceased with the sound of shattering glass, and her parents burst out of the room like two tourists fleeing a bear's cave. After a few moments, Lish emerged wearing her usual crooked smile. I was amazed! I would have been in tears. The only reminder that her parents had come was the disappearance of the incense candle holder--reduced to glass shards--and the lingering stench of Macy's perfume.

The next night, while I lay on my pink comforter watching <u>The Cosby Show,</u> my phone buzzed. It was my parents giving me the usual razor-sharp threats to do well in my classes. After our yelling match, I slammed the phone down, pounced on my bed, and smothered my face in my pillow.

Immediately there was a timid knock, and I was amazed and a bit frightened to see Lish. She wore Mickey Mouse slippers and a pink flannel nightgown as she shuffled onto my robin-egg blue carpet.

 ## DIALOGUE

Like other aspects of describing people, **dialogue must be distinctive**—your characters shouldn't sound like *you* but like themselves. If you use real people in your story, listen for their **unique speech patterns and quirks of language.** If you live in the northern states and have a person from the South in your story, he may use the words "polecat" instead of "skunk," "sack" instead of "bag," or "depot" instead of "station." To a southerner, a Bostonian forgets r's, as in "A bahbah cut my heyuh," but adds r's as in "That's a good idear." When I moved to Rochester, New York, I had to learn that asking for a "red hot" and a "pop" was not provoking a brawl but a request for a "frankfurter and a soft drink" (or is it a "wiener and a soda"?). Be careful of stereotypes, however. Few Californians really use Valley-talk ("like gag me with a spoon, dude"); few southerners say, "Y'all come back fo' grits, dahling"; and few people from New Jersey refer to their state as "New Joysee."

More important are individual speech characteristics: the person who says "hey" or "ain't" or "prevarication" or who addresses people as "honey" or "pal" or "sir." **Education levels** show up in dialogue too. "You ain't puttin' nothin' ovah on me," and "I'm inclined to disbelieve that assertion" come from two different people saying the same thing. **Age, use of slang, environment, and hobbies all influence our choice of words.** People who are into computers, cars, television, or the military use vocabulary that reflects their interest, no matter what they talk about. Take a minute to think of a friend or relative who has a unique vocabulary or style of speaking.

A storyteller must try to **capture the speaker's voice.** As you see, it's legitimate to break spelling and grammar rules in dialogue for realistic effect. A street punker may not say, "We had quite a blast last night" but, "Freakin' blast last night." Describe these speakers based on their style:

"Isn't that the cat's pajamas, honey? We sat on the same stoop and I didn't recognize him! Mr. Mahoney, the grocer! He could have been the man in the moon!"

"We can say with firm assurance that no such knowledge of any event could proceed without the bureau chief's tacit or at least implied consent."

"He's a rem. Bag him and book with me, babe."

"It's time for lunch, right? So I get him, right? We meet at the mall, right?"

"Ice it, pops. You beat up your chops too much."

Someone once said, "Dialogue is what people *do* to each other." In stories, you shouldn't pass the time of day in small talk. Skip hello, introductions, goodbyes, and "please pass-the-butter" talk. Concentrate on the meaningful scenes. **Each piece of dialogue must move the story along.** Dialogue can carry scenes in which important revelations are made about a character, the action, or the theme. For example:

The father rumbled into my office. "Why the hell didn't you put her on the goddamned bus if she ain't sick? I got work."
"Your daughter has several bruises on her lower rib cage," I said, "and I suspect she may also suffer—"
"I feel fine, Daddy," Rachel whispered.
The man stared at her, his thumb working in his belt loop. "Yeah," he said. "You look awright."

How does the dialogue reveal all three characters in a short time?

Here's an example of how dialogue and brief description create an intense scene:

> Everyone from the hood had come up to the court to watch the homies play some b-ball. We were soaking up rays when a gold metal-flaked Honda pulled up with Speed and Little Man and a Puerto Rican girl, Blue Eyes. Blue Eyes remained in the car. Speed and Little Man's pants hung off their butts and showed their boxers. Blue bandannas were tied around their heads. Little Man grabbed a 16-year-old boy named Angel.
>
> "Yo, man! Why you be dissing my home boy? What's up with tha? You best chill 'fore I pop a cap in yo ass!"
>
> Angel pulled away and tried to reason with Little Man. "Bro, I don't even know your home boy."
>
> Little Man pulled a small silver hand gun from his boot, held his arms out straight, legs spread apart. His arms shook as he pointed it with two hands at Angel's chest. Angel stepped back, hands up, and pleaded, "Yo! Yo, ain't nobody dissing your homie, Bro. It ain't like that."
>
> People ran from the line of fire. Speed yelled, "Do him! Do him!" Little Man stood, arms shaking the gun pointed at Angel's chest. "You ain't got no props if you don't do him!" Speed yelled. The gun jerked. Again! Smoke rolled from the barrel.
>
> Angel's eyes opened wide. "No!" he mouthed. "No." His head bounced as it hit the ground and his blue tee turned deep red.
>
> Speed cried, "Snap! Snap! Let's be chillin' 'fore five-oh gets here."
>
> *—Dawn M. Schranck*

What parts seem most realistic? How does the dialogue advance the action? Are there any word choices you question?

▲ **PRACTICE 10-11:** Create four or five lines of dialogue for the people in your story. Work on realistic style and reveal character.

 # HOW TO SAY SOMETHING WORTH SAYING

How can you make a story convey a good theme?

Tell the truth. Now that sounds simple, but the fact is that the most difficult lies to brush away from the truth are the ones we tell ourselves. Does the theme of your story sound too simple because you've given yourself a candy-coated cliché or a safe, predictable message? You must *re-feel* the events, ask yourself at every turn if you missed something or closed your eyes to something. Use the brain teasers on unquestioned ideas and clichés and alternate viewpoints to help break into new truths. But don't worry at the outline stage if your theme isn't outstanding. Theme requires drafting and revision to emerge.

Question your own motives along with everyone else's. Be honest about aspects of the story that contradict your main idea. If the ending was basically good or optimistic, look for darker meanings lurking there. If it was a sad ending, look for positive aspects. Doing this will separate the superficial paper from the one that's probing. The poet Coleridge once said, "No man does anything from a single motive." Look for multiple causes for your actions and the actions of others.

Why have a theme? Why not just tell what happened? Because how you feel about what you did or what happened to you is more important than the act itself. A reader may make up his mind on his own, but he also wants to know how you interpret it. Working on theme also makes us learn something new.

Here's how one student handled theme in a story about a car crash that horribly maims a young man. Steve's girlfriend, Amanda, helps to nurse him despite his disfigurement and brain damage. Months later, the narrator accompanies Amanda to visit Steve at the care facility for the final scene:

We wheeled Steve out to the sunporch, a place where we often spent our time. Amanda could barely stand to look at him. Steve was paralyzed from the neck down. He had permanent facial scars and was completely deaf, and both his eyes were damaged. His brain was severely injured. Although he could mutter a few sounds, he seemed to comprehend little of what he said. Amanda said, "I don't look forward to this. I'd like to stop visiting him. It hurts me too much."

"How can you abandon him, Amanda?" I said. "I thought you loved him."

"The person I fell in love with is dead, damn it! All that's left is a pile of mush, some *thing* that can't move, hear, see, or talk. Or even understand who I am or was to him! It's not fair!"

Would it have been better if Steve died in the accident? Maybe Amanda was right. As we walked out of the center that afternoon, I noticed Amanda gently embracing her stomach with both her tiny hands. She rubbed her swollen belly delicately and then smiled slightly. She had lost the most important person in her life. But Steve was still a part of her.

—*Christine D. Reber*

Commentary

The author shows life in its honest complexity. Amanda is neither a saint nor an ogre, but an honest woman who gives what she can. I might wish life were different; it would be so much neater if she would devote her life to Steve and be an angel—or run off thoughtlessly to another man and be a devil. Do you like the last paragraph and what it implies?

▲ **PRACTICE 10-12:** Make a rough statement of what you learned from one conflict you've had—perhaps from a previous practice exercise. Now look for a contradiction or opposite message that you could have drawn from the same experience.

Highlights of Chapter 10

- Telling stories is a powerfully visual way to convey a point and to explore personal experiences more deeply.
- Conflict is the heart of narration; it focuses your story and makes readers turn the page.
- Stories are most often spoiled by not getting to the conflict soon enough, by giving away the outcome too soon, and by continuing after the conflict has ended.
- Stories should begin in the middle of conflict, complicate the initial conflict, and force the people in the story to make tough decisions.
- Create breathing, walking people in stories through their physical appearance, habits, dialogue, possessions, and gestures. Details that symbolize their beliefs or personality will be the most powerful.
- As with all other types of writing, honesty—a questioning attitude—will lead to a theme that tells the truth about some segment of life and will guard you from predictable clichés.

Writing Suggestions and Class Discussions

1. Tell your best family story.
2. Tell a story of a run-in you had with a relative, but tell the story with the relative as the narrator and you as his or her antagonist.
3. Write a narrative essay about an intense event in your life that changed your philosophy or way of seeing the world. Be honest.
4. Dialogue Practice: Write how *you* would ask where the rest room is at a restaurant. Now, ask as an Englishman, a Texan, or a New Yorker, an elderly schoolteacher, a street kid, and a construction worker might ask. Choose words and style carefully.
5. You are 85 years old, and your friends are gathered around your hospital bed. Before you die, you want to tell them one story of the many you've experienced, a story that will reveal to them who you really were and what your life meant. Tell that story. (It should be something that has not yet happened to you.)
6. Description Practice: Describe the eyes, mouth, and one other feature of someone close to you. Make a list of potential descriptions, then

choose the most revealing for character. Turn in one finished paragraph, and also turn in your brain teaser.

7. You are a drug rehabilitation counselor and have been asked to address a group of high school students on the dangers of drug use. You're afraid they'll be bored if you start out preaching, so you decide to tell a dramatic story to lead into your point. Write this speech.

8. Tell a story that brings an abstract idea to life. It may be true or fictional. Use one of these topics:
    - Courage
    - Prejudice
    - Failure
    - Cheating

9. Alternate Viewpoint Practice: A mother (or father) aged 39, daughter (or son) aged 18, and a grandmother (or grandfather) age unknown, live together. The grandparent wants to remarry. Break the class into groups of four—one for each part and one to record notes. Present possible ideas each character would have.

10. Describing People Practice: Use the list of character features on pages 157–158 to create a page of details to describe either yourself or a close friend. Go beyond the obvious.

11. List five conflicts in your life that could be potential narrative essays. Under each specify the opposing forces and mention a key incident in which the conflict came to a head.

12. Do several brain teasers on the best conflict in number 11 and write a two- or three-page essay.

13. Tell your peer group a story you're thinking of writing. Then ask each peer to express the ideas and feelings of one person in the story.

14. Read and discuss the student narrative essays "Pa's Secret" and "Bastard" in Chapter 15, "The Mower" in Chapter 9, and "Spring Break 1989" in Chapter 3.

Sample Student Narrative Essay

LIVE ABORTION

Beatriz Valle

opening conflict

flashback

Cooky's baby was born fourteen weeks premature. She was on a ventilator and losing ground. The Hospital, Centro Medico de Mayaguez in Isabella, Puerto Rico, was supposed to have an advanced neonatal intensive care unit. That's why Cooky chose it. My sister had had two miscarriages.

Her doctor had even performed a cerclage, tying her cervix shut to prevent one miscarriage that happened anyway. This time the baby was alive, but she weighed only one pound, ten ounces.

adds a new complication

Jessie, Cooky's husband, and I left the tattered furniture in the lobby and rode the elevator to the sixth-floor nursery area. Its dreary yellow curtains were closed. I rang a bell, and a long while later a nurse appeared. "May I help you?" she asked. Jessie couldn't utter a word. His face was drained.

"Yes," I said. "We are here to see Rebecca Rivera's baby. This is the father." As I touched Jessie's arm, my voice broke.

dialogue raises new conflict and complications

"It isn't visiting hours yet," the nurse answered, pointing at the sign on the door.

"He's her father! What if she dies before visiting hours?" I snapped back.

"She is considered a live abortion," the nurse replied, but she signaled us to move to the window.

I could never have prepared myself for what I was about to see. Her head was no bigger than a tangerine. Her eyes were horizontal slits. She had no eyebrows, eyelashes, or hair. Her hands were no bigger than the tip of my finger. Hoses and tubes jammed into every orifice of her frail body. If I could pick her up, she would easily fit into the palm of one hand. I hugged Jessie and we cried.

description draws us in

Later we were told if the baby survived 24 hours and then died, the family would have to make the funeral arrangements. If she died prior to then, the hospital would not release the body. Which was better? I wondered.

more complications and inner conflict

Cooky was anxiously awaiting us so she could see her baby for the first time. Jessie wrapped his arms around her as we shuffled to the nursery. Cooky pressed her face against the window and waited for the curtain to open. When it did, she whimpered. Jessie embraced her and she sobbed.

That evening Dr. Gomez said, "Don't expect to take her home. Don't expect her to leave the hospital alive."

new conflict complication

Cooky turned on him. "You are <u>not</u> God. I <u>will</u> take her home alive."

Months later, four-pound Rebecca Beatriz Rivera left the hospital. During that time she survived two heart attacks, fought for each ounce she gained, and was scarred all over from the tube insertions. But we were elated.

complications

Valle 3

complication

> Chicky, as she's now called, celebrated her sixth birthday last Sunday. Her vision is very poor and only recently did glasses give her a clear picture of the world. She walks on tippy-toes and often stumbles and falls.

complication

> The hospital is not being held accountable for what happened. We found out later that after the birth, Chicky had been placed on a paper-lined tray to be disposed of. After several minutes, she cried. A nurse scooped her up and ran her to the neonatal intensive care unit. Only then did she receive adequate care. Because she suffered from lack of oxygen, she now has a mild case of cerebral palsy.

Commentary

Opening: The opening establishes immediate conflict.

Ideas: Complications build quickly. Cooky has already lost two babies. The nurse's coldness, and later the doctor's, add person vs. person conflict to the baby's battle against nature. When the narrator worries what's best, we have some inner conflict too. The conflict is directly related to the theme. This child was given no chance to live and was treated as if she were already dead, yet life can beat the odds. In the end the author seems to suggest that although the hospital was not held legally accountable, its presumption of death led to Chicky's cerebral palsy. I like the honest inner battle the author wages: part horror, part love, part anger.

Details: The description of Chicky is powerfully honest and vivid. Comparing her to a tangerine and suggesting what's missing ("no eyebrows . . .") demonstrate that the baby is not visibly human. Yet the family refuses to accept the appearances. The sharp one-word descriptions of the hospital furniture and curtain are enough for background. More could be done with Chicky's description at age six; we need to see her in full humanity now to prove the theme.

Dialogue: The "live abortion" comment and Cooky's defiance of the doctor are strong. I'd like to hear Cooky say something when she first sees her baby. It seems like an important moment. Punctuation and paragraphing are fine.

Ending: The author did not give away the ending, but a new conflict is raised and left dangling. Although I favor short endings, I'd like the author to tell us how she feels about the hospital's responsibility. Another possibility is to give this information earlier—perhaps as a complication occurring before she leaves the hospital.

✓ **PEER REVIEW CHECKLIST FOR NARRATION**

Author: _____

A question you have for the reviewer: _____

_____

_____

Reviewer: _____

	STRONG	AVERAGE	WEAK
OPENING—Opening Sentence			
Early Conflict			
IDEAS—Complications of Conflict			
Honesty/Depth of Theme			
DETAILS—People are vividly described			
Actions are vividly described			
DIALOGUE—Realistic and sharp			
Punctuation, Paragraphing			
ENDING—Ends with a punch			

The most vivid aspect of this story is:

Respond to the author's question. Offer several suggestions if possible:

Make another two or three suggestions about the story and discuss them with the author. Start by helping with areas you marked less strong in the boxes.

✓ SELF-EVALUATION CHECKLIST FOR NARRATION

Instructions: Evaluate your own narrative essay, rating it for each item. You may rate it "A" through "F" or "Good," "Average" or "Poor." Explain what you might do to improve the weaker areas.

CONFLICT:
   Impact of Conflict(s)
   The Turning Point or Interesting Character

COMPLICATIONS:
   New Complications
   Competing Explanations or Choices
   Not Giving Away the Ending

ORGANIZATION:
   Early Conflict
   Smooth Flow
   Concise Ending Resolves Main Issues

DESCRIPTION OF PEOPLE AND ACTION:
   Vivid
   Some Symbolic Detail
   Dialogue Is Vivid and Realistic

THEME:
   Honesty and Depth

PROOFREADING/GRAMMAR/MECHANICS:

The part of my paper I like best is:

The reason I like it is:

The part of my paper I'm least pleased with is:

One way I might revise it would be to:

Right now this paper deserves an overall grade of _____.

CHAPTER 11

Informative Writing

Telling Your Audience What It Doesn't Know

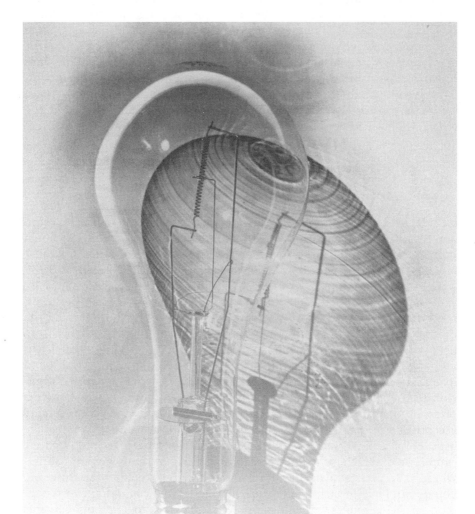

Nothing can be loved or hated unless it is first known.

LEONARDO DA VINCI

There's something in life that's a curtain, and I keep trying to raise it.

MAXINE HONG KINGSTON

Men occasionally stumble over the truth, but most of them pick themselves up and hurry off as if nothing had happened.

WINSTON CHURCHILL

A college student using *Ideas and Details* wrote me a note asking, "Why does a person who is going to be a television technician need to know how to write informative essays?" He'll find out. Most college graduates are surprised by how much writing is required in their careers. Nurses, social workers, police officers, technicians, and businesspeople discover writing fills far more job time than they ever anticipated. One engineer recently estimated that she spends 50 percent of her office time writing, not calculating or sketching plans. And of the writing you will do as a college graduate, more will be informative than any other kind: technical and business reports, memos, brochures, summaries of meetings, letters, speeches, and perhaps research projects or articles for professional journals or newsletters in your field. We live in an era known as the "information age." The person who can convey instructions, facts, summaries, and analyses *concisely, clearly,* and *vividly* will have an edge in becoming a valued employee or leader.

AUDIENCE AND TONE

Informative writing strives for *objectivity.* This means a reader must be moved by your *information, not by your opinions.* Using facts to support personal opinions is persuasive writing—discussed in the next chapter. In informative writing your tone should be unbiased; you should not think of yourself as converting your audience but rather as educating it.

For example, you can write an informative essay explaining how an abortion is done or you can contrast the pro-life and pro-choice positions, but **you should not argue your personal views.** If in describing the process of an abortion, you write, "the baby is then ripped in agony from his mother's womb," you have loaded the dice with opinion. Likewise, if you write "the reproductive wastage is cleaned from the uterine wall," you load the dice the other way. Another aspect of objectivity is **your obligation to present all major *legitimate* viewpoints where there is difference of opinion.** Which are legitimate? They must be either widely accepted or verifiable through science or direct observation. Many people believe that a newly conceived fetus has a human soul, so even though we cannot prove it scientifically, you ought to include that viewpoint somewhere in an informative paper contrasting positions on abortion. However, you do not have to include the supermarket tabloid claim that aborted fetuses are being implanted with computers and grown to be robotic servants of the FBI. The source is untrustworthy and the claim has not been verified by reputable observers. Scientists do disagree, however, about whether a fetus feels pain during an abortion. They debate how developed the nervous system is at various stages, so both theories should be presented.

But don't think of informative writing as dull or boring, a mere reciting of facts. The writer's job—*always*—is to keep the reader awake, no matter what the topic. Unless your audience requires stiff formality—as in a lab or business report, for instance—occasional humor, vivid anecdotes, and lively words are usually welcome.

Writers do adjust their tone in informative writing for the audience. The amount and kind of information you might use writing about an archaeological dig will vary greatly depending on whether you write a paper for your anthropology professor, a letter to your mother, or a section of a job application. The professor will want technical and interpretive information; your mother may find the events of the trip more important; a potential employer may be most interested in the skills you learned and how well you meshed with the rest of the team.

Suppose you are writing an informative paper entitled "The Gift of Life"—donating your organs to sick people when you die. How would your tone and information differ for the following audiences?

- A sociology professor
- Transplant surgeons
- The family of a dying person
- The general public

To illustrate, here are some details about the procedure. Which of the preceding audiences especially would or would not want to know the following?

- In a way organ donation allows the dying person to continue living.
- The donor is usually brain dead (a flat EEG line), but the heart is still beating and a ventilator keeps the person breathing during the removal of transplant organs (organs deteriorate quickly without blood and oxygen).
- A neurologist is consulted to declare the person brain dead.
- The transplant doctor does *not* decide when it's time to save the organs.
- The hospital *does* notify transplant doctors of likely cases so they can prepare ahead of time. They contact the receiving family and wait anxiously with equipment poised for the word.
- The Uniform Anatomical Gift Act allows your spouse, child over 18, parent, or adult sibling to donate your body even if you have not signed a donor card.
- Doctors refer to these as "organ harvests."
- It is a rapid operation without anesthetics. The body is simply sliced open—"peeled back" as one doctor said in a professional journal—to save time. The desired organs are removed as quickly as possible. Then the breathing machine is turned off and the person dies.
- The body cavity can be packed and stitched up for a funeral.

As you can see from the facts just listed, an informative writer must be sensitive to the intended audience. Even in this list there is obvious slanting of the facts presented. I aimed at a general student/teacher audience, easing back on the technical information.

Failure to consider the intended audience has led to some absurd "informative" writing. In 1919 British prime minister Lloyd George wrote an informative report to the Italian government on the economics of growing bananas, concluding by advising them to plant great banana plantations to reduce their trade deficits. He didn't know that bananas can't grow in Italy.

PACKING IN DETAILS

Here we are again. There's no way to write well without details, and the informative essay should bristle with them. During the prewriting stage, **tease your brain by asking reporters' questions.** You might start with this overall one: "What would *I* want to know about this topic if I could ask any expert?"

Suppose your topic is the effects of a nuclear war. *Ask personal questions:* What would happen to *me* if a nuclear bomb struck a half-mile away, a mile away, five miles, fifty miles? Ask for graphic details—what would happen to my skin, bones, hair, eyes, sexual function, and digestion? How would it affect me if I survived? How would I eat? Who would I live with? What would be the odds of finding friends or family? What aspects of society would remain?

Ask less personal questions: How would the living deal with all the dead and dying? Would society revert to a primitive cave culture as some people predict? Would the survivors be inspired to deeper comradery? Would there be just a few bombs or would the warring countries let loose hundreds? Would the atmosphere be poisoned for all life on earth as in Nevil Shute's *On the Beach?* How likely is the nuclear winter that Carl Sagan and other experts predicted—should the sun be blocked by billions of tons of dust thrown into the atmosphere? How would we respond if it was terrorism and not war? Can you add three or four questions to this list? Try it now for practice.

It's easier to ask questions, of course, than to answer them, but in asking sometimes answers emerge. In asking you also mark which territory you will be able to handle best when you focus the topic more. So the first step is to ask the honest questions—the ones you really care about. Tough questions require tough, gutsy details. They'll help point you toward a good paper.

▲ **PRACTICE 11-1:** Ask four or five tough questions about the topics below. Suspend what you do know about them and ask what you really should know:

- Drug use in junior high school
- Television nature programs
- The value of a college education

SURPRISE VALUE

Good informative reports or essays should *surprise the reader with new information.* If you only tell us what we already know, you are really not informing us of anything. For instance, most people know that nuclear bombs generate great heat and do awful things to human flesh. But when you read John Hersey's book *Hiroshima,* you learn that some people caught within a quarter mile of the blast were vaporized so suddenly that they didn't even have time to scream or turn away. How do we know? Because they stood between concrete walls and the blast, and exact, perfect outlines of their bodies are preserved on the concrete—a painter raising his brush, a mother straightening the blanket on her baby. Their bodies shielded the wall from the intense heat just enough to imprint their silhouette.

That is information. Give your reader the same kind of **essential, inside information.** "General" information and "official" information usually tell readers only what they already know, unless you pick exotic topics—like spelunking (cave exploring), cooking Indonesian food, or teaching sign language to the deaf.

Do you have to do original research to write informative essays? In a sense, yes. However, you don't have to travel to Japan or work ten years in a lab. Your eyes, ears, fingers, and brain are researching the world every day. If you can imagine a world without electricity, family, schools, police, hospitals, or law enforcement, you may be able to create a plausible essay on the world after nuclear war. If you can use your human experience to imagine what it might be like to see a dying relative put on a respirator and can honestly picture a doctor asking you to sign over the person's organs, you can write about some of the issues in the "gift of life" topic.

Here's an example of meticulously detailed information based on personal observation. It's from a student essay titled, "Dealing with the Dragon":

When he returned to the car, Mayito pulled out a syringe from its orange and white shrink wrap and a tiny brown cellophane bag with a palm tree stamped on it. His hands shook as he tore the top and poured the brown powder into a tarnished silver spoon. He meticulously drew up 20 cc of water from a puddle he poured in his palm. With the needle, he stirred the water into the powder in the spoon. He then held a lighter to the belly of the spoon until the mixture bubbled. He uncapped the syringe with his teeth, stuck it into a piece of filter from his cigarette, and drew up the amber liquid. He then jabbed the needle into a bulging vein in his arm with the skill of a sharpshooter. As he pulled back on the plunger, blood mixed with the drug. He told me, "turn your head!"

But I couldn't turn away. As he depressed the needle, the fluid returned to his vein, and I felt nauseated. I knew this was how it was done, but to see it! I threw open the car door and stood on the pavement, the sun beating on my head. I was sure I would throw up, but I didn't. Mayito stepped out and stared at me. Tears rolled down his cheeks as he buried his face in his hands.

—Janice Mundorff

Many informative papers you do for college *will* require some outside research without being full-scale research papers. Be sure to document these sources (see Chapter 14). Here's an example by a student who was writing on bulimia, or binge eating. To enhance her personal knowledge, she cited two sources with surprise value in details:

Jessica, a 36-year-old financial analyst from California, gorges herself, then takes three hundred laxatives. She has done this each day for sixteen years. A teenager with bulimia starved herself, gorged herself, and made herself throw up. She died while retching over a toilet bowl (Cauwels 2). Suzanne Abraham recorded one patient's "bad binge": she ate a bag of potato chips, a jar of honey, a jar of anchovies on bread, one pound of rolled oats, two pounds of pancakes, one pound of macaroni, two instant puddings, four ounces of nuts, two pounds of sugar, one box of Rice Crispies, a pound of margarine, two quarts of milk, a gallon of ice cream, a pound of sausage, a pound of onions, twelve eggs, a pound of licorice, a dozen candy bars, and ended with a bottle of orange cordial. This totals 1,071 grams of protein, 1,964 grams of fat, and 14,834 grams of carbohydrates (85). These violent abuses of the body profoundly affect bulimics' social life, self-esteem, and psychological functioning. It may cause death from suicide or cardiac arrhythmia.

—Andrea Macaluso

▲ **PRACTICE 11-2:** Write a sense and example brain teaser about a natural disaster you know about: windstorm, earthquake, blizzard, or fire, for example. Be especially alert for details with surprise value—little things that many people might not know.

POOR INFORMATIVE TOPICS

Introductory topics, such as "How to Play the Piano," can lead to disaster. There's so much basic definition and terminology, it is very hard to write an interesting paper. You might do better to focus on "How to Handle Your First Piano Recital" or "What Makes Jazz Piano Sound Different." Another problem with introductory topics is that most educated people will be familiar with the basic information. Picking topics such as "Techniques of Safe Driving" or "Basics of Gardening" will bog you down saying the obvious. Pick an *aspect* of the topic that promises more surprise value: "Why Truck Drivers Are the Safest Drivers" or "Garden Health Hazards."

Broad topics, such as "What Is a Good Marriage?," can also doom your paper. You'll only be able to say the most general and superficial things about this topic because you promised more than you can fulfill in sharp, gutsy detail. Better choices: "How to Handle a Family Argument over Money" or "Six Questions to Ask Your Fiancé before Walking Down the Aisle." Notice that in both of the narrower topics, the opportunity exists for a definition of a good marriage to emerge.

CHOOSING GOOD TOPICS

Lurking inside all poor topics are potential good topics, and keeping two things in mind will help you recognize which kind you have. First, has it been **limited to an aspect you can cover *in depth*** in your allotted pages? Can you really tell us something fresh and fill the essay with vivid details? Second, do you have **a specific slant or message** to convey—a thesis? To help you arrive at a thesis, let me explain a half-dozen time-tested ways that people have structured informative writing. This illustrates an important point that sometimes gets lost: The steps in writing an essay are really interdependent—the thesis helps determine structure; the structure helps create ideas. The four steps of the writing process described in this book—Getting Ideas, Order, Draft, and Revision—in actual practice constantly play back and forth to each other.

▲ **PRACTICE 11-3:** List three or four potential topics for your own informative essay. Narrow each so you can cover it in depth in a few pages. We will be building on these topics throughout the chapter.

ORGANIZING INFORMATIVE WRITING

After narrowing your topic somewhat and doing some brain-teaser lists, you can invent your own scratch outline for the material. But here are six common structuring and thinking devices people use to convey information. If you start with one early in your prewriting, focusing and structuring your informative writing will be easier. This is not to say you should always rely on these devices—the most creative topics often break new ground.

- The Process or "How-to"
- The Essentials or "What-is"
- Causes or "Why"
- Effects
- Comparison or Contrast
- Classification

The last two were brain teasers from Chapter 3. The other four are also brain teasers. All not only dig into corners of your brain for ideas, but suggest a focus and structure as well. Let's look at each in some detail.

The Process or "How-to"

One way of focusing and organizing information is to present it as a *process*. Imagine yourself telling the reader *how to do* something: "How to Skydive," "How to Con a Professor," "How to Teach Children Manners." Process can also be used to focus on issues simply for *understanding:* "How the Serb–Bosnian Civil War Started," "The Stages of Juvenile Delinquency," or "The

Fall of Communism in Eastern Europe." Your scratch outline will consist of *chronological steps*. Try several scratch outlines until you're satisfied. If, for instance, you find yourself with three stages that have very little information and one bloated with examples and ideas, you probably need to divide that step and combine the smaller ones. If I was writing on skydiving, for instance, I don't think the following outline would work well:

- Saying goodbye to family
- Arriving at the airport
- Preparing your equipment
- The flight up
- Diving
- Cleaning up

The first, second, and last items don't deserve full steps in the process. They can be brief transitions. Preparing equipment seems reasonable as a main heading, but the dive seems most important and ought to be divided into several stages itself: the (ulp!) leap, the free fall, opening the chute, and the landing. Organizing chronologically does not imply that you must give equal time to each element. Focus on the key moments and divide the steps accordingly. Slowing time down at a key moment can heighten the informative effect.

The Georgia Paramedics Against Drunk Driving, for instance, published an effective brochure that describes the process of an accident at 55 mph. This brochure describes the one second after a car smashes into a solid object. In the first tenth of the second, the bumper and grille collapse. In the second tenth, the hood crumples and hits the windshield. The car frame stops, but the rest of the car still travels at 55 mph. The driver braces his legs against the crash, and they snap at the knee. In the third tenth of the second, the steering wheel shatters. In the fourth, the front two feet of the car collapse while the rest still moves at 35 mph. The driver is still traveling 55. In the fifth tenth, the driver is impaled on the steering column and blood fills his lungs. In the sixth tenth, the impact can rip his feet out of tightly laced shoes, the brake pedal snaps off, and the driver's head strikes the windshield. In the seventh tenth of the second, hinges pop and seats break free, hitting the driver—who is now dead.

After deciding on your scratch outline, brain-tease again and add details and ideas to each heading. This is true for each of the outline patterns that follow.

▲ **PRACTICE 11-4:** Describe a process in slowed-down fashion, as the Georgia paramedics did. Try a kiss, falling down stairs, or your own topic from Practice 11-3.

The Essentials or "What-is"

This approach informs a reader of *essential* characteristics of your topic. For example: "The Essentials of a Good Photograph," "Problems Children Have

When Parents Divorce," "What's Really Bad about Rats," or "What Is Unique about Adrienne Rich's Poetry." Your scratch outline consists of each key element you will explain. For instance, for children involved in divorces, you might have:

- Loss of a father/mother figure
- Dealing with parental sorrow and grief
- Feelings of guilt about causing the parents' divorce
- Often loss of home when property is sold and divided
- New "uncle-daddies"/"aunt-mommies" in the home
- Loss of friends if the family moves

Under each of these you can list the examples, facts, questions, or bug items from your brain teasers. If you find some items have little information, omit them. If one item draws most of your attention, you might focus more exclusively on it. For instance, one common thread I notice in the previous example is that of *loss*. I might decide at this point to focus on "Things Children Lose during Divorce."

▲ **PRACTICE 11-5:** Make a list of the essentials of a good relationship with a boss or the essentials of a good shopping mall.

▲ **PRACTICE 11-6:** State your best topic from Practice 11-3 as an "essentials" topic and make a scratch outline of main headings.

IS THERE ONE "RIGHT PATTERN" FOR YOUR ESSAY?   The topic on good photographs and the one on divorce would also be possible as process essays, describing the stages of taking a good photo or the stages children go through during a divorce. The organization of the paper changes, but it might be equally effective. On the other hand, the topic on rats might not work so well as process—unless you wanted to tell the story of one incident ("Our Apartment Building's Battle with Rats" or "Chicago's History of Rat Control"). The real point here is having a *plan that does not mix approaches.* That might confuse a reader—and *you.*

Causes or "Why"

Organize the paper by informing the reader of the causes of a particular situation. Here are the same topics from cause perspectives:

- What motivates (causes) a person to skydive?
- What were the reasons the United Nations sent troops to Bosnia?
- What causes a rat infestation?
- Why do children feel guilty during a divorce?
- How are juvenile delinquents created?

List as many causes (reasons or motivations) for the situation. Each may become an outline heading and eventually a paragraph in the paper.

▲ **PRACTICE 11-7:** Make a list of possible causes for one of the cause topics.

▲ **PRACTICE 11-8:** State your best topic from Practice 11-3 as a "cause" topic and list three or four headings for an outline.

Effects

Instead of looking backward for the source of the situation, look forward to the effects or consequences of a situation. Explaining our topics from this perspective we have:

- Long-term effects of skydiving on your body
- How Bosnia affects U.S. foreign policy
- The psychological effects of rat bites
- When children of divorce marry
- The effects juvenile delinquents have on their peers

To develop one of these, I would list as many effects or consequences as possible. Under each effect, I would list details.

▲ **PRACTICE 11-9:** Create an effects approach for each of the following topics. Then list four to five possible effects one of them leads to.

- Drunk driving
- The 12-month school year
- A change in your neighborhood
- Dating through the Internet

▲ **PRACTICE 11-10:** Create an effects approach for your best topic from Practice 11-3 and draw up a scratch outline of headings.

REASONABLE CAUSES AND EFFECTS   Suggesting causes and effects for events may be controversial or lead to logical errors. The informative writer must try to avoid arguing and instead suggest all reasonable causes and effects without bias. For instance, the following would be reasonable causes of the computer revolution:

- To improve business efficiency and reduce human errors
- To reduce information storage space
- To speed up communications
- To save money by eliminating jobs

But how about these?

- To bend the minds of children away from religion
- To help government gain secret control of people's finances

The last two demand a lot of arguing to prove they're true and are more appropriate for persuasive papers than informative ones. "But," someone might say, "look how children *are* turning away from religion just as computers became widespread! It's a fact!" No, it's an opinion without the widespread acceptance the first four causes would have.

Here is an objective example of cause analysis that explains what clues tell fire investigators that an arsonist has set a fire. Notice how the student explains the whys behind the causes:

> The color of the flames is a clue that a fire might have been caused by arson. An arson fire burns hotter than a normal fire, creating brighter flames with less smoke. Due to the heat, there is purer combustion and less smoke. Unintentional fires usually start small, so when bright red and yellow flames roll out the windows, firefighters should be suspicious.
>
> When fire spreads, it moves up and away from its origin and leaves a "V" mark on walls. If the floor is burned from one end to the other, this may be a sign that an arsonist spread gasoline or kerosene. If there is a lack of deep char around the point of origin, it indicates a fast-spreading fire that may have been helped by an accelerant.
>
> *—Bruce Teague*

▲ **PRACTICE 11-11:** Explain the causes of some social problem today, *or* if you could change one decision you made in the past—at least one year ago—describe the effects a different decision would have had on your life. Be as honest and objective as possible.

Comparison or Contrast

Let's try our topic list for comparative structure:

- Skydiving is safer than hang gliding
- Bosnia and Iraq: Two ways of handling the media
- Rats vs. cockroaches: If you had to choose
- Is it worse for a parent to die or to divorce
- Teaching manners to kids in the United States and in Italy
- Juvenile delinquency today and in 1960

Next you would list your points of comparison as headings and support each point with details.

▲ **PRACTICE 11-12:** Develop a brain-teaser list of comparisons or contrasts for one of the topics just listed.

▲ **PRACTICE 11-13:** Create a comparison or contrast approach to your best topic from Practice 11-3 and draw up a scratch outline of headings.

Classification

Here are some of the topics structured by classification (you can refresh your memory on pages 42–44):

- Three types of governments emerging from former communist regimes in Eastern Europe
- Four kinds of excuses to use on your professors
- Five skydiving styles
- Three common reaction patterns for children of divorce

After deciding on your main points, fill in each category with details describing it. In your draft, each heading will become a paragraph.

▲ **PRACTICE 11-14:** Create a classification approach to your best topic from Practice 11-3 and draw up a scratch outline of headings.

▲ **PRACTICE 11-15:** Pick one of the following topics and try to see it in five of the six thinking structures. Create a one-sentence statement for each:

- Evolution (or any other scientific concept)
- *Romeo and Juliet* (or any other literary work)
- Schizophrenia (or any other psychological term)

▲ **PRACTICE 11-16:** Create a brain-teaser page exploring the most promising of your topics.

Highlights of Chapter 11

- Adjust your approach to audience in informative writing.
- Pack in plenty of details with surprise value. Ask questions and use other brain teasers to stimulate ideas.
- Narrow your topic to one you can handle in your allotted space. Avoid broad, introductory topics and pick ones with a sharp *focus.*
- Consider *several* options when organizing an informative essay. Create your own pattern, describe a process, explain the essentials, explain causes, explain effects, compare or contrast, or classify.
- Don't mix organizing patterns in short essays.

Writing Suggestions and Class Discussions

1. List five topics on which you think you can write a nonresearched, informative essay. Highlight the ones you think will offer the most surprise value for a general audience.
2. Write an "Ask Questions" brain-teaser list (with answers) and one other brain-teaser list for two of the best topics from number 1.

3. Narrow the best topic further and write three scratch outlines (just main headings). Use three different organizing patterns.
4. Using the same topic, decide which organization plan conveys your message best and fill it in with details from your brain-teaser lists.
5. Write the paper and revise it.
6. Audience and Tone: Suppose you were writing an informative letter entitled "My First Semester at College." How would your tone and information included differ depending on to whom you were writing?
   - The college president
   - Your boss (who reimburses your tuition)
   - Your best friend (who is not attending college)

   Make a list of information for each letter.
7. Rewrite these weak topics into sharper, more interesting ones still related to the originals; give two alternatives for each:
   - How to bowl
   - What is classical music
   - How to balance a checkbook
   - Police brutality
   - Smoking is bad for your health
8. Ask five tough questions about each of the following topics, questions that will lead to surprise value information:
   - Teenage marriages
   - The future of gasoline consumption in the United States
   - Community colleges vs. four-year colleges
   - Television satellite dishes
9. Write a process or how-to essay, packing as much information as you can into one or two pages. Concentrate on vivid details and smooth organization. Topics:
   - How to drink with style
   - How to meet men or women at college
   - How to deal with a sexist (or racist) boss
   - How to give an "A" oral report
   - Open topic
10. Suppose you land the job you want. Write a letter to clients or employees explaining a process to them. Choose something you're learning in your major now: "How to extract wisdom teeth," "How to help austistic children respond," or "How to conduct a mar-keting survey for our new product—the solar popcorn maker."
11. Class Exercise in Process Writing: Create a diagram or doodle of your own of about the same complexity as this one: Write a process description of it so someone else can draw it without seeing the doodle. Proportion is important, but actual size is not. You will have

10 minutes. Members of the class will try to draw it only from the read-aloud instructions—no changes allowed from your written text.

12. Write an Essentials essay on one of the following, packing as much information as possible into one or two pages:
    - A good love letter
    - A top action film
    - The most common clichés of television situation comedies
    - Handling being an older adult student in college
    - Open topic

13. Write a Causes *or* Effects essay on one of the following, packing in as much information as possible in one or two pages:
    - Loss of wildlife habitat
    - Democratization of Russia
    - High salaries for athletes
    - A recent career change you made
    - Open topic

14. Write a one- to two-page informative essay comparing or contrasting two of your current textbooks. Evaluate them based on the standards established in this chapter for conveying information: adaptation to audience, surprise value, and covering the tough questions readers have. Quote examples to support your views.

15. Write a classification essay on one of the following, packing as much information as possible in one or two pages:
    - Male attitudes toward women
    - Female attitudes toward men
    - Levels of racism in the United States
    - Open topic

16. Inform a person you're attracted to of your essential personality features. This should *not* be a sell, but an *honest* appraisal. Offer at least three key aspects about yourself that a future spouse should be aware of. Pack in vivid, supporting detail.

17. Write an informative essay on the essentials of a career you're considering. Interview a person in the field, asking real questions you have. Here are some all-purpose starter questions:
    - What do you like best about your job?
    - What one piece of advice would you give to someone wanting to enter this career?
    - What qualities are most important to be a successful _____?
    - What are you most proud of in your career?
    - What part of your job would you gladly give to someone?
    - What most frustrates or disappoints you about it?

    Before calling for an interview, read page 260 for proper etiquette and techniques of interviews.

    A sample career research paper is on p. 303.

18. The class will be divided into six groups. Each will apply a different one

of the six informative organizing patterns to the same topic. Each group should write a focus sentence, an outline, and some details for each heading.

19. In addition to the informative essay that follows, read the student informative essays on pages 297–311.

Sample Student Informative Essay Using Classification

WHEN THE BOUGH BREAKS: BLACK CHILDREN IN CRISIS

Tokeya Young

Millions of black children live in crisis today: crises of violence, poverty, and ill health. Their families, their communities, and their government have failed them. Most people have heard of the failures of some families and communities, but in 1991 the United States was one of only a few nations not to ratify the Rights of the Child Treaty sponsored by the United Nations that would have set standards for "basic safeguards any civilized nation must provide for its children" (Cottman-Becnel 94).

Many black children don't live to see their 18th birthday. In 1990, almost two thousand Black youths were killed by guns. Every day in America, an average of four black men under 19 are murdered (Weathers 70). It saddens me that the value of a young life can be measured by the price of designer sneakers, leather jackets, gold

INTRO classifies three crises

violence

jewelry, or "gang turf." In urban areas, a young black man is more likely to die from violence than a soldier was on a tour of Vietnam (Weathers 70). Inner cities are battlegrounds filled with children armed for war. Sixty percent of all deaths of black boys between 15 and 19 are from guns (Weathers 71).

poverty

ill
health

Many black children are growing up poor and in ill health. Almost half of black children live in poverty (Cottman-Becnel 94) and for that reason many are never immunized against childhood diseases and are malnourished. Black babies are twice as likely as white babies to die within their first year (Johnson 74). Another health problem is children with AIDS. There are eight in Monroe County who have full-blown AIDS, and in New York State over 1,300 (Machuca). Half of all youngsters nationwide with AIDS are black (Johnson 83). There are also thousands of cocaine babies. Their parents' prenatal use of cocaine causes these innocent victims to suffer withdrawal and often physical and learning disabilities the rest of their lives. In 1991 in Monroe County, there were 197 reported cocaine babies, 84% of whom were black (Machuca). Other causes of child-hood ill health are improper nutrition and lack of immu-nization. If more clinics offered free immunization, underprivileged youth could be protected against child-hood diseases. One and a half million American children--many of them black--don't have health insurance (Johnson 74).

Black children live in a crisis not witnessed since   conclusion

slavery. Violence, poverty, and ill health disrupt their

lives and threaten society's future.

WORKS CITED

Cottman-Becnel, Barbara. "Poverty as Policy." Essence

   Dec. 1993: 92-94.

Johnson, Kirk. "Alive and Well." Essence Dec. 1993: 74-83.

Machuca, Paola. Telephone interview. 2 May 1994.

Weathers, Diane. "Stop the Guns." Essence Dec. 1993:

   70-71.

Commentary

Surprise value: Because people know *generally* that African American children often face great stress, the essay's surprise value lies in specific data. People who assume the United States champions child rights would be surprised by the veto of the child rights treaty. I thought the paragraph on violence had the best surprise value in statistics. The fact that the author made a personal call (to AIDS Rochester) to get local facts would appeal to her class audience.

   Details: Some were vivid. Comparing children's survival rates to soldiers in Vietnam was powerful. More detail was needed on poverty—the skimpiest of the three sections.

   Organization: This is a classification essay. The introduction states three types of crises. Violence is handled cleanly, but poverty and ill health mix in the third paragraph. The poverty section needs more hard detail and its own paragraph. The conclusion is concise.

   Tone: Mostly objective. Only "it saddens me" in the second paragraph is personal and her call in the third paragraph for free immunizations verges on argument.

   Audience: Her classmates: a local but general audience. The style is clean, nontechnical, and accessible to average readers.

   Research: The documentation format is fine, but notice that all three published sources come from the same issue of one magazine. Essence is respected, but other sources would strengthen her impartiality. Her sources could also be more up-to-date because they rely on statistics.

Questions the essay should answer but doesn't: Why is poverty such a crisis? We need details. Second, what diseases do African American children suffer from because of lack of immunization?

Strongest aspects: Specific statistics and clean style.

Additional suggestions: I think there's room for examples, perhaps based on the author's observations. Name a child who died in a crossfire or describe a family who lives in poverty. She doesn't have to become opinionated to describe some people up close. The essay's reliance only on statistics keeps the reader at arm's length from the little kids she obviously cares about. Second, she should identify her phone interview source in the body of the paper. Who is Paola Machuca? What's this person's position?

✓ **PEER REVIEW CHECKLIST FOR INFORMATION**

Author:_____

The organizing pattern I used for this essay is: _____
Describe it if you created your own pattern.

I'd like help with this paper in this area:

Reviewer: _____

	STRONG	AVERAGE	WEAK
IDEAS—Surprise Value			
DETAILS—Vivid			
Enough Detail			
ORGANIZATION—Clear/easy to follow			
Transitions/paragraphs mark major shifts			
TONE—Unbiased, informative			
AUDIENCE—Style suits audience			
RESEARCH (if used) Documentation			

Do you agree with the author's assessment of the organizing pattern?
Explain where/how it might be strengthened.

Respond to the author's request for advice:

Evaluate the essay's surprise value. What was new; what wasn't?

What questions about the topic should the essay answer that it doesn't?

What is the strongest part of the essay to you?

Give two additional suggestions for revision:
1.

2.

CHAPTER 12

Persuasive Writing

Seeking Agreement from an Audience

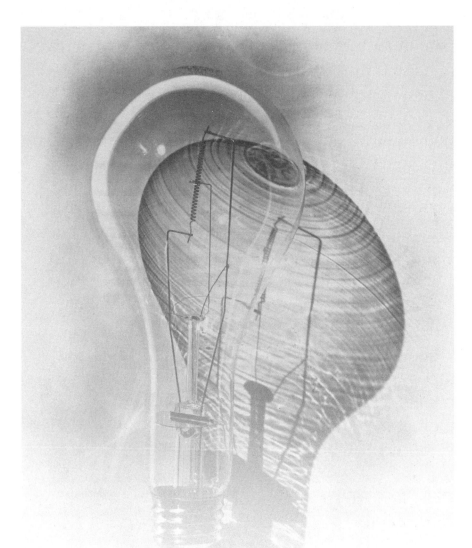

The aim of argument should not be victory but progress.

JOSEPH JOUBERT

The civilized world represents the victory of persuasion over force.

PLATO

Persuasive writing has a bad reputation. At its worst we picture a slimy hoodlum twisting someone's arm to "persuade" him to tell where the diamonds are. We think of battleships and bombers hovering off the coast of a tiny country to "persuade" its government to change its policies. Cigarette advertisements in magazines "persuade" men that one brand will make them feel as if they're riding a snorting stallion on the range while another brand will make women feel daring and rebellious. How about empty political campaign speeches or a father screaming at his late, tipsy teenager at 2 A.M.? Persuasion is commonly pictured as forcing, tricking, seducing, or lecturing people to buy or do something not really in their best interests. Too often these tactics work. But that's not the kind of persuasion we're interested in here.

Honest, ethical persuasion means bringing readers—through their own reason and emotions—to believe or act as the writer does. In this sense, readers willingly and *consciously* discover that it is in their best interest to agree. This type of persuasion, which will be required of you in many college assignments and in most persuasive writing done in business, professional, and technical careers, is an *honest appeal to reason and feeling.*

AUDIENCE AND TONE

Advertising, political speeches, and barroom debates often imply the audience is so dumb or so bullheaded that it must be pounded into submission. Reasonable persuasion assumes your audience is uncommitted (unless you know for *sure* you are dealing with supporters or those holding opposite views). It assumes your audience is educated and will weigh your arguments reasonably. This audience wants facts and logic, expects you to be ethical, will be critical of shortcomings in your position, and will not fall for the gimmicks of advertising.

This means that you, as a persuader, must achieve a good persuasive tone. You do not have to be somber or dull. In fact, humor not only enlivens persuasion but can demonstrate the writer is broad-minded. Overall, strive for perspective and common sense. Sentences like "All people who support abortion are murderers!" and "Antiabortionists want to enslave women!" share the same hysterical tone. Wild, undisciplined language usually results from wild or undisciplined thinking, and smart readers will be skeptical about such statements. Assume your readers are intelligent, present many facts and reasons for your position, and trust readers will see the logic. If you try to bully readers into agreement with shouting, they won't be convinced—they'll only want to get away from you.

Several years ago I received an anonymous letter from a student. The fact that it was anonymous made me question the writer's integrity from the start. The student was complaining about the revealing clothes a woman in the class wore, arguing that they were out of place in college. I admit the woman's clothes lacked taste, and if I'd received a reasonable letter, I may have gritted my teeth and spoken to her about it—even though I don't think a teacher should be a police officer. But the student's letter used numerous profanities to describe the woman—"slut" and "bimbo" being among the nicer. It ended: "I want action! Have *YOU* any sense of decency??!!" Me? Me?! The student steamed and frothed so much that he totally lost perspective. He was attacking his reader, not the opposition, and he lost whatever chance he had of persuading me to act as he wished. I felt more inclined to counsel *him* than the woman in question.

Before we agree with an argument, we must trust the arguer. **Give readers reasons to trust you.** Is the persuader ethical? Knowledgeable? Reasonable? Your credibility is damaged by using profanity, bullying, ranting or threats, by twisting facts or calling rumors "facts," and by relying on slogans, clichés, stereotypes, or other oversimplifications. The writer who calmly *helps* a reader sort through the complexities of a situation, who honestly *shares the difficulties* of right and wrong in the issue, and who *respects the truth* will open doors with a quiet knock. The persuader who approaches with a battering ram or who tries to sneak in a back window is the one against whom readers build barricades.

So before you begin persuading readers, try to put yourself in an honest, helpful frame of mind; open yourself to alternate viewpoints in the early stages especially, so the point you set out to prove is as reasonable and fair as it can be. Keep Joseph Joubert's statement in mind: "The aim of argument should not be victory but progress."

As long as you consider your audience's reactions, are willing to modify your ideas to strengthen them, and use many brain teasers to open the topic, you will make honest progress. If you seek victory over a reader, ignore or hide facts that shake your plan, or lose control of your emotions, your case will start to crumble.

▲ **PRACTICE 12-1:** Recall two persuasive situations you've been in: one that led to hot tempers and anger, one that led to "progress." Think about the attitude of the people involved in each.

To help achieve a good tone, **write to real people for a real reason—** actually send your ideas to someone. My students' persuasive papers have been published in the college newspaper, city newspaper, Humane Society newsletter, Ukrainian Club newsletter, and several magazines. One wrote a proposal to a bank to finance a towing company; another asked a museum curator to reinstate cancelled free art classes for poor children; another used the class paper as an opportunity to answer her supervisor's negative job evaluation of her. One of my students wrote to her town school board to protest a policy against students using calculators during tests. Irene's dyslexic son knew his math, but made simple errors, such as writing "45" instead of "54," without a calculator. Her letter brought a state assistant secretary of education to a board meeting and the rule was changed. Irene was later asked to address a convention of 500 educators on the topic and help rewrite the state rules. There's no inspiration like writing to real people for real reasons.

You can write to your student loan service center with suggestions, to your boss at the retail store about changing an exchange policy that costs the store thousands of dollars, to a local high school principal to persuade him to make driver's education a required course, to the campus facilities director to add a bus route for the dorm in the woods, to a father to persuade him not to retire from racing, to the Hallmark Company persuading them to sell Christmas jewelry you designed, to Apple Computer proposing a software registration plan that will keep prices low and prevent others from duplicating the software. These are all recent papers my students wrote—and mailed. Going "live" instead of writing only for your professor can be some of the best education you will have in college. But do wait for peer and/or your professor's reactions before sending out your ideas.

 ## PERSUASIVE TOPICS

When choosing a topic for persuasion, **you have basically two choices: to take a stand on an existing controversial issue or to make a proposal to solve a problem.** If you choose to take a stand, you will have the advantage of some preexisting arguments but will need to find additional arguments and examples of your own. Freshness of idea will be difficult with some topics like pornography, nuclear power, and drug laws because most supporting arguments on *both* sides are well known. If you make a proposal of your own—a new solution to a problem—you will have to invent all your own arguments. But you will have the advantage of freshness. Proposals sound more stimulating:

- "Students with 'A' grades in a course will receive free tuition; those with 'D' or lower will pay double tuition."
- "No politician should serve more than one term in office."
- "Put a $1 per gallon tax on gasoline and use the receipts for solar research."

But proposals require more careful thinking: Can you think of a serious objection to each of these proposals as well as a positive benefit?

In career writing, of course, you will be writing proposals 98 percent of the time. Most employers pay people for new concepts and plans, not rehashing of old issues. Persuasion will be needed to convince your supervisor and colleagues and more persuasion needed to sell clients, government agencies, customers, and other institutions. The higher you rise in your career, the more persuasive proposals you will write, and in fact, writing proposals for new ideas is one way to rise rapidly. How would your employer react to receiving proposals like these from you under your own initiative?

- We can draw more customers to the store by providing a shuttle bus service from three locations.
- Bookkeeping at the company can be simplified if we adopt the following plan. . . .
- The summer recreation program can be improved if we stagger the children's nap times and alternate quiet tasks and outdoor activities.

▲ **PRACTICE 12-2:** Write a trial proposal for your employer, college, society or family. List a few details of the plan.

▲ **PRACTICE 12-3:** State your stand on three controversial issues today. We'll be developing these throughout the chapter. Try to pick ones for which you have some mixed feelings so you'll have a more honest paper.

RAISING PROBLEMS

As in the preceding examples, your thesis should be stated in a single sentence, and in most persuasive writing it appears at the end of the introductory paragraph. This is not unalterable law, but it is a pattern that makes reading easier to follow. It's a mini-map for reader *and* writer. Short persuasive essays may defer the thesis until the conclusion, especially in cases when the writer finds both sides appealing. It is used less often simply because it's trickier to bring off successfully. What does the rest of the introduction do? It makes the reader care about the problem. The introduction can also establish your reasonable tone. For example, one might start the essay on "Grades and Tuition" this way:

```
Teachers complain many students are unmotivated. Colleges
don't figure transfer grades into one's grade-point average--
"C" is good enough for credit. Many graduates wonder if work-
ing hard for a high cumulative GPA is really worth the effort
when they might get a job based on their personality. Many good
students just slide through with little effort, and the tax-
payers foot much of the bill. Perhaps we can motivate students
with something closer to home: cash.
```

At this point the writer has established a problem and has shown she's considered it from several angles (teachers, transfer colleges, several types of students, and taxpayers), and she probably has the reader saying something like this: "Yes, motivation is poor; what should be done about this?" In other words, by showing us a problem, by showing how extensive it is, the writer has made the reader hungry for an answer. Then the thesis is presented as the last sentence of the paragraph followed by the essay that supports it.

The proposal for the shuttle bus might begin this way:

A customer who wants our product circles the store three times. Our tiny parking lot is full; street parking is full. Will that customer ever return? Unlikely. No one in the area will sell us space for parking, the city has refused to run a bus route nearby, and we have already made our employees park six blocks away. If we can shuttle them, why not our customers?

One way of starting to think about persuasive writing tasks is to raise all the problems you can about a topic—perhaps by writing a brain-teaser bug list. Much of this may turn up in your introduction.

▲ **PRACTICE 12-4:** Take an issue you find important—perhaps one of your topics from Practice 12-2 or Practice 12-3—and write three or four sentences explaining why it is a tough problem. Be fair to all sides. Then, if you think there is a way to solve this problem, write a trial thesis sentence.

▲ **PRACTICE 12-5:** Think about a decision you must make, writing three or four sentences explaining why it is a tough problem. At the end write a trial thesis you could defend.

 ## SUPPORTING EVIDENCE

A reasonable person expects reasonable evidence before believing something. In the previous examples, you'd want to be convinced that cash motivation would work for grades: that it would be fair, that the specific economics of the plan would fly, and that it would be good for students and teachers. Can you imagine three or four questions you'd want answered before investing in shuttle buses if you were the store's manager? **Always anticipate your audience's barriers to belief.**

When you argue persuasively, pack in as much supporting evidence as possible. Think of yourself as a lawyer convincing a jury. There are three types of evidence:

- Facts
- Appeals to values
- Logic

These are new brain teasers for persuasive writing. Make a list of all the facts you know (or need to know so you can research them later), all appeals to value you can use, and all logical arguments you can use.

 ## FACTS

Statistics are one type of fact you can use to support a thesis. A proverb says, "There are two kinds of lies: regular lies and statistics." It means that statistics can be twisted to bolster weak arguments. Maeir's law even says, "If the facts do not conform to the theory, they must be disposed of." This attitude may be held by less reputable advertisers or politicians, but in honest, ethical persuasion, you must be especially careful to **handle your statistics fairly and accurately.** If we say, for instance, "A recent study found that 94 percent of people surveyed believe the ban on television advertising for cigarettes is unfair," our reaction to this statistic changes if we learn it was conducted by a tobacco company in the town where its factory is located. An ethical arguer must reveal such information or not use the statistic.

The source of your fact strengthens or weakens its impact. Generally, **your facts will be more credible if they are based on recent research conducted by an expert and published in a reputable journal, Web site, or book.** Material from *The National Enquirer,* material assembled by astrologers, or work done 30 years ago in fast-changing fields like psychology or physics is generally not considered reliable. Even experts are not absolutely trustworthy. Lord Kelvin, Leonardo da Vinci, and Sigmund Freud all made whopping errors in their fields.

Another problem with statistics is simply making the reader *see* them clearly. Today we are bombarded with numbers: billions of dollars, millions of highway deaths, thousands of recalled products. Despite our modern sophistication, big numbers seem unreal for most people, and **the writer must help the reader *see* what the number means in a concrete way.** When the United States went past the $1 trillion mark of indebtedness, for instance, most people simply shrugged until one representative of Congress found a way of visualizing the statistic. He calculated that if we stacked $1 trillion one-dollar bills on top of each other, the pile would reach the moon! That gave people an image of $1 trillion dollars they could visualize, and it persuaded many people to demand government action, as the representative had hoped.

Here are three facts. Which is the most visual?

- 200 million tons of dirt/rocks were dug to create the Panama Canal.
- A typical hurricane releases 50 times the energy of the first atomic bomb.
- Hoover Dam holds back 10 trillion gallons of water.

I'd pick the second example because we can see 50 atomic bombs (even if we cannot fully comprehend the impact), but without careful calculation I couldn't even tell whether 200 million tons of dirt or 10 trillion gallons of water would be the bigger volume.

▲ **PRACTICE 12-6:** Take a minute to creatively visualize in words those other two facts for a reader.

▲ **PRACTICE 12-7:** State two facts or statistics you know about a topic you chose for Practice 12-2 or Practice 12-3. Then help a reader creatively visualize them through a concrete comparison.

Plan on doing occasional research for persuasive writing. The facts I just gave took me five minutes to locate in a geology textbook. Statistics give authority to your persuasive voice.

Some statistics can come from your own observations. In a letter to the Vice President for Facilities Management at the State University of New York at Buffalo, a student proposed that the college expand its parking facilities. At one point, she produced her own statistics by driving around campus counting spaces:

> It may also be possible to turn parts of faculty lots into student parking, since faculty lots are seldom full. There are 27,000 students and 4,000 faculty members at UB. All 19,000 commuter students, and, I estimate, one quarter of the 8,000 who live on campus drive to class. There are eight student lots on North Campus, three of which hold approximately 300 cars, five of which hold 200 cars, for a total of 1,900 spaces. Yet there are five faculty lots with a total of 1,000 spaces. On the South Campus, there are four student and two faculty lots, each accommodating 200 cars. I calculate the ratio of faculty to parking spaces is three to one and of students to student parking spaces is eight to one. After viewing the parking lots throughout the semester, I believe you can afford to transfer at least several hundred spaces to students.
>
> —*Tina C. Maenza*

There's a second kind of fact, one handy for all of us: **examples.** Use examples from (1) what you've seen; (2) what your friends and families have seen; (3) historical or current events; and (4) hypothetical cases.

If you're writing about the law that forbids those under a certain age from drinking alcohol, for instance, you probably know a dozen cases that could support either side—from firsthand experience, from what others have told you, and from the news. Everyone can dig up a couple of examples of drunken teenagers causing fatal accidents—or of drunken middle-aged people killing sober teenagers; of teenagers bribing an adult to buy illegal liquor—or of responsible teenagers arranging a designated driver who will not touch alcohol during the evening.

Historical and news stories carry more weight with a reader—she can think, "Oh yes, I remember that." It is verifiable. **Personal examples** may make the reader wonder if you've colored the facts; however, your own examples give you the chance to write vividly. You can describe the accident scene, quote dialogue from the beer party, build narrative conflict, and write with a freshness you can't with historical cases—and you should. **Examples you heard from your friends** are less satisfactory because, as lawyers say, it is "hearsay" testimony. It is one step further removed from the reader and hence less reliable. We all know truth has a way of getting watered down (or spiced up!) as it gets passed along.

Hypothetical examples are necessary to fill in gaps when facts are not available or to project future events for which there are no facts. Hypothetical examples are simply made-up cases of things *likely to happen.* In the abortion debate, for instance, several hypothetical cases are usually raised: "Suppose a woman gets pregnant through rape . . ." or "Suppose a pregnant woman discovers the fetus is badly deformed." Both scenarios are likely to happen sometime in our society. We might be able to track down facts about actual women in these cases, but if we can't, a hypothetical example can appeal to the reader's common sense. The reader will test your common sense in explaining the hypothetical case as well. You would be on shaky ground, I think, to portray a woman pregnant through rape as a person who should forget how she became pregnant and within months develop normal maternal tenderness, or look forward to the experience of childbirth the way an intentionally pregnant woman would. There are noble people who can do this—but wouldn't you agree that they are rare? It would be equally unlikely for most normal women, even under such stress as this, to be driven to suicide should they not be allowed to have an abortion.

Facts and examples are important support for most arguments; pack plenty in your essay, and use them fairly and vividly. Rely most on firsthand experience and reliable sources. Secondhand and hypothetical examples should be used as last resorts.

▲ **PRACTICE 12-8:** Use a reference book to find two strong facts you could use to support your topic from Practice 12-2 or Practice 12-3. Then add three examples—yours, your friends', historical and/or hypothetical.

 ## APPEALS TO THE READER'S VALUES

People are persuaded not only by facts but by realizing that your proposal supports *values* they believe in. Facts without a context of values seem meaningless much of the time. Amory Lovins, an energy expert, calculated in 1980 that if the United States were to take all cars off the road that drove less than 15 miles per gallon and were to replace them with cars that drove at least 35 miles per gallon, the United States could reduce its gasoline consumption by 15 percent. Ho-hum, right? Well, it becomes more interesting when Lovins reminds us today that if we reduced oil consumption 15 percent, we would have needed to import no oil from the Mideast, need station no ships in the Persian Gulf, risk no soldiers' deaths, perhaps have fewer diplomats, reporters, or businesspeople there who might be taken hostage. This puts the fact about gas mileage into a values context.

Some values that writers consider in persuasive writing are *economics, fairness, health, safety, love, environmental impact, freedom, beauty.* As Abraham Maslow showed in his hierarchy of needs, certain basic needs must be met before people are willing to consider others. We are, therefore, unlikely to consider an appeal to our sense of beauty (put up a gorgeous city sculpture display that will delight our minds) if the project will bankrupt us or be dangerous for children to play on. Maslow said we must have safety and basic physical needs met before we strive for "higher" values like fairness and freedom. After we achieve *them*, Maslow argued, humans will give priority to love, beauty, and spiritual matters. Here is a simplified list of Maslow's values, starting with the most basic:

- Physiological (food, shelter, water, health)
- Safety (security, order, stability)
- Belongingness and love (family, friends, social groups)
- Esteem (status, power, recognition, money)
- Self-actualization (reaching your *individual* potential; for example, oneness with God, nature, or lover; creativity, justice, beauty, and freedom)

Maslow was being descriptive of how he saw people behave, not how he thought they *ought* to behave. By contrast, most philosophies and religions insist spiritual values are more important than, say, status, recognition, or even safety. People like Martin Luther King, Jr. or Mahatma Gandhi, as well as millions of unknown people, have put justice, freedom, creativity, or love above personal health, safety, and status.

You will have to decide for yourself if Maslow is right about what values motivate people the most. Would *you*, for instance, bulldoze a beautiful neighborhood park for an industrial plant if it meant secure jobs for your family? Would most people? Germany, where most wilderness has been devastated, values nature preserves more than Brazil, which is burning down its vast tropical rain forest for industry in hopes of improving its people's standard of living—what it sees as a higher value. One of the more interesting aspects of persuasive writing is dealing with the changing, conflicting values of people and groups.

A student of mine served several hitches in the U.S. Navy SEALS. This young man had been in Lebanon when a terrorist drove a truck filled with explosives into a Marine barracks, killing nearly 300 men. He vowed revenge. In one paper he announced he was going into counterterrorist activity so he could torture terrorists and kill them. He described in vivid, gory detail what he would do to his country's enemies and concluded by saying, "I'm doing this so my future children can grow up in a decent, moral world." What hierarchy of values does he hold? Do you agree?

▲ **PRACTICE 12-9:** Make a list of *your* most important eight to ten values, trying to include several not already listed here. Star the two or three values you think are most important.

In practical terms, the persuasive writer might start thinking about defending a proposal by going down a checklist of values, asking how each value can suggest new arguments to support his position. It's another brain teaser. Suppose I am proposing that my state outlaw legal gambling and close betting parlors. The list of values below is written so you can use it as a brain teaser to think up support for many topics.

- What *economic* benefits will my position have? For whom? How much?
- Will it increase people's *security or satisfy basic needs?*
- Is it *fair* to all parties involved? Think through—one at a time—how various other people might see it.
- Will it enhance or limit anyone's *freedom?*
- How will my plan affect *families?*
- Will my plan appeal to the reader's concern for *beauty?*
- Will my plan affect the *environment?*
- Will my plan build *self-esteem or status* for anyone? Who? Why?
- How might this help people *actualize their potential?*
- List *other values* of importance to yourself. How can they be appealed to by your proposal?

▲ **PRACTICE 12-10:** Go through this list to see what support it triggers to ban legalized betting. Some questions will lead nowhere; just move on.

For example, let me respond to the first question. Outlawing gambling may prevent some bettors from losing (or winning) money, but I suspect many would then bet illegally. This would actually increase the gambler's odds of economic success because the government keeps a higher percentage of money bet than bookies do. Outlawing gambling would deprive the state of this money and perhaps cause taxes to rise. If other states don't ban gambling, my state may lose some tourist dollars as well. I realize now I need to research how much is spent in my state on the lottery and horse racing and how much the state keeps. Right now, these ideas offer more potential as refutations rather than direct support.

▲ **PRACTICE 12-11:** Try the same list (and perhaps your own high-ranked values) with these proposals, looking for support:

- The United Nations ought to be given command of a permanent, powerful military force.
- Evolution ought to be the only creation theory taught in public schools.
- Churches should pay property taxes.
- The Internet must be censored for pornography and dangerous information like bomb instructions.

▲ **PRACTICE 12-12:** Try the same list to create more supporting arguments for your topic from Practice 12-2 or Practice 12-3.

LOGIC

Logic alone rarely persuades people, but it draws together facts and appeals to values. In its simplest form logic takes one fact (the minor premise) and one value (the major premise) and shows if they both are true, that a reasonable conclusion drawn from them must also be true. Let's take an example.

Suppose I want to persuade people abortion is morally wrong and ought to be illegal. To do this I present a value—killing a human being is morally wrong and illegal. Then I present a fact—that a fetus is a human being. If these two are true, then the conclusion is inevitable: Killing a fetus is wrong and should be illegal. Someone who disagreed with me, however, might argue that one or both of these premises are *not* true. With the abortion issue, people usually question whether a fetus is really a human being. Do you see how the logic of my claim disintegrates if that "fact" is proved false? The opposition might also question my other premise by pointing out that killing humans *is* morally or legally acceptable in a number of circumstances. Can you name some?

Logic, then, is rarely perfect. One or both of the premises can be questioned. There are about a dozen common flaws writers fall into when using logic. We call these "logical fallacies" because they make any argument that uses them invalid. They are forms of dishonest persuasion. Here are eight of the **most common logical fallacies.**

1. Endorsement. Michael Jordan likes a certain hamburger. The commercial claims you will like it too. "Doctor" Peter Benton (of TV show *ER*) recommends a particular kind of coffee. Are you persuaded to buy it? Obviously we suspect that these people's recommendations are strongly influenced by what they are paid. But the endorsement's fallacy isn't really lying, but logic. There is no necessary connection between the tastes of one person and another. Had a genuine doctor recommended a coffee for its health effects, we might have had a stronger case. An athlete endorsing a hamburger is far less effective than an athlete endorsing sneakers. In such cases there should also be an explanation of *why* the product or viewpoint is correct. Does the hamburger use highest quality meat, cost less, or avoid dangerous preservatives? These are the real issues. This applies to experts you may quote in your papers as well. It's not enough to say Abraham Maslow or Rachel Carson believed something. For the reader's understanding you also need to explain how the theory works or what the facts are.

2. Hasty Generalization. I hate Professor Smith. My friends in the class hate him. Therefore, Professor Smith must be an unpopular teacher. Sorry. You need more evidence. Several students from a class of 25 are too few to support such a claim. Perhaps your group is on Professor Smith's bad side because of poor performance or attitude. How about this: The Democrats always start America's big wars—Democrats were presidents when Vietnam, Korea, World Wars I and II started. This is also hasty generalization—can you explain why?

A hasty generalization means you base a conclusion or claim on too few examples or oversimplified evidence. You can overcome this in your essays by deluging your reader with cases and examples. If you're worried you have so many facts and evidence that you may be boring a reader, list the "excess" in a note at the end of the paper.

3. Bandwagon. This is similar to the endorsement, except that instead of picking a prominent person who supports your claim, you say your position must be right because many people support it. There's a quick cure for this fallacy: Just remind yourself how many millions of people thought Hitler and Mussolini were saviors. Closer to home, remind yourself how President Richard Nixon won a landslide election and resigned a year later for dishonest and illegal activities. Was his presidency justified because so many people supported him? No. What makes an argument right is that it *is right,* not that millions of people *believe* it's right. Your job is to show how it's right, not how it's popular.

4. Tradition. "It's always been done this way" or "My parents taught me to believe . . ." This is a copout from thinking. You're hiding behind someone else's thinking instead of walking the reader through the arguments themselves. There's a quick reminder you can use if you're tempted to rely on this fallacy: Suppose the first human beings one million years ago had latched onto this principle? "We've always eaten our meat raw and slept in trees. No fire, no caves!"

Traditional beliefs prevent people from rushing to each wild, untested idea that floats along, but the fact that a belief once may have been valid does not mean it still is. Tradition fights new good ideas as well as bad ones.

5. Unqualified Generalization. In our enthusiasm for a claim we sometimes exaggerate: "Television game shows are the worst thing for our children's minds today." Really? Worse than pornography? Worse than fighting parents? Worse than an abusive teacher? A statement like the previous one shows the person has simply not thought *through* the idea. *Qualifying makes it more acceptable.* "Television game shows are bad for children's minds." It is now no longer at the head of a list of *everything* bad. You could also say, "*Some* TV game shows *may* harm a child's mind as badly as pornography." The reader cannot toss these away at first reading—she must first see how you support such a view. Avoid words like "all," "always," "never," "nobody in her right mind," or "everyone." Use considered words like "most people," "usually," or "under normal circumstances."

6. Faulty Cause and Effect. This means claiming one thing caused another to happen when the only tangible relationship between the two things is that one preceded the other. You may be able to prove the one did indeed cause the other, but a simple time relationship alone does not. "My parents got divorced after I was born. Therefore, I broke up their marriage." Or, "Everytime I get a day off, it rains." Or, "The family has deteriorated in the last 20 years—since feminism became strong. That proves how harmful feminism has been to America." None of these holds water as complete arguments. In the first case you need to prove that your parents' marriage was solid before you came along and that you were the key problem in arguments your parents might have had. In the second, you'd have to establish that meteorological powers infuse your body on a day off. With the antifeminist statement, think of all the competing explanations for why the family has deteriorated: decline in church-going, increased violence, increased sexual activity outside of marriage, increased drug use, increased materialism, worse public morals, a more highly mobile society. All three cases need to show a *connection* between cause and effect.

7. Sentimentality. This means pleading a cause based on your feelings (usually misery) rather than on its merits. "You've got to give me a 'C' in this course or I won't graduate"; "You can't withdraw me for absences; I'll lose my state aid." Sorry. The grade in a course says you have performed at a certain level, and your misery at not doing well should not persuade a professor your merit is greater than it is. Your state aid is given assuming you will attend class; you earn it by attending and performing at an acceptable level. "A promotion will make me so happy!" By itself, not good enough. The logical questions are Did you earn it? Do you show potential?

8. Attacking Your Opponent. Instead of attacking a position, value, or fact to advance your case, you attack the person who made the proposal. "Don't support President Clinton's health care plan; look at the scandals he caused." To a fair-minded reader, this is con artistry. The bill and its sponsor are two separate issues, and the plan should be discussed on its own merits. How about these cases; are they valid criticisms?

- "We should not elect Al Gore president; he was vice president for Bill Clinton."
- "We shouldn't do business with the Captain Computer Company; its head salesman smokes pot."

▲ **PRACTICE 12-13:** Think of two arguments that infuriate you: political, parental, peer, or commercial statements. Now, using the eight fallacies as a guide, expose the logical flaws in these arguments.

▲ **PRACTICE 12-14:** What is one argument dealing with your topic from Practice 12-2 or Practice 12-3 that relies on a logical fallacy? It will be easier to find an opposition argument, but be honest enough to look for one on your side.

An Example of Support and Logic

In the following selection from a student essay, Candace Northrup proposes that we ought to allow doctors to prescribe marijuana for medical purposes under strict hospital supervision. Here is one of her support paragraphs:

```
    Marijuana has been shown to help people with many ill-
nesses. For glaucoma patients, marijuana reduces fluid pres-
sure in the eye that causes the person to lose vision. AIDS
patients use marijuana to increase appetite and decrease
nausea. Some multiple sclerosis patients claim marijuana
improves their motor functions and reduces muscle spasms
```

and pain (Dickinson 135). Healthy people may not realize the pain these patients endure. My aunt, who has multiple sclerosis, can barely walk because the pain eats away at her. If marijuana was legal, she would suffer less.

Commentary: This scores high for packing specifics into a short paragraph. By listing the benefits of pot for three types of sufferers, Candace shows the issue affects many people. If she had mentioned only one of the diseases, it would lack punch. Notice also that Candace explains *how* pot helps each disease–giving her authority as a persuader and educating her audience. She appeals to the **values** of health and fear from pain, but also makes an **emotional appeal** to the reader's pity for the sufferers. The concluding example of her aunt personalizes the medical facts.

Candace's essay next raises several **refutations:**

How many people already use marijuana for medical purposes? One researcher says, "Six hundred thousand people now have criminal records because marijuana is not legal for medical use"; as a result, California and Arizona have passed initiatives approving the medical use of marijuana (Ziegler 70). So the government has been forced to look at the issue. Yet General Barry McCaffrey, head of drug policy, was quoted as saying, "Just when the nation is trying its hardest to educate teenagers not to use drugs, now they are being told that marijuana is medicine. There could not be a worse message to young people" (Stiefell 9).

This is one argument against legalizing marijuana--that children will see it as medicine and might think it is all right to smoke for recreation. As a teenager, I don't see that threat. Marijuana was around my small town. Legalizing marijuana for medical purposes is not going to cause much increase in teen usage. I don't see where General McCaffrey gets off saying, "The nation is trying its hardest to educate children on drugs . . ." because I haven't seen much education from the government. Even if we were educated, would it really stop the use of marijuana? Teenagers are curious and oblivious to the world. If teens have their minds set on smoking marijuana, then they are going to smoke it. Even though General McCaffrey opposes medical use of marijuana, the government recently agreed to spend $1 million to look into it (Stiefell 10).

Another question often raised is why legalize marijuana if THC, the main ingredient, is already being prescribed? THC is available as a legal pill (Brookhiser 28). Unfortunately, the pill can take hours to begin working. Smoked marijuana is effective within minutes (Dickinson 135). Second, treating nausea with a pill is not the brightest idea because nauseated patients may not be able to keep the pill in the stomach long enough for it to begin working. One report found that "Oral THC is metabolized through the liver, which neutralizes more than 90 percent of the chemical; smoking delivers the THC--as well as sixty other unsynthesized cannabinoids, many of which are therapeutic too--directly to the bloodstream" (Dickinson 135). Marijuana also seems safer than oral THC. The DEA's own administrative judge, Francis L. Young, declared, "Marijuana is one of the safest therapeutically active substances known to man" (Dickinson 135).

Commentary: The first two paragraphs fairly raise an objection based on the consequences to youth of legalizing pot, but Candace falls into three fallacies in responding: unqualified generalization, bandwagon, and attacking one's opponent. The unqualified generalizations occur in her description of teenagers as "oblivious to the world." Qualifiers like "some" or "many" or examples are needed. Where are the other two fallacies?

Candace's third paragraph raises another refutation: Why not prescribe the chemical in pot without legalizing pot? This is a good objection and one many readers may not have heard. An unethical arguer might have ignored it. She does a fine job of responding with facts to refute this objection, providing details of why smoked pot works better for sufferers. At the end of the paragraph—when she quotes a DEA official to contradict the DEA position—is this an endorsement fallacy or a valid point?

Now look at Candace's **sources:**

Works Cited

Brookhiser, Richard. "Pot Luck: Any Sick Person Who Wants to Use Marijuana to Help Himself Has to Break the Law." National Review 11 Nov. 1996: 27-28.

Dickinson, Ben. "What If Weed Is Exactly What You Need?" Esquire Oct. 1997: 134-35.

Stiefell, Chana Frieman. "Marijuana on the Ballot: Should a Menacing Drug Treat Some Chronically Ill Patients?" Science World 21 Feb. 1997: 8-10.

Ziegler, Jan. "Up in Smoke." Hospitals and Health Networks 20 June 1997: 70+.

The first is politically conservative, the second liberal, and the last two scientific/medical. Should we care? Does her list of sources create a stronger image of the writer?

 ## STRUCTURING THE PERSUASIVE ESSAY

If you have the time and creativity to invent your own persuasive structure, do it. But over two thousand years from Roman orators to today's editorialists, one model structure stands out.

Not only does this model help you organize your ideas, but it generates new ideas and makes sure you cover key aspects of any persuasive presentation. The four-part structure is Introduction, Main Supporting Ideas, Refutation Section, and Conclusion.

The **introduction** should begin by intriguing us with a concrete problem that is difficult to solve and end with your solution to this problem, your thesis. You establish a reasonable, ethical, knowledgeable tone here by showing the reader your familiarity with several issues involved.

The introduction should also outline in detail exactly what you are proposing. *Explain* how your plan will work, define key terms, who will do what, how it will be funded, what the timetable or stages are. Before you defend it, show the reader exactly what you propose. A complex plan may require several paragraphs to explain. Don't skimp here!

The **main supporting evidence** should be arranged tightly, one paragraph or two perhaps for each main supporting idea and the paragraphs filled out with examples, facts, appeals to value, and logic that support the idea. In papers of three to five typed pages, you should have room to develop three to four supporting ideas. In papers of one to two pages, two supporting ideas may be all you can support in depth.

To outline, list the main arguments and fill in support from brain teasers under each. Try several scratch outlines until your main headings are crisp and distinct. The Roman orators believed support should start strong and end strong and that the less strong arguments should be in the middle. Their rule of thumb: Second strongest argument comes first, strongest comes last, and the others in the middle. If you have a flimsy argument, put that in your wastebasket.

▲ **PRACTICE 12-15:** Drawing on your notes from other practices, make a scratch outline of your main supporting ideas for your topic in Practice 12-2 or Practice 12-3.

The **refutation section** comes next in the paper. After raising your main supporting ideas, take time to consider one or two major objections someone might have against your views or proposal. Some people may ask "Why should I attack my own case?" Why indeed? Well, in a written persuasive paper, as contrasted with a debate, you have total control over the presentation of ideas; there is no one else who can raise questions about your ideas—*except the reader!* And believe me, when someone is trying to persuade a person, she or he will raise objections. Most people love to find reasons why things cannot be done. Hiding weaknesses in your position won't work with a good reader. So be honest. Also, if you don't consider objections, chances are good you'll get carried away and end up with something superficial or full of holes. By considering objections, you can modify and improve your ideas to be more convincing. It's not only honest but in your best interest as an arguer and will help you improve your ideas. As John Locke once observed, "To judge other men's notions before we have looked into them is not to show their darkness, but to put out our own eyes."

In the refutation section, **one strategy is to show how the objection is flawed.** You must state opposition ideas with full honesty—so it would satisfy the opposition. Present these as valid questions, not as pesty troublemakers. Then, pinpoint *fallacies* in the objection, correct *"facts"* the objection may have mistaken, or question the *values* in the objection. In other words, the same brain teasers used to create support can also create refutations to an objection.

Suppose you have written an essay defending television, saying it contributes much to American culture and is a great educational tool. In your refutation section, you must consider objections people might have to your view. One objection would be that television watching has caused a decline in children's ability to read. This contradicts your claim of television's educational value. To be an honest arguer, you might point out that children do seem to watch television more than they read books; perhaps you might acknowledge that reading scores on standard tests have declined steadily in the past 15 years. How do you refute this now? Begin by seeing if the objection falls into a logical fallacy. Faulty cause and effect, for instance, seems to apply. Just because a decline in reading scores followed an increase in television watching does not prove one caused another. We have had Republican presidents most of the past 50 years; can we claim *they* caused a decline in reading scores? Of course not. In refuting, you should also suggest possible causes of the decline other than television. Perhaps the schools aren't teaching reading the best way; perhaps school discipline problems disrupt the teaching of reading; perhaps the lack of family togetherness (reading aloud after supper, discussing the newspaper) has contributed. Perhaps today society as a whole values reading less.

Question the facts. Perhaps the reading tests are outdated. Do the lowest test scorers watch the most television or do the best readers also watch television? You can get examples from your classmates or perhaps do some quick research. You can also *question the values* behind the objection. You might argue it's too easy to blame a machine for our problems as a society when we ought to blame ourselves for not working hard enough to learn, support, and teach reading.

A second way of handling a refutation is to concede some truth to the objection. "Television has probably contributed somewhat to a decline in reading ability. However . . ." *Then* writers usually say despite this drawback, there are too many good reasons to let this one objection stand in the way. This is often the only solution where there is no compromise possible, usually due to moral issues. If you were in favor of allowing abortions, for instance, you may have to concede that aborting a fetus really is the taking of a human or potentially human life. You might even acknowledge this would be wrong in a perfect world, but that the misery an unwanted or deformed child endures is worse yet.

Another type of concession offers compromises. People who are against abortions, for instance, might reluctantly agree that a woman in danger of dying in childbirth may be granted an abortion. But they should probably add that the principle of the sanctity of human life is still not compromised—that the taking of a life is to save a life.

The refutation section of a persuasive essay is perhaps the most important; it establishes your integrity as a writer, it forces you to consider your thesis more deeply, and it gives you the chance to make your argument even stronger. Refutation may be placed in a separate section of the essay, or you may handle it as objections might be raised against your supporting points.

▲ **PRACTICE 12-16:** Raise two objections to one of these proposals (from Practice 12-11) and then see if you can refute the objections through logical fallacies, facts, or values:

- The United Nations ought to command a permanent, powerful military force.
- Evolution should be the only creation theory taught in public schools.
- Churches should pay property taxes.
- The Internet must be censored for pornography and dangerous information.

▲ **PRACTICE 12-17:** What two major objections might someone raise to your position in Practice 12-2 or Practice 12-3? Refute them with logic, values, or facts; concede; or compromise.

The **conclusion** in persuasive writing can be a simple reaffirmation of your thesis, but it's usually better to look forward. You might paint a picture of the world in which your plan is enacted, or you might paint a picture of how less effective plans than yours would affect people's lives. Or you might end with a dramatic statistic or example.

Highlights of Chapter 12

- To find a persuasive topic, use a bug list, fantasy, or ask questions. To develop your argument, use the special brain teasers for persuasion, making a list of facts (including all the examples, statistics, and hypothetical examples you can think of, as well as from research you do) and making a list of values supporting your proposal. To develop the refutation, you need to see from alternate viewpoints and then use fallacies, facts, and values to break down the objections.

- The traditional order for persuasive writing is introduction, support, refutation, and conclusion.
- While drafting your persuasive paper, write a concrete, problem-solving introduction, adopt a reasonable, honest tone (be a host, not a preacher), speak to your audience, and visualize statistics and examples.
- In revising your persuasive paper, ask if the thesis is clear, if there is sufficient support, if you fall into any logical fallacies, if your audience would object to anything, and if you are being fair and reasonable. Test your word use to qualify generalizations and eliminate extremist language.

Writing Suggestions and Class Discussions

1. a. Make a list of five topics you could develop into persuasive essays. Try for a mix of personal, career, and social issues. Choose topics that matter to you.
   b. Develop one of these into a proposal, explaining your plan.
   c. Use several brain-teaser lists to develop supporting ideas and details. Begin developing a refutation idea.
   d. Order the essay in a scratch outline.
   e. Draft and revise the essay.
2. Read the letters-to-the-editor section of several papers and pick out an example of a letter with an appealing tone and a letter whose tone put you off. Explain why one works and why the other doesn't. Bring the letters to class.
3. Write an introductory paragraph for a paper on teenage sex. Your job is to show the reader how difficult the problem is to solve and also how important it is to solve. Establish a tentative thesis by the end of the paragraph.
4. List a page of statistics, examples, and hypothetical examples that could be used to support one of these theses:
   - Baseball is America's most exciting game.
   - Most white people have little idea what subtle discrimination most minorities suffer in an average day.
   - The rules of normal life are suspended once you enlist in the armed services.
   - Raising a child isn't as sweet as many people believe.
   - High school is a time of continual humiliation for many students.
   - Old age can be the best time of a person's life.
5. a. Make a list of the *ten* values you hold highest. This will be a brain-teaser resource for persuasive papers.
   b. Use this list to support or refute the following proposals:

"The government should bring all children of American servicemen and Vietnamese women to this country and provide homes and education for them."

"Gay or lesbian teachers should not be hired in elementary schools."

"Public television stations ought to be supported by a special tax of $50 on all television sets sold."

6. What *values* would you use to support these two statements?

"I am a citizen of the world."

—*Socrates, Greek philosopher*

"I have no responsibility to save the world."

—*Richard Feynman, Nobel Prize winner in physics*

7. Write examples to illustrate five fallacies. These can be real or made up. Label each example with the fallacy it demonstrates.

8. Pick out a magazine or newspaper advertisement, and write a paragraph explaining a fallacy in logic in the ad.

9. If you could change one historical event, what would it be? For examples, have Jesus not be crucified or warn the United States of the surprise attack on Pearl Harbor. Speculate on the hypothetical effects this change would have; then defend your change by appeals to value.

10. Write a response to an essay read in your reading text. Respectfully disagree with the author. In your introductory paragraph, accurately and fairly present the author's views; then work on refuting logic, facts, and/or values.

11. Write a letter to persuade your mother you really are working hard at college. Help her visualize the amount of work you're doing by making the statistics (number of pages read, papers done, hours studying, and so on) more visual. (1 paragraph)

12. Write a one-page letter to yourself, persuading yourself to reform some habit or trait you know is wrong. Be sure to consider a refutation.

13. Write a one-page persuasive essay on some subject of college policy. You will be expected to send a copy to the student newspaper.

14. Write a letter persuading a company to change its television advertisement that you find offensive. Address it to the Public Relations Department and provide a stamped envelope so your professor can mail it.

15. Write a newspaper or Internet advertisement to sell a product you like. Use facts, values, and logic, and be ethical.

16. Write a letter to any bureaucratic official, persuading him or her to change some policy or activity you don't like.

17. Write a proposal to your employer to solve a company problem. After revision, send it to your supervisor.

18. Write a proposal of your own—some new idea that would solve a current problem—and defend it.

19. The United States has just discovered a $100 billion vein of gold on federal property and Congress is debating whether to use the money (1) for increased antiterrorist units; (2) to lower the national debt; (3) for space exploration; or (4) to feed starving people in developing nations. Use Maslow's list of needs/values and make up a *list of arguments* based on those values for the plan you would support.

20. Read and discuss the sample student persuasive writings in Chapter 15.
21. Write a job application letter for yourself. Apply for an actual job you want now or imagine one you will want after graduation. Honestly sell yourself by referring to your main accomplishments, skills, experience, and personal qualities. If there is an obvious refutation (your lack of experience, for instance), answer it.
22. Group Activity: Open Hearing. The class will be divided into four groups. Each will develop its own proposal to solve a local or college problem, doing research and brain teasing for supporting facts, values, and logical arguments. Each group will present its plan to the rest of the class in an open hearing for feedback: refutations, suggestions for additional research, new ideas. Then each student will write a persuasive paper on the topic.
23. Group Activity: Bring to your peer group a thesis and two or three main supporting ideas for a persuasive paper. Each member of your group will role-play a person or group who is likely to have a strong view about your proposal and express how that person or group might argue for or against your thesis.
24. Group Activity: Predict the arguments the following groups would make about this proposal: "The Internet must not be censored in any way."
    - A parent of school-age children
    - A Chinese pro-democracy leader
    - A white supremacist militia man
    - An FBI official
    - A wheelchair-confined person

Sample Student Persuasive Letter

```
                                          22 Anyplace Road
                                          Rushville, NY 14544
                                          June 14, 2000

Eileen N. Iannuzi
Director of Student Loans
Sallie Mae Corporation
Loan Servicing Center
Box 352
Waltham, MA 12534

Dear Ms. Iannuzi:

Recently while contacting your agency concerning the

status of my loan, I was told by several unknown voices,
```

anecdote to draw interest

"No, I'm sorry. We have no record of that conversation taking place that day. . . . We can't release any information to you unless you are the authorized party . . . I'll send you another form immediately." These nameless voices who know little about my account create a frustrating communication barrier almost every time I call.

thesis

I would like to suggest three changes to increase cooperation and communication between the loan holder and the Loan Servicing Center.

point 1

First, please consider documenting all calls concerning an account, so your representatives will know more about the callers. I have called the center many times to inquire about changes in my loan since Chase Manhattan transferred my loans to Sallie Mae. Consistently being told there was no record of any previous conversations with your agents irritates me. Documenting the date, time, and matter of each call could eliminate further confusion and frustration for both your agents and the loan holders.

point 2

Second, you should establish <u>joint accounts</u> for loan holders so other family members can receive information. For example, I have called several times to check on my parents' loan, since I will be the one to pay it back. But I am often told no one except my father can receive certain account information. Your representatives have an obligation to keep financial information private; yet the loan holder could sign a release of information to other parties. The company would benefit by not having

refutation 1

to wait so long to receive important papers when other parties are involved.

Finally, why not assign one agent to each account? Having one agent follow an account would decrease mix-ups and lost information. Within the past six months, I have spoken with a dozen different agents concerning my loans. Frequently, because these agents know little about my account, they just send me another form to fill out. One authorized agent with knowledge could check his or her records for definite answers.

point 3

I recognize Sallie Mae handles a tremendous number of loans and can see how easy it might be to confuse, misplace, or lose valuable information. These ideas might help. The cost would be minimal to activate these ideas. You would lower mailing costs since there would be fewer forms sent out, and hours spent on the phone would be drastically reduced.

refutation 2

The growing cost of higher education continues to astound college students, and loan agencies like Sallie Mae that relieve the pressure need to be more efficient. Open lines of communication between agents and loan holders, joint information request forms and recorded conversations could help eliminate confusion and frustration and give peace of mind to worried college students. Thank you for your time and consideration.

conclusion

Sincerely,

Amy Meritt

Amy Meritt

Commentary

Introduction: The anonymous, bureaucratic voices draw us into the paper. The thesis in paragraph 2 is direct, but unspecific. We must read the entire letter to learn her three points. So I'm glad she uses clear markers like "second" to keep us on track. Her plan could be more specific in point 1—how would these calls be documented? Tapes? Notes written by the agent?

Tone: The author is "irritated," yet avoids abuse or sarcasm. She makes "suggestions," not demands.

Ideas: Is it a fresh idea? I'd never heard of this problem. But as a topic, I wonder how many people aside from students with loans will be interested.

The audience: It is directly targeted and several times she shows sympathy for the corporation.

The number of arguments: Three points and a refutation are fine for a short letter. The power of the arguments was good, but not highly creative. Why not computer access?

Details: Supporting facts: Her support needs more "oomph." Perhaps add an example from a friend's experience?

Visualization of facts: Recreating actual conversations makes her reader see better.

Values appealed to: cooperation, communication, efficiency, accuracy, economics, and peace of mind. I particularly like the way she stressed that the loan company and students' interests are linked through shared values.

Logic: I saw no blatant fallacies. She might have fallen into sentiment (parading her suffering), but doesn't. She avoids unqualified generalizations by saying, "*almost* every time I call," (not "every time") and "voices who know *little* about my account" (not "*nothing* about my account"). I'd ask her to specify how often she received the runaround—to prove it's not hasty generalization.

Refutation: The essay raises two refutations, but only the first is well answered. In paragraph 4 she concedes that "your representatives have an obligation to keep financial information private." She breaks this objection by suggesting her father be allowed to sign a release and by appealing to efficiency (the corporation would receive forms faster if the author could fill them out).

The next-to-last paragraph acknowledges the "tremendous number" of loans the corporation handles. She's polite, but has not deeply visualized an agent's job. Could one agent remember details of several thousand loans? I suspect these telephone agents don't stay long on this job—would she be dealing with new people anyway just from turnover? Wouldn't delays be longer if you had to get to just one agent instead of the first open line?

The strongest aspects of this essay are its tone and organization.

I'd suggest building up the details and going deeper into the second refutation.

Sample Persuasive Essay

HOMOSEXUALS ADOPTING CHILDREN

Kerry Burton

In some states gays and lesbians are allowed to marry legally. In this country, homosexuals should be free to live as they choose, but children should not be involved. Homosexual couples, married or not, should not be allowed to adopt children.

Even in our modern age, homosexuality is still taboo. People laugh and say, "God created Adam and Eve, not Adam and Adam." When Ellen Degeneres, the sitcom actress, came out of the closet, it was a big deal, a TV "event." But homosexuals adopting kids is more serious. A study was done by British researchers to see if there was a significant difference in the sexual orientation of kids raised by homosexual versus heterosexual parents. They monitored 46 young people over 16 years. Among the lesbian mothers, 23 kids were straight and 2 gay. Among heterosexual mothers, 21 kids were straight, none gay (Dunlap 15). This could be interpreted two ways. If you do not support homosexuals as parents, those two kids who turned out gay are significant. When kids are raised with gay parents, that's what they see and what becomes normal to them. But in our society, homosexuality is not normal. If you support homosexuals adopting kids, you might think two kids out of 46 is not significant and may be what you'd find if all the kids were raised by heterosexual parents.

Everywhere you turn, people are saying how wrong homosexuality is. One of the biggest reasons I think it is wrong is that kids need a mother and a father. Sometimes it can't be helped if kids grow up without a mother or father, but with homosexuals adopting kids, it can be helped. Times are hard enough with the social issues today's kids must cope with: popularity, peer pressure, drugs, alcohol, and violence. Why would any homosexual adult add to a child's pressure by adopting him or her? Imagine the ridicule that kid will endure in school. In one story I read, a mother had to give up her son for adoption. But when she discovered that her son was going to be adopted by a gay couple, she tried to reverse the adoption. She said, "Every child needs a mother and a father" ("Mother" 8). For this reason and others, adoptions by homosexuals are prohibited in Florida and New Hampshire ("Mother" 8).

This issue is difficult and controversial. Many studies prove that you do not have a choice to be gay; it is already built into your DNA when you are born. It would not matter if you are raised by straight parents, gay parents, or a pack of wolves--there would be no influence on your sexual orientation. One might also ask if it really matters if a kid has a mother and a father as long as the kid is truly loved. If a homosexual couple loves a child unconditionally and wants it strongly, they should make excellent parents. Many kids today do not have two parents who love them like that. Perhaps a homosexual couple could substitute a friend or family member to supply the missing role of the opposite sex. Of course those homosexuals who do get pregnant or get someone pregnant should be permitted to raise their biological children.

But only heterosexuals should adopt kids. A kid's life is tough these days. Why should we make it harder on them? It's not fair to do it for the selfish reason of wanting a child.

WORKS CITED

Dunlap, David W. "Homosexual Parents Raising Children."
   New York Times 7 Jan. 1996, Sec. 1: 15.

"Mother Fights Son's Adoption by Homosexuals." New York
   Times 1 Jan. 1994, Sec. 1: 8.

Discussion

Evaluate this essay as persuasion, using the **peer review checklist** on the following page as your guide.

✓ **PEER REVIEW CHECKLIST FOR PERSUASION**

Author: _____

Author should underline the proposal or position.

Author's intended audience (explain background if necessary):

_____

One concern or problem the author has with the paper is:

Reviewer: _____

	STRONG	AVERAGE	WEAK
INTRODUCTION: Grabs my attention			
Raises problem			
Thesis proposal is clear			
Plan is detailed			
TONE: Respectful, open-minded			
IDEAS: Thesis is a fresh idea			
Ideas target the audience			
Number and power of arguments			
DETAILS: Supporting facts			
Visualization of facts			
Appeal to values			
Logic			
REFUTATION: A major objection is raised and answered			
DOCUMENTATION: Sources are credited			

Respond to the author's concern:

The strongest part of this paper is:

Here are two things you might work on in revision:

1.

2.

CHAPTER 13

The Literary Essay
and Review

In every work of genius we recognize our own rejected thoughts.

RALPH WALDO EMERSON

Men take possession of art as a means of covering their nakedness
a little.

PABLO PICASSO

During college you will probably be asked to write papers about literature—poems, plays, fiction, or essays. Why? Partly to practice critical thinking and writing. But also because literature's great works often fully express our own unborn or rejected ideas. Writing about literature not only teaches us how the best writers write; it helps develop thoughts we have not been able to ripen alone. Literature's compact intensity often reveals patterns, emotions, and ideas clearer than in real life—which is watered down with trivia.

Exactly what is a literary essay? What does it do? First, it is *persuasive,* for you must convince a reader with evidence that your analysis is valid. It's *informative* as well because most literary essays strive for an objective tone and reveal something about the work, not just your feelings. Some require *research.*

At heart, the literary essay *explains* or *analyzes* a literary work. It is *not a summary.* Analysis seeks the *why* under the surface of a literary work. It discovers not-so-obvious organization, style, or ideas. Analysis creates a *thesis* to be proved about the work:

"*Moby Dick* is a book about hunting the God who runs this world, not about hunting whales."

"In Frost's poem 'Stopping by Woods on a Snowy Evening,' the horse represents civilization and order."

"*The Glass Menagerie* uses music and lighting to create a mood of fantasy."

Notice that each thesis requires supporting evidence from the literary work, and each says something *about* the work that the work's author does not state; it does not simply retell the story.

Here are the same three theses stated as vague summaries—theses that will lead you to "D" papers or worse:

"*Moby Dick* is about a man obsessed with killing a white whale."

"Stopping by Woods on a Snowy Evening" tells how a man is tempted to enter a beautiful woods instead of going home."

"*The Glass Menagerie*'s main character is a frustrated young man who lives with a bossy mother and a fragile sister."

A good thesis may also compare or classify several works:

"Modern detective stories still use Poe's tricks."

"Marlowe's *Dr. Faustus* and Goethe's *Faust* portray two very different men who sell their souls to the devil."

"We can see Sylvia Plath's changing view of death if we compare one early and one late poem."

▲ **PRACTICE 13-1:** Explain what a writer would have to do to prove each of the six good theses listed above.

Here are some preliminaries: Read the literary work *slowly* (fast reading is for newspapers). Allow the story or poem to lead you into its world. Suspend judgment at first. Say to yourself, "maybe what's going on here is . . ." rather than committing yourself to one idea. Read it again, marking passages that strike you as important or meaningful. These may not always be something you understand; in fact, sections that seem irrelevant or puzzling may be the most fruitful because you hope to explain the not-so-obvious.

At this point, an *idea* for a thesis may occur to you. The marked passages will be handy *details* for evidence. But if no thesis pops up automatically, common ways of thinking about literature can be applied as brain teasers. I'm going to suggest four major approaches to get ideas about literature:

- Use your own gut reactions.
- Try to discover the author's intention.
- Use one of several common critical perspectives.
- Explicate or analyze the words in the work.

Like most literary critics today, I lean toward the last approach and will spend more time focusing on that, but all four have virtues and in fact often combine in one paper.

 ## BRAIN TEASERS

1. Use your own gut reactions. Reading is a *collaboration* between writer and reader. Writers are helpless without readers' imaginations. They rely on readers to catch suggestions, to feel sad or afraid. Your response is part of the literature.

Start by listing your thoughts on a literary work. Simply freewrite impressions and observations. Begin by describing the emotions the literature made you feel, what you thought about after reading it, or how you might behave if you had been in the same situation as the main character. Reread the work's significant passages to restart the flow when you stall. If an idea sizzles, continue in paragraph form until the spell cools; then start new ideas.

The drawback to gut feelings is that they may not be in the work. If you enjoyed pet garter snakes as a child, for instance, you may allow this personal experience to misread a poem like Emily Dickinson's "A Narrow Fellow in the Grass." Dickinson's comment that snakes make her feel "zero at the bone" does not allow a cuddly snake interpretation. *You* may write such a poem, but Dickinson didn't. As I will point out in the fourth brain teaser, you must be able to *support* your gut reactions with evidence from the work.

2. Explain the author's intentions. This involves researching what authors have said about their work or biographical events that relate to the work. Poet T. S. Eliot attached more than 50 notes to "The Wasteland"—most readers need these comments and explanations to understand the poem. Another example is poet and novelist Thomas Hardy, who often wrote about chance and fate. Two biographical incidents may explain why.

Doctors pronounced Hardy stillborn at birth, but he was revived by a skeptical nurse. Weeks later, he was found with a poisonous snake sleeping beside him. These stories, vividly told to young Hardy, may have influenced the accidents and twists of fate that afflict his characters.

There are dangers in biographical analysis. A book does not necessarily reflect an author's life. Writers often disguise their personal lives, create purely from fantasy, or build a mythical public image of themselves. Robert Frost cultivated the kindly, simple New England farmer image, but his poetry was cynical and elegant. Ernest Hemingway's books are tough and antireligious, yet we know he was a soft touch for friends in need and often slipped into churches to pray. Robert Browning raised another problem. A popular English poet, Browning was asked late in life to interpret one of his first poems, "Sordello," because no one had ever understood it. Browning stared hard. "When I wrote 'Sordello,'" he said, "only God and I knew what it meant. Now only God knows." He could no longer explain his own poem! The point is that authors aren't omniscient about their writing. Their intentions—if we can really discover them—may strike readers quite differently. It's perfectly reasonable to disagree with an author's interpretation of her own work—*if* you can prove the words support your view. If you do find an author's life or philosophy relevant to the work, you must also show evidence from the work. Most professors will be uneasy with a totally biographical interpretation of a literary work, but some connections may help develop your ideas.

3. Condsider critical perspectives on literature. Like biographical interpretations, these ways of thinking step outside the strict boundaries of the text. They relate the literary work to ideology or social issues. Here are some common ones:

- **Political perspective.** You can interpret literary works as expressions of common social problems. John Steinbeck's *The Grapes of Wrath* or *In Dubious Battle,* for instance, can be interpreted as attacks on capitalism during the Depression and as portraits of the struggle to establish labor unions. Your paper could discuss the accuracy of Steinbeck's portrayals of history or the new ideas he created for social justice. Edward Abbey's novel *The Monkey-Wrench Gang,* which advocates sabotaging bulldozers, driving spikes into trees (to ruin saw blades), and blowing up dams, inspired the "Earth First!" group that actually does some of these things. A historical approach could compare Abbey's ideas and Earth First's or debate the ethics of his philosophy as expressed in the book.

- **Feminist perspective.** You can evaluate literary works' portrayal of women. Shakespeare often gets credit for creating smart, witty, independent, strong women like Portia but criticized for paper dolls like Ophelia who falls apart or for shrews like Kate who is "tamed" into meek obedience by her loudmouthed oaf husband. Or, as some critics suggest, has Kate learned to play along with male egos in public so she can be free in private? Your paper can evaluate or define how women and gender roles are handled in the work.

- **Ethnic perspective.** Mark Twain's *Huckleberry Finn* has come under attack lately for its portrayal of African Americans. After an explosion, someone asks if anyone was killed. A boy replies, "No . . . only a nigger." Was Twain a racist or using irony to attack racism? Twain's life, we are fairly sure, showed respect and love for African Americans, and most critics believe he wanted to make white readers feel the ugly horror of racism. To write a paper on this topic, you would have to dig up ethnic references from the book and use them to support a thesis. Shakespeare's portrayal of the Jew Shylock in *The Merchant of Venice* has been considered anti-Semitic. Your paper could gather references in the play, research the way Jews were seen and treated in Shakespeare's day, and draw comparisons to current literature.
- **Other perspectives.** Critical perspectives give you new ways to think about a literary work. Indeed, *any* belief system can be a brain teaser. You can analyze any literary work from a Christian, Hebrew, Hindu, or Muslim perspective. Or from a psychological or sociological perspective. All are brain teasers that open up ideas and angles to write from.

   The danger of critical perspectives is that you may distort the literary work to make it fit your idea. Freud's Oedipal theory applied to Hamlet—a latent sexual attraction toward his mother—is a notable exaggeration. As with biographical interpretations, you must return to the words in the text for supporting evidence.

   4. Focus on the words. Most literary critics today stress the work itself—the words and form. They say an author's atheism or comments made to friends and the work's connection to politics are secondary. They say because words create meaning, the analysis should focus on them. This school has convinced most other critics that *any* analysis should include some *explication of the text*. This means a close reading of the text in detail. Your entire paper may be a line-by-line interpretation of a poem or a selection from a short story or, more often, may explicate several short sections to show how the literary work supports your thesis. At the brain-teaser stage, work through key passages, explaining lines and tying ideas together. Here's an example from Thoreau's *Walden:*

> Time is but the stream I go a-fishing in. I drink at it; but while I drink I see the sandy bottom and detect how shallow it is. Its thin current slides away, but eternity remains. I would drink deeper; fish in the sky, whose bottom is pebbly with stars.

Brain Teaser: Time is like a stream. Okay. What are the fish? He also drinks from time--we all do. Time nourishes us--like food and water. But Thoreau sees through time and realizes it is "shallow" and "sandy." These aren't really negative words, but they do show how small and impermanent time is--which is ironic because time seems immense to most people. Time flows away and is thin because the present moment is all we can ever grasp and that's gone as soon as it comes. He compares time with eternity. He wants to be nourished by something deeper than time. The sky is like a giant stream, or ocean and stars like pebbles. Magnificent--the cosmic beach. This contrasts with the shallow, sandy stream of time. The sky at night does resemble a giant ocean, but he's talking about it on a deeper level, about the soul or heavens perhaps, finding nourishment from things that do not change and slide away but which are permanent. How do we grasp that, find it? Thoreau's two years at <u>Walden</u>, then, may have been a kind of fishing in time. Self and even nature are incredibly tiny fish.

A few observations on this process: My rough brain teaser opens up potential ideas but must be focused when I develop a trial thesis. Second, notice how long the explication is compared to the original. That's normal—works of genius compress much into a small space. Third, notice that a rough explication moves backward and outward for connections; you cannot simply plod through line by line. Tie ideas together.

BRAIN TEASERS FOR EXPLICATION

1. Theme. Don't settle for the first idea you see. Make a list of possible themes. Very few literary works have one underlined purpose. And often the first ideas that occur to you, as with any brain-teaser list, will be superficial. Also, don't think of theme as the ultimate point of a literary work. Literature is not a sermon in rhyme or dialogue, but an experience of life. There's more to it than a moral.

In its proper form a theme must be:

- a complete statement, not just a single word.
- stated in terms outside the literary work—stated in universal terms.

> **EXAMPLE:** The theme of *Romeo and Juliet* is that romantic love cannot exist in this corrupt world.

> **WEAK:** The theme of *Romeo and Juliet* is love. (What *about* love?)

> **WEAK:** The theme is that Romeo loves Juliet too much when their families are fighting. (This is not universal.)

How do you figure out what a theme is? There's no formula, but you might start by putting into words what the main character learns or why the work ends as it does. Start with a topic word like *jealousy* or *freedom* and try to say what the story or poem **demonstrates about the topic.**

2. Conflict. List the forces in tension in the work. In the quote from Thoreau, "time vs. eternity" is most obvious, but you could also list "earth vs. heaven" or "permanence vs. impermanence." In a short story or play, conflict occurs between characters, in a character's mind, or between a character and society or nature. List all the conflicts and fill them out with examples or evidence from the story. Then draw a conclusion about the conflict, and you have your thesis:

■ In *Walden* Thoreau struggles toward heaven but is unwilling to let go of earth.
■ In *The Sun Also Rises* the conflict between the matador and bull in the bull-fighting scenes reflects the conflicts among Jake, Brett, and Robert Cohn.

Your paper must then illustrate and prove its thesis with detailed evidence.

3. Character. Drama, fiction, and some essays and poems can be approached by thinking about character. Start with gut reactions, but also apply these questions:

■ What *consistent* qualities does a character have?
■ What *motivates* the character?
■ What *complexities* does the character show?
■ Does the character *change* and how?

To discover ideas, comment on each question and note details from the work for support. In *The Great Gatsby*, for example, Jay Gatsby is *consistently* polite, gentle, a big spender, mysterious, and somehow detached from real life. He's *motivated* most obviously by wealth and the desire for Daisy, the rich girl he loved but who married someone else. Underneath, there's also his motive of wanting to live in the past. He's *complex* because he has contradictions and inner conflicts: He has gangster pals and a poverty-stricken past and yet can be naive and gallant and really doesn't care about money except to attract Daisy. Does he *change?* Scholars have debated this point since the book was published. This brain teaser can supply ideas and details for any paper on fiction or drama.

4. Images. Most literature can be analyzed through its images and symbols—pictures and other sense details. Scan the work, listing images, searching for patterns and repetitions. In *Romeo and Juliet,* for instance, Shakespeare uses religious images (saints, prayer books, a shrine) to refer to Juliet to suggest both love's holiness and Romeo's melodramatic excess in Act I. In *The Great Gatsby,* the author repeatedly mentions the green light on Daisy's dock across the bay. Perhaps Gatsby wants a green "go" light from Daisy to pursue his romance, but this hazy, uncertain light may represent Daisy, who likes the youth and fun Gatsby brings her settled life but who is too selfish to risk herself. Like the light she is a tease. There's usually something significant behind a repeated image. Write down page references and your first interpretations.

5. Form/Style. Each genre or type of literature has its own principles of style and form. *Poetry* can be analyzed by looking at the rhyme, rhythm, sound devices, and format (sonnet, ballad, and so on). But you can't just *describe* rhyme pattern, for instance. Show how it relates to the overall meaning of the poem by having a *thesis* about the rhyme.

SAMPLE THESIS: e. e. cummings uses rhyme that doesn't quite match (off-rhyme) in "when serpents bargain for the right to squirm" to show that humans are not in harmony with nature.

Fiction can be analyzed through narrative point of view (who the speaker is and how much he or she knows of characters' thoughts) or by explaining how the time sequence is constructed. As with poetry, show how the form or style contributes to the story's overall effect:

SAMPLE THESIS: Nick narrates *The Great Gatsby* because Gatsby is too ignorant of himself and too blind to Daisy to tell the story honestly.

Drama's unique element is staging—the props, actors' gestures, lighting, the set, and visual effects. Show how these elements contribute to the overall themes/conflicts:

SAMPLE THESIS: The main sets in *Romeo and Juliet*—the street, the bedroom, and tomb—set up the three main conflicts in the play.

All literature can be analyzed for word choice and "tone" or "mood"— what we might call the writer's *attitude* toward the subject:

SAMPLE THESIS: When e. e. cummings distorts ordinary, simple English words, he is showing his real theme: We ought to pay such close attention to the simple, basic things in life that they become strange and new to us again.

▲ **PRACTICE 13-2:** Read this poem by Robert Browning:

Meeting at Night

The grey sea and the long black land;
And the yellow half-moon large and low;
And the startled little waves that leap
In fiery ringlets from their sleep,
As I gain the cove with pushing prow,
And quench its speed i' the slushy sand.

Then a mile of warm sea-scented beach;
Three fields to cross till a farm appears;
A tap at the pane, the quick sharp scratch
And blue spurt of a lighted match,
And a voice less loud, through its joys and fears,
Than the two hearts beating each to each!

First reading: What's going on? Is a character or the author telling the poem? Any vocabulary you need to look up? First reactions?

Brain teasers: List the conflicts. Who is meeting and why is it so secret? List the images—what pattern emerges? Is there meaning in this? Regarding form, how do the two stanzas mirror each other? Listen to the sounds by reading the poem aloud, especially the end of stanza one and the middle of two. Does this poem have a theme?

After answering some of these, formulate a thesis you can defend in discussion with supporting evidence from the poem. Is it possible our close reading and interpretation will create ideas an author did not intend? Of course—although we are far more likely to underestimate a professional's rich use of words. The point of literary interpretation is not to hit exactly what an author meant to say, but to exercise and develop our minds to see and think more deeply and to help a reader see new possibilities of meaning in the literary work. Your interpretations will be legitimate as long as you can support your ideas with details from the literature.

 ## ORGANIZING LITERARY ESSAYS

Many approaches can lead to a paper, but you must focus on an aspect of the work—a *thesis* like those shown already; only short poems or very brief stories can be adequately analyzed as a whole in a short paper. In developing a thesis, examine your notes for an idea *worth* proving—one with some complexity. In literature this often means recognizing *multiple truths*. Good vs. evil rarely occurs cleanly in life or good literature. More often we face a choice between two partial goods or two partial evils. Gatsby, Hamlet, Ahab, and Hester Prynne interest people because good and evil mix in them. An honest thesis embraces ambiguity. A categorical thesis suggests that either the poem or the interpretation is superficial.

> **WEAK:** Daisy in *The Great Gatsby* is an evil woman who doesn't care what harm she causes.

> **BETTER:** Daisy causes much evil from weakness, fear, naïveté, and selfishness.

> **WEAK:** Ahab in *Moby Dick* is a lunatic, pure and simple.

> **BETTER:** Ahab may be crazy, but it's a magnificent, sane madness.

After focusing your thesis, assemble evidence from the literary work—quotes, incidents, details of character—whatever interesting, relevant bits you have combed from reading, brain teasers, or research. Place like material together until you have solid outline headings.

 ## THE DRAFT

A good way to start a literary essay is to explain why your thesis is important or puzzling. This should lead to your support. During drafting, constantly clarify and support your ideas with quotes from the literature. Explicate to *show* how it supports your thesis. Don't fall into summary. Strive to see deeper into each quotation used.

The following is a nice example of a student assembling evidence to build a point. "Revelation," a story by Flannery O'Connor, is about an older woman, Mrs. Turpin, who feels morally superior to other people. While in a doctor's office, a young woman, Mary Grace, grows upset with Mrs. Turpin and finally throws a book at her and calls her "an ugly old wart hog from hell." The girl has a seizure, so Mrs. Turpin tells herself the girl was crazy and the ugly one. But Mrs. Turpin's superiority is shaken, and she has a vision of being one of the last summoned to heaven. The student's introduction asserts that Mary Grace is not a lunatic but "a manifestation of a supernatural being representing goodness or oppressed suffering," and that Mrs. Turpin, although she represents herself as a charitable, God-fearing woman, may be evil. In this section, the student supports her idea of Mary Grace as supernatural force:

The most obvious clue that something supernatural is going on is the end when Mrs. Turpin watches the parade of souls going to heaven. However, the whole work is peppered with symbols representing supernatural things, beginning with the title, "Revelation." The "Grace" in the girl's name could be religious imagery suggesting goodness. Then there's this description of Mary Grace: "She was looking at [Mrs. Turpin] as she had known and disliked her all of her life--all of Mrs. Turpin's life, it seemed too, not just the girl's life" (121). The idea that the girl's hate goes back before her mortal life began hints that Mary Grace is not simply a mortal, sensitive teenager. An examination of the waiting-room scene shows that Mary Grace flares up angrily when Mrs. Turpin merely thinks evil thoughts. An example is when Mrs. Turpin is thinking about how white trash are beyond help:

> All at once the ugly girl turned her lips inside out once again, her eyes fixed like two drills on Mrs. Turpin. This time there was no mistaking that there was something urgent behind them. (123)

If Mary Grace were mortal, her flare-ups, dirty looks, and scowls would be limited to those times that Mrs. Turpin glares at someone or says something nasty. But if she represents the spirit of God's intention that we live in harmony, her anger would rise against the oppression and ridicule in Mrs. Turpin's mind.

—Marjorie Pixley-Ketzak

Copy **quotations** accurately. If three lines or less, incorporate them into your paragraphs. Should you quote poetry this way, you must use a slash to indicate the actual line ending as in this example from Marvell's "To His Coy Mistress": "Had we but world enough, and time, / This coyness, lady, were no crime." If a quote is more than three lines, set it off like this selection from Tennyson's "Ulysses":

> The lights begin to twinkle from the rocks;
> The long day wanes; the slow moon climbs; the deep
> Moans round with many voices. Come my friends,
> 'Tis not too late to seek a newer world.

The lines are *indented* ten spaces for both poetry and prose, and *no quotation marks* are used. Some people double-space all indented quotes and others stick to the older practice of single spacing. See Chapter 16 for punctuation of tag lines for quotations. Try not to pour on quote after quote. Quote the best, paraphrase the rest. (For documentation of quotations, see Chapter 14.)

REVISING LITERARY ESSAYS

Revise for ideas first. Does your thesis still fit what you wrote? Some parts may have to go, or the thesis may need to be rewritten. Have you wrenched the literary work's main idea out of line to make your point? Cut where you dwell on the obvious. Beef up interesting ideas treated too briefly.

Revise details. Too little support? Too many quotes? Are your explanations sharp and vivid?

Revise mechanics and style. Literary essays use the present tense to describe the work (after all, literature is immortal), so you would say, "Flannery O'Connor says . . ." even though she is dead and "said" it years ago.

THE REVIEW

Related to the literary essay is the review—of books, restaurants, plays, concerts, art shows, speeches, films, or any other event or work that can be judged by *standards of performance*. Like literary essays, reviews persuade readers through supporting details. If it was a bad dinner followed by a worse speech, describe the limp green beans and mushy potatoes as well as the speaker's bad jokes. Like a literary essay, a review can interpret the purpose or themes of its subject.

Reviews differ from literary essays, however, in several regards. First, **descriptive summary** *is expected.* Up to half of a review may inform readers accurately about the topic. Assume readers of literary essays are already familiar with the work being discussed, but a review must help readers sample the unknown. Second, **the review emphasizes** *evaluation.* Your purpose is to make a judgment of value and then support that judgment with evidence. As with any persuasion, make your **standards of judgment** clear. Specify what you mean by "good service" at a restaurant. Some people like a server to check on their needs every few minutes; others consider that pesky. In an art review, does "old-fashioned" art mean the red barn school of painting or anything that does not use lasers or computers?

Chances are good you will write reviews in your career and in college. In your career, you may be asked to review a new product your boss is considering buying or to review another employee's job performance. You will need to set up standards of performance and interpret how well they have been reached and will need specific, descriptive details to support your point. For a product, some standards might be:

- Efficiency
- Ease of use
- Price
- How necessary it is
- Safety

Can you add others? Under safety, for instance, you might point out that the new computer tends to give some employees a tan after a week's use. For a job evaluation, common standards of performance are:

- Amount of work done
- Quality of work
- Reliability
- Ability to work with others
- Initiative

What else would you add? You might outline your review with these headings, then comment on each with details.

You will likely review books or theories for college courses. Your psychology professor may ask you to contrast how behaviorist and humanist psychologists would deal with a teenage alcoholic and then evaluate which will succeed best. What should be the standards of success?

Although people don't usually write reviews of dates or parenting style, in your private life you can use the techniques of a review to help decide what car you want to buy or which college you want to attend. Prioritizing standards and a sharp eye for supporting detail can help you evaluate with more depth and clarity.

▲ **PRACTICE 13-3:** Make a list of *your* top five standards of performance for one of the following: art, restaurant, book, film, or theatrical event. Now apply these standards to one specific painting, concert, work, or performance.

Highlights of Chapter 13

- A literary essay explains or analyzes a literary work. It is *not* a summary. You aren't ready to begin until you have a thesis to be proved about the literary work.
- These four brain teasers can help you to a thesis:
  - Freewrite or list your own gut reactions.
  - Discover the author's intention through biographical research.

- Use a common perspective: politics, history, feminism, ethnic perspective, religion, psychology, and myth.
- Explicate the text itself. Most literary analysis today closely examines individual passages. You might limit yourself to one aspect: theme, conflict, character, images, or form.

- During the drafting of a literary essay, you must continually *prove* your thesis with evidence, so before starting, assemble a list of quotations and significant incidents from the work that support your idea. As you draft, explain these passages in detail.
- The review, like the literary essay, supports a judgment about someone else's work with evidence, but its scope includes performance or written work. It both summarizes *and* evaluates.

Writing Suggestions and Class Discussions

1. Write a review of a restaurant, film, art show, or other subject with performance standards. Make your standards clear, and support your opinion with specific details.
2. Write a review of your essays written so far for this course. Establish standards of performance and evaluate your work, quoting from past papers to support your points.
3. Write a job evaluation review of someone who works with you. Fairly and specifically evaluate their work, with supporting details. Conclude with a recommendation.
4. Read the sample student review in Chapter 15.
5. A peer group will research and analyze a literary work. One person each will (a) research the author's life and connect it to the work; (b) apply critical perspectives to the work, doing necessary research; (c) explicate theme; (d) explicate conflict or character; (e) explicate images and symbols; and (f) explicate style. The group will discuss and combine ideas and then report to the class.
6. Choose a literary work. Do preliminary brain teasers and turn in three possible thesis statements you might defend. After review with peer groups or professor, organize, draft, and revise the paper.
7. Compare and contrast works by two authors on the same topic (Wright and Walker on racism, Millay and cummings on love, for examples).
8. Study how one poet or fiction writer deals with a narrow topic (Yeats on escape, Lawrence on love, Hopkins on nature). Support your thesis with explication of several works and any other evidence you can find.
9. Six poems follow. Although from different historical ages and using different forms, all deal with the idea of time. Here are several ways you can use these poems to improve your ability to analyze literature.
   - Pick one poem and come to class with ideas to discuss about it. Formulate a tentative thesis.

- Look for similarities and differences among the poems. Consider theme, imagery used, and form. Have specific evidence from each poem to support your ideas.
- Research the author's life for one poem and see if you can draw some connections to the poem. Does the poem alone support your biographical interpretation?

POEMS FOR EXPLICATION AND DISCUSSION

Sonnet 73

That time of year thou mayst in me behold
When yellow leaves, or none, or few, do hang
Upon those boughs which shake against the cold,
Bare ruined choirs, where late the sweet birds sang.
In me thou see'st the twilight of such day
As after sunset fadeth in the west;
Which by and by black night doth take away,
Death's second self, that seals up all in rest.
In me thou see'st the glowing of such fire,
That on the ashes of his youth doth lie,
As on the death-bed whereon it must expire,
Consumed with that which it was nourished by.
    This thou perceiv'st, which makes thy love more strong,
    To love that well which thou must leave ere long.
                    —WILLIAM SHAKESPEARE

VOCABULARY *thou:* you; *mayst:* may; *boughs:* branches; *fadeth:* fades; *doth:* does; *perceiv'st:* understand; *ere:* before.

To the Virgins, to Make Much of Time

Gather ye rosebuds while ye may,
    Old time is still a-flying;
And this same flower that smiles today
    Tomorrow will be dying.

The glorious lamp of heaven, the sun,
    The higher he's a-getting,
The sooner will his race be won,
    And nearer he's to setting.

That age is best which is the first,
    When youth and blood are warmer;

> But being spent, the worse, and worst
>   Times still succeed the former.
>
> Then be not coy, but use your time,
>   And, while ye may, go marry;
> For, having once but lost your prime,
>   You may forever tarry.
>   —ROBERT HERRICK

VOCABULARY *ye:* your; *succeed:* follow; *coy:* shy or flirtatious; *tarry:* linger behind.

Ozymandias

> I met a traveller from an antique land
> Who said: "Two vast and trunkless legs of stone
> Stand in the desert . . . Near them, on the sand,
> Half sunk, a shattered visage lies, whose frown,
> And wrinkled lip, and sneer of cold command,
> Tell that its sculptor well those passions read
> Which yet survive, stamped on these lifeless things,
> The hand that mocked them, and the heart that fed:
> And on the pedestal these words appear:
> "My name is Ozymandias, king of kings:
> Look on my works, ye Mighty, and despair!"
> Nothing beside remains. Round the decay
> Of that colossal wreck, boundless and bare
> The lone and level sands stretch far away.
>   —PERCY BYSSHE SHELLEY

VOCABULARY *antique:* ancient; *visage:* face.

A Noiseless Patient Spider

> A noiseless patient spider,
> I marked where on a little promontory it stood isolated,
> Marked how to explore the vacant vast surrounding,
> It launched forth filament, filament, filament, out of itself,
> Ever unreeling them, ever tirelessly speeding them.
>
> And you O my soul where you stand,
> Surrounded, detached, in measureless oceans of space,
> Ceaselessly musing, venturing, throwing, seeking the spheres to
>   connect them,
> Till the bridge you will need be formed, till the ductile
>   anchor hold,
> Till the gossamer thread you fling catch somewhere, O my soul.
>   —WALT WHITMAN

VOCABULARY *promontory:* a peak of high land overlooking the sea; *spheres:* planets or stars; *ductile:* plastic or stretchable.

To an Athlete Dying Young

The time you won your town the race
We chaired you through the market-place;
Man and boy stood cheering by,
And home we brought you shoulder-high.

Today, the road all runners come,
Shoulder-high we bring you home,
And set you at your threshold down,
Townsman of a stiller town.

Smart lad, to slip betimes away
From fields where glory does not stay,
And early though the laurel grows
It withers quicker than the rose.

Eyes the shady night has shut
Cannot see the record cut,
And silence sounds no worse than cheers
After earth has stopped the ears.

Now you will not swell the rout
Of lads that wore their honours out,
Runners whom renown outran
And the name died before the man.

So set, before its echoes fade,
The fleet foot on the sill of shade,
And hold to the low lintel up
The still-defended challenge-cup.

And round that early-laureled head
Will flock to gaze the strengthless dead,
And find unwithered on its curls
The garland briefer than a girl's.

—A. E. HOUSMAN

VOCABULARY *chaired:* carried; *betimes:* early or promptly; *laurel:* a tree whose branches were woven into victory wreaths worn on the heads of ancient athletes; *rout:* crowd; *lintel:* top of a door frame; *challenge-cup:* trophy; *garland:* victory wreath.

Childhood Is the Kingdom Where Nobody Dies

Childhood is not from birth to a certain age and at a certain age
The child is grown, and puts away childish things.
Childhood is the kingdom where nobody dies.

Nobody that matters, that is. Distant relatives of course
Die, whom one never has seen or has seen for an hour,
And they gave one candy in a pink-and-green striped bag, or a
    jack-knife,
And went away, and cannot really be said to have lived at all.

And cats die. They lie on the floor and lash their tails,
And their reticent fur is suddenly all in motion
With fleas that one never knew were there,
Polished and brown, knowing all there is to know,
Trekking off into the living world.
You fetch a shoe-box, but it's much too small, because she won't
    curl up now:
So you find a bigger box, and bury her in the yard, and weep.

But you do not wake up a month from then, two months,
A year from then, two years, in the middle of the night
And weep, with your knuckles in your mouth, and say Oh, God!
    Oh, God!
Childhood is the kingdom where nobody dies that matters,—
    mothers and fathers don't die.
And if you have said, "For heaven's sake, must you always be
    kissing a person?"
Or, "I do wish to gracious you'd stop tapping on the window
    with your thimble!"
Tomorrow, or even the day after tomorrow if you're busy having
    fun,
Is plenty of time to say, "I'm sorry, mother."

To be grown up is to sit at the table with people who have died,
    who neither listen nor speak;
Who do not drink their tea, though they always said
Tea was such a comfort.

Run down into the cellar and bring up the last jar of raspberries;
    they are not tempted.

Flatter them, ask them what was it they said exactly
That time, to the bishop, or to the overseer, or to Mrs. Mason;
They are not taken in.
Shout at them, get red in the face, rise,
Drag them up out of their chairs by their stiff shoulders and shake
    them and yell at them;
They are not startled, they are not even embarrassed; they slide
    back into their chairs.

Your tea is cold now.
You drink it standing up,
And leave the house.

—EDNA ST. VINCENT MILLAY

Sample Student Literary Essay

STRUCTURE AND FEELING IN "CHILDHOOD IS THE KINGDOM WHERE NOBODY DIES"

Carrie Gaynor

"Childhood is the Kingdom Where Nobody Dies" by Edna St. Vincent Millay captivated me with its vivid images and emotional confessions. It defines what it means to grow up. Childhood is a vast place, a kingdom wrapped in the innocence that allows us to act as though time were on our side. But that all changes when the people who matter most to us are snatched away, along with the deception of security. When you grow up, you realize how exposed and vulnerable life is. In order to convey these feelings, Millay blends images with various structures.

The poem is presented in two parts. The first deals with what it means to live in the kingdom of childhood. Millay then creates visual images that intensify to an emotional climax. To support this progression, she starts with distant relatives, then comes closer to home with the family cat. In describing the distant relatives, Millay speaks in third person in a long, rambling structure. This makes it go fast and seem insignificant:

Distant relatives of course
Die, whom one never has seen or has seen for an hour,

[margin annotations: why she chose topic; thesis; outline overall approach in paper]

supporting quote

And they gave one candy in a pink-and-green striped
        bag, or a jack-knife,
And went away, and cannot really be said to have lived

page reference

        at all. (286)

Notice the matter-of-factness of the words and the
lack of emotion. A family gathers and <u>one's</u> great uncle

explication

brings a piece of candy. He has nothing to do with your
life, and his death is no event.

style analyzed by comparison

In the next stanza, Millay begins to draw the reader
into a comparison of sorts. <u>You</u> are home, and your cat,
full of life and fleas, lies on the floor, dead. And you
place the cat, now in rigor mortis, into a box and bury
it under a tree. You weep. Millay creates a personal
sense of loss by switching from third-person to second-
person narrative, directing the image at the reader:

You fetch a shoe-box, but it's much too small,
        because she won't curl up now:
So you find a bigger box, and bury her in the yard, and
        weep. (286)

explication of quote

The use of the box symbolizes the child's need to
expand her view of the world to match her experience.

The next stanza continues to make you feel words in
your belly. The rambling sentence plays with your adrena-
line. There is no ambiguity about what now defines childhood:

But you do not wake up a month from then, two months,

quote needs explication

A year from then, two years in the middle of the night

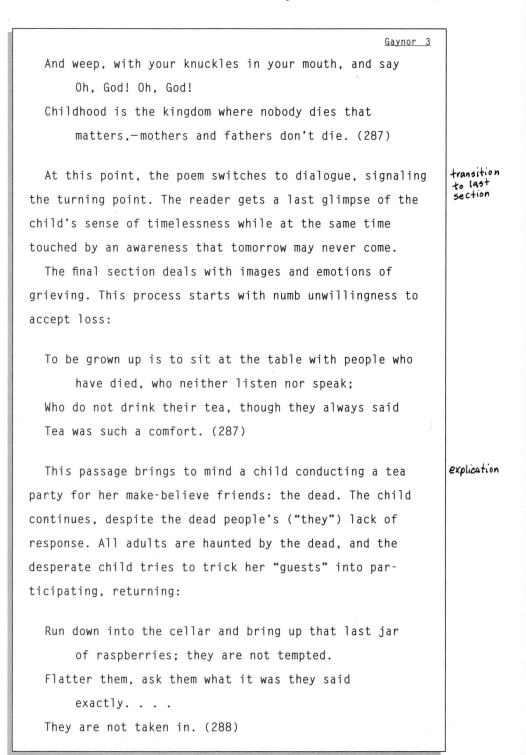

And weep, with your knuckles in your mouth, and say
        Oh, God! Oh, God!
Childhood is the kingdom where nobody dies that
        matters,—mothers and fathers don't die. (287)

At this point, the poem switches to dialogue, signaling
the turning point. The reader gets a last glimpse of the
child's sense of timelessness while at the same time
touched by an awareness that tomorrow may never come.

The final section deals with images and emotions of
grieving. This process starts with numb unwillingness to
accept loss:

To be grown up is to sit at the table with people who
        have died, who neither listen nor speak;
Who do not drink their tea, though they always said
Tea was such a comfort. (287)

This passage brings to mind a child conducting a tea
party for her make-believe friends: the dead. The child
continues, despite the dead people's ("they") lack of
response. All adults are haunted by the dead, and the
desperate child tries to trick her "guests" into par-
ticipating, returning:

Run down into the cellar and bring up that last jar
        of raspberries; they are not tempted.
Flatter them, ask them what it was they said
        exactly. . . .
They are not taken in. (288)

*transition
to last
section*

explication

These passive, rational attempts abruptly change to
aggression:

quotes
need
explication

> Shout at them, get red in the face, rise,
> Drag them up out of their chairs by their stiff
>   shoulders and shake them and yell at them;
> They are not startled, they are not even embarrassed.
>
>   (288)

conclusion

The final act of growing up is learning to accept what
is. The last stanza reflects the change from the absence of
any control to very careful control. Millay switches back
to a matter-of-fact tone as she ends the tea party. Time
has passed, the tea grown cold. The child stands. She is
no longer part of the delusion and leaves the house. Leaving the house suggests what being grown is: when one is
completely exposed, deprived of all security. The last
words are small, the last lines short, and they make the
reader feel that way--exposed at the end of the page.

WORK CITED

Millay, Edna St. Vincent. <u>Collected Poems.</u> New York:
   Harper & Row, 1956.

Commentary Based on Peer Review Sheet

Ideas: Insight. This essay has some wonderful depth of interpretation. Her
last paragraph asserts potent truths about childhood. Although the author
does not raise her personal experience, I sense the poem touched her.

Sticks to thesis: The opening prepares us for analysis of theme, but the second paragraph announces she will use a section-by-section analysis that combines structure and imagery. How about a sentence telling us that the structure and imagery support the theme she's discussing?

Details/Amount of support: Plenty. Every section is supported with several direct quotes and other references.

In-depth interpretation of quotes: At times the quotes fly too thick without explication. Just before the concluding paragraph there are eight lines of poem with only one line of explanation. In those quotes I'd like to know if the "cellar" and "raspberries" have deeper significance. A cellar is like a grave, and raspberries, once juicy live fruits, are now preserved there. Since she's been discussing living, dead, or dead-while-alive relatives, this must mean something. Generally, her paper has fine depth. For instance, she perceptively lays out the switch from the impersonal "one" to "you" and ties it to her thesis.

Organization: It's smooth with nice transitional markers ("In the next stanza," "At this point," and "The final section . . .") to help the reader.

Format: A fine model for handling quotes/citations.

Most creative interpretation: I'm impressed with how she blends idea and style. She shows how the relaxed, rambling sentences give way to abrupt, hysterical ones, reflecting the change in the child from calm to shock.

Adjectives to describe the essay: Careful yet passionate.

What else ought the writer explain? She ignores the scene in which the dead people sit at the table with the child. It's the boldest, most puzzling part of the poem to me. Are they memories? Ghosts? Living people who act dead? Wishful thinking?

Poem and Sample Student Literary Essay

Batter My Heart, Three-Personed God

Batter my heart, three-personed God; for You
As yet but knock, breathe, shine, and seek to mend;
That I may rise and stand, o'erthrow me, and bend
Your force to break, blow, burn, and make me new.
I, like a usurped town, to another due,
Labor to admit You, but O! to no end;
Reason, Your viceroy in me, me should defend,
But is captived, and proves weak or untrue.
Yet dearly I love You, and would be loved fain,
But am betrothed unto Your enemy.
Divorce me, untie, or break that knot again;
Take me to You, imprison me, for I,
Except You enthrall me, never shall be free,
Nor ever chaste, except You ravish me.

— JOHN DONNE

Vocabulary *o'erthrow:* overthrow; *usurped:* taken by force or trickery; *fain:* gladly; *betrothed:* engaged; *enthrall:* enslave.

THREE-PERSONED GOD

Nancy L. Galleher

In "Batter My Heart, Three-Personed God," the narrator addresses the three facets of God's Trinity: Father, Son, and Holy Ghost. The poem uses images relating to battle and capture to describe man's heart. For the narrator-- like all men--has been captured by God's enemy, Satan. The line, "I, like an usurped town to another due" (5), de-scribes this surrender. The word "usurped" means seized or taken possession of by force, wrongfully.

The poem separates the Trinity or "Three-personed God"(1) into three intertwined entities that struggle to redeem man's heart. Whenever God is mentioned in the poem, the words "You" or "Your" are capitalized. The line, "for You/As yet but knock, breathe, shine, and seek to mend" (1-2) describes the Son sent by God the Father to redeem man with tenderness and love. The words all suggest a gentleness embodied by the lamb of God. The word "knock" reminds me of a mural behind the altar in the church I attended as a child. It is a picture of Christ gently knocking on a gate to a lovely garden-- which symbolizes the door to man's heart. "Breathe" and "shine" are words of life. "Seek to mend" suggests the care and concern God the father has for man, which is why he sent his son. Man instinctively recognizes and loves his heavenly father in whose image he was created: "Yet dearly I love You" (9) and is desperate that God love him: "and would be loved fain" (9). He works hard to give God access to his heart: "I . . . Labor to admit You" (6), but he fails:

> . . . but O! to no end;
> Reason, Your viceroy in me, me should defend,
> But is captived, and proves weak or untrue. (6-8)

Man's heart is a prisoner of war, "captived" by the en-emy. "Proves weak or untrue" suggests betrayal under the pressure of captivity. Man has been given reason by his creator to govern his actions, just as a viceroy who

represents a king is expected to rule and carry out his
king's wishes. God expects man's reason to defend him
better.

In scripture, Jesus is compared to a bridegroom at
a wedding feast. He lived among men, died, and was resur-
rected by God to prepare the wedding feast at God's table
in heaven. Man's heart is often referred to as Jesus'
beloved or bride. With this in mind, the poet effectively
uses the image of marriage in these lines:

> But am betrothed unto Your enemy.
> Divorce me, untie or break that knot again; (10-11)

"Betrothed unto Your enemy" means promised in marriage to
Satan, which occurred when man first sinned in the Garden
of Eden. Man knows the only way this unholy relationship
can be severed is by divorce, which will "untie" or
"break the knot." Marriage is symbolized by the knot, an
intertwining of two souls. The word "again" refers to the
time when man's heart belonged to God alone, before it
was captured by Satan.

Man has been given the Holy Spirit to empower him to
wage war against Satan. The lines:

> That I may rise and stand, o'erthrow me, and bend
> Your force to break, blow, burn, and make me new. (3-4)

describe the bestowing of this gift. When Jesus ascended
to heaven, he promised his disciples a power to enable
them to carry on his battle against evil. At the Feast
of Pentecost, the force of the Holy Spirit sounded like
a strong wind blowing ("blow"); tongues of fire appeared
and touched every person there ("burn") and filled them
with the Holy Spirit ("make me new"). This empowers man
to do God's work and resist evil. Man's will must be
broken and the wall surrounding his heart penetrated.
This is suggested in the plea: "Batter my heart, three-
personed God" (1). "Batter" suggests ramming down barriers by repeated attacks that overwhelm and subdue. When
God "batter[s] my heart," He breaks those walls that have
kept Him out. The force increases in intensity from lines
two to four: "Knock" becomes "break," "breathe" becomes
"blow," "shine" becomes "burn," and "mend" becomes "make
me new." The narrator wants to be recreated, not just
repaired.

Man must be a servant--but to which master, God or Satan? He pleads:

    Take me to You, imprison me, for I
    Except You enthrall me, never shall be free,
    Nor ever chaste, except You ravish me. (12-14)

He recognizes that even though he knows which master he wants to serve, the only way he can be certain to serve God is to have his free will taken away and his soul captured. "Enthrall" means to hold or reduce to slavery, as well as to spellbind. However, man has been given free will and is continually asked to make choices about which master he will serve. The last line, "Nor ever chaste, except You ravish me"(14) creates two contrasting images. "Chaste" means pure, holy, and without sin. A person who is chaste is in control of his impulses and actions. The word "ravish," in contrast, implies being overcome by force or rape. How can a person become pure by such an act? The poet seems to suggest that the only way a man's heart can become pure is if his will becomes subdued. Then, and only then, will he be truly free of Satan's grip on his soul.

Discussion

Using the Peer Review Checklist for ideas, comment on the strengths and weaknesses of Nancy's analysis. What else did you see in the poem that she does not mention? What words or phrases might be taken in a different sense?

✓ **PEER REVIEW CHECKLIST FOR LITERARY ESSAYS**

Author: _____

I would especially like the reviewer to comment on:

Reviewer: _____

State the author's thesis as you see it. Author and reviewer should discuss the accuracy of this statement:

	STRONG	AVERAGE	WEAK
IDEAS: Insight into literary work			
Sticks to thesis			
DETAILS: Plenty of supporting evidence			
In-depth interpretation of quotes			
ORGANIZATION: Smooth and logical			
TRANSITIONS: Mark ideas			
FORMAT: Page citations for quotes			
Punctuation of quotations			

What was the most creative interpretation the paper made?

Respond to the author's request:

Use several adjectives to describe this essay:

What else about the literary work ought the writer explain to prove the thesis or to dig out its complexity? What questions do you have that are still unanswered after reading the paper?

✓ **PEER REVIEW CHECKLIST FOR REVIEW**

Author: _____

Question or problem for reviewer:

Reviewer: _____

	STRONG	AVERAGE	WEAK
IDEAS: Standards of performance are clear			
Depth/creativity of analysis			
DETAILS: Support for evaluation			
Visualization (vivid description)			
ORGANIZATION: Clear and logical			
TRANSITIONS: Mark ideas			
TONE: Reasonable			

Respond to the author's question:

What do you think is the best part of the paper?

What standards does the author seem to value most? What others might be used?

Is there anything the author ought to cover in more depth or to cut? Explain:

Offer a possible refutation to the author's evaluation (Hint: See the evaluation from the viewpoint of the person being evaluated):

Offer two other suggestions for the paper:

CHAPTER 14

Research

Written with
Christopher Otero-Piersante

When I slept, armies of footnotes marched across my dreams.

—TED MORGAN

Do not complain about the truth.

—I CHING

It's 2 A.M. Books are piled on the desk and floor. A thousand scraps of paper snow you in. Blank, fanned-out 3 × 5 note cards await entries. You've quoted so much, your paper will be one long footnote. You've been waiting for someone to return your most important book to the library, and you forgot to copy a source's publication dates and pray to the demon god of the Internet that the link will still be there tomorrow. In 12 hours your finished copy is due.

or

It's 2 A.M. Five weeks ago, the day your research paper was assigned, you typed this schedule:

WEEK ONE:	Do general reading—reference section
	Narrow topic choice
WEEK TWO:	Assemble books, magazines, and Web sites
	Join an online newsgroup
WEEK THREE:	Read sources and take notes
	Record bibliographic information
WEEK FOUR:	Weigh all evidence
	Decide on thesis
	Create outline
	Write rough draft
	Bring draft to peer group
WEEK FIVE:	Revise paper
	Type Works Cited list
	Print extra copy for security

Beside each item, as relentless as marching soldiers, checks appeared as weeks passed. *You* took all the books first, and there was time to contact the Web site owner, who updated the missing link. Your notes stacked aside, you're about to proof the paper. The only thing wrong, really, just nagging the back of your mind, is that your paper seems bland.

The first scenario is full of chaos, and the second is idealized, but overly mechanical. Although both are exaggerated, they are stereotypes that give research a bad reputation. If you learn to balance these two extremes, you might even enjoy research. You must use deadlines to keep you on track, but also allow yourself a little chaos to be creative.

 ## RESEARCH SKILLS: PROFESSIONAL, ACADEMIC, AND PERSONAL USES

Think of your career goals. If you become a financial advisor, you might research new stocks, investment trends, and inflation rates for your clients. As a civil engineer paving the courtyard of an apartment complex, you might need to learn about new tools or techniques to make your job easier or more creative. As a social worker, you might have to learn more about new medications for AIDS clients. It's important to enter the work force ready with information, but it's just as important to be able to discover information when you don't know it.

Think of your academic studies. Use your research paper to learn more about a topic that the class discussed superficially. Choose something your professors didn't cover, and you may stun them! If you have an interest in some aspect of your major not discussed in class, this is your chance to educate yourself. When your class doesn't directly relate to your major, create a connection. For example, if you're a computer science major taking a literature class, find a way to link the values of technology with the poems you're studying. If you're a psychology major in a history class, apply a leading theory of aggression to your studies.

Think of your personal life. A friend of mine who had been sick for the last two years learned that she had sarcoidosis, an noncontagious disease that affects people before they're 40. She suffered from labored breathing, sharp eye pains, and kidney stones. After five referrals, she finally was diagnosed with a disease that has no real cure except for time, and it might take up to 20 years. She immediately got on the Web and learned more about what she could do to ease some of her symptoms. She even provided her doctors with information about the disease.

A student who rented an apartment from her sister thought her sister was taking advantage of her by charging excessive rent, by barging in without knocking, and by not maintaining the place (it had broken windows, a loose door lock, and a mouse scuttling in the ceiling at night). Isabelle researched current housing regulations and wrote a formal complaint letter. She also used personal arguments—an appeal to sisterly love and a hint she would inform Mom and Dad, who lived in another city. The sight of the written facts and ideas prodded Isabelle's sister to action. "Now she knocks! She actually knocks!" Isabelle told the class.

 ## RESEARCH AND THE WRITING PROCESS

This chapter will give you enough information to write short research papers and introduce basic research methods. For papers over ten pages—especially in the sciences or psychology—you may need more guidance. Whatever length the research paper, though, it usually follows the same writing process as any other writing:

- Thinking
- Organizing
- Writing
- Revising

FINDING RESEARCH PAPER TOPICS

Choose a topic you care about. If the paper becomes a pointless exercise done just to get a grade, you've missed an opportunity to empower yourself. When professors assign a research paper, they encourage individuality and creativity—so seek it. Find the exciting example within the broad, bland topic. Remember this: In most cases, your reader cares about your topic only half as much as you do. Your enthusiasm will spread to your readers. Inspiration is as contagious as boredom!

Seek connections between your personal experiences and your class requirements. If your assigned topic for a history course is World War I and you're interested in cars and engines, research transportation technology during this era. If you love sports, study new sports emerging from World War I or games soldiers played. If your boyfriend is in the armed forces, you might research how wives and girlfriends handled loneliness or grief. Or you might research the way women military aides were treated. If you fear you're narrowing the topic outside the professor's limitations, simply ask.

Thinking is messy and redundant. You already know that narrowing the topic and creating a thesis is not as simple as the schedule at the beginning of this chapter suggests. Before, during, and after your research, refine and rewrite your topic and thesis. Keep a separate pad of paper nearby to allow new ideas to surface.

▲ **PRACTICE 14-1:** This exercise will be referred to throughout the chapter. Find at least two research topics that interest you inside three of these subjects (six topics total):

- Your own topic
- Criminal psychology
- Astronomy
- Blues music
- Children's literature
- Advertising

ESTABLISHING KEY RESEARCH QUESTIONS

Before you begin to research, ask questions you want answered. Finding the answers will be your research. For instance, suppose I decided to research the African roots of the blues. These preliminary questions occur to me:

- What features of African music are in the blues?
- How did slavery contribute to the blues?
- What stages did African music go through before becoming the blues?
- When did these stages occur?
- What African tribes had the most impact on the blues?
- What do the two sound like?

Key questions keep your focus on the important issues as you dive into research. But open yourself to new questions and scrap ones that grow stale or seem obvious.

Use other brain teasers to draw out what you already know. On the blues topic, a sense details brain teaser could record your impression of the music. Get a CD of African music and contrast it to a CD of the blues. Listen for similar riffs and refrains. Create a list of the different instruments used in each. Classify the African music into spiritual, festive, and folklore. Compare them to the different types of blues (e.g., Delta, Texas, and Chicago).

Be an active thinker. Figure out what's important. Keep asking "why" and "how" at each step.

▲ **PRACTICE 14-2:** For one of the topics in Practice 14-1, create a list of four key research questions, and do a half-page brain teaser to see what you already know.

 # LIBRARY RESOURCES: LIBRARIANS, BOOKS, JOURNALS, AND COMPUTERS

The library contains four main sources of information. The first source—often overlooked—are librarians. They can guide you through pamphlet files, computer indexes, microfilm, and the Web. Just a brief caution. To keep this primary resource on your side, come prepared with specific questions, not just a general topic like "war" or "music." The more specific you are, the better information you'll get. Do the obvious work *before* asking for help—check out basic references, card catalogs, and periodical indexes.

The Reference Section

The reference section includes dictionaries, encyclopedias, almanacs, and other books that summarize large bodies of information and provide raw facts and statistics. If you want to write on the dangers of importing Mideast oil to the United States, the *Information Please Almanac* will tell how many billions of barrels of oil the United States imports from a country. If you're researching the blues, you might go to an encyclopedia for a general history of the blues before writing your list of key research questions. However, don't rely on encyclopedias as main reference sources—they're too superficial for college papers. Here are some recommended reference books. Most can also be accessed through the Web (some provide free trial memberships):

General Background

- *Encyclopaedia Britannica* (www.eb.com)
- *Van Nostrand's Scientific Encyclopedia*
- *Encyclopedia of World Biography*
- *Occupational Outlook Handbook* (stats.bls.gov/ocohome.htm)

Facts and Statistics

- *Information Please Almanac* (United States, world facts; www.infoplease.com)
- *The Statistical Abstract of the United States* (www.census.gov?stat_abstract)
- *Rand McNally Commercial Atlas and Marketing Guide* (business statistics)
- *CIA World Fact Book* (www.odci.gov/cia/publications/factbook/index.html)

I recommend browsing in such books as *The Statistical Abstract of the United States*. Curiosity and a few minutes can dig up strong facts on almost any topic. If I were writing on gun control, I'd find this fact powerful: 68 percent of all murders in the United States are caused by guns; 2 percent are caused by human hands only (213). If I were writing on the death penalty, I would include that of the 299 people sentenced to death in 1996, only 15 percent have been actually executed (231).

▲ **PRACTICE 14-3:** For the previous practice topic you developed, list the reference works you'd use, the specific headings you'd search under, and the specific facts/statistics you'd like to find.

Finding Books

The card catalog, whether traditional or computerized, **only lists books your library has,** not all books written on the topic. Electronic card catalogs allow you to access other online libraries as well. Now study the sample online catalog card you might find under the subject of blues music on the opposite page.

How do you decide if you want to read this book?

- **Think about how closely the title relates to your topic.** This title looks good, but makes no direct connection to African origins of jazz.
- **Compare the number of pages in the book with the size of the topic suggested by its title.** A history of music in 400 pages will be more superficial than a history of the blues in 200 pages. This book is only 64 pages long, so it's bound to be superficial.
- **Think about the author's credibility.** Is this author an expert? I searched Amazon.com, an Internet bookstore, and the OCLC, an online reference to books in print, and found nothing else by Elmer. I'll remember this as I examine his credibility.
- **Check the date.** How important this is depends on your topic. Scientific and technological topics often must be published within the last five years to be up to date. Psychology considers ten years old to be out of date. In books about historical events or music, "recent" can mean something published 25 years ago. Elmer's book was published in 1999.
- **Check the book format.** This book is formatted for a child. But I'm not about to give up on it yet. Although it might be oversimplified, it may give me a quick overview of the history of the blues.
- **See if the source has an index.** An index helps you scan the book's subjects before you read the entire work. This book does have one.

- **Try to use the book to help you find more sources.** This book includes a discography (a list of popular musicians and titles) and a bibliography (a list of works the author used to write the book). Published in 1999, it might include some other contemporary titles, or it might identify important ones that have survived the decades. Referring to bibliographies saves you time researching. Why repeat someone else's research? This probably isn't a book I'd cite in my essay, but it could be solid start. Besides, you should always gather more books than you'll need, so you can choose from the best.

Author	Elmer, Howard
Title	**Blues**: its birth and growth/Howard Elmer.
Publisher	Rosen Pub. Group, 1999.
Paging	64 p.: ill (some col.); 25 cm.
Series Stmt	The library of African American arts and culture
Notes	Discograpy. p. 58–59 Includes bibliographical references (p. 60–61) and index.
Summary	Traces the origins of blues music, its evolution in the United States, and its influence on jazz and rock and roll.
Subjects	**Blues** (Music) History and criticism Juvenile literature. **Blues** (Music) History and criticism.
Format	Child

Full Status

Branch	Location	Date	Call Number	Status
EXT		05/20/99	j781.643 ELM	Not Checked Out
MGRW-E	Child	06/14/99	781.643 ELM YA	Not Checked Out
WHEAT		07/12/99	YA 781.643 E38b	Not Checked Out

For books worth scanning, write down the title and call number. When you find good books in the library stacks, cruise the adjacent books. Related books hang out together. If you're working online, you can print out bibliographic information—and use the back of the sheet for note taking.

To locate books not in your library, check *Books in Print,* which lists all books currently being sold, or visit the Online Computer Library Center (OCLC), a worldwide card catalog that connects 11,000 institutions with access to 22 million volumes. You can call up the complete books and articles from over 800 popular titles published since 1994. You can *read,* but not duplicate, the online texts. Search online bookstores like Amazon.com <www.amazon.com> or Barnes and Noble <www.barnesandnoble.com>. Write down the publisher and date, so you can ask the librarian to order a loan copy, which will take about a week to arrive.

▲ **PRACTICE 14-4:** Find two book titles for your topic from your library's card catalog and two from either *Books in Print*, the OCLC, or an online bookstore. You do not have to read the books, but do record complete bibliographic information.

Finding Magazine and Newspaper Sources

Why would you want magazine and newspaper articles if you have a book? Because, most new books are already one to five years old the minute they reach the bookstore. This is the time lag in writing, editing, and producing books. Magazines and newspapers are more current. Also, magazines can cover topics too small for books; so you may find ten or fifteen articles on blues musicians James Ingram or Bo Diddley but no book. Last, researchers can read many writers' ideas in magazine articles in the time it takes to read one book.

Periodical Indexes

Periodical indexes are catalogs for magazines and newspapers. They list all articles written on a topic, giving the author, magazine, date, and sometimes other information (abstracts, for instance, summarize the article). Because thousands of magazines exist, there are many indexes, each covering up to 400 magazines.

Choose the appropriate index for your topic. If you use the book versions you must examine the 1999 indexes for the war in Bosnia or the 1993 indexes for the attack on the Branch Davidian compound in Waco, Texas. Here are some major indexes and the dates they started:

- *Applied Science and Technology Index* (1958)
- *Art Index* (1929)
- *Business Periodicals Index* (1958)
- *Computer Literature Index* (1971)
- *Criminal Justice Abstracts* (1968)
- *Education Index* (1929)
- *Environmental Index* (1971)
- *Hospital Literature Index* (1944)
- *The Humanities Index* (1974)
- *The New York Times Index* (1913)
- *The Reader's Guide to Periodical Literature* (1900)
- *The Social Science Index* (1974)

The most commonly used general indexes are *The Reader's Guide* and *The New York Times Index*. *The Reader's Guide* lists all the articles written in over 200 magazines with the largest circulations—magazines like *Redbook*, *Time*, and *People*. Many of these magazines are thought provoking and carefully researched, but some are too lightweight for college research.

Use specialized indexes for more detailed and scholarly information. In-depth research on Michelangelo's paintings, for example, will more likely turn up in magazines listed in *Art Index* than in magazines listed in *The Reader's Guide*. *Hospital Literature Index* is not the place for general medical information on natural childbirth; however, if you are a nursing student writing a term paper on natural childbirth procedures, it will provide stronger sources than *The Reader's Guide*. *The Reader's Guide*'s articles give statistics and general information; specialized journals provide information on the experiments that produced the statistics. This is especially useful when you need to discuss the validity of the information you provide. In freshman English, *The Reader's Guide* and *The New York Times Index* may do quite well, but as you take upper-level courses, you'll need to know how to use specialized indexes. Here is a sample entry in the 1999 *New York Times Index* for the topic "The Blues."

```
Peter Watrous tribute to BlueNote Records, jazz label that
marks its 60th Anniversary; Bruce Lundvall, who revived
label in 1984, comments, interview; Photo. Jan. 10, II, 37:1.
```

This might have historical information because it covers 60 years, but because it does not immediately focus on the African roots of blues, it would be a low priority source. Let's look elsewhere now.

 # COMPUTER INDEXES TO MAGAZINES AND NEWSPAPERS

A wide variety of computer indexes are rapidly replacing bound indexes. What any library may have varies greatly, but here are six common computer indexes:

- *ArticleFirst!* (full-text articles from sources similar to those in *The Reader's Guide to Periodical Literature*)
- *Expanded Academic Index* (full-text articles and sources from magazines and Internet sources)
- *First Search* (humanities, business, and science indexes)
- *NetFirst* (resources for Web pages, listservs, and newsgroups)
- *ProQuest* (*New York Times* and hundreds of periodicals)
- *Wilsonselect* (gives ten-year chunks of *The Reader's Guide*, *Business Periodicals Index*, and other indexes; provides full-text articles)

A popular index like *ArticleFirst!* provides some full-text sources. It's one-stop searching at its best. You can view the article itself on your monitor. Most computerized indexes work similarly. The first screen is where you enter your search information. After you click on the Start Search button, the next screen lists your hits, prioritized by your likely interest. A note of caution, though. Just because the database says the hits will match your needs, it doesn't mean they will. I went through 45 records before I found one that seemed useful.

▲ **PRACTICE 14-5:** Which of the articles in the following illustration promises to be useful for the topic "African Roots of the Blues"?

Netsite: 🔍 [   ] 🔘 What's Related

43. The Rise of Gospel Blues: The music of Thomas Andrew Dorsey
in the Urban Church.
Author: Harris, Michael W.; Baldwin, Lewis V. **Source:** Church history.
Year: 1995 *Tag Record* ❑

44. SONG - Led by harmonica wizard John Popper, whose girth matches
his talent, the boys in Blues Traveler may not be much to look at, but
to growing legions of fans their music is a thing of beauty.
Source: People weekly. **Year:** 1995 *Tag Record* ❑

45. The Rise of Gospel Blues: The Music of Thomas Andrew Dorsey
in the Urban Church.
Author: Harris; Boyer, Horace Clarence **Source:** Ethno-musicology.
Year: 1995 *Tag Record* ❑

46. The moan within the tone: African retentions in rhythm and blues
saxophone style in Afro-American popular music.
Author: Miller, Doug **Source:** Popular music. **Year:** 1995 *Tag Record* ❑

47. Top of the pops: Net surfers love MP3 but it's giving record companies
the blues. Now the industry is trying to stop the music.
Author: Moody, G. **Source:** New scientist. **Year:** 1999 *Tag Record* ❑

48. Festivals.
Source: Amusement business. **Year:** 1995 *Tag Record* ❑

I selected Doug Miller's article (record 46) because its title seemed to match my subject. After clicking on the article's title, I can print out the next screen (see example shown on page 253).

Hints for Using Computer Indexes

- **Use indexes before you search the Web.** They're as easy as searching the Web, and they are more organized and more reliable than Internet sources.

```
Netsite:                                                        What's Related
```

Next	Previous	Libraries with Item	Get Item	Change Database

Ownership: Check the catalogs in your library.

AUTHOR:	Miller, Doug
TITLE:	The moan within the tone: African retentions in rhythm and blues saxophone style in Afro-American popular music
JOURNAL NAME:	Poplular music.
VOL, ISSUE:	Volume 14, Number 2
PAGES:	pp. 155
YEAR:	1995
TYPE:	Article
ISSN:	0261-1430
J ALT NAME:	Popular music (Cambridge Unversity Press)

- **Start specific, and then broaden searches.** Type in your most specific topic first ("Blues"). If your results are minimal, try broader categories ("Music"), and then scroll the list until you discover a better subheading.
- **Reduce the number of records.** If you get 88 hits as I did under "Blues" on *WilsonSelect*, combine words and phrases ("Blues History" or "Roots of Blues") to reduce the number of hits. Keyboarding in "The Blues and Africa," I landed 5 articles. You can also limit your searches by date. When I narrowed my search for articles only between 1990 and 1999, I found 10.
- **Change your search options.** A topic search gave me 663 hits, but a keyword search turned up 2,015. I found no hits for the origins of blues in one year of periodicals covered by *ArticleFirst!*, but in a previous year there were 11. Each database is like a door in a house. You need to look in all the rooms to find the best information.
- **Think of different words to express your topic.** Most indexes come with a thesaurus and also list topics related to your search. In *ArticleFirst!* I clicked the Browse Index button and typed in "blues." It gave alternatives like "blues-band," "blues-inspired," and "blues-jazz" along with a record listed for each.

▲ **PRACTICE 14-6:** Which periodical index(es) on page 250 would you use to find articles on these topics? List three or four headings you might search:

- Your topic from Practice 14-1
- Employment potential in hotel management
- Welfare fraud

- Aristotle's philosophy
- Junior and high school violence
- End of time prophecies

 ## GETTING CONNECTED: RESEARCH ON THE WEB

To illustrate how Web sites are typically organized, let's look at the U.S. Census Bureau's site, an excellent source of social data. Here's its home page:

All Web sites have addresses, called URLs (universal resource locators):

- Http is the computer language that Web sites use.
- WWW stands for World Wide Web.
- The next portion of the Web site abbreviates the name of the organization that maintains it (in this case "Census" for Census Bureau).
- The end tag indicates what type of group maintains the site:
     gov—government offices, departments, and agencies
     edu—educational institutions
     mil—U.S. military links
     org—organizations and associations
     int—international organizations
     com—commercial and business sites
     net—networking organizations

The Census Bureau's home page allows for many points of entry, which helps me not have to sift through the entire site to look for my information. For example, I can click the "Subjects A to Z" index to locate "Household Income Rates." I can click on "Population Clocks" and learn that for every U.S. citizen who dies, two more are born. Or I can enter "Related Sites" and access 70 other statistical agencies. This site is reliable, but others aren't so easy to evaluate for credibility.

Finding Reliable Web Sites

- **The Internet is unregulated.** Anyone can create and post information. No official verifies that it's true. Although published authors make mistakes and distort facts at times, editors correct them and readers cancel unreliable publications. Reviews crush weak books. There's incentive to be accurate. The library staff only picks survivors to shelve. Your odds of reading trustworthy information in a college library are a lot better than when you plug into Smokin' Billy's Web site.

- **Knowing the type of Web site you're viewing will help you evaluate it.** For example, the National Rifle Association <www.nra.org> is a nonprofit organization, but its commitment to a cause means it often provides biased information. Educational institutions usually are the most objective. Commercial sites are bound to slant information, but they often have a resource-filled links page associated with their product. For example, a company that sells toddler car seats might provide articles on car safety.

- **Avoid Web sites with more than three advertising banners.** These sites are more interested in pocketbooks than library books.

- **Look for a menu or site map button to help you browse the site.** These indexes will help you filter needless information.

- **Web sites with their own search engines tend to be the best organized.** These internal search engines let you pinpoint links within a specific site.

- **Find counters that display the number of visitors to the site.** But remember that counters are about popularity, not validity. A new worthwhile site might not have had time to attract visitors.

- **Check for the site's last update.** If the page hasn't been updated for six months, it tells you about the care and reliability of the page's creator. Forget it.

- **Review the site's "Link" page.** Scan the links and click on a few to learn more about the person who maintains this page (some come with a résumé of the site's owner). It might make you decide to try another site.

- **Identify personal Web pages by looking for a tilde (~) within the Web site address.** The BluesWEB site is <www.island.net/~blues>. Although the address contains no personal name, the tilde indicates that it's a personal page provided by Island Internet, an Internet service provider. To learn what network housed the site, I went to <www.island.net> to see what it was. The slash between *net* and *~blues* means this Web site has many directories, and one of them houses BluesWEB. Because there's a tilde in the Web site doesn't mean you should pass it up; it is a warning to be sensitive that the page may reflect its owner's biases. Knowing who houses the site can help assess the site's reputability.

Searching the Web

Search engines   Search engines attempt the impossible—to categorize the entire world's Web sites. In 1997 a new Web site emerged every minute! But their creators reported their presence to only *some* of the search engines. This means different engines will give you varying results, even when you use the same keyword search.

Start your searches at institutions related to your topic, not at general search engines. With a social or economic topic, I recommend going to institutions like the U.S. Department of Justice, which links to federal sites such as the Department of Agriculture, Department of Defense, the Food and Drug Administration, Department of Housing and Urban Development, and Legal Services Corporation. You can find these links and more at <www.usdoj.gov/02organizations/index.html>. For **up-to-the-minute information,** search news media sites:

- ABC News <abcnews.go.com>
- CNN News <www.cnn.com>
- MSNBC News <www.msnbc.com>
- National Public Radio Online <www.npr.org>
- New York Times Online <www.nytimes.com>

Refine your searches   If you use quotation marks around a phrase ("blues and African roots"), your search will only show results with that exact combination of words. To search for two subjects at once, use *and* between words. For example, you can search for sites that include the word "blues" *and* the exact phrase "African roots" by typing: *"blues" and "African roots."* If your search gives you pages loaded with text, you can locate your subject words by using your browser's Find command under its Edit menu. Your screen will scroll down and highlight the keywords when it finds them.

A search engine that ranks: *Lycos*   Lycos's advanced search <lycospro.lycos.com> lets you limit searches by pictures, books, home pages, and sounds. It also lets you limit searches to only the top 5 percent of Web sites—sites that Internet users have critiqued for credibility. If you're researching Michelangelo's painting, *Lycos* can show you images of the Sistine Chapel. *Lycos* will provide you a list of links that are ranked according to their relevance to your word search. Some search engines display relevance either by stars (three out of four stars is very relevant) or percentages (85 percent of 100 percent is decent). Remember, though, this is the search engine's judgment of *your* interest, so use these indicators cautiously. As a general rule, if you don't find a significant link within the first 60 results, try a new phrase or another search engine. If you learn to use *Lycos*, other engines will come easy to you. Here is a *Lycos*'s screen:

A search engine that categorizes: *Yahoo!* When I searched "blues music," *Yahoo!* <www.yahoo.com> gave me a screen full of potential categories to narrow my topic. The most appropriate was Entertainment > Music > Genres > Blues > History. Within the history subcategory, I found two links on the history of the blues and African roots. Did you know that in 1807 Washington Irving used the term "the blues?" That he borrowed it from the sixteenth-century British who used "blue" to emphasize a state of sadness? That Native American tribes from the Memphis area helped contribute to the rhythm of the blues? What a coming together of three cultures! If I find more, I might consider changing my focus to British or Native American roots of the blues.

A search engine that searches other engines: *MetaCrawler* *Metacrawler* <www.metacrawler.com>, like *Lycos,* ranks your search hits. But it also "crawls" through popular search engines to give you only their top hits. It saves you from retyping phrases, and it gives you a good overall view of what's on the Web to help narrow your search.

Other popular search engines on the Web:

- *Altavista* <www.altavista.com>
- *Excite* <www.excite.com>
- *Infoseek* <infoseek.go.com>
- *Hotbot* <hotbot.com>
- *Infomine* <infomine.ucr.edu>

Searching for multimedia resources After skimming the Web for about three hours, I modified my search from text articles to multimedia. I remembered, after seeing some sites with blues music, that I needed some recordings to compare and contrast musical styles. MP3 files (CD-quality sound files) are available. I located and downloaded five songs. I could potentially use one song to discuss the *ArticleFirst!* resource, "The Moan within the Tone: African Retentions in Rhythm and Blues Saxophone Style in Afro-American Popular Music." I also decided to go to Broadcast.Com <www.broadcast.com>, a site that provides free access to audio books. I found one called *A Short History of Africa*. I also went to the site's music link and watched Big Jack Johnson and the Oilers, a blues band, during its February 1999 concert in Dallas, Texas. Throughout the concert, Johnson provided historical comments on the music.

▲ **PRACTICE 14-7:** Search three engines using the same word or phrases for a topic of your choice, and analyze your search results. Which engine gave you the most credible results?

Electronic Mail and Newsgroups

E-mail an author. When giving a presentation during a literature class, one group stunned us. They read aloud a letter they received from Ron Carlson, a well-known short fiction author. They learned that he taught at a Midwest school and e-mailed him questions about his story. Within a day, they got a two-page response! E-mail can be a great way to interview an expert. If you don't have access to e-mail at home, you can get a free Web-based e-mail system, and access it free from your college's electronic learning center.

Visit college Web sites and find professors' e-mail addresses who might give you some insight. Or visit an "Ask the Expert" Web site. Because e-mail is essentially an interview, be professional. Do some homework to avoid asking obvious questions. Let the person know in advance what your assignment entails, what your goals are for the interview, where you are located, and what class you're taking. This openness will likely lead to a conversation. As a kind gesture, send the person a copy of your paper, along with a thank you note.

Register your e-mail address with an online newsgroup that discusses specific topics. Whenever an article or response to an e-mail is posted, it's automatically mailed to you. I went to *Reference.com* <www.reference.com> and *Listz* <www.listz.com> and found two groups related to blues and another two on West African music. I might meet people willing to share resources with me; I might even meet a well-known blues singer. Because responses to notes may take a week, join a newsgroup as soon as your research paper is assigned.

▲ **PRACTICE 14-8:** Go to *Reference.com* or *Listz*. Find at least two newsgroups related to your paper topic.

OTHER RESOURCES

Use the Yellow Pages telephone directory as a powerful brain teaser. One of my students concerned about pollution in the lake near his home did library research on general background, but he discovered specific information about pollution in Long Pond by calling local conservation departments. They told him which species of fish and turtle were dying, the specific sources of water deterioration, and current pollution levels. A student researching funeral rituals called several undertakers for information and got not only an interview but a *very* detailed tour of the facilities. She learned far more than most books would have taught her. Food, death, sports, housing, technology, child care, and a host of other topics all have local experts, including people who sell related products or services. Most will give information over the phone to courteous callers.

Find online Yellow Pages that are linked to your favorite search engine. They let you search by subject and city—as well as provide maps for addresses. If businesses are online or have e-mail, they'll be listed in the company's description. Use these:

- *Yahoo! Yellow Pages* <yp.yahoo.com>
- *GTE Superpages* <yp.superpages.com>
- *Yellowpages.com* <www.yellowpages.com>

Create your own good sources for research. A student wanted the college to offer more televised courses. She called the local public broadcasting station to find out how many were offered in the area and how many nationwide. To project how popular telecourses might be, she conducted an informal survey in several of her classes. She also used an almanac to discover that 88 percent of American homes with television sets now have VCRs, and she concluded that colleges could offer telecourses at unpopular time slots because most people can now tape programs. She found no books, but a smattering of magazine articles did show up in *Education Index*. Her own brain-teasing ideas were that telecourses might relieve our college's classroom shortage, attract students with irregular schedules, and reduce traffic and parking congestion. Her proposal went before the college curriculum committee.

Collect your own research firsthand. Here's an example of a student gathering her own research simply by counting. This paragraph comes from a letter Jennifer Wheeler sent to her employer's retail clothing store. She wanted the store to recycle or eliminate plastic wrapping to "do its part in saving our planet":

```
During a typical week in the Ladies Sportswear Department at
my store, we receive approximately fifteen rolling racks of hung
clothing and between five and ten racks of boxed clothing. Each
individual piece of merchandise is needlessly prepackaged in
plastic that is thrown away. Weekly, we throw away approximately
3,000 plastic bags and 2,250 plastic hangers. This is only Ladies
```

Sportswear. My manager informed me that monthly our store discards one ton of plastic. Many of these bags can be reused and all the hangers can be used in the store instead of switching the clothes to our store hangers. This would save salesclerks six hours of work in our department each week.

▲ **PRACTICE 14-9:**   Who can give you nonprint information for your topic from Practice 14-1? List at least four questions you'd ask.

Tips for Soliciting Research in Person

- *Ask* for the person's time a week ahead, and explain exactly why you want it. Suggest a few sample questions and how much time you'll need. (I recommend 30 minutes.)
- Do your preliminary reading first. If you show some awareness of the topic, the interview will stimulate your source to provide better information.
- Prepare questions, but be open to new ideas during the interview.
- Come with paper and pen. If you want to tape a formal interview, ask permission.
- Dress professionally—you will get better information.
- Start with an easy question to loosen things up, but move to the key research questions quickly, so you don't run out of time before asking them.
- *Immediately* after an interview, fill out your notes and record your reactions before they go cold. Be sure to indicate which are quotes, paraphrases, and personal reactions.
- Send a typed thank you note, along with a copy of your paper.

 ## NOTETAKING

There is no "right" way to take notes; they are as unique and messy as other brain teasers. But here are some suggestions:

- **Skim your list of sources before reading any.** Read only the most recent, most expert, or most relevant to your topic. When you do have full text on screen or in hand, scan the headings, index, or table of contents to find the best information quickly.
- **3 × 5 note cards provide two advantages.** They stack neatly and easily fit in book bags, unlike a ragged mess of papers. Second, cards can be easily rearranged when you organize the paper—provided you limit yourself to one fact or one idea per note card. With two ideas on one card wanting to go different places in the essay, you'd be like Solomon, debating how to divide the brain child.

- **Large loose-leaf paper gives you space to write reactions, but will tempt you to put too many ideas on one page.** When it's time to organize, use color highlighters to identify related ideas or facts.
- **Use Post-it notes as tabs in the margins of the references.** Label the tab with a topic heading, and next to it write down questions and reactions.
- **Paraphrase instead of copying long quotations.** Condense the original, and quote only key sentences or phrases. This will help *your* voice control the draft. It's best not to look at the original as you paraphrase so you don't risk plagiarism. After reading the source, ask yourself, "What is the one key point I want for my purposes from this source?" Then write. Of course, if you unearth an absolutely sparkling paragraph, take it whole. In notes, always quote accurately: Use quotation marks and record page numbers.
- **Comment on and analyze source material while reading.** You are not a stenographer but a thinker when you take notes. Raise an objection to the author, add a personal anecdote, or connect sources. This is easy on full-size notebook paper. For note cards, use a separate card to react to sources. In either case, be sure to label "My Ideas" or "My Comment" at the top so you never confuse your ideas with research. Staple or clip comment cards to the source cards. This example on blues music shows actual notes that the student, Carol Nobles, wrote. Notice the blend of paraphrase, quotation, and commentary:

Bibliographic Information

Blues People, Le Roi Jones. Wm. Morrow and Co. N.Y. 1963
Yoruba tribesmen from Dahony thought "the universe is ruled by fate and the destiny of each man worked out according to a predetermined scheme." Music was one of the few ways they defied fate (p. 9).

Page Reference

Comment Card

MY IDEAS HERE - - Did this belief in fate allow them to be made slaves to people who believed in free will? How did it affect their music? Blues may be music of defiance of establishment rules. Goes way back.

One Card
Combines
Comments with
Source Matter

> *Black Music in America*, John Rublowsky, Basic Books, N. Y. 1971
>
>   On Sundays slaves dressed in "hand-me-down" finery from the big house and would do a "take-off on the high manners of the white folks" by prancing and high-kicking. Then the "masters" would gather and watch, awarding a cake to the fanciest dancer (that's how "cakewalk" got its name), not knowing that they awarded a prize to the one who mocked them the best. (p. 96)
>
> MINE - - Is this how they used music to get even with the gods/fate?

- **Record the complete bibliographic information with your notes—** as Carol did in her notes. Write page numbers after each paraphrase or quotation. You don't want to lack a publisher or date after the library closes for the weekend or discover the Web site you've used has been deleted. Some researchers record complete bibliographic information on separate "bib" cards, which are easy to reshuffle and rearrange when it's time to write the bibliography. In this system, cards with ideas on them only list the title and page number.

▲ **PRACTICE 14-10:** Fill a note card or sheet of paper on your topic from Practice 14-1 based on a source you found. Paraphrase most of your source but include a short quotation. Be prepared to read and compare the source's words to your paraphrase during class.

ORGANIZING RESEARCH PAPERS

Organize research papers as you would informative or persuasive writing. Review Chapters 5, 11, or 12. If you used note cards, place them into related piles and create headings. Another option is to read through your notes and put them aside. Then, focusing only on your main ideas, list the main points you want to cover. With long papers, it's especially important to formulate a working thesis before attempting an outline, to help create a structure for your blizzard of notes. Read through your notes, marking ones that relate to the thesis. Or read through your notes and make a list of trial thesis sentences from them. Remember: Make your thesis a statement, not a question. One sentence is preferred.

If you find that some statistics or quotations don't fit into a category, they may still fit your introduction or conclusion. Now is a good time to look for gaps in your research. Write a list of missing information that you'll need to improve your essay.

Many professors require students to submit parts of their research papers in stages for approval. Try not to think of this as an extra chore, but as an aid in writing: It forces you to think and organize early, stimulating your subconscious to incubate, and it provides feedback before a grade is at stake. Get used to preliminary reports. Often business and professional research requires an "abstract"—a statement of thesis and a paragraph summary of the main points. This is usually submitted for approval before the paper is written and may accompany the final paper.

▲ **PRACTICE 14-11:** Formulate a thesis and headings for your topic from Practice 14-1.

WRITING THE RESEARCH PAPER: HANDLING SOURCES

Drafting a research paper involves the same process discussed in Chapter 6. A sharp introduction should grab the reader with an anecdote, key research questions, or a strong fact, and lead to a clear statement of thesis. Often the introduction previews the areas you will cover and explains why you will not cover others. Work quickly on the first draft, so you don't get hung up correcting little problems. Your main goals are to clarify your sketchy ideas and to visualize them with sharp details.

Because what's unique about research papers is using sources, the rest of this section deals with that. Incorporating research into essays requires four parts: the tag line, paraphrase/direct quote, commentary, and citation.

Use Tag Lines

Tag lines make quotations, paraphrases, and facts flow with your paper. Tag lines introduce the source before you present the quotation or paraphrase: "As one social researcher says . . ." or "After thirty years as a judge, Deborah Paine believes . . ." Tag lines not only prepare us for a new voice but tell us *what authority* your source has.

Should You Paraphrase or Use Direct Quotation?

Paraphrase all but the most important passages. You cover ground faster with paraphrase, and strings of quotations frustrate readers, who assume correctly that the real message is in your voice. If two or three writers agree on one point, quote or paraphrase the best one, and simply mention that others agree; don't drag a reader through redundant quotations. Here's an example of a good student paraphrase mixed with bits of quotation from a clinical description of an animal test by Mindy Reynolds:

```
The Draize Test involves testing cosmetics for eye damage that

might occur to humans. Reports describe how researchers smear  Tagline
```

Paraphrase and Quotation

mascara, for example, over the eyeballs of rabbits. Unlike humans, rabbits have no tear glands to wash it off. The animals are "immobilized" in a stockade device. In some cases their eyes are held open with clips. As a result, they cannot blink to get even a moment's relief and ultimately suffer "eye ulcers, bleed-

Citation
Author commentary

ing, and blindness" (O'Connor 94). And for what purpose? The tests do not even resemble how humans use the product.

Should you need a **long quotation** (four lines or more), indent the entire passage five spaces. The quotation's font and line spacing remain the same as the rest of your essay. No quotation marks are needed. Use this block quotation very sparingly.

Comment on Your Sources

Don't just report source material. Your commentary ties the source to your essay—makes everything fit smoothly. Agree, disagree, expand, or clarify the idea of the source when you comment. When you don't comment, the reader may misinterpret your information or simply not understand how it supports your thesis.

Here's an example from an essay against the banning of handguns. It's from the student's refutation section, where Barbara Collins considers arguments opposing her thesis. Notice how she leads us back to her thesis:

Tagline

According to a U.S. News and World Report study, police argue

Paraphrase and citation

that a gun is six times more likely to be shot at a family member or a friend than at an intruder (Baer, Gest, and Anderson 35). This, however, does not justify banning guns. Let's take

Commentary

the husband who goes mad and wants to kill his family. He goes to the gun case and notices his gun is missing. Does he change his mind and decide to let them live? No. People in a rage use knives, clubs, or their bare hands. The weapon isn't the gun; it's hatred and insanity.

Handling Statistics

Like quotations and paraphrases, you must comment on statistics or you will lose your reader. Imagine reading a political science essay on voting, and in the middle of a page you run into this table lifted from *The Statistical Abstract of the United States.*

No. 462. Voting-Age Population, Percent Voted, 1996

Characteristic	Voting Age Population	Percent Voting
Total	193.7 million	54.2
18–20 years old	10.8 million	31.2
21–24 years old	14.9 million	33.4
25–34 years old	41.6 million	43.1
35–44 years old	41.9 million	54.9
45–64 years old	50.9 million	70.0
65+	31.9 million	70.1
White	162.8 million	56.0
Black	22.5 million	50.6
Hispanic	18.4 million	26.7
School Years Completed		
8 or less	14.1 million	28.1
9–11	21.0 million	33.8
12	65.2 million	49.1
1–3 years of college	50.9 million	60.5
4 years of college	42.5 million	73.0
Employed	125.6 million	66.2
Unemployed	6.4 million	37.2

Honestly now, if you're like me, you skimmed this table and little sank in. In the middle of a research paper, it'll have the same zero effect. To make it count, you must *draw conclusions* about the statistics. Here's my point as it might appear in a draft (without the table):

> Research shows that older, better educated Americans vote more and consequently have more power getting their candidate in office. People more likely to be poor--the young, minorities, less educated and unemployed--all vote

Author's idea

statistic supports idea

less than their counterparts. For example, in the 1996 elections, only 31.2% of 18- to 20-year-olds voted, while people over 45 voted at a 70% rate (<u>Statistical Abstract Online</u> n. pag.). Is it any wonder that Congress makes Social Security a priority while it cuts college loans and job programs?

Commentary

Statistic

Likewise, while 56% of whites voted, 50.6% of blacks and only 26.7% of Hispanics voted (n. pag.). Of course, the language and cultural barrier may keep many Hispanics home,

Commentary

but which came first? Do they not vote because the politicians ignore them, or do the politicians ignore them because they don't vote? The unemployed voter--who should have high stakes in electing people to create jobs--only

Statistics

voted at a 37.2% rate compared to 66.2% for the employed. And those with college degrees were more than twice as likely to vote as those who never finished high school (n.

Conclusions

pag.). The young, minorities, less educated, and unemployed should be better motivated to have their voices heard. Yet it is the "haves" who vote most often. Perhaps because they are "haves," they believe in the system and keep it going. Those who are alienated may feel the system will not listen to them anyway and don't vote because it best expresses how they feel.

Notice how commentary alternates with hard statistics—ideas alternating with details. But two flaws in my paragraph must be dealt with. First, I did not mention that the voting age population includes noncitizens—a footnote in *The Statistical Abstract*. This affects my interpretation of the Hispanic voter, since large numbers of Mexican and Cuban immigrants in the United States cannot vote. Perhaps if noncitizens were left out, the statistics would show that Hispanics vote at much higher rates. I need to find out! To be an honest researcher, you must present and account for all factors in the statistics that might affect your conclusions. The second flaw is an unstated assumption that groups vote as a block in their own self-interest. But a grandmother may want students to have loans, and an employed person may want better job-training programs. Can you think of any other issues the statistics and my conclusions raise?

Citations

- **Always use citations in the text to document sources.** A citation is the material in parentheses that follows any ideas taken from a source. For your English papers, use the **Modern Language Association (MLA)** format.
- **Citation format:** Simply list the author's last name, and give the page number where the material was found, like this: (Toutelli 52). Notice there are no commas or abbreviations for page. The reader can locate the entire source at the end of your essay in the Works Cited List—arranged alphabetically by the authors' last names.
- **Author's name used in tag line:** If you've used the author's name in the tag line to your quotation or paraphrase, as in "Professor Toutelli declares . . ." then the parentheses would only include a page number, like this: (52).
- **Source with no page number:** In the voting example, I downloaded the statistics from the Web, which doesn't have page numbers, so I used "n. pag." Do the same if you refer to a pageless lecture or interview.
- **Two sources by one author:** If you use two or more sources by the same author, you must indicate which one the material came from in the parentheses, like this: (Toutelli, *Demon Data* 52). Use ellipsis points to shorten long titles (Toutelli, "Finding . . ." 12).
- **When no author exists:** When no author is named, use the title of the work in the citation, like this: ("Internet Excess" 31).
- **A source within a source:** In this case, you're using Richland's idea quoted in Toutelli's work. Include both names like this: (Richland qtd. in Toutelli 30).
- **American Psychological Association (APA) variation:** There's one glitch in this scheme. Most social and natural sciences papers require the date of the publication just after the author's name and a "p." or "pp." before the page number(s): (Toutelli, 1999, p. 226). A page reference is only needed if you give a direct quotation or statistic; general summary needs only a name and date, like this: (Toutelli, 1990). Use this format for citations in papers you write for psychology, sociology, and science courses.

▲ **PRACTICE 14-12:** For your note card or sheet from Practice 14–10 write a brief paragraph that introduces the source smoothly and uses a proper citation.

◆ AVOIDING PLAGIARISM

Under current copyright law everything anyone writes, including student essays, is copyrighted—that is, protected by law from being used by anyone else without written permission. Copyright laws protect authors and publishers from other people profiting from their efforts. However, this would create havoc if 12 million college students needed publishers' permissions to quote sources in papers. So all have agreed that proper documentation will substitute for written permission to use copyrighted material for scholarship. You document sources, then, to show your material came from reputable sources, and also to "pay" an author and publisher by acknowledging them for using their work.

The reader should never doubt which ideas are yours and which are from sources. **Use introductory tag lines to tell readers where source material begins, and use the citation parentheses to mark the end of source material.** Anything else you are claiming as your idea. "Naked" quotes or paraphrases without citations create doubts, and may result in a teacher accusing you of plagiarism—academic stealing. The following must have citations:

- Quotations
- Paraphrases or summaries in your words
- Statistics or facts

Rewriting does not make an *idea* yours; it only makes the *words* yours. A citation credits the *idea* to someone else. Quotation marks credit the *exact* wording to someone else.

Common knowledge. The core of knowledge possessed by most educated people is called "common knowledge" and does *not* require citations or Works Cited entries: It is considered the common property of society. This includes famous quotations like these:

- "I have a dream."—MARTIN LUTHER KING, JR.
- "Oh that this too, too solid flesh would melt."—SHAKESPEARE
- "I am not a crook."—RICHARD NIXON

Common knowledge also includes ideas:

- The first Amendment to the U.S. Constitution protects the right of free speech.
- Capitalism stresses individual rights, while socialism stresses group rights.
- Most religions say death is a release from the pain of life, not a dreaded event.

Common knowledge can be facts and statistics as well:

- Shakespeare lived in England 400 years ago and wrote the plays *Hamlet* and *The Tempest*.
- DDT spraying 40 years ago still pollutes water today and kills fish and birds.
- Michelangelo painted the Sistine Chapel.
- The speed of light is more than 186,000 miles per second.

Expert knowledge. Higher degrees of specific knowledge ceases to be common knowledge. If, for instance, you quoted the rest of Hamlet's speech, or discussed the debate over the approval of the First Amendment that took place in 1790, or described the specific chemical reaction DDT causes in bald eagle eggs, it would cease to be common knowledge for the public. Among *experts,* this information may still be considered common knowledge, but until you establish yourself as an expert, you must document.

Anything you learn from reading specifically for a paper must be documented. If you read something three or four times in different sources, you can suspect it is common knowledge. Ask your professor if you're not sure.

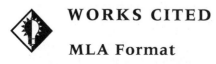

WORKS CITED

MLA Format

MLA Works Cited Format

- The entire *list is alphabetized* by the author's last name, so citations are easy to locate.
- If there is no author, alphabetical order is determined by the first main word of the title.
- Indent second and third lines five spaces to keep the author's name visible.
- Double-space.
- Follow punctuation and order of items exactly.
- Title the list "Works Cited" on a separate page at the end of the paper (but don't use quotation marks around it).
- Include only works you actually cite (not everything you read for the paper).

Here's how an MLA Works Cited list might look at the end of your paper:

Works Cited

Abbey, Edward. <u>The Monkey Wrench Gang</u>. New York: Avon, 1975.

"Fatherhood in America." <u>Fathers and Families: Advocacy for the Father Child Bond</u> 22 Mar. 1999. 27 Aug. 1999 <http://www.fathersandfamilies.org/about/fathers.htm>.

Jervis, Nancy. "Waste Not, Want Not." <u>Natural History</u> May 1990: 70–74.

The first is from a book, the second from the Web, and the third from a magazine. When you do your own Works Cited list, find the proper format for each source and follow it exactly.

Works Cited Formats

Basic book format—author, title, place of publication, publisher, and date published. Use the latest date listed on the copyright page. You may use a short form for publishers ("Harcourt," instead of "Harcourt Brace").

> Abbey, Edward. The Monkey Wrench Gang. New York: Avon, 1975.

Book with editor—but if the editor's introduction or notes were what you quoted, list the entry under "Gregory" and put the author after the title.

> Anderson, Sherwood. The Portable Sherwood Anderson. Ed. Horace Gregory. New York: Viking, 1972.

Book with two or three authors—second and third authors' names are in normal order.

> Auden, W. H., and Louis Kronenberger. Aphorisms. New York: Penguin, 1981.

Book with more than three authors—"et al." means "and others."

> Axon, Pamela, et al. Juggernaut. New York: Smith, 2000.

Book not in first edition—after title, specify edition.

> Breland, Osmond, et al. Principles of Biology. 3rd ed. New York: Harper, 1964.

Book that collects the works of various authors—if you only use the work of one author, list the author of that work first, then the title of her work, then information on the book. Page numbers are needed.

> Bambara, Toni Cade. "The Lesson." American Mosaic: Multicultural Readings in Context. 2nd ed. Eds. Barbara Roche Rico and Sandra Mano. Boston: Houghton Mifflin, 1995. 417-23.

Book in more than one volume—cite volume used before city.

> Bradstreet, Ann. "Contemplations." The American Tradition in Literature. Ed. Scully Bradley, Richard Beatty, and E. Long. Vol. 1. New York: Grosset, 1967. 39-44.

Common reference books—complete publishing information not needed. Edition date only. List the entry under the heading where your information was found.

> "Fauvism." Encyclopaedia Britannica. 1968 ed.

Lecture—speaker, title of lecture, sponsoring group, location, and date.

> Gould, Steven Jay. "Wonderful Life." Rochester Arts and Lectures, Rochester, NY. 26 Apr. 1990.

Monthly magazine—author, title of article, magazine, and date. Abbreviate months except for May, June, and July. Pages of entire article listed. If the article skips pages, use a "+" instead of listing all pages. For the following example, it would be "70+."

Jervis, Nancy. "Waste Not, Want Not." <u>Natural History</u> May 1990: 70-74.

Weekly magazine—specific date included.

Kael, Pauline. "The Current Cinema." <u>The New Yorker</u> 29 Nov. 1982: 162-65.

Quarterly magazine—volume number after magazine title and the year in parentheses. If magazine pages are numbered continuously throughout the year, do not include the season in parentheses. The "9.1" here means it is in volume 9 and the first issue of the year.

Meek, Jay. "The Farmhouse." <u>The Iowa Review</u> 9.1 (1978): 32.

Newspaper—include section with page number. If the section here had been a number instead of a letter, you would write "sec 5: 25."

Quindlen, Anna. "Forward March." <u>New York Times</u> 7 Jan. 1990: E25.

No author listed—with any source not naming an author, start with the next item needed, alphabetized by its first letter.

"Rating Desktop Computers." <u>Consumer Reports</u> Sept. 1996: 22-24.

Newspaper without city in title—include after title in brackets.

"Reports of Clashes Among Mohawks." <u>Democrat and Chronicle</u> [Rochester, NY] 29 Apr. 1990: A17.

Interview—use book or magazine format if you read the interview, but use the following if you conducted the interview yourself.

Raines, Tim. Personal interview. 18 May 2000.

Corporate or group author—specific unit listed as author and larger company or group listed after title.

Microsoft Product Support Services. <u>Getting Started with Works 2000</u>. Microsoft. 1999.

Pamphlet—author, title, place of publication, publisher, and date, if available. Try to follow the book format. In the following entry, the city of publication was not named.

Forestry Office. <u>Trees and Shrubs in New York</u>. New York State Department of Environmental Conservation, 1999.

Television program—program title, director ("Dir."), narrator ("Narr.") or writers ("By"), station name, location, and date.

<u>CBS Evening News</u>. Narr. Dan Rather. KTVT. Fort Worth, TX. 4 Jan. 2000.

Videotape, No Author—episode, title, then series' title as shown here. For single productions, simply underline title.

"Why Write?" <u>The Write Course</u>. Videotape. Developed by the Center
for Telecommunication. Dallas County Community College District,
1983. 30 min.

Audiocassette—composer or author, title, format, producing company,
identifying number, date.

Winter, Paul. <u>Canyon</u>. Audiocassette. Living Music, LC 0006. 1986.

Electronic Sources

Because new technology changes rapidly, so do the ways we access information, making it difficult to standardize citation formats for electronic
sources. The Internet is unregulated, so many submissions often don't come
with complete source information. To help simplify documentation, first
classify your source into two categories: previously published and previously unpublished.

**1. Previously published material you read from a full-text index, CD-
ROM, or the Internet**—give the original publication information first, then
the computer information. When items are not listed or not applicable, just
skip to the next. Format them on the page as you would any other works cited
entry, but present items in this order:

- Author
- Title of article or book
- Name of editor(s)
- Title of journal or database name (for periodicals)
- Volume and issue number (for periodicals)
- City and publisher (for books)
- Date of original publication
- Name of database underlined (<u>ProQuest</u>, <u>Infotrac</u>, <u>ERIC</u>, <u>NY Times
  Online</u>, etc.)
- Publication medium (online or CD-ROM)
- Name of computer service or producer (Nexis, BRS, Prodigy, AOL, etc.)
- Date you looked it up if online; date of electronic publication if CD-
  ROM
- Complete Web site or file transfer address (be exact—one missing let-
  ter will create an incorrect link)

The computer service was not available in some of the examples here—
a common occurrence.

Articles on a CD-ROM, Internet database, or Web site:

Clines, Francis. "An Ode to the Typewriter." <u>New York Times</u> 10 July
1995: A3. <u>ProQuest</u>, CD-ROM. Jan. 1996.

Miller, Doug. "The Moan within the Tone: African Retentions in Rhythm and Blues Saxophone Style in Afro-American Popular Music." <u>Popular Music</u> 14.1 (1995): <u>ArticleFirst!</u> Online 7 Sept. 1999 <http://www.ref.oclc.org/:next=NEXTCMD"/FETCH:next= html/fs_record.htm:recno=1:resultset=3:format=M:numrecs=1: /fsrec6.txt"%3Asessionid=1523396:6>.

Book on the Internet that was previously published:

Mandela, Nelson. <u>Long Walk to Freedom: The Autobiography of Nelson Mandela</u>. New York: Little, Brown, 1995. <u>Open Book Systems</u>. Online. 10 Sept. 1999 <http://www.obs-us.com/obs/english/books/Mandela/Mandela.html>.

2. Previously unpublished material you read on the Internet—much information may not be shown, but give whatever you can find in this order:

- Author
- Title of material
- Title of database or Web site home page (underlined)
- Name of institution associated with the site
- Date the information was placed online
- Date you accessed the source
- Internet or file transfer address

Article: author, title, place of publication, date published, date of your access, Internet address.

Galewitz, Phil. "Milestone for America's Richest: Group Passes $1 Trillion Mark." <u>ABCnews.com</u>. 23 Sept. 1999. 24 Sept. 1999 <http://www.abcnews.go.com/sections/business/DailyNews/ forbes990923.html>.

E-mail communication: author, title of message taken from subject line, recipient of e-mail, date.

Rock, Sarah M. "Blues History." E-mail to Jason O. Tollers. 14 Sept. 1999.

Newsgroup or bulletin board posting: author, title of submission taken from subject line (in quotation marks), online posting, date material was posted, name of forum, date of access, online address of newsgroup or bulletin board:

Sanchez, Ramon. "This Too Shall Pass." Online posting. 19 Oct. 1999. <u>True Freedom</u>. 30 Oct. 1999 <www.truefreedom.com>.

Professional or personal site: author, title of article, name of home page, date of your access, Internet address.

Smith, Gary. "King of the Delta Blues." <u>BluesWeb</u> 29 Aug. 1999
<http://www.island.net/~blues>.

Sound recording or clip: author, title of file, name of record or audio
label, title of Internet site, date submitted to Internet, date of access, Internet address.

Lanegan, Mark. "Little Sadie." Sub Pop Records. <u>RealGuide Jukebox</u>.
Sept. 1999. 10 Oct. 1999 <http://realguide.real.com/category.
rxml?category_uid=405&artist=Mark_Laneg>.

Missing Works Cited Information

Some publications omit identifying information. Substitute these abbreviations for missing information:

- np (no place of publication listed)
- nd (no date given)
- n. pub (no publisher given)
- n. pag. (no page numbers given)

To see MLA format in action, look at the sample essay "Pigs as Pets" at the
end of this chapter, or consult the *MLA Handbook for Writers of Research Papers* (5th ed., 1999). John Barzelay's paper on page 325 illustrates electronic
sources.

APA Format

The American Psychological Association prefers a slightly different format.
In a bibliography for a social or natural science paper, observe the following
changes from MLA format:

APA Reference List Format

- Only initials are used for first names.
- "Works Cited" is called "References."
- Capitalize only the first letter of all titles of articles and books.
- The date appears immediately after the author's name.
- The year always appears first in any dates used.
- Quotation marks are not used around the titles of articles from mag-
  azines or newspapers.
- "p." or "pp." is used before all page numbers; "p." is for single pages,
  "pp." for consecutive multiple pages.

Here are two sample entries done in APA format:

Book:

> Sobel, D. (1999) <u>Galileo's daughter: A historical memoir</u>. New York:
> Walker.

Weekly magazine:

> Hanson, David. (1999, Dec. 13) EPA struggles with human testing issue.
> <u>Chemical & Engineering News</u>, 34.

For additional examples of APA format, see the student essay titled "The Teenage Pregnancy Epidemic" in Chapter 15. Consult the *Publication Manual of the
American Psychological Association* (4th ed., 1994) for complete information.

Note to Students: Yes, this dual system ought to be united into one simple, logical form of documentation for all areas of study, so researchers can
concentrate on ideas and evidence, not on format. Perhaps the APA and
MLA will cooperate one day. For now, check with your professors to see
which system you should use.

▲ **PRACTICE 14-13:** Compose a Works Cited page using all the sources you
found in researching your topic from Practice 14-1.

 # REVISING RESEARCH WRITING

Revising research papers proceeds as any other revision. Start
with the big things first: the thesis and supporting detail. Then move to
paragraphs, sentences, and word choice, and finally proof for mechanics.
See Chapters 7, 8, and 16. Here are new items for revising research papers:

- Edit long-winded quotes or paraphrases. Pick the most vivid or relevant; eliminate the rest.
- Make sure each source has a smooth introductory tag line, citation
  with page numbers at the end, and your own commentary tying it to
  the thesis.
- Research papers usually restate the thesis in the conclusion.

Writing Suggestions and Class Discussions

1. Ten years from now—in your chosen career—what two research projects might likely come your way?
2. What research does your employer need done now?
3. List three topics you'd like to research in college for personal use—
   consumer, health, or hobby topics, for instance.
4. Take one topic from number 3, and do a brain-teaser list of key research
   · questions. What do you want to know?

5. Narrow two of these topics until they interest you:
   - Changing family patterns
   - Advertising
   - Medieval castles
   - Religious principles
6. Make a list of key research questions, and do a brain-teaser list on one narrowed topic from number 5.
7. Suppose you had to write a research report on one of the following. Without actually doing the research, make up a list of places to go for information—in the library and elsewhere. Be specific about the headings you'd search under in catalogs or indexes:
   - Violent patients in hospitals
   - Abstract art
   - Solar-heated houses
   - Students' rights in college
8. Library Scavenger Hunt: Pick any one topic you listed in numbers 1 through 7 and find information on it from each of these sources:
   - A computer index
   - The *New York Times*
   - The Internet

List the source in proper works cited format and then write—in note card form—several lines paraphrasing what you learned.

9. Pick any famous historical event that happened since 1920: the stock market crash of 1929, the bombing of Pearl Harbor, the first moon landing, for examples. Use the *New York Times Index* to locate an article written on the topic, and use *The Reader's Guide to Periodical Literature* to locate a second article. Or use a computerized index to find two articles. Find and read the articles, summarizing both and quoting one strong sentence from each. Turn in your notes with complete works cited information attached.
10. Do the same as number 9, but use the Internet to find two sources.
11. Do the same as number 9, but use a book and a reference section book as sources. You only need to read enough to fill out one note card for each.
12. Look up the *New York Times* for the day you were born. What were the main headlines for the day? For fun, name a headline that secretly "announced" your birth ("Budget Deficit Again" or "Madman Holds Bank at Bay" for example). Explain why it fits you.
13. Do the same as number 12 for a weekly magazine like *Time*.
14. Using *The Statistical Abstract of the United States* or another almanac, find an interesting fact about each of these topics. Be sure to include complete bibliographic information and page numbers. Comment on the significance of each statistic:
    - Crime
    - Marriage
    - Sports

- Ecology
- Your own topic

15. Find a nonreference section book source for one of the topics in number 14 and quote a short section that you find interesting. Then paraphrase and condense the material, keeping only a key phrase or two in quotes. Comment on the material and include bibliographic information.

16. Combine 14 and 15 into a short (one- to two-page) research paper.

17. Peer groups will develop research questions for one of the following topics and establish a list of sources to contact or read:
    - Doctor-assisted suicide for the terminally ill
    - Overcrowded national parks
    - Spending the federal budget surplus
    - Laws protecting homosexuals from discrimination
    - Illegal immigrants
    - AIDS testing confidentiality
    - Single fathers
    - Self-defense murders of abusive spouses/parents
    - Pregnant drug addicts
    - Crime victims' rights

18. Works Cited Exercise: Find ten sources on a topic on which you might write a research paper. Try for a mix of books, reference works, magazines, newspapers, and Internet sources. Assemble it in proper bibliographic form.

19. Find two reviews of a book you loved or hated. Try *Book Review Digest* (which includes abstracts of the reviews) or *The New York Times Index.* Write a one-page paper summarizing the reception the book had, citing each source, giving a proper bibliography, and also commenting on the reviews.

20. Write a research paper (consider expanding any of the preceding assignments).
    - Choose a topic and narrow it.
    - Make a list of key research questions.
    - Assemble a list of sources to answer these questions.
    - Take notes and comment on the sources.
    - Write the draft.
    - Revise the draft.

21. Write a career research paper to investigate thoroughly a career you're considering. Combine library and nonlibrary resources, including one formal interview with a person who holds the kind of job you want. Your list of key research questions should include all the hard information you want to know about the career—the gutsy, naked truth about its ecstasies and agonies. Finally, evaluate your research and decide if this career fits your interests and abilities.

A student who interviewed a lawyer found there was "no gavel-pounding or cries of 'order! order!' but simple, solemn procedure." The lawyer admitted liking pinstripe suits and shiny black briefcases from "the horn of plenty." A student interviewing a special education teacher for emotionally disturbed children was taken to a developmental center for half a day where "it is a major accomplishment to have a kid say 'hi' to you." A student interviewing a reporter was quickly disillusioned about the job's status, glamour, and danger. The working reporter noticed only low pay, stress, dull hours in police stations, and editorial interference.

For more information on this topic, see the end of Chapter 11 and two sample student essays on pages 303–08.

✓   **PEER REVIEW CHECKLIST FOR RESEARCH**

Author: _____

One aspect of this draft I'd like the reviewer to comment on is:

Reviewer: _____

	STRONG	AVERAGE	WEAK
INTRODUCTION: Purpose is clear			
IDEAS: Freshness, insight			
DETAILS: Plenty of them			
Vividness			
ORGANIZATION: Logical/easy to follow			
CITATIONS: Proper format			
Research smoothly worked in			
WORKS CITED: Format			
Strength of Sources			

My response to the author's question:

The strongest part of this paper is:

Two suggestions I have are:

PIGS AS PETS

Annette McFarland

Pigs should be pets, not sandwiches. These animals are not the smelly beasts most people think. In fact, pigs are clean, intelligent animals that make great household pets.

Thesis

According to Tony J. Cunha, chairman of the Department of Animal Science at the University of Florida, "People who see pigs wallowing in mud often consider them dirty and stupid. But hogs keep themselves cleaner than most farm animals. Hogs are also intelligent" (250). Although it's time to shatter anti-pig prejudice, few publications are dedicated to this animal. However, there are personal accounts. Singer Belinda Carlisle admits to having two pet pigs. Does she wallow with them in mud or rearrange the silk pillows on her Henredon sofa for her pink pals?

Scientist quoted

Personal story

Not so glamorous an owner was Buddy Thorne, an ex-rodeo rider. He found a baby javelina pig in the Texas brush. It was alone, starving, and so young its umbilical cord was still attached. Buddy took the baby home to his wife and teenage daughters, who nursed it to health. Bubba slept in a doll carriage under blankets, with his forearm wrapped protectively around an orange teddy bear. The family fell in love with him. Bubba watched TV and butted Buddy's mattress each morning to wake him for breakfast. A single scolding taught Bubba not to jump on the bed. Bubba would sit beside the girls every morning as they brushed their teeth, waiting for <u>his</u> daily brushing. It

Anecdote

took just 24 hours to paper-train Bubba (it took weeks to train our dog, a supposedly smart seeing-eye breed). Buddy claims Bubba was smarter than any dog or horse he'd ever known. Bubba ate from spoons, loved beer poured down his throat, and chewed slowly to savor his food. He'd place his head in a lap and fall asleep if his ears were scratched. "I'm sure other families have loved an animal like we love Bubba," Thorne says, but I'll be darned if I know any. . . . He was like one of our kids" (Coudert 144-48).

Author's Commentary

This should be our image when we think of pigs. All too often we picture pigs in a sty or lying appetizingly between two slices of bread. But this endearing creature was never meant to be food. Deuteronomy says, "Of their flesh ye shall not eat, and their carcass shall ye not touch; they are unclean to you" (14:8).

Religion and science

For those who like the scientific stamp of approval, modern science verifies this biblical law. In the Bible, animals listed as clean to eat were cud-chewing vegetarians with divided hooves like deer and cows. Their sacculated alimentary canal and secondary cud receptacle (basically three stomachs) purify their food--which takes over 24 hours to be converted into flesh. Swine, on the other hand, will eat anything. The pig has a single badly constructed stomach and limited excretory organs. In about four hours, its foul digested food becomes flesh, which humans eat (Josephson 45-46).

Health Issues- toxins

The hog was created as a scavenger to clean the earth, like a vulture or a maggot. He eats anything dead and

decaying on the ground (Josephson 46). If you think farm
pigs raised for human consumption don't have access to
repulsive matter, you're mistaken. Farm pigs eat and
drink the excretions of other animals. They chew the can-
cers growing on other pigs (Josephson 48-49).

Pigs have running sores under their hooves. With a little
squeeze, green matter oozes from outlets designed to rid
the pig of poisons he ingests. Sometimes this artery clogs,
so toxins back up inside the pig, forming internal green
growths. A meat packer testified, "We're instructed to just
trim them off, and when the meat inspector comes, he puts
his stamp on" (Josephson 50). Considering that humans eat
what was cancer and fecal matter only hours before, it's
no wonder God ordered men not to eat pigs.

Here's another thought: 40 percent of all Americans are
20 pounds overweight (Avon 100). Almost 50 percent of
American women are trying to lose weight ("Watching Our
Weight" 530). *Mademoiselle* magazine points out that
"everyone knows ham is fattening"("The Most Unwanted
List" 244). In fact, the meat with the most calories is
cured pork (bacon) at 750 calories per 4 ounces. In comparison, barbecued chicken has only 225 (A to Z 82-83).
The solution to America's weight problem may be the
porkless diet. It's been around for centuries.

Let's look at other health problems. Many authorities
accuse pork of causing blood disease, weakness of the
stomach, liver troubles, eczema, consumption, tumors, and
cancer (Josephson 47). Dr. Laird Goldborough writes, "In
the pork Americans eat there too often lurk myriads of

Health Issues— fat

Health Issues— sickness

baffling and sinister parasites . . . minute spiral worms called <u>Trichinella spiralis</u>. . . . A single serving of infected pork--even a single mouthful--can kill or cripple or condemn the victim to a lifetime of aches and pains. . . . The trichinae are often so minute and so nearly transparent that to find them, even with a microscope, is a task for expert scientific inspectors. 'US Government inspected' does not mean that any official inspection whatsoever has been made as to whether this pork is trichinous or not. It has merely passed the routine inspection" (Josephson 58).

[margin note: Quotation shortened with elipses]

Many think cooking prevents trichinosis. But a university lab tested infected hog flesh. Even when heated to incredibly high temperatures, worms still lived (Josephson 59). Anyway, who wants to eat dead worms?

[margin note: Health Issues- spoilage]

The butcher/owner of a supermarket adds, "When pork begins to get bad, it spoils from the inside out, where it is noticed last. On the other hand, when beef breaks down it starts on the outside" where it can be detected at once (Josephson 55).

There is no profit for anyone persuading you not to eat pork. But the pork industry has billions of dollars at stake to persuade you to eat it, even at the expense of your health. And, if by chance you don't care about

[margin note: Conclusion]

your health, don't you even at least want to look svelte in a bikini in the few years before you develop a serious disease?

As an alternative, make pigs into pets. If you can't eat 'em, join 'em.

MacFarland 5

WORKS CITED

A to Z Diet Guide Calorie Counter. Miami: Merit Publica-

   tions, 1977.

Avon Products, Inc. Looking Good, Feeling Beautiful. New

   York: Simon & Schuster, 1981.

Coudert, Joseph. "Where's Bubba?" Woman's Day 27 Oct.

   1987: 144+.

Cunha, Tony. "Hog." World Encyclopedia. 1970 ed.

Josephson, Elmer. God's Key to Health and Happiness.

   Newark: Fleming, 1976.

"The Most Unwanted List." Mademoiselle Aug. 1986: 244.

"Watching Our Weight." Vogue Oct. 1986: 530.

Commentary

Introduction: The thesis seems clear and sharp, but it's contradicted later when the writer describes how filthy pigs are.

Ideas: It's fresh and insightful. It's a topic few students write on and makes a serious point. It's also creative to combine scientific and religious evidence. Third, she uses humor—although it fades about halfway through, then returns at the end.

Details: The number of details is good: We learn a lot about pigs. The vividness is excellent. Several students each year tell me after reading this essay that they will never eat pork again. Most vivid were the pigs' hooves, spoilage, and trichinosis. Notice, she doesn't just say pork is bad for our health; the gory details teach us why.

Organization: It's easy to follow because she divides it into three main parts: personal, biblical, and health reasons not to eat pigs. Transitional expressions like, "Let's look at other health problems" keep us on track.

The logic is flawed, however. Her biblical and meat-packing facts contradict her thesis that pigs are clean.

Citations: Proper format: Yes. Page references in parentheses follow each paraphrase or quote. The author's name is included if it didn't appear in the tag line. Anonymous articles are listed by the first item in the bibliography for easy cross-reference.

The sources are smoothly worked in. Tag lines prepare us for source material, and notice how she begins paragraphs with an overall point of view of her own. She summarizes most sources or, as in the third paragraph, combines a few direct quotes with summary. The one long quote (in paragraph 9) has been condensed by using ellipses. These features keep it from being drawn out.

Works Cited format: This is a fine model to follow.

Strength of sources: Her first source is reputable—and she lets us know it through her tag line—but Buddy Throne and Avon's credibility are weak. The three popular magazines have only average authority for a college paper. She relies too heavily on one source—Josephson—but by quoting Dr. Goldborough in Josephson (and letting us know he's a doctor in the tag line), she tries to overcome this. The sources (and the paper) are from the 1980s. But I have seen no newer evidence to refute her claims.

Strongest part of the paper: The vivid details.

Suggestions: To straighten out the contradiction about pigs' cleanliness, she might suggest that when pigs are treated individually as pets they are clean, but the overcrowding caused by raising them for food drives them to filthy habits. A second suggestion is to get at least one more strong source. College papers should show more in-depth research. A student wrote to me with another suggestion about this essay. Akilah Stevens said, "One thing Annette failed to speak about. In Timothy, God says to Peter, 'Do not call anything I make unclean.' As long as you bless the food, it will be all right." Do you agree?

CHAPTER 15

A Collection of Student Essays

Go into yourself.

RAINER MARIA RILKE

Look the world straight in the eye.

HELEN KELLER

JOURNALS

Journals preserve our thoughts, give us a place to be brutally honest without committing ourselves publicly, and remove the pressure of grammar and spelling. You write journals freestyle, not to create a finished product, but to stir up your mind. Journals help us realize how much there really is to our lives. Journals should closely record sights, sounds, facts, and conversation—the hard details of life. They preserve the history of your life. But they should also search for meaning behind those details. A diary records what you did and when and superficially tells how you felt. A journal explains the significance of what happened. It seeks intense moments, insights, conflicting feelings. You can reflect on events in your life or the news, describe a person, place, or thing, remember your past, react to books or films, or record ideas for papers.

SELECTIONS FROM JOURNAL

Richard L. Shields

Nov. 2

I'm sitting on a wooden bench in a holding cell. It's 7 am. I'm writing this on toilet paper. It's Monday. If I were home the TV would be on. My orange back pack would be lying on the carpet beside the couch. My homework would be strewn across the coffee table. If I didn't crawl out & clean up pretty soon I'd be late for KW's math class. I'd feel good about being fifty and going to college--if I was home.

A deputy turns the lock and gestures with his finger. "Time for prints Mister Shields," he says as he holds the cell door open. I follow him to the printing area. There are cells on either side of the main corridor. Arms and hands hang out. Black, white, old & withered, restless & youthful. Faceless with one bond in common. We've all been accused.

My life is spinning backward, like reverse English on a cue ball. Slowly at first--then gaining momentum. Faster and faster. Left hand corner pocket. Scratch! You lose.

Dec. 12

Grandpa was a little guy. He wore a black derby, a gray overcoat with a black velvet collar and high-top black

broughams that shone like ice in moonlight. And the old
man strutted like a rooster. My mom claimed I was his
spitting image, but I couldn't see it. Going on 6, I was
almost up to him. He was bald, but I was nappy-headed. I
was skinny as a rail in my knickers and sockless PF Keds,
and he was a short and stocky fashion plate.

"What have those two sisters of yours been up to since
I was here last?" he'd ask when he got off the bus in
front of Critie's Ice Cream Parlor. I'd hesitate then because I knew I'd have to make up some exciting gossip for
him. He'd reach way down into his pants pocket and drag
out that long leather change purse with silver clasps.
He'd rummage around until my lips puckered up a story and
then go into Critie's Ice Cream Parlor--and my lying ass
right behind him.

Feb. 20

The minute I saw the words "Highland Park" in the newspaper headline, I found myself standing in a bygone era.
I was 10 and blazing a trail through Highland Park. My
knapsack was filled--rib-sticking peanut butter and jelly
sandwich, Oreos, Milk Duds, and Black Crows. Also 2 creme
donuts, licorice twists, and Mary Janes I'd been stashing
in a shoebox under my bed. I even had Daddy's thermos
brimmed with life-saving lemonade. Oh, I remember.

My ears were finely tuned to autumn leaves as they
crunched and knuckled under each trail-blazing step. I
was on a mission. No longer was I Dickie Shields. I was
Crispus Atticus. I was Nat Turner. I was Harriet Tubman.
Leading a band of rag-tag runaway slaves through the
dense underbrush along the park perimeter.

"Look out boy!" I'd shout. "Dontcha get too close to de
edge! Goodman Road out yonder. Ol' massa's men be comin'
long dat road afore long. Y'll keep up now."

I crawled along the hill, stopping only to put my ear
to the ground to listen for horse hooves. Steam fogged my
coke-bottle glasses. My hands sweat. Weak from exposure, I
began to hear the howl of bloodhounds. "You got to go on!"
I whispered through clenched teeth. I groped feverishly in
my empty knapsack, curling around one last melting Milk
Dud. It was mangled, fuzzy from knapsack innards. My face
squinched as I thought of typhus, gangrene, and TB.

What would ol' Frederick Douglass do? What would
Harriet Tubman do? Die on the underground trail and leave
her runaways to fend for themselves, their dream of
Canada shattered? Or would she risk disease by eating a
fuzzy, melted Milk Dud? I broke into whispered song: "Go
down Moses, way down in Egypt Land, Tell ol' Pharaoh, let
my people go!" I knew what I must do. I blew hard on the
Milk Dud, kissed it to God, and plunged it into my mouth.
And my strength returned. "C'mon, y'all," I shouted.
"Canada!"

Discussion

1. If you were advising Richard to develop one of these journal entries into
   an essay, which would you push hardest? Why?
2. Write your own journal entries on a low point in your life, a family
   member, or a childhood fantasy.

SELECTIONS FROM JOURNAL

Tina Thompson

1.

I can't forget the things my mother did to me and move
on with life. I want to forgive and forget but don't know
how. Maybe if I write it all down, I can get it out of my
system, stop feeling sorry for myself and begin to have a
normal relationship with my mother.

2.

My sister and I had torn a pair of stockings. "Do you
think I am made out of money?" my mother said. "Do you
think I can go stand on my head and spit money to replace
everything you ruin?" In her hand was the belt! It
dangled, quivering like a snake having an epileptic
seizure. My stomach lurched. I scurried on hands and
knees to reach my sister. We had to hide! She put her
hands over her head, pleaded with Mom not to. But nothing
could stop her in a rage. The strap swooshed and the

heavy buckle jingled. Then WHACK! WHACK! Leather and metal against my back. The air rushed from my lungs and it hurt breathing again. My sister's eyes bulged. We scratched and clawed our way onto the bed as the belt stung us. My back throbbed like a thumb hit with a hammer. When we were driven against the wall, we scaled it like rock climbers for the window ledge above us. Somehow we scrambled on the two and a half-inch sill.

Mom laughed at our climbing, her round body shaking like Santa Claus. Then she turned and stalked out. My sister and I fell from our perch onto the mattress. Our backs were bruised and bleeding. Our hearts pounded like scared rabbits. We grabbed our blankets and dove under the bed. Maybe we would be safe in the dark for a while.

3.

When I turned 18, my boyfriend gave me a puppy. He was gray with white specks but had a face swollen like a blow-fish. He was so bloated that his ears stuck out like Yoda's in Star Wars, so I named him Yoda. He was big, wild, and slightly retarded, but he was all mine! He slept with me every night. I even got him his own pillow and blanket. When I came home from school, Yoda would be waiting by the door, his whole body wagging.

One day my mother thrust my brother's glasses into my hand. The lenses were gone and the frame was mangled. It looked like someone had them for lunch. "Do you know how much these glasses cost me? 170 bucks! Your brother found Yoda eating them."

"Where is he?" I knew something was wrong, horrible.

"Hah! I took him to the pound." She gloated.

"You fat, ugly witch!" I knew I was in trouble as soon as I said the words, and ran into the dining room. She bounded after me like a crazed elephant on the warpath. She didn't bother going around the table, but scrambled right across it and dug her nails into my shoulder. But I was so furious it didn't hurt. She'd beaten so much hatred into me, I had plenty to spill out. I dug my nails back into her. She screamed at me and threw me into the wall and yanked my hair, throwing me on my back onto the dining room table. She punched me, each blow like a sledgehammer to my ribs. My legs kicked to keep her off, so she pinned me under her 300 pounds. The old table cracked. My brother screamed. When the table collapsed, I was pinned between the splintered wood and her body. My sister tugged at Mom, yelling, "Are you crazy? You'll kill Tina!" Then Mom took after my sister. Then all of us jumped our mother, writhing and thrashing around the room, stumbling over broken table legs, crashing chairs and pictures to the floor. "This'll be the last time you ever lay a hand on us," we vowed. And she never did again. After the police broke it up, I left home for good. I could no longer take her rage and I realized I could no longer contain my own.

   To this day I don't know how to act around her. She owes us an explanation and an apology we've never gotten. Maybe someday, if she can't find the courage to talk about it, I will.

Discussion

1. Tina was willing to share this personal journal with others because she wanted to go one more step. What would you say to her if you could write her a letter in response to this journal?
2. Write your own series of journal entries focused on exploring your memories of a close relative. Don't worry about making it all stick together yet.
3. Describe a pet and what it meant to you.

 NARRATIVE/DESCRIPTIVE ESSAYS

PA'S SECRET

Carol Nobles

   My great-grandfather died on a Monday--which upset my grandma's schedule. On Mondays, Grandma changed the bedding, hung up the week's wash, and sliced Sunday's leftover roast beef. But this Monday there were arrangements to make.

   Actually, she'd already begun preparations the day after Pa (my great-grandfather) was taken to the nursing home. Grandma had wedged open his bedroom door and hammered at the sealed windows. Pa was forever cold, even in summer, so they hadn't been opened in years. Panting from the exertion, Grandma said to me, "We've got to air this room out. God knows it needs it."

I only half listened, for I'd never been in Pa's bedroom even though he lived with us two years. I was eight when his second wife died and he moved in. His bedroom door was always shut, but occasionally I'd pass through the hall as he emerged, and a warm, spicy odor sneaked out behind him. The scent reminded me of an old crumpled tobacco pouch I once found hidden in the barn. Maybe Pa had something like that hidden in his room. Why else would he lock his door? If something was in there, now Grandma would find it. She never missed anything.

Grandma watched Pa closely during his last year because he began losing his mind. Today we call it Alzheimer's disease, but back then Grandma only saw it as another chore thrust on her. Pa spent mornings reading the newspaper while huddled next to the kitchen stove, occasionally puffing a cigar suspended from his mouth. Some days he'd forget to flick the ashes, and when they'd drop to the floor Grandma dove on him like a hovering hawk. She'd shriek, "Pa, put that thing out. One of these days you'll start the house afire. You shouldn't smoke those filthy things anyway." Pa never answered, never. He'd just puff and read and reread.

One Sunday, I sat at the table sticking Silly Putty against the comics, imprinting and then stretching Dagwood into all sorts of disproportions, when some live ashes must have embedded in Pa's sweater. Grandma yelled, "Pa! You're on fire!" He just sat there, little smoke streams lifting off his sleeve, while Grandma poured water on him. Only when he felt the wetness did he finally look up with a confused expression. I laughed so hard.

Once, a neighbor called to announce that Pa was "going pee" under the maple tree. Grandma was so mad she must have forgot I was only 10. "That old man's lucky I took him in," she sputtered. "He never cared for me when he was supposed to. My mother died when I was 13, and he took to drink and stayed away nights. Left me all alone for days. But when he asked to live here, I never said a word, just took him in. Not a word! And what gratitude do I get? That dirty old man!"

What angered Grandma most was when he got a girlfriend who lived in the old people's home. Grandma would whisper, "Just watch now. That old fool's in the bathroom sprucin' himself up for that old biddy up at the home. At his age!"

One afternoon, Grandma and I stood in a crowd at the bus stop when she spied Pa strolling down the street with his lady friend. As the bus arrived, she pushed our way to the front and dragged me to a seat so she could watch them pass. "Look at that now, will you? She's got a corsage pinned to her dress. So that's what he's doing with his money. The old fool."

The courtship was short-lived because within months Pa began to shuffle to breakfast unshaven and soon lost his appetite completely. So Grandma called the doctor. A few weeks later I awoke to strange voices on the stairs. Peeking out the door, I spotted two men in white jackets maneuvering a cot around a corner of the hall--headed for Pa's room. Muffled voices were drowned by Pa's "No, no. Don't take me. No." Pleading cracked his voice. Grandma tried calming him, but he wasn't listening, and he moaned steadily.

Later I heard Grandma on the phone saying they'd taken him to St. Mary's Nursing Home: "He's all swollen up down there. The doctor said he only had a few days, but it was going to get messy and this was the best way. I hated to do it, Rose, but I just couldn't handle him anymore."

The next afternoon, Grandma took me to see Pa because it might be for the last time. I asked her, didn't she think I was too young, but she said it was the right thing. At the front desk, a nun glided to us. Tucked into her waist, her rosary beads clicked together as we wordlessly followed her to the room.

It had three other beds. You couldn't see the sick people in them, but you knew they were there by the bulges. They lay flat, motionless, sunken under sheets. I didn't look. I didn't want to see their faces.

"He's in the corner," whispered the nun. She tugged a wooden dowel, opening curtains that hid his bed. It didn't look like Pa, but more like a bunch of bones jutting at funny angles. His pale, wrinkled nightshirt was pulled above his waist, his knees tucked into a fetal position. His legs seemed forced apart by a bulging, angry purplish-red swelling that he fingered.

"Pa! Stop that! Don't do that," Grandma hissed. She
tugged at his nightshirt, trying to cover him, but it
only made him moan. She grabbed at his hands to stop him
from touching himself, but it only made him try harder.
The nun whipped up the sheet wadded at the bottom of the
bed and covered him, but then he wailed. That's when I
left.

On the way home, curled in the back seat of the bus, I
tried to remember Pa rocking in his chair, Pa playing
cards with me, Pa any way but how I'd just seen him. If
he had any more secrets in his bedroom, I hoped Grandma
wouldn't tell me.

Discussion

1. What aspect of this essay seems strongest to you? If you could suggest
changes to the author in a workshop, what would you say?

2. Study how the author creates conflict. Does the essay start *en medias res*?
Point out all the conflicts. Describe how conflict grows more complicated.

3. Study character. There are three vivid people here; how are they made
distinct through dialogue and descriptive details? Discuss Grandma's motivation and complexity.

4. The young girl takes little direct part in the action. What does she contribute to the story?

5. Outline the time sequence in the essay. Can you explain why the author
might have arranged some parts as she did? Is it too complicated?

6. Study some of the little telling details: Pa's locked room getting aired out
and its "spicy" odor; the Dagwood and Silly Putty; and one other you
found significant. What do they add to the story?

7. Comment on the last line of the essay. How has the author grown or
changed? Why?

8. What is the essay's message or theme?

9. Freewrite a page about a family secret or an eccentric relative in your
family.

Revised Narrative Essay (Original in Chapter 7)

BASTARD

Miguel Martinez

A child born out of wedlock is called bastard, illegitimate, or lust child. I know. I am a bastard. When I was five, I asked my mother where Daddy was. I only had a vague idea of what a daddy was. I had heard the word used in kindergarten, but didn't understand the principle behind it. Among the many misconceptions about one-parent children is that we feel as though something is missing. We don't. There is no instinct telling us there should be another. We just accept the one parent we have.

My mother told me the best lie she could. She explained that my father had died shortly after I was born. He was supposed to have been a college professor. I accepted this. But her uneasiness about him kept me from asking more.

I have always been gentle with my mother. When she was young, her mother abandoned her, her three sisters, and a brother. They were all placed in a Catholic orphanage. Two of her sisters found good foster homes, and had decent chances at life. Not my mother.

Earlier this year I was required to get a copy of my birth certificate. I learned there were two kinds. The common one states that you were indeed born. The actual file copy, however, is loaded with information. I examined this one carefully. No father was listed. I had given up on learning anything new about my life when I caught a glimpse of the previous children section. It tells how many times the mother has carried to term, how many were born alive or stillborn prior to the birth certificate. I found out my mother had a child before me.

When I first saw that, things clicked into place. My mother had always vowed she was going to keep me. She struggled raising me, working as a waitress, and keeping odd hours. She was paranoid about someone finding me left by myself. I can look back now and see why.

As I won't ask her what really happened in her youth, I can only guess. I think she used sex as a love substitute, looking to men to give her the love she was not getting at the orphanage. I assume she got pregnant while living there and was forced to give the child up for adoption. This would explain why she would always tell me, "No one is going to take you away from me." By 18, she was probably defiant, and went out and lived. I can see a wild streak in her now, when she refers cryptically to New York City bars and roller skates or firecrackers in birthday cakes. I guess she met my father there, and on a fateful November evening, I came into being.

She tells me that shortly after I was born, she moved to North Rose, where she took a job as a live-in caretaker for an elderly couple. I am told that she wasn't allowed in her mother's house with me, and my grandmother once refused to loan my mother money for a needed hospital visit. It makes you wonder about family.

As for me, I grew up basically alone, as my mother would either be working or sleeping when I was at home. I don't resent that, if the alternative was an orphanage. My mother protected me with her lie about my father being dead; imagine what school would have been like for me if it was known I was a bastard. As it was, my friends sympathized.

Looking back, I think I should have realized something was amiss earlier than I did. A certain conversation always haunted me. It took place with a school administrator, who asked, "What was your mother's maiden name?"

I replied, "Martinez."

"No," he'd say, "I want your mother's maiden name."

"Martinez."

"That's her married name. I need her name before she was married."

Again, I would respond "Martinez" and get flustered. I suppose I didn't want to know.

I never really thought of my father. It seemed silly to wonder about someone who had no influence on my life. Nor can he ever. If I do wonder, maybe it's just a selfish desire to know if I have any inherited health problems.

I finally found out that I was a bastard when I joined the Navy. I had quit school and traveled around the country for a year, with no direction in my life. My mother despaired--pleaded with me to enlist. This was the only time she admitted I needed a male influence in my life.

Martinez 3

While I didn't agree, I felt that I had failed her by quitting high school and I agreed to join.

As I glanced through the mound of government forms before me, I saw a paper that my mother had signed stating that I had been born out of wedlock, and that my father did not support me. I think she had to submit this to allow me to join the service as a minor. When I saw the paper, I was surprised, but didn't care. What influence did this man have on my life? Didn't he just supply the raw material? To acknowledge that he had any claim on me would be just as absurd as saying a marble stonecutter can lay claim to an artist's sculpture.

The night before I left for boot camp, before I went out for my last fling with the guys, my mother sat me down and told me that my father was still alive. She told me his name and the city he lived in. She said she was telling me in case I wanted to contact him. I remember my mother was nervous, and I sensed it was a sort of loyalty test, for if I did seek him out, it would have been a slap in her face. I responded that I didn't want to contact him; there was no need. She smiled. I had kept her fragile world intact.

In time, I did get curious enough to look up his phone number, but not to call him. I think I just wanted to affirm that he was. The only thing about fathers I really wonder about is what kind I will make.

Discussion

1. You may want to read the early draft of this essay in Chapter 7. How has the writer responded to peer comments and suggestions? What has the essay gained in revision? Has it lost anything you liked about the early draft?

2. What suggestions would you make if the writer were to revise this draft?

3. The author says his grandmother abandoned his mother and then refers to the grandmother refusing to lend money to his mother. Should he explain how they met again later in life or would it pull the essay off track?

4. Free write a page starting a story about a label people have put on you and the conflict it created. How do you deal with it?

5. Write a letter to the author of this essay, explaining what the concept of "bastard" means to you.

INFORMATIVE ESSAYS

Informative Contrast Essay

FOOD FOR THOUGHT

Yeou-jih Yang

Mr. Chen took a short break from the steamy kitchen. Even though he was sweaty, he had a sense of accomplishment and satisfaction. He ducked out of the kitchen and scanned the dining room. Most tables were full. He watched a man shaking something vigorously into his food.

"What's that, Daddy?" asked a little girl who sat beside him.

"Soy sauce; you're supposed to put it on Chinese food."

Chen's heart sank. He retreated into the kitchen. "You should see what they do to my dishes!" he exclaimed. "After I spend so much time blending just the right seasoning, plup! It's all gone!"

Welcome to the West, or conversely, to the East. Dining experience is often a gate through which we can peek into a different culture. By examining it, you can not only enjoy food better, but also understand another culture and people, maybe even getting along better and promoting peace.

In Chef Chen's case, he had cut the meat and vegetables into bite-size pieces. He had chosen bright orange or red carrots, thick round scallops, curly pink shrimps, tender beef, green tree-shaped broccoli, yellow bamboo shoots, mixed them and gave a quick stir in the wok over intense flames. Then he blended in the sauce that he created. His masterpiece! Its smell provoked the gastric glands. Its appearance had a master painter's color and composition. Its taste made the tongue sing. It was a culture communicator inviting the eater to examine it and appreciate it. Just like tasting fine wines or desserts, we shouldn't just flush or gulp it down the throat. The stomach may be filled, but the head will stay empty and the senses idle.

Chinese dining is filled with loud greetings, bright lights, and crowded seating. In contrast, American dining appears quite harmonious--candlelight, soft, soothing music, and well-matched tableware. Peeling off this superficial appearance, we will find a different philosophy underneath.

To understand, first you must know that the Chinese believe the universe consists of two opposite forces: yin, a negative force, and yang, a positive force. Only if these two are balanced can there be harmony and peace. This applies to food too. Meat is usually yang and vegetables are yin. A balance produces a peaceful dish. The Chinese avoid extremities. For example, they don't drink icy cold water while eating a hot dish. They avoid conflict. For the same reason there are no knives at the table. Everything needing cutting is already done in the kitchen. The Chinese can't understand the western style of cutting meat at the dinner table, nor the swing from ice water to hot soup back to cold salad followed by a hot entrée and ending with a cold dessert. To Chinese, this causes conflict and unbalance.

"Would you pass the mashed potatoes, please?" someone may politely request at the end of an American rectangular table. With these interruptions, cutting food with two hands and switching the fork from one hand to the other, it can get pretty busy. The Chinese prefer a round table so everyone has equal access to the food. The use of chopsticks with precut food doesn't require switching, so everything is more direct and peaceful.

One day last summer while visiting from Taiwan, my in-laws, armed with a dictionary, local map, some basic sentences, and a lot of curiosity, ventured into town by themselves. When they returned, my father-in-law said, "When I order a steak, the waiter bombed me with a chain of questions: 'How would you like your steak, sir: well done, medium, or rare? What kind of dressing would you prefer? We have French, Italian, Thousand Island, and house. Potato? Baked, mashed, or fried?' There! I thought steak was a simple American food."

My mother-in-law nodded. "All I wanted was an American hamburger, but they asked me how do I want my burger done, do I want lettuce or tomato on it or both? Leave out onion? Keep pickle in? Do I want ketchup, mayonnaise, or mustard in it?" She continued, "Like a tailor, they will make exactly what you want. The problem is, I don't

know what an American burger should be. A Chinese chef
doesn't make you make all these choices to enjoy it."

When we go to different restaurants, we have the chance
to fill our stomachs, but also to fill our thoughts.

Discussion

1. Rate this essay for surprise value in ideas and detail. What do you know
   now that you didn't before?
2. How does the author enliven this comparison of Chinese and American
   eating habits?
3. How is the essay structured?
4. Think of two types of food or eating styles from different cultures. Draw
   up a list of comparisons or contrasts, looking for some "food for thought"
   behind the surface differences.
5. If you read this essay in a class workshop, what suggestions would you
   offer the author?

Informative Process Essay

THE AUTOPSY

Gregory F. Matula

The county hospital. People come here to mend broken
bodies, but it's also where those whose time has been cut
short are sent to find out why. In the back, almost like
an embarrassing family member kept out of sight, is the
medical examiner's office. This is where the fine art of
forensic medicine is practiced.

Above the door a sign reads, "What you see, what you
hear, when you leave, leave it here!" A reminder of the
sensitive investigations conducted here. There is complete silence except for a constantly ringing telephone.
Three walls in the holding room are covered with tile and
the fourth with what appear to be metal refrigeration
doors.

This is the world of Dr. Nicholas Forbes, the medical
examiner who will be performing today's autopsy. When

he enters, his assistant briefs him about the corpse's death. She was a 59-year-old woman whose automobile struck a tree during good driving conditions with clear visibility.

I follow Dr. Forbes into the examining room, and I'm given a gown and mask to protect myself and my clothes from flying debris and blood. In the center are two metal beds that work like draining boards. Holes in the top layer allow water running beneath to wash away the blood that spills. There are instruments, wash basins, and hoses placed around the room for easy access.

On one metal bed lies the naked body of the dead woman. Stitches stretch from the navel to rib cage and continue under each breast almost to the armpit. This is from a brief preautopsy exam performed just after the accident. Abrasions cover her body. Dr. Forbes's job is to determine what might have caused the car accident.

As he disappears to scrub up, his two assistants diligently reopen the cuts made the night before, and the room fills with an aroma best described as that of menstrual blood. One inserts a long needle into the woman's eyes to draw fluid. From this fluid they can determine if there was alcohol in her system. After exposing the rib cage by moving the breasts up and to the side, the gentlemen use a plier-like tool to cut the ribs and remove them. Now the lungs are visible.

With the precision and delicacy of a butcher, one assistant lifts and cuts out organs. The lungs and heart are plopped on the table. A hose suctions out a pool of dark blood from the cavity. From a brief inspection, the man notices that her liver is badly mangled and adds it to the vital body parts. When the pile of organs grows too large for the table, he pulls out a metal bin and dumps them in.

Is this what life is to become? A bunch of scraps thrown in a pile, like giblets for the gravy? It's been said we are "food for worms." I wonder if worms like giblets. Humans tend to think "It won't happen to me," "I can handle it," or "Only old people die." However, the Bible says in James 4:14, "whereas ye know not what shall be on the morrow. For what is life? It is even a vapor, that appeareth for a little time, and vanisheth away." How fragile we really are.

My thoughts are interrupted by a high-pitched whizzing sound. The man has completely gutted the corpse. All that remains is the empty cavity of the woman's torso with her head and appendages. The sound comes from a saw that looks like a drill with a disk. In the empty cavity the man saws the woman's backbone. After a moment he pulls out what looks like a flat oval-shaped dog biscuit. He explains it's a vertebra--to be used for a bone marrow specimen. He points out the spinal cord. It's thin and flimsy, like thick thread.

Next, the man walks to the head of the table, and without a word about what's next, grabs her scalp at the center of her head and folds it over her face. There, directly before me emerges a human skull. Not a picture, not a movie, not a computer replica, but a real skull fresh from its fleshy cage. He wipes it so it almost shines, as if gloating about its ability to protect its cargo. The saw resumes, and its pitch drops under the strain. Then the man uses a small prying instrument to pop the cap he'd just cut.

I'm privileged to see firsthand the most perplexing organ of the human body. The brain is creamy with black-etched grooves. It's so powerful yet so delicate that it indents like a sponge when the man takes hold and removes it. This magnificent piece of flesh isn't just thrown into the bin like the rest. It's treated royally, set apart on the examining tray. It will be saved for last.

After scrubbing up, the doctor reappears, steps to the table, and makes a visual inspection. He presses a foot pedal and talks into a microphone. In his foreign accent, he announces the time, then picks through the organs in the bin for the heart. He weighs it and announces the result into the microphone. He cuts the heart open for an internal examination and records a few observations. Then, like a butcher discarding excess fat, he drops the organ into a pail lined with a plastic bag.

One by one, the doctor examines each organ externally and internally in the same manner. He has obviously conducted this procedure more often than he might care to calculate.

Dr. Forbes pauses for a moment. In deep thought, he taps a tune on the examining tray with an instrument. For the first time I realize there's an actual person behind that surgical mask. He calls me over to see something un-usual in the lung. He explains how he determined she had sclerosis. I'm lost in the medical terms, but it doesn't stop him. He jokes about the red lungs with black tobacco spots having beautiful color just before he throws them into the pail.

Next is the trachea. He explains how it changes as a woman ages and causes her voice to deepen. He cuts intri-cate samples of each piece of flesh. He begins to quiz me on my knowledge of bodily organs and, like a game show host, he gongs me when I'm wrong.

Dr. Forbes appears to be surprised, when examining the stomach and liver, to see there is no gallbladder. He checks the bin and motions an assistant to look for a scar on the woman to see if it had been removed by surgery. No scar. The doctor notes this into the microphone. He then makes an incision into the stomach to empty its contents into a sample cup. "Well, look what we have here!" he says, as about thirty little yellow pills appear.

At this point, Dr. Forbes realizes this is a suicide. So far, he's determined she did not die on impact, because pieces of her liver were found in her lungs, proving aspiration after the accident. The pills in the stomach weren't even slightly digested, suggesting that she took them just before getting into her car. Due to her frenzied state, she must have driven her car into the tree because she couldn't wait for the pills to take effect. The doctor briefs me on the mental state of suicides.

While Dr. Forbes turns over the pills to the toxicol-ogist for further examination, his assistant returns the skull cap and sews the scalp back together. After in-specting all the organs, Dr. Forbes cuts into the brain as easily as slicing paté. I cringe at the thought of all the memories it once held. It's almost as if with each cut, 59 years of history are erased bit by bit. To me, the inside of the brain is the most beautiful part of the body. The white portions are distinct, highlighted with a creamy layer and graceful lines. If one glance at it doesn't cause you to believe in Creation and the miracle of humankind, then nothing ever will.

Done, Dr. Forbes presses the microphone pedal and announces, "Cause of death, pending toxicology report. Autopsy complete at 11:32."

Discussion

1. What are the steps in the process described? Which steps does the author dwell on and which skim over? Say why you agree or disagree with his emphasis.
2. This is mostly an objective, unemotional informative essay. Do the passages in which the author muses on the meaning of what he witnesses fit? Defend your position.
3. For most people, this essay rates high in surprise value. Think of how you could use firsthand witness to write a great informative essay. List three processes you think readers and you would be interested in, and a few notes about how you would go about it. Greg received permission to observe the autopsy simply so he could write a college paper.

CAREER RESEARCH PAPERS: USING THE INTERVIEW AND MLA-STYLE DOCUMENTATION

RADIATION THERAPY AS A CAREER

Lorrie Hartz

To help understand a career in radiology, I toured the radiation department of Strong Memorial Hospital in Rochester, New York, and spoke to Dr. Raymond Sweredoski and Dr. George Uschold. I wore an employee's white lab coat. They wore a small device clipped to their pockets that resembles a magnet. This "film badge" is worn for a month to monitor radiation levels you may be exposed to. Dr. Sweredoski noted that this information is filed to keep track of your cumulative lifetime dose of radiation.

I viewed many x-ray machines built to accommodate different body parts. Some were stationary; others moved around the patient or moved with the patient on them. I felt as if I should have worn my Spock ears for an espisode of <u>Star Trek</u>. I witnessed an angiogram (in which a tiny "camera" is inserted into the patient's blood vessels near the heart), and was surprised that the blood didn't bother me. I was told a radiographer must be in all operating rooms during surgery to take x-rays at a moment's notice. I also observed a computerized tomography scan, a computer-enhanced cross section of the body.

The machine resembled a tunnel and the patient moved into it. It's painless, but I was warned that claustrophobic patients may present a problem.

The radiation therapy center is more somber. I don't know if this is psychological or real, but the hallways and waiting room felt like a gloomy March day. The staff moved as if they were robotic, and I had a hard time telling if their smiles were real or stale half-moons pasted beneath their noses. I witnessed a child being measured with laser beams to determine the exact spot for treatment. Here you treat the same people over and over; you watch the effects of radiation on them: skin irritation, weight loss, nausea, hair loss, and depression.

The radiation therapy room resembles a maze. In reality, it is. This mazelike hallway acts as a barrier to radiation. The three-foot-thick concrete walls and lead doors absorb radiation and prevent the beams from continuing to where staff and patients are. Because of their weight, the doors are operated electronically.

The doctors explained that radiographers and patients wear lead aprons over areas you don't want exposed, and the radiographer stands behind a clear leaded-glass panel during the x-ray. Studies prove we're exposed to radiation every day of our lives from natural causes: from "the sun and stars, radioactive elements in the earth such as uranium, radium, and thorium, and radioactive substances such as radiopotassium and radiocarbon, which are found in foods, drinking water and air. . . . This accounts for over half the amount of exposure we receive" (Callaway 213).

Mental stress is the number one drawback to this profession. In therapy the burnout rate is high. The doctors said some radiation technicians find it hard to work with infants, friends, or family. This isn't a career for you if you can't stand the sight of blood or if the thought of giving a barium enema repulses you.

What you need is sympathy toward the patient. Eye contact, clear communication, and effective listening are important. It's better to say "I _think_ I know how you feel" rather than "I _know_ how you feel." A good sense of humor, self-confidence, and self-esteem convey a professional image.

Sixty percent of radiologists are employed by hospitals: the rest work for private physicians or clinics
("Radiology" 198). Dr. Sweredoski said hours vary from 8
to 4, 4 to 12, or 12 to 8 with a rotation of weekends and
hours on call. Job sharing or part-time employment is
also popular, and starting salaries range from $12 to $18
per hour ("Radiology" 198-99).

I have yet to decide if I will choose this career. I
want to do something that will make a difference and help
people. I have been a hairdresser, and it bothers me to
hear people say, "how I feel depends on how my hair
looks." This is trivial when I can ease the pain in an
ill person.

WORKS CITED

Callaway, William, and LaVerne Gurley. Introduction to
  Radiologic Technology. 3rd ed. St. Louis: Mosby Year
  Book, 1992.
"Radiology." Occupational Outlook Handbook. May 1992.
  Bulletin 2400.
Sweredoski, Dr. Raymond. Personal interview. 17 Nov.
  1992.
Uschold, Dr. George. Personal interview. 17 Nov. 1992.

Discussion

1. What is your personal assessment of this career after reading this essay? Why would you be interested or not in a career as a radiologist?
2. What areas does Hartz cover best? What additional information would you like to have?
3. Make a list of the top five things you want from a job. How does your present job or the one you are pursuing through college match up?
4. Create a list of 10 questions to ask someone who has the kind of career you want.

CAREER IN IMAGINATION

Rob Banwar

When *Star Wars* first came out in 1977, audiences were amazed at the effects: huge ships exploding in space, swords made of light, and laser blasts that defied reality. Yet special effects from such multi-million dollar movies are common now in $50 video games. I was raised on those movies and video games, and I want to be the person to create these awesome effects in 3-D design. But I wondered about three things when I started exploring this as a possible career: How much schooling is needed? How do you apply for a job like this and what salary would I earn? Last, and maybe most important, is it really as much fun as it seems to be, or does being in entertainment ruin it for a person?

When I interviewed John Romero of Ion Storm Entertainment in an online conversation, he told me, "Gaming is a metaphor for reality. In games we can live lives we can't normally have." Mr. Romero was the founder of the gaming company ID Software, which started the first-person perspective gaming with *Doom.* Using a primitive gaming engine and simple eight-bit textures, this game became a benchmark and is still widely played. This game embodies the graphical design career world (Romero n. pag.).

In my research I learned that computer and console games such as *Nintendo* and *PlayStation* are made using 3-D technology. First, CAD (Computer Aided Design) editors use wire frames to construct a model for a character, a level or even an entire scene. They then use textures created by a desktop publisher or graphics artist to bring these lines to life. The rock that passes by as mere glitter in a game is, in fact, an individually modeled polygon that has been texturized using a series of texture maps. This requires three people: a programmer, a 3-D modeler and a texture artist (Activision n. pag.). The aspect that interests me the most is the texture art work.

This field is often ignored. 3-D modeling generally pays more and has a larger market since it is used more often in movies. But 3-D creates just the skeleton of an image. Texture is what a gamer remembers. Not the shape of the rock, but how it looks. Was it dark gray? Light green? Wet? Pitted? (Wilmore 112).

Texturing and graphic design salaries typically start at $70,000 a year and can rise into the millions in some markets. Usually an associate's degree in graphic design is all that is needed, but those with master's degrees often start at the higher salaries and work the industry's better jobs (Heckbert n. pag.).

Blizzard Entertainment uses the standard method of hire for these jobs. Applicants send in a demo tape showcasing their best graphics: still frame animation, special effects, or video and code for a game. This way, it is not just credentials that get a person a job; it is talent. For this reason, many people in the field are often college dropouts or fresh out of high school working beside experienced artists with college educations (Blizzard n. pag.).

I wonder about the long-term effects of such a career. Would a career in special effects ruin my imagination? So many games and movies mimic the popular ones to rip off their success. Look at how *Scream* failed so badly to recreate *Psycho*. The masterful effects were just tired and overused. How can the industry stay fresh enough to keep new ideas constantly flowing? When I wonder about growing stale, I think of the president of the United States Patent Office who once declared "All that can be invented, has been invented"; but he said this in 1899! (Wilmore 371).

But even Mr. Romero mentioned burnout. People who draw from their imaginations each day may just run out of ideas. The fun, the entertainment, is sometimes lost in the job's repetition (Romero n. pag.). I don't see this. I love working with my imagination. My job would be crafting imagination and provoking thought. How could creating the impossible ever grow stale?

One last reason I am interested in this career is because it influences culture. People grow up on television, computers, games and movies. Having influence in shaping young people's minds intrigues me.

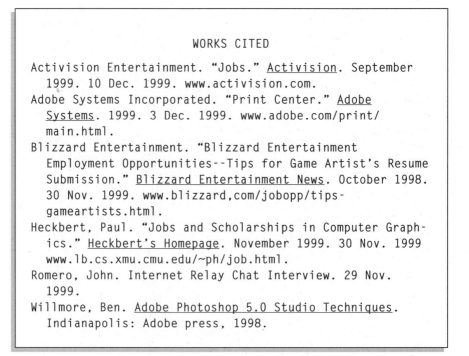

WORKS CITED

Activision Entertainment. "Jobs." Activision. September 1999. 10 Dec. 1999. www.activision.com.

Adobe Systems Incorporated. "Print Center." Adobe Systems. 1999. 3 Dec. 1999. www.adobe.com/print/main.html.

Blizzard Entertainment. "Blizzard Entertainment Employment Opportunities--Tips for Game Artist's Resume Submission." Blizzard Entertainment News. October 1998. 30 Nov. 1999. www.blizzard,com/jobopp/tips-gameartists.html.

Heckbert, Paul. "Jobs and Scholarships in Computer Graphics." Heckbert's Homepage. November 1999. 30 Nov. 1999 www.lb.cs.xmu.cmu.edu/~ph/job.html.

Romero, John. Internet Relay Chat Interview. 29 Nov. 1999.

Willmore, Ben. Adobe Photoshop 5.0 Studio Techniques. Indianapolis: Adobe press, 1998.

Discussion

1. What is your personal evaluation of this career after reading this essay?
2. What aspects of this career does Rob not discuss that you think are key issues?
3. How does this essay compare to Lorrie Hartz's career paper in the amount of information and evaluation the writer provides?
4. Evaluate the concluding paragraph.

INFORMATIVE CAUSE ESSAY: APA-STYLE RESEARCH FORMAT

THE TEENAGE PREGNANCY EPIDEMIC

Hollie Salphine

The statistics are startling: American girls, on average, begin having sex at age 16, boys at age 15. By the end of their teens, 70% of girls and 80% of boys have been sexually active (McBee, 1986, p. 8). One of every ten teenage girls in the United States becomes pregnant every year, and almost half of these pregnancies result in births--30,000 to girls under the age of 15 alone (Stark, p. 1986, p. 28).

What appeared over 20 years ago as a threat has esca-lated into a full-fledged disaster that is rapidly making its mark on America. News commentators are calling it an epidemic, a word previously reserved for a disease. The teenage birthrate in the United States is among the high-est in the world for developed countries (Oettinger, 1989). Why?

Social workers are almost unanimous in citing the influ-ence of popular media--television, rock music, videos, and movies--in directing the trend toward premature sexu-ality. How can teens learn the value of abstinence while watching tails wagging lustfully in TV commercials for tight jeans? How can we expect them to "be careful" when, by the estimate of one family planning group, there were 20,000 instances of "suggested sexual intercourse" in one year's TV programming--without a single mention of birth control or disease prevention? (Van Biema, 1987, p. 111).

Lately, of course, the media have edged a tiny step closer to providing American teenagers with a better un-derstanding of sexuality. A groundbreaker was an August episode of <u>Kate and Allie</u> in which Allie has a heart-to-heart talk with her daughter, who is thinking about hav-ing sex with her boyfriend. On April 5, the television show <u>Daddy</u> made one of the bluntest statements yet about teen pregnancy when it demonstrated the high price of parenthood.

Teenage pregnancy can also be blamed on such unreliable methods of birth control as withdrawal or rhythm. Nearly two-thirds of unwed sexually active teenage girls either never or inconsistently practice birth control. Why are teenagers so careless when it comes to contraception? Karen Pittman, a sociologist at the Children's Defense Fund in Washington, D.C., explains that, "Many teenagers can reconcile their sexual activity if it's spontaneous or unplanned" (Stark, 1986, p. 30). In many cases a teen-ager's desire for completely spontaneous sex is tied to the belief that being "swept off your feet" or "carried away" is forgivable, but having premeditated sex is not.

Third, sex requires a responsibility that most teen-agers don't accept. Most are simply not capable of dealing with the emotional impact of premature sexuality. According to Irma Hilton, a psychologist at the Ferkauf Graduate School of Psychology, "Young people just don't have the psychological strength to recognize the consequences of their actions" (Wallis, 1985, p. 84). Teenagers tend to be impulsive and have trouble making long-range plans to provide contraception.

Another probable cause of increased teen pregnancies is the fact that sex without marriage nowadays is gaining social acceptance. The Gallup Poll reveals that over the past ten years 16% more of us have come to accept the idea, bringing total acceptance of premarital sex to 48% (Oettinger, 1989, p. 48). Our liberal attitude makes teens feel nonmarital sex is perfectly acceptable.

No simple solution for teenage pregnancy is available. Adolescents today face a rapidly spreading epidemic that even they may not be able to stop. Although we cannot be sure of one major cause to focus on, we can be sure of the disastrous effects.

REFERENCES

McBee, S. (1986, December 22). A call to tame the genie of teen sex. U.S. News & World Report, p. 8.

Oettinger, K. B. (1989). Not my daughter: Facing up to adolescent pregnancy. Englewood Cliffs NJ: Prentice Hall.

Stark, E. (1986, October). Young, innocent and pregnant. Psychology Today, pp. 28-35.

VanBiema, D. (1987, April 13). What's gone wrong with teen sex? People, pp. 111-21.

Wallis, C. (1985, December 9). Children having children. Time, pp. 78-90.

Discussion

1. Outline this essay. Are the causes distinct and separate, or do they blur into others?
2. Can you think of any other causes for teen pregnancy?
3. Rate this essay for surprise value and packing in details.
4. Is the conclusion satisfying?
5. Contrast the "feel" or "mood" of this informative essay with "Food for Thought." How do they differ in their approach to informing a reader?
6. Think up a list of three or four causes for a topic of your choice. List some facts or statistics you'd like to research for support.
7. This essay is 10 years old, what changes have occurred since then that could update it? Consider TV, advertisements, birth control education, and other factors.
8. Use the Internet to get the latest numbers on teenage sexual activity and pregnancy rates.

THE PROFESSIONAL LETTER

You will write many business or professional letters in your life: cover letters for job applications, letters of recommendation, letters to co-workers, bosses, employees, government agencies, and clients. You will write letters to lawyers, banks, medical organizations, and credit card companies disputing charges or asking for information or help. Your writing must look professional to be taken seriously.

The professional letter follows a strict format, and you can model yours on either of the first two that follow. Letters are **single spaced** with double spaces between paragraphs. **Do not indent paragraphs.** Write your address in the upper left corner with the date below it. Skip a line and write the person's name, title, and address to whom you're writing on the left; then skip another line and write the salutation ("Dear Ms. Lesser:" for example). The body of the letter should state its purpose in the opening paragraph and clearly state what you want your reader to do. The closing ("Sincerely," for example) goes on the left side of the page. Skip several lines where you will sign your name, and type your name.

Persuasion Using Description

Hanson Street ICF
Newton Area NYDA

June 13, 2001

Brad A. Walker
Director of Employee Relations
New York Developmental Association
Newton, NY 14620

Dear Mr. Walker:

At 6:03 as I enter the group home I am bombarded by screaming and banging. Don, a co-worker, is slumped against the door of the time-out room, hand diligently on the doorlock. Dark circles hang under his eyes. He is utterly exhausted. "Long night?" I ask. He can't hear me. Inside the room, G. L. pounds her fists against the metal door.

As a residential treatment specialist at the Developmental Association, I experience stress on many levels. I have begun to pop Rolaids like candy, and my body is bruised and scratched. I deeply enjoy most aspects of my job: helping residents use a toothbrush, participate in sensory stimulation, or practice sign language. I am part physical therapist, part social worker. Working with the retarded is both important and inspiring.

But we have a 75 percent turnover rate of employees every two years. The house is in a constant state of retraining, which detracts from the quality and amount of goal work with residents. Someone hired a month ago cannot relate well to residents or implement programs. We need to make changes to prevent the burnout caused by unnecessary stress.

One cause of stress is the time-out room used by three of the ten residents at my house. According to G. L.'s plan, for instance, when she becomes disruptive or assaultive, she will be "escorted" to the time-out room. The escort requires two staff members trained in SCIP (strategies in crisis intervention and prevention) to physically relocate G. L. Her arms are held, SCIP staff secure her between them with their hips, and she is forcibly moved. In her agitated state, she lashes and thrashes feet, arms, and head to cause damage. This occurs daily, up to five times in a single afternoon. She is kept in the time-out room for up to an hour where she will yell and bang the electromagnetically locked door. Staff must hold the button at all times or she can exit.

H. T. also exhibits violent behavior. He becomes impatient and disruptive if forced to wait--for dinner, for instance. If ignored, he hurls anything within reach at staff, engages in SIB (self-injurious behavior), breaks windows or furniture, and assaults staff members. He is strong enough to dislocate arms and snap wrists.

Here are some strategies to reduce these stresses.

We could introduce a more dynamic program to vent staff frustration. Our present biweekly meetings deal with modification-to-behavior plans. We could devote more time to good old-fashioned gripe sessions. These would be confidential, nothing would be taken personally, and nothing would be exempt from discussion. Empathy from administration during these meetings is crucial. I have observed that older NYDA administrative members tend to dismiss our grievances--when we do voice them--by saying, "Boy, you should have been here ten years ago. That was stress." Maybe so, but it is exhausting now, and they should be more receptive to our suggestions.

We should have access to stress management courses designed for our specific work problems, as well as to teach us how to catch up on sleep after an overnight and manage time better. A group membership at the local YMCA could vent pent-up anxiety and frustration. Ideally, we should have access to deprogramming sessions with a psychologist after particularly bad episodes. We are expected to fulfill our responsibilities regardless of how angry we are at getting spit on, slapped, scratched, bitten, and pulled by the hair. We're frustrated having a behavior plan work successfully one day and blowing up the next. We know each resident has potential; when this potential is not realized, we blame ourselves. We need to know our supervisors support our efforts and understand; we often feel they do not. Making available any of these suggestions will show we are taken seriously, respected and appreciated.

My duties at NYDA are not without rewards, but it is increasingly difficult to feel the enthusiasm I once did. Walking into the Hanson Street ICF is like entering a pro wrestling match that does not let up until my ten-hour shift is over. My ears often ring on the drive home.

These stresses detract from my goal: to do something positive and learn about myself and the human condition, not just turn a profit with my head in the sand. I do not regret working with the mentally retarded, but at the current stress level, I do not think I will continue after finishing my education. I don't want to be a coffee-gulping, chain-smoking burnout by the time I'm twenty-five. Please consider these proposals for the good of all of us.

Sincerely,

Craig Lammes

Craig Lammes
Residential Treatment Specialist

Discussion

1. What are the main ideas of this letter; what are the best supporting details?
2. The author is writing for an audience who knows something of the subject. If you are not familiar with the operation of group homes, you may feel a bit left out as an audience. Find some word choices that indicate this.
3. What does the author say to avoid sounding like a mere complainer?
4. Write a formal letter to your employer or a public official to suggest a policy change (one page maximum, single spaced).

Persuasive Letters

84 Somewhere Drive
Brighton, NY 14623

April 25, 1997

John D. Perry
New York State Senate
506 Legislative Office Building
Albany, NY 12247

Dear Senator Perry:

I am a registered Democrat residing in your 54th Senate
District. I am writing this letter to seek your help in
stopping antiabortion demonstrations that block access
to doctors' offices, clinics, or hospitals. These demonstrations not only inconvenience medical professionals
and patients trapped in a facility invaded by antiabortionists, but they threaten the health of women there
for medical attention. Please help by sponsoring legis-
lation that would classify trespassing which prevents
administering health care to any patient as an offense
punishable by up to one year in prison and up to a
$1,000 fine.

I am sure you are aware of the increasing number of
antiabortion demonstrations around the state and nation
where demonstrators occupy obstetrician-gynecologists'
offices, hospitals, or abortion clinics. The demonstrators call these invasions "rescue missions" and justify
them on the grounds that they are rescuing "unborn children" from "death." There have been three such demonstrations in Monroe County since the end of December. These
resulted in 28 arrests, mostly for trespassing. In all
three incidents, women waiting for doctor appointments
were prevented from receiving needed medical care. A
Democrat and Chronicle article about a December 28 "rescue" reported that one patient fainted while detained by
the demonstrators; Democrat and Chronicle reports of a
March 29 demonstration indicated one patient became hysterical because demonstrators would not allow her to
leave the office.

Although some demonstrators were arrested for more serious charges such as resisting arrest or obstructing a police officer, most were charged with either third-degree or second-degree trespassing. Third-degree trespassing carries a maximum sentence of 15 days in jail; second-degree trespassing, a class B misdemeanor, carries a maximum three months. If previous experience holds true, most of those arrested will receive minimal punishment such as a suspended sentence, a small fine, or an alternative penalty such as writing an essay on civil disobedience (the essay was actually imposed by a Rochester City Court judge on antiabortion demonstrators at Highland Hospital last year!). Those jailed will spend a month at most behind bars.

While the punishments fall within sentencing guidelines, they are too lenient to deter demonstrators. We require a law matching the punishment with the gravity of the offense. New York needs a statute that makes it unlawful for anyone to deny a person access to health care as a result of trespassing. While this will not eliminate all "rescue missions," it will make demonstrators weigh the consequences before occupying a doctor's office, clinic, or hospital.

Denying access to a medical facility is not the same offense as refusing to leave someone's yard when requested by the owner (third-degree trespassing). It threatens the health of patients trapped in the facility or who are outside and need medical care. Although antiabortion demonstrators insist that the only patients inconvenienced are those seeking abortions, both the trapped doctors and patients stated in the newspaper that there were no scheduled abortions those days. The occupied offices are obstetrician-gynecologists' offices, not "abortion clinics" as claimed. As such, many or most of the women there were seeking medical care ranging from regular examinations to prenatal care to emergency treatment. Even if the offices had been abortion clinics, the demonstrators would have prevented women from receiving legal medical treatment.

Denying access to a doctor's office violates the inalienable rights of life and liberty. Newspaper accounts indicate that patients are often detained against their will.

Indeed, the March 29 demonstrators refused police access
to the hysterical woman. Most patients are innocent
bystanders. In addition, these demonstrations threaten
the delicate confidentiality of doctor/patient relationship by exposing it to public confusion and
chaos. Finally, the minimal punishments given convicted
demonstrators weaken respect for the law and encourage
others.

Some people may argue that denying access to a medical
facility warrants penalties no harsher than trespassing,
since these are acts of political free speech. Although
no reasonable person would deny antiabortion advocates
the right to speak against abortion through picketing,
public forums, advertising, and lobbying elected of-
ficials, these acts differ from occupying a doctor's
office. Genuine acts of speech do not violate the lawful
rights of other people.

Antiabortionists may also justify doctors' office occupa-
tions on the grounds that they are saving lives of unborn
innocents; the inconvenience patients experience is justified by the higher value of life if abortions are prevented. However, the news media in Rochester have never
indicated that any abortions have been prevented.

Health worker unions may wonder if harsher penalties
against demonstrators blocking health care facilities
might be used against their members in a strike at a
hospital. These fears can be eased by drafting the law
so that nondisruptive political speech, such as informa-
tional picket lines, would be permitted.

Harsher laws against denying access to health care are
not unlike laws that prohibit disruption of a religious
service. Such an act is classified as aggravated disorderly
conduct, a class A misdemeanor under New York law punishable by up to one year in jail. Disrupting a church service and blocking access to health care both deny basic
rights: the freedom to worship as one chooses and the
right to medical treatment. Both acts are morally repug-
nant and can inflict deep psychological scars. Disrupting
a church service raises the specter of religious persecu-
tion; denying access to health care violates doctor/
patient confidentiality.

Senator Perry, I thank you for your staunch support of
abortion rights through the years. Increasing the penalty
for denying access to medical care through trespassing
will help assure those rights. I hope you and your staff
draft such a law and that you sponsor it in the Senate.

Sincerely,

Timothy C. Dewart

Timothy C. Dewart

Discussion

1. What is the proposal? What are the elements of the plan?
2. How does the author aim this proposal at his specific audience? How
   would he have to change things if it were written for a general audience?
3. What are the author's supporting arguments? What values does he
   stress?
4. Does he fairly represent opposition viewpoints? Analyze the refutation
   section (paragraphs 7, 8, and 9). Is it effective? What other objections
   can you raise?
5. React to the last two sentences in paragraph 5.
6. Is the analogy in paragraph 10 a false analogy or valid?
7. Write a draft letter to one of your local representatives about a law you
   would like enacted.
8. This letter is long. If you had to cut 25 percent, argue which sections
   contribute the least.

NOTE: This essay is a letter the student wrote to her boss, the owner/
director of a dance studio where the author worked as a dance instructor.

Dear Shirl Bonaldi:

There are a few things I would like to discuss with you.
I feel your business needs extreme improvements.

First, your attendance record lacks by a lot. You are the
director of a dance studio, and you have put in only two
full weeks this whole year. At least one day a week you
have cancelled class or gotten another teacher to cover
for you. As a result of these constant absences, students

have lost confidence in you. For example, one of your
most advanced students, Kelly Fisher, refused to do
competition because she felt she wouldn't get enough
practice. A student can only practice so much on her own.
She needs a teacher's advice and corrections to really
improve and be successful in competition. Your students
are beginning to doubt your ability because they don't
see it very much.

Secondly, you have lost your enthusiasm. You used to come
to class with your tights, leotards, and proper shoes.
Now you wear jeans and sneakers. It is a bad influence on
the little kids. Now they come unprepared. When asked
where their stuff is, they say, "Miss Shirl doesn't have
her things, so why do I need them?" You never dance anymore. You just sit in your chair and dictate what you
want done. You make it easy on yourself. You take all the
advanced classes and leave the other teachers with the
beginner and baby classes. Where is your desire to teach
and dance? You have already lost two students, and you
will continue to lose more if you don't think about what
I'm saying.

There is one last point: the treatment of your employees.
I have been working for you for three years, and I've
gotten the same pay all that time. I'm teaching as many
classes as you are. I also pay $104 a month to take les-
sons from you. When I finally had the nerve to ask for a
raise, you laughed at me. I understand you may not have
been able to afford it, but you were inconsiderate.

The students miss how you once were: energetic, enthusi-
astic, and caring for all of us. You could use these
again. Please think about it. Thank you for your time.

Sincerely,

Tina Maenza

Tina Maenza

Discussion

1. Comment on the tone of this letter. How do you think the author's audience would react or feel? Suggest where and how you might revise it
   for tone.

2. Outline the letter. What are the key arguments? Discuss their validity. Are they supported with sufficient detail?
3. If you have complaints about your boss or place of employment, write a brain-teaser list. In peer groups or in class, discuss how to achieve the proper tone in presenting them.
4. How does this letter's format fall short?

 PERSUASIVE ESSAY

A VOICE AGAINST NEEDLE EXCHANGE

Raymond Santiago

The Needle Exchange Program attempts to reduce the AIDS epidemic by providing sterile syringes to intravenous drug users. Vans usually distribute these syringes in local neighborhoods. Addicts are supposed to give their names, turn in their used needles, and get a new pack. There are about 75 needle exchange programs in 55 cities (Leary 1). However, I believe we need to hear the voice of the inner city. It has plenty of needles, but it doesn't have enough outreach into the streets or good drug treatment facilities. The Needle Exchange Program had to be thought up by people who don't understand the inner-city mentality.

Studies show that this program does slow the spread of AIDS, and that it puts many addicts into contact with health care services, including drug rehabilitation programs. It is reported that the spread of AIDS among intravenous drug users has dropped in every city with this program.

The media, however, has not reported the bad side. I've worked as a volunteer outreach worker in the inner city among Hispanic and black communities with high rates of AIDS. I know from my experience in the streets that chronic heroin and crack addicts are irresponsible and extremely difficult to reach. They don't show up for appointments. Many have lost their families because of irresponsibility. When they need a fix, they use the first available needle. How can these people be counted on to turn in dirty needles or to give their real names to keep track of them?

Here are three other problems. Many dealers sell drugs with needles for extra money. Where do they obtain these needles? From the helpful vans, of course! Second, while we make needles easy for addicts to get, diabetics whose lives are also at stake must pay for their insulin needles. Third, what would happen if someone were to die of a drug overdose while using a needle from a Needle Exchange van, and the family sued the program?

This program means well, but treatment is still the best avenue. Addicts hooked on heroin and crack today have to wait so long for treatment that by the time they do get help, most are already infected with the AIDS virus. And let's remember this: it costs taxpayers about $2,000 a year to treat an addict, but $40,000 to put them in prison, and $100,000 to care for them as they die of AIDS (Garcia 14).

Fresh needles can make other problems worse. A television documentary recently reported on the exchange program in Philadelphia. They stationed the van near schools and children saw them operate. Residents also found themselves collecting pails of discarded used needles from their sidewalks. Cars from New Jersey and Delaware cruised in for needles. This van was stationed in an area plagued with crime, abandoned houses, and economic problems. The residents didn't want the program and these additional problems there. But it was the perfect place for those who run the program: it had no voice, no way of fighting the program.

Corrine Jennings, a woman who lives on the Lower East Side of Manhattan, said addicts "urinate, defecate, and vomit on my steps." She washes blood from her steps after addicts shoot up "with syringes they got from the van down the street" (Monte 6). Residents also complain that drug users come from New Jersey for the clean needles. Yet discarded needles are still picked up in her area--and used again. And the discards endanger everyone. A toddler was found playing inches from a syringe discarded near a church (Monte 6). It's hard to pick them all up, because the program on the Lower East Side dispenses over 20,000 needles each week ("Legalizing Syringes Won't Curb Abuse" 22).

The program came to my city also--against the inner city's wishes. Drug counselors, volunteers, addicts, and ministers spoke against the program at meetings before it arrived. I met the program's promoters. Many seem as if they have never dealt one-on-one with an addict. They showed high education on addiction, but little true knowledge about how an addict thinks, feels, or functions.

Addicts spoke at the meeting, including some already with the AIDS virus. One woman, who had been an addict for years, spoke about the time she shot up with a girl who was eight months pregnant. She told the girl that she had the HIV virus, but the girl responded, "that she didn't care, that she needed a fix right away." So they shared needles. She came to the meeting to speak against the Needle Exchange Program because addicts are desperate, indifferent, and irresponsible. One by one other speakers shared similar experiences and opinions, all falling on deaf ears.

A friend of mine, a drug counselor and ex-addict, said giving an addict needles is like writing him off. I'll translate Julio Cuevas's statement from Spanish: "You don't need a needle exchange program to save their lives. You need to give them hope, and if you give them needles, you're closing down their last hope--that their lives will change" (Cuevas 13). Giving an addict clean needles is like helping him pull the trigger of a gun to his head.

I know many addicts who kicked drugs. I was there once myself--seven years ago--drowning my pain with drugs, trying to hold on to some hope I could overcome this demon. If someone had handed me a needle every time I needed one, I would never have made it out of drug addiction.

WORKS CITED

Cuevas, Julio. "A Quien Pueda Interesar." La Prensa Hispana 1 Nov. 1993: 13.

Garcia, Andres. "The Latino Community." La Prensa Hispana 1 Nov. 1993: 14.

Leary, Warren E. "Report Endorses Needle Exchange as AIDS Strategy." New York Times 20 Sept. 1995: A1.

"Legalizing Syringes Won't Curb Drug Abuse." New York Times 12 Sept. 1995: A22.

Monte, William. "Neighborhood Report: A Rough New Neighbor in a Rough Old Neighborhood." New York Times 19 Mar. 1995: B6.

Discussion

1. The author supports his position with personal experience as well as research. What are you still wondering about that he could answer either with more research or personal observations?
2. He fairly presents the facts around the Needle Exchange Program in the opening paragraph. But what refutations might the promoters or you raise against his argument?
3. Go through the essay and list the various arguments he uses against needle exchange. What values does he stress? What values would you stress to argue *for* needle exchange?
4. Write a position statement on some issue for which you have firsthand experience. You might use the author's approach: arguing against outsiders who think they know best.

 REVIEW

DANCE RHYTHMICS

Tina C. Maenza

"Dance Rhythmics" was performed at the old St. Agnes Church by the dancers of Dance Attitudes who ranged from three to fifteen years old. They performed tap, jazz, and ballet to an almost full house. Despite some interesting dances, songs, and costumes, the recital as a whole was a disappointment. It simply needed more preparation and organization.

Even considering that this was only the second recital for this school and most of the students were beginners, the girls were unorganized and unprepared for an audience. As dances were in progress, a dancer's head would turn to a fellow dancer to imitate moves. They were not in synch and lacked confidence and grace. It distracts the audience when a ballet dancer jumps in the air and lands with a big thud.

The class mothers were unprepared and unorganized themselves. Their job is to prepare dancers before going onstage and show them their way once off. Yet there were long stale breaks between dances. Instead of twenty seconds, breaks lasted two minutes. One could hear chaotic movement behind the curtain. There were no props, so what was the problem? And once the red velvet curtain raised, the dancers were still fidgeting into position.

The mistakes and lack of synch in the young girls were cute, acceptable, and expected in their amusing "Hippity Hoppity Frog" and "Jump Shout Boogie." But the dance teachers' numbers, "Swing the Mood" and "T.B.A. Flipper," were unimpressive, not good examples for the young dancers. The moves were simple and boring and almost easy enough for some students.

The older girls were weak too. In "Fantasia Overture" performed by seven, eleven, and twelve-year-olds, the girls leaped like cattle roaming open land. The hollow stage echoed after each jump. Six of the seven girls were overweight, yet dressed in short red tutus that barely covered their rears. This color was probably chosen to coincide with the music, but only drew viewers' attention to the size of their bodies. Another performance where appearance made a difference was "Kiss the Girl." The costumes were unnecessarily revealing, for with almost every little bounce their breasts seemed about to burst from their costumes.

Overall, this performance was a disappointment. The commotion in the audience and exiting of people after almost every dance showed they were not interested. With organization and practice, the girls are likely to perform better next June.

Discussion

1. What are the author's standards of judgment in this review?
2. Although support does she give for her views?
3. Although the review is negative overall, how does the author strive for balance and fairness? Does she succeed?
4. Write a review of a recent performance you witnessed in sports, the arts, film, or television.

LITERARY RESEARCH PAPER USING COMPARISON

RESPONSIBILITY AND THE <u>ODYSSEY</u>
John Barzelay

In the first pages of Homer's <u>Odyssey</u>, the Greek God Zeus introduces the theme of responsibility: "Ah, how shameless--the way these mortals blame the gods. From us alone, they say, come all their miseries. Yes, but they themselves, with their own reckless ways, compound their pains beyond their proper share" (Homer 78). The tale will demonstrate how irresponsible men are held accountable for their excesses. It will take twenty years to transform Odysseus from a fearless, irreverent, reckless boy into a responsible, self-controlled man.

Now consider the controversy surrounding attention deficit disorder--and how the <u>Odyssey</u> addresses this problem. ADD is used to describe an inattentive, overactive, noncompliant child with poor impulse control (Breggin n. pag.) Four million ADD-diagnosed children each year are prescribed Ritalin, a stimulant medication (Diller, "Nearly" n. pag.).

In a letter to the <u>New York Times</u> one physician asks whether vague and subjective symptoms including "often fights with hands or feet or squirms in seat . . . leaves seat in classroom" and "has difficulty awaiting turn" could be explained by something other than a neurological problem. He suggests that many factors may lead children to behave this way: "a spirited, creative nature that defies conformity . . . inconsistent discipline or lack of unconditional love . . . boring and oversized classrooms . . ." In short, the ADD label is "attached to children who are in reality deprived of appropriate adult attention" (Breggin n. pag.). The National Institute of Health admits that there is no valid diagnostic test for ADD (Huffington n. pag.). Neurologist Fred Baughman cites estimates of the frequency of ADD that vary from 1 in 3 to 1 in 1,000 and asks, "Is ADD, after all, in the eye of the beholder?" (Breggin and Breggin n. pag.).

Early in the book, Homer describes the misery that Odysseus's wife and son endure at the hands of brazen suitors who hope to wed the supposed widow, Penelope. Odysseus's son, Telemachus, blames the god Zeus for his misfortune: "Zeus is to blame. He deals to each and every laborer on this earth whatever doom he pleases" (Homer 89). These are the words of a boy who sees himself as a helpless victim. This self-image perpetuates his victimization.

But growing up means becoming responsible for oneself. And Telemachus's transformation from child to adult begins when the goddess Athena arouses his dormant manhood by instructing him: "Think how to drive these suitors from your hall at daybreak. Summon the island's lords to full assembly, give your orders to all and call the gods to witness. Tell the suitors to scatter sail in quest for news of your father. Then . . . think hard for a way to kill these suitors. You must not cling to your boyhood any longer. It is time you were a man" (86-89). She shows Telemachus he is not helpless, that passivity makes him guilty of complicity.

This same phenomenon occurs with children diagnosed with ADD. Studies show that labeled children tend to hold themselves less accountable for their behavior. The ADD label encourages victimlike passivity or a sense of per-secution. One author says, "Self-image for children is highly dependent on peer opinion. . . . Once labeled, it may take them well into adulthood to learn that they have a choice" (Diller, "Culture" n. pag.).

The suitors indignantly deny any responsibility for de-vouring Odysseus's family's worldly goods by blaming Penelope for being so attractive (Homer 96-99). By fixing blame on her, they rationalize their outrageous behavior.

Just so, we find that diagnosing children as ADD merely relieves us of responsibility. Diller says, "Parents of children who receive the diagnosis often describe the event as tremendously liberating and empowering. The idea that their problems are not of their own making but con-trolled by skewed brain chemistry and genetics represents salvation from a sense of failure" ("Culture" n. pag). Shockingly, while prescriptions of Ritalin to children diagnosed with ADD jumped 20% since 1989, the percentage of those receiving psychotherapy dropped from 40 to 25% (Huffington n. pag.). Such statistics show that health-care providers prefer relatively cheap drugs to costly

therapy. It also demonstrates our lazy culture's inclina-
tion to medicate social problems rather than act on them.
Diane McGuinness describes the crossroad in the debate
concerning ADD: "Research . . . indicates that ADD and
hyperactivity as 'syndromes' simply do not exist. We have
invented a disease, given it medical sanction, and now
must disown it. The major question is how we go about destroying the monster we have created . . . and still save
face" (Breggin n. pag.).

The brazen suitors show that to enjoy one's folly, a
man will embrace with dogmatic fervor any explanation
that relieves him of responsibility, even if the consequences of doing nothing are horrible. Odysseus re-
venges himself on the suitors, cracking open their skulls
and washing the floor in their blood (Homer 448-51).

The failure to correct the ADD fallacy will also have
serious consequences. One developmental psychologist at
UC Berkeley reports that children on Ritalin are three
times more likely to develop a taste for cocaine. The
Drug Enforcement Agency reports increasing Ritalin abuse
among adolescents. Huffington concludes, "When the government spends $16 billion a year on the drug war, and when
more than half those in jail are nonviolent drug offenders, isn't it time we connect the dots between prescription drugs and street drugs? How many more prisons do we
have to build to jail offenders who, earlier in life, we
have drugged with abandon?" (n. pag.). Not only are we
turning out Ritalin zombies; we have made the concepts
of self-discipline and freedom of choice obsolete. This
indicts our society, but the real tragedy is the child
whose life is needlessly and irreparably harmed.

In Odysseus's encounter with Polyphemus the Cyclops,
both Polyphemus and Odysseus first reject responsibility.
Polyphemus, the son of Poseidon, harbors no fear of Zeus.
For when Odysseus entreats him for hospitality in the
name of Zeus who guards all guests, the Cyclops contemp-
tuously eats two of Odysseus's men. Likewise, Odysseus,
whose lineage springs from Zeus, blinds the one-eyed son
of Poseidon to escape.

As the crew escapes, Odysseus taunts the Cyclops and
proudly announces who has humiliated Poseidon's son.
Polyphemus groans back: "Oh no, no--that prophesy years
ago. It all comes back to me with a vengeance now!

Telemus warned me all this would come to pass someday, that I'd be blinded here at the hands of one Odysseus. Come here, Odysseus, let me give you a guest gift and urge Poseidon . . . to speed you home. I am his son . . . and he will heal me if he pleases" (Homer 227). Polyphemus realizes his own reckless sacrilege caused his pain. Offering a guest gift shows his respect for Zeus.

Odysseus, however, brimming with indignation and pride, shows contempt for Poseidon in responding, "Heal you . . . Would to god I could strip you of life and breath and ship you down to the House of Death as surely as no one will heal your eye, not even your earthquake god himself!" (Homer 227-28). Odysseus's blind arrogance incurs Poseidon's wrath, and it takes 20 years of pounding, rocking, sea-sickening misery to clear his vision. Home at last, he must face another disaster his blindness allowed to happen--the suitors for his wife's hand.

Like Odysseus, we are no longer blind. Twenty-five years of drifting on a fallacy and sowing the seeds of disaster have passed. As the evidence mounts, we can no longer plead ignorance. ADD simply does not exist as the widespread condition psychiatry once claimed. Society must now decide whether it will acknowledge its culpability and minimize the damage, like Polyphemus, or turn a blind eye to the disastrous long-term effects, like Odysseus. Society should leave behind its fantastic explanations and prescription drugs, stop avoiding responsibility, and liberate itself from victimhood.

WORKS CITED

Breggin, Peter R. "Whose Attention Deficit Disorder Does Ritalin Test?' Center for the Study of Psychiatry and Psychology Online. <http://www.breggin.com/newyork times.html>. 2 Mar. 1999.

Breggin, Peter, and Ginger Ross Breggin. "The Hazards of Testing 'Attention-Deficit/Hyperactivity Disorder' with Methylphenidate (Ritalin)." Center for the Study of Psychiatry and Psychology. Online. <http://www.breggin. com/newyorktimes.html>.2 Mar. 1999.

Berzelay 6

Diller, Lawrence H. "The Culture of ADD." Online. n. pag.
    <http://www.docdiller.com/html/six-1.htm>.2 Mar. 1999.
Diller, Lawrence H. "Nearly 5 Million Americans Take
    Ritalin Daily." n. pag. Online. <http://www.docdiller.
    com>. 2 Mar. 1999.
Homer. Odyssey. New York: Penguin, 1997.
Huffington, Arianna. "U.S. Attention Deficit On Legal Drug
    Risk." Center for the Study of Psychiatry and Psychol-
    ogy. Online. <http://breggin.com/ritalinAH2.html>.
    2 Mar. 1999.

Discussion

1. Evaluate the sources used in this essay.
2. Is the author's focus primarily on the *Odyssey* as literature or on ADD?
3. Are there any flaws in the comparison between the two?

CHAPTER 16

Handbook of English

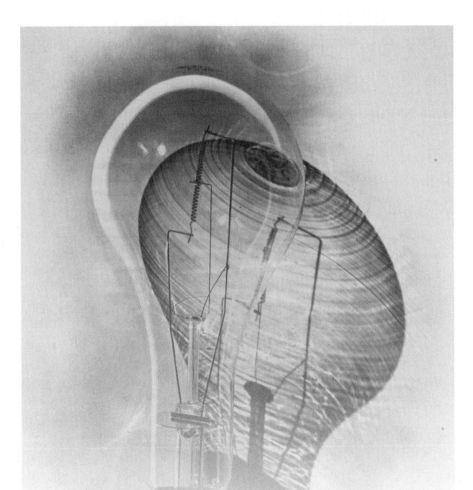

Sanity is perhaps the ability to punctuate.

W. H. AUDEN

You just can't trust the English language.

NEDRA LAMAR

There's only one "z" in "is."

GEORGE S. KAUFMAN

This handbook covers the most common, serious errors in punctuation, sentence structure, and usage. Refer to it *after* you've written your paper. Don't let commas distract you from stringing good ideas together or from searching for vivid, exact words to express your ideas. But *do* use the handbook before your final draft is printed. A great idea described with sentence fragments is like the Mona Lisa smoking a cigar—who could appreciate its beauty? In the résumé that lists your academic achievements, should you stumble over those three stooges—"their," "there," and "they're"—a potential employer may decide you might not be able to tell the difference between a debit and a credit either. When I started as a professional writer for magazines, an editor returned one of my submissions with four or five errors circled. He wrote, "I don't trust a person who can't spell."

CORRECT WRITING AND THE ENGLISH LANGUAGE

You know grammar is confusing. However, don't blame your English teachers. Our language's complicated rules simply record the various ways we use our language. If people hadn't been creative hundreds of years ago, we wouldn't have irregular verbs. If people in the past hadn't sometimes left out connecting words in sentences or experimented with new sentence structures, that tiny terror—the comma—might not even exist today. English teachers only report people's standard practice.

Imagine for a moment what it was like before we had a grammar system. William Caxton, the man who compiled the first English dictionary back in 1490, did so because he was fed up with all the varieties of English being used. There were no formal rules for language then, and people became so inventive, Caxton said he couldn't understand a book written in the English of 200 years earlier. The language had changed tremendously even since his own birth. Once, not far from his London home, Caxton grew hungry and knocked on a farmhouse door. He asked the woman who lived there if he could buy some eggs ("eggys") from her. The farm wife answered she didn't speak French. Caxton snapped back that he wasn't speaking French but "goode englishe." They needed a mediator to translate his "eggys" to her "eyren." After many such confusing incidents, Caxton decided the country needed a dictionary to make the meaning and spelling of words the same throughout the land. Over the next 200 years, people decided you should no longer capitalize or punctuate according to individual feeling, but only for definite reasons. Grammar "rules" were born.

Rules not only help us understand each other today, but slow down the historical evolution of English so we can understand our past and so future people can understand us. Study the following versions of the same biblical passage from different years. They are all correct English for their day:

About 1000 A.D.: Ure Faedir, þu þe eart on heofonum, si bin nama gehalgod. Tocume þin rice. Geweor þe þin willa on eorþan swa-swa on heofonum.

About 1390: Oure fadir that art in heuenes, halewid be thi name. This kyngdom come to. Be thi wille don in earthe as in heune.

1611: Our father which art in heauen, Halowed be thy name. Thy kingdom come. Thy will be done, in earth as it is in heauen.

1952: Our father who art in heaven, Hallowed be thy name. Thy kingdom come, Thy will be done. On earth as it is in heaven.

Notice how much more our language changed in the early years. This was largely the result of not having fixed rules. When the Normans invaded England in 1066, thousands of French words, spellings, and sentence structures simply mixed haphazardly with what the native English already spoke and wrote. Different regions went their own way, making governmental, cultural, educational, and even religious communication a nightmare. Caxton's dictionary and in 1611, King James's Bible, standardized English vocabulary, grammar, and usage.

Notice also that while change has slowed, it hasn't stopped. People are too creative for that. Grammar rules don't squash creativity, but they do make new ways of writing or talking prove themselves over time and across many regions of the country. Otherwise, thousands of new words and expressions like "bad" (meaning "good"), "gag me with a spoon," or "interface" (computerese for "communicate") would quickly become entrenched and make our communication problems worse. If new ideas weren't tested over time, a common ungrammatical expression like "alot" (a lot) might be accepted as standard English. Fine, except then future generations would need a new rule like this added: "You use an article ("a") before nouns except in the case of 'lot,' where it is incorporated into the noun itself." If millions of people do decide to break the current rule for several decades, "alot" will probably become standard English, and future students will ask, "What was wrong with those people?"

Many accepted contradictions exist as it is. It's spelled "realize" in Chicago, but "realise" in London. "The government *have* decided . . ." is correct in England because the British see collective nouns as plural. Americans see collectives like "government" and "committee" as singular, so they say, "The government *has* decided . . ." English can be plain weird: quicksand is slow, a boxing ring is square, and we park on a driveway and drive on a parkway.

▲ **PRACTICE 16-1:** Think of five contradictions in local, regional, or international English spelling, word meanings, or usage.

Rules of language are a *convenience*. There's no reason why "cat" can't be spelled "rat," "hat," or "lypd." The letters and sound of the word have no logical connection to the object they represent. **Language is simply an agreement people make that they will share these arbitrary definitions.** Communication and complex thoughts would be impossible without such an agreement. That agreement is called "standard English" and it is *the language used for government, education, business, and publishing—in other words the language that provides a person with money, prestige, power, and status.* Other, nonstandard forms of English, including "street" language, black English, teen slang, and others, compete with standard English for the "vote" of agreement about what means what. Nonstandard English is often creative and dramatic, but incorporating it into standard English complicates an already difficult system.

PUNCTUATION

Punctuation is a quiet signal to an experienced reader. You don't stop to think "What does that comma mean?" You absorb the punctuation without thinking, as you do with small words like "if" or "and."

When you mispunctuate, a reader can usually figure out what you intended to say. But you make her read twice what should only have to be read once, and you may give her an entirely wrong idea. For instance, reread the first sentence in this paragraph without the comma. Doesn't it sound for a second that you're punctuating a reader? Sometimes punctuation errors can be more serious. Look at these two sentences:

- All foreign fruit plants are free from duty.
- All foreign fruit, plants are free from duty.

The first means that young trees and bushes that will bear fruit may enter the country without paying an import fee. The second means all fruit as well as plants are duty free. The comma in 2 means two items are duty free. Number 1 was what Congress intended in a law it passed. But a congressional clerk punctuated incorrectly as it is in 2 and the error cost the United States $2 million in lost import taxes before the law could be reapproved without the comma.

＇ Comma

＇ 1. USE A COMMA TO SEPARATE AN INTRODUCTORY CLAUSE OR PHRASE FROM THE MAIN SUBJECT AND VERB OF THE SENTENCE. The comma signals the end of introductory words and the beginning of the sentence's main subject and verb. The typical English sentence starts with its subject (a noun), tells you what the subject does (the verb), and usually ends with a modifier that further explains what these two are up to.

Subject Verb   Modifier

    S   V   M

Amy reads science fiction novels.

    S   V   M

Jeremy hit a home run yesterday.

Even when sentences are more complicated, the "normal" pattern still holds:

              S   V   M

In a minute Cindy will drive us to the late show.

          S   V   M

My friend Diana wore a silver wig at the café after work on Tuesday.

If you *vary* this pattern by delaying the subject and verb, the comma tells the reader where the main actor and action of the sentence begin. When the modifier comes first as it does in this sentence and the reader is desperately looking for the main subject and verb, the writer must help the reader by marking the end of the introductory words with a comma (after the word "verb").

         INTRO   S V   M

If I get an "A" in Chemistry, I think I'll explode with joy.

Wearing only his track shoes and a smile, John dashed out of the locker room into class.

Since starting her new job this year, Marcella has been promoted twice.

MISLEADING: Thinking time had not been called Benny kept running toward the goal. (Time's name is not Benny. Insert a comma after "called.")

MISLEADING: Because he came back to school, after four years in the navy, Kevin thought he would forget all his math. (The first comma misleads us—delete it so a comma comes only at the *end* of the introduction.)

If it's a very short introductory phrase, there's no need for the comma because a good reader can see the entire sentence as a unit. Even if it's short, however, words that would confuse a reader if unpunctuated or words that are place markers need to be separated:

```
     INTRO      S   V   M
In a moment we'll join you.
```

When it rains I get so depressed.

Next to Janis, Bob is ugly. (Bob looks ugly when compared to Janis. If the comma followed "next," it would mean that Janis thought Bob was ugly.)

Secondly, the war proves humans still have a lot to learn. (place marker)

, **2. A COMMA SEPARATES ITEMS LISTED IN A SERIES.**

Mario walked into the faculty locker room by accident and found a pile of moldy papers, a textbook, and a retired Latin professor on the floor. He dropped his sneakers, socks, and towel.

The comma before the conjunction is preferred, but not necessary.

This rule also applies to a series of adjectives modifying the same noun—but *only* if you can substitute an "and" for the comma.

The Latin professor gave a long, musical, sputtering snore. His nose was a pinkish red and matched his pink, red, and tan socks.

WRONG: The professor gave a most, musical snore.

, **3. A COMMA SEPARATES TWO GROUPS OF WORDS THAT COULD BE PUNCTUATED AS SEPARATE SENTENCES WHEN THESE SENTENCES ARE JOINED BY A CONJUNCTION.** These are the conjunctions.

and

but

or

nor

for

so

This comma tells readers a complete thought has just ended, and they must regroup to look for a new subject and verb.

```
     S       V                    M                    C
Mario nudged the Latin Professor with one foot, and
```

```
        S         V              M
the professor muttered a few phrases from Cicero.
```

He could scream for help, or he could leave quietly and say nothing.

If the reader sees an "and" or other conjunction and *no comma,* the signal is different. It tells the reader that whatever is on the other side of the conjunction still refers back to the subject or verb on the first side:

```
     S      V  ┌───────M───────┐ ┌──────C──────┐
    Mario asked if the professor was hurt or if he could get

       ┌────────────────┐
    him a Latin text. ("Mario asked" applied to both "if" clauses.)
```

The professor grunted and said, "Julius Caesar was a Roman geezer." ("Professor" before the "and" applies to both verbs "grunted" and "said.")

Summary: When you come to any conjunction, separately read what is written before the conjunction and what is written after the conjunction. If *both* could be punctuated as complete sentences, you need a comma. If either part is a fragment, don't use a comma.

,   4. COMMAS SEPARATE NONESSENTIALS FROM THE MAIN SENTENCE.
This is one of the uses of commas that frequently occurs when you hear pauses in a sentence, but you will do better if you understand the logic behind it. When you have a *parenthetical comment,* that is a comment like this that sounds as though it belongs between parentheses, you need to separate it from the main sentence. It signals the reader that we are making a side trip into a less important area. To test whether you need commas, see if the sentence makes sense if you leave out the words in question.

```
     S   ┌───────M───────┐ ┌───V───┐ ┌M┐
    Mario, his pulse starting to race, began backing toward

       ┌────────────────┐
    the locker room door.
```

The Latin professor, who wore only gray tweed undershorts, shouted, "*Illiterati non carborundum.*"

Mario, however, was racing for the health office.

Remember, if the words in question are essential to understanding the sentence, *don't* use commas; they are meant only to set off extra information. Compare the following, both correct as they are:

George Smith, who plagiarized a term paper, was expelled from college.

All students who plagiarize term papers should be expelled from college.

The following sentences are both correct as they stand but have quite different meanings:

The president of the college says the professor is misinformed.

The president of the college, says the professor, is misinformed.

How would this sentence from the *Wall Street Journal* change if we removed the comma?

In the past decade small stocks returned 13 percent, above their 12 percent annual gain since 1926.

A group of words at the end of a sentence can also be considered extra information. If the words are necessary to the main idea in the sentence, *do not use a comma.*

Write all test answers in the blue book, remembering to skip lines. ("Remembering . . ." is extra information.)

The war is over because we starved the enemy into submission. (The *reason* the war is over is the key idea, so "because . . ." is necessary.)

Don't leave the party if you've been drinking. ("If . . . " is necessary.)

5. USE A COMMA TO SEPARATE QUOTATIONS FROM TAG LINES. (See the section on quotations on page 342.)

6. USE A COMMA AFTER THE GREETING IN A PERSONAL LETTER. BUSINESS LETTERS ARE INTRODUCED BY A COLON.

Dear Wendy,
Dear Senator Cumulous:

7. USE A COMMA TO SEPARATE DIRECT ADDRESS OF SOMEONE.

Sarah, would you come here?
I wish you'd look at this, Doctor.

8. USE A COMMA TO SEPARATE THE DAY FROM THE YEAR IN A DATE:

September 19, 2001.

9. USE A COMMA TO SEPARATE WHAT WOULD BE SEPARATE LINES IN AN ADDRESS:

I visited my former lawyer at Cellblock 33, 12 Dawson Street, Sing Sing Prison, San Francisco, California 92758.

▲ **PRACTICE 16-2:** Illustrate the first five comma rules by creating a sentence for each that uses commas correctly.

▲ **PRACTICE 16-3: Comma Exercise.** Correct any comma errors in the following:

TO: ALL STUDENTS   OCTOBER 31 2000

FROM: Dr. R. J. FACTOTUM, Dean of Academic Studies

RE: GRADUATION COMPETENCY EXAM

The college is instituting a competency examination which must
be passed to graduate so all students should study the follow- 5
ing questions carefully.

BIOLOGY PRACTICUM, Part 1. Create life with your Bunsen burner
a test tube and two spoonfuls of the cafeteria's jello.

Part 2. After your professor approves your life-form you should
make it evolve to the level of an earthworm or a TV talk show 10
host whichever comes first.

BIOLOGY WRITTEN TEST. The platypus lays eggs like a bird, swims
like a fish, and has hair like a mammal but it has no wings,
gills, or eyelashes. If a female platypus were to mate with a
polar bear describe the genetic makeup of the offspring and 15
draw an accurate lab sketch.

PHILOSOPHY. Using Socratic and Aristotelian methods of inquiry
explain life. What will humans assuming they still exist then
believe life means in the year 2050? Be concise, and specific.

ENGLISH. From memory, rewrite <u>Moby Dick</u>, also called <u>The Whale</u> 20
or <u>Hamlet</u>.

MATH, Part 1. Applying the principles of probability studied
in Math 151 you must defeat your math professor at blackjack
poker or gin rummy. A deck of unmarked unopened cards must be
supplied by the student.   25

Part 2. Students must divide any number by zero, and record the
result if they live.

Answer Key to Comma Practice 16-3

Line
  1. Separate day from year in date. "... 31, 2000 ..."
  5. Separate two complete sentences joined by a conjunction. "... gradu-
     ate, so ..."
  8. Separate items in a series. "... burner, a test tube ..." Comma after
     "tube" is optional, but be consistent.
  9. Separate introductory words. "... form, you ..."

11. Separate nonessential information at. ". . . host, whichever . . ."
13. Separate two complete sentences joined by conjunction. ". . . mammal, but . . ."
15. Separate introductory words. ". . . bear, describe . . ."
17. Separate introductory words. ". . . inquiry, explain . . ."
18. Separate parenthetical, nonessential information. ". . . humans, assuming they still exist then, believe . . ."
19. No comma before conjunction unless there are two sentences. ". . . concise and . . ."
20. Separate end of parenthetical material. ". . . *Whale*, or . . ."
23. Separate introductory material. ". . . 151, you . . ."
23. Separate items in a series. ". . . blackjack, poker . . ." Comma after "poker" is optional.
24. Separate items in a series. ". . . unmarked, unopened . . ."
26. No comma before conjunction unless there are two sentences. ". . . zero and . . ."

; Semicolon

; SEMICOLONS CONNECT TWO COMPLETE SENTENCES THAT ARE CLOSELY RELATED. To test whether a semicolon is correct, read the words on each side of the semicolon; each side must stand independently as a complete sentence.

> Hawaii has the Liberty Bowl; Florida has the Gator Bowl.
>
> We can satisfy almost all our energy needs with solar power; the main energy needed is the effort to pass the laws.
>
> **Wrong:** Our soccer team lost by a 7–4 score; even though they had twice as many shots on goal as our opponents.
>
> **Wrong:** There are two billion hungry people on earth, that's more than all the people who lived in the entire nineteenth century!

Do *not* use a semicolon when two sentences are joined by a conjunction; a comma is used there.

> **Wrong:** The boss wants sales; and he wants them now.

Do use a semicolon if two sentences are separated by what's called a conjunctive adverb. You don't need to memorize that term, but recognize the most common ones, which are "however," "therefore," "yet," and "nevertheless."

> Colorado River University may have carp in its river, but Colorado Creek College has trout in its pond.
>
> Colorado River University may have carp in its river; however, Colorado Creek College has trout in its pond.

⦂ Colon

A COLON'S MAIN USE IS TO EMPHASIZE A SHARP BREAK BETWEEN A STATEMENT AND SOMETHING THAT FOLLOWS: A LIST, A COMMENT, A QUOTATION, A QUESTION, OR AN EXPLANATION. Hint: Think of a colon as meaning "that is" or "namely." If one of these sounds right, a colon is your best choice.

> Three things would make the Student Union perfect: a popcorn vendor, sawdust spread on the floor, and a ringmaster.

> Everyone should remember Henry David Thoreau's last words: "Moose, Indian."

Because the colon is used only when you want to make a dramatic break, do not use it when your list or explanation follows *smoothly* from what comes before:

> **WRONG:** This handbook consists of: rules, rules, and more rules.

▲ **PRACTICE 16-4:** Create a sentence using a semicolon correctly and another correctly using a colon.

Other Punctuation

! **EXCLAMATION POINT** They're overused! They shout too much!! Save them for big moments!!! Don't use more than one!

— **DASH** You are never required to use a dash—commas, colon, or parentheses can always substitute for the dash, for it **separates a nonessential part of the sentence from the main idea** (see comma rule 4). A dash has more flair than commas, and for this reason poets—Emily Dickinson, for instance—like to use them.

> Professor Snerdman—a burly bull of a man with a flaming shock of red hair—charges into his lectures just looking for a student foolish enough to wave his hand.

- **HYPHEN** A hyphen indicates **a word split** at the end of a typed line. *Only divide words at syllable breaks*—which are indicated in dictionaries. Hyphens also **connect groups of words that function as a single unit:** a happy-go-lucky boss is not a happy boss, go boss, or lucky boss. If you can substitute an "and" at the problem location, use a comma.

> sister-in-law
>
> my thirty-first birthday
>
> two-thirds vote
>
> the hairy, old horse

( ) **PARENTHESES Parentheses separate nonessential information** (definitions, citations for sources, or by-the-way comments like this) from the main text. No punctuation marks should precede a parenthesis, and all punctuation that normally would come at that point should follow the end parenthesis mark. (The exception is a parenthetical statement that is a complete sentence, like this one.)

> When General Motors fired the Flint auto workers (7,000 in August and another 6,000 in October), the city's tax base collapsed.

> General Motors fired 13,000 Flint auto workers in August and October. (The city's tax base collapsed.)

" " QUOTATION MARKS

1. Put quotation marks around the titles of short works. (poems, articles, chapters of books), but use italics or underlining to indicate works long enough to be published on their own (books, long plays, magazines, newspapers).

> In his research paper, Michael documented the following sources: <u>The Missoula Times-Union</u>, O. Henry's "The Gift of the Magi," <u>Jaws</u>, a <u>Newsweek</u> article called "Bloodshot in Boise," and the entry "Worms" in <u>The Encyclopedia Americana</u>.

" " 2. Use quotation marks to indicate speech reported word for word. If you're doing research, you must record exactly what the writer wrote. If you want to leave out some of what was said, use ellipses marks (3 or 4 dots). Three dots mean you've left out part of a sentence; 4 dots mean you've left out a sentence or more or you've left off the end of the sentence you're quoting.

> The press secretary reported, "President Nixon left 3,500 hours of tapes, 10,650 pages of diary . . . and 45 recorded dinner conversations with his wife."

> Joseph Campbell's best advice was, "Follow your bliss."

If you're writing **dialogue in a narrative,** you also must use quotation marks around what the speakers say. If you don't feel you can report accurately, summarize and *do not* use quotation marks.

> "What a blast!" Billy yelled as he lit the fuse.

> As he lit the fuse, Billy said he was having a blast.

If people speak aloud in anything you write, these guidelines clarify what's happening:

- Never quote two or more people in dialogue in the same paragraph. If a second person speaks, start a new paragraph, even if only for one word.

- Use *tag lines* to identify speakers. A simple "he said" is usually better than "he threateningly implied." In dialogue between only two people, you may leave the tag lines out once in a while if it's clear who is speaking.
- Punctuate tag lines with commas.
- People's thoughts are *not* put in quotation marks.

Sample Dialogue

> Greg approached the registration counter waving a letter. "This says I can't graduate," he said.
> "That's right," the secretary said. "See, you haven't completed your program's new course in witchcraft."
> "Witchcraft! I'm going into computers."
> "Well," she said, "maybe the college curriculum committee thinks you need a broader perspective." Great, Greg thought.

66 99   **3. Use quotation marks around a word or phrase being referred to as a word.**

> The word "computer" comes from "compute."

> I want to examine the term "software."

6 9   **4. Use single quotation marks for quotations within a quotation.**

> Doctor Seaver says, "We must understand poverty, not simply 'pity the suffering of the poor,' as my colleague stated."

Single quotation marks are made by striking the apostrophe key on keyboards.

66 99   **5. Punctuating Quotations.** At the end of quotations, periods and commas go before the quotation mark; semicolons and colons follow it. Question marks and exclamation marks go before the end quotation if they are part of the quotation, after it if they apply to the sentence as a whole.

> Merle said, "trick or treat"; then he snapped open his suitcase.

> How can we elect a man who says, "Kiss my grits"?

> Darren's last question was, "What's for supper?"

Do *not* combine a comma with other punctuation marks in quotations.

9   **APOSTROPHE**

1. Use an apostrophe to form a contraction; the apostrophe is located where the missing letters normally would be.

> don't (do not)

> who's (who is)

❯ **2. Use an apostrophe to form possessives.** To form the possessive of *all singular nouns* (including those already ending in "s") and *plural* nouns *not* ending in "s," simply add " 's."

> Pete's ball
>
> James's hat
>
> men's cars
>
> people's park

For plural nouns already ending in "s," only add an apostrophe.

> schools' rules
>
> enemies' weapons
>
> cats' tails

What does the following sentence mean? "I saw cats' eyes staring at me from the woods." It means more than one cat was staring. If it had been "cat's," only one cat was staring.

When grammarians codified the English language, the apostrophe's two uses ran into conflict where they overlapped: at the possesive pronouns. They decided to award the apostrophe to the contractions—who's (who is) and it's (it is)—and to allow the possessive pronouns to be possessive even though they don't have apostrophes: whose, its, his, ours, hers, and so on.

> It's raining outside.
>
> The sky let loose its heavy rains.
>
> Who's coming to the party?
>
> Whose party is it?

▲ **PRACTICE 16-5:** Write a series of sentences that correctly use a dash, a hyphen in a compound word, titles of a chapter and a book, a quotation, a contraction, and a possessive plural. Circle each use.

CAPITALIZATION

1. Capitalize the first word in every sentence or intentional sentence fragment.

2. Capitalize the first letter of all words in a proper noun.

A proper noun is the name of a specific person, place, thing, organization, or event.

Frederick Douglass

South Carolina

Orange County

Cobb's Hill

Lake Ontario

the planet Earth

October

the Northeast

Kodak Corporation

Webster's New World Dictionary

Tuesday

Grandma (but "my grandmother")

Do *not* capitalize the seasons (winter) or general directions (Go northeast a mile).

3. Capitalize the first word and all important words in a title.

The Moon and Sixpence

A Dance of Thieves

"Rommel the Desert Fox"

▲ **PRACTICE 16-6: Punctuation Exercise.** Correct any errors in punctuation and capitalization in the following:

May 2, 2000
12 Pit Road
Citrus, FL 32881

Marla G. Snooker
President   5
Snooker sales corp.
17 Lemon Lane
Citrus, FL 32881

Dear President Snooker,

I regret that my wife Loretta and I will not be able to attend   10
the companys annual dinner dance at the Elegant Memories diner.
Since Loretta returned to college full time I'm living with a
human volcano and its tough keeping up with her. She tears
through four classes, and three hours in the library. When
Loretta and I arrive home she's still full of energy, however,   15
I'm ready for a nap.

All of a sudden she knows about Psychology and even talks to me in spanish. She wants to discuss "Hamlet" and Ode to Joy with me. It's wonderful she's learning so much but I'm worn out listening. At 2 a.m. she'll be reading that yellow marker at- 20 tached to her hand.

"Do you feel like discussing picassos paintings?" she'll say. "It's 2 a.m.!" I'll groan. "Put some zip in your life," she'll say.

A four-hour party will kill me and Loretta has to finish her re- 25 search paper about illegal whale hunting. There's one thing I need most rest. I hope that you our president will understand.

Sincerely,

Boris Backwater

Boris Backwater

Key to Practice 16-6

Line

6. "... Sales Corp." Capitalize proper nouns.
9. "... Snooker:" Colon used in greeting of formal letter.
10. "... wife, Loretta, and ..." Separate interrupter with commas. Dashes acceptable instead of commas.
11. "company's" Possessive requires apostrophe.
11. "Diner" Capitalize proper noun.
12. "... time, I'm ..." Comma separates introductory material.
13. "... volcano, and ..." Comma separates two complete sentences joined by conjunction.
13. "it's." Contraction, not possessive.
14. "... classes and ..." Comma before conjunction *only* if it joins two complete sentences. There's just one here.
15. "... home, she's ..." Comma separates introductory words.
15. "... energy; however ..." Semicolon joins two complete sentences when "however" or "therefore" is used. A comma would be used if "but" had been used.
17. "psychology" It's generic, not a proper noun.
18. "Spanish." Capitalize words derived from proper nouns (Spain).
18. Hamlet should be underlined or italicized as a book-length work.
19. "Ode to Joy" must have quotation marks around it—title of a short work.
19. "... much, but ..." Comma separates two complete sentences joined by conjunction.
20. "... reading, that ..." Comma separates nonessential information (unless she's really reading the marker).

22. "Picasso's"—Capitalize people's names and use apostrophe for the possessive.
24. New paragraph before "It's." A new paragraph starts when there's a second speaker quoted.
24. New paragraph before "Put."
25. "... me, and ..." Comma separates two complete sentences joined with a conjunction.
27. "... most: rest." Colon (or dash) should mark the sharp break.
27. "... you, our president, will ..." Commas separate nonessential interrupters. Dashes OK too.

 ## SENTENCE STRUCTURE

Sentence Fragment

The "normal" English sentence has a subject, verb, and possibly a modifier. Anything less is a sentence fragment or incomplete sentence. Why do English teachers make a big deal about it? Because it shows whether or not you recognize the basic unit of the language.

Most sentence fragments are not like the following: "John the house early" or "Left the house early." Most fragments occur in complex collections of words where one of two things usually happens: the writer, nervous about writing a long sentence, makes a break even though there's no grammatical reason, or the writer confuses a verb *form* with a main verb. Look at these examples:

FRAGMENT: Margaret put away her teddy bear, kissed her goldfish goodbye, and tore up the photos of her high school boyfriend when she headed off to college. Which turned out to have more fish than good-looking guys.

FRAGMENT: The first college guy she dated reminded her of her guppy. Because he puckered every time she looked at him.

FRAGMENT: Margaret asked the guy to take her to the aquarium to meet his family, and he agreed. Making her wish for the boys of high school.

All three examples are typical fragments that should be attached to the previous sentence. There's no theoretical limit to the length of an English sentence (James Joyce may hold the record with a 50-page sentence in *Ulysses*). The first example lacks a subject in the second part—it needs to refer back to "college" to make sense. The second fragment does have a subject and verb, but it also begins with a "because," which turns what follows into a *dependent clause*. It *depends* on the first part to have complete meaning. The third has a verb form ("making"), but it is a participle, not a main verb, and lacks a subject.

Beware of these key words:

- because
- since
- if
- although
- as
- who
- which
- verbs ending in "ing"

If any of these words begin a sentence, it should be in an introductory phrase or clause with a comma separating it from the main subject and verb. If there is no such place, you've probably written a sentence fragment that should be joined to the sentence that preceded it.

There are legitimate uses of sentence fragments: use them to answer your own rhetorical question or in dramatic scenes to create a fragmented impression.

LEGITIMATE FRAGMENT: Why do politicians lie to the public? Because the public wants to be lied to.

LEGITIMATE FRAGMENTS: Whack! The stick caught the side of his head. Whack. Dizzy. Spinning images of the windows. Whack! Sal went down.

Run-On Sentence (Comma Splice)

A *run-on sentence is two sentences joined together without proper punctuation.* What difference does it make? Here is an actual invitation some professors at my college received for an end-of-the-semester party: "Come to the party and forget your exams, spouses and other attached persons are welcome." We all thought it was going to be a wild party until realizing, at the end of the sentence, that we were only to forget exams. In this case the writer should have either substituted a semicolon for the comma or put a period there and capitalized the "s" in spouses.

RUN-ON: From the parking lot, Emily listened to the roar of the jets landing at the airport she wished she were going somewhere. (Period or semicolon needed after "airport.")

RUN-ON: Tom's biology experiment had an unexpected result, his frog grabbed a scalpel and hopped for freedom. (Semicolon needed after "result.")

RUN-ON: The security guards pursued the frog toward the student cafeteria, however, the amphibian made good its escape. (Semicolon needed before "however." If a "but" had been there, a comma would be proper.)

It may help you to understand sentence structure better if we examine the **three types of sentences: simple, compound, and complex.** The following abbreviations are used:

S—subject of sentence

V—verb of sentence

M—modifier

C—conjunction

DCl—dependent clause

                                                              S   V   M

Simple Sentence (SVM): Tran Loc wished to study English.

                                                                S   V   M

Compound Sentence (SVM, CSVM): Tran Loc wished to study English,

C S V   M

but it was painfully slow work.

                                                                          DCl

Complex Sentence (DCl, SVM *or* SVM DCl): Because there were so

                                            S   V   M

many irregular verbs, learning English was painfully slow work.

                                                                       S   V

Compound, Complex Sentence (SVM, C DCl, SVM): Tran Loc wished

         M   C   DCl   S V

to study English, but because there were so many irregular verbs, it was

        M

painfully slow.

▲ **PRACTICE 16-7:** Write one sample sentence of your own to illustrate each of the four types of sentences. Label the parts as illustrated here.

Misplaced Modifiers

A modifier is a word or group of words that describes or adds details to another word or group of words. Italicized sections are modifiers:

He played *the Baldwin grand piano.*

With tenderness, Randolph rocked *the beautiful, bald baby.*

The modifier must be placed next to the thing it modifies, or it may accidentally describe something else with comic results:

MISPLACED: For Sale: One maple table by elderly lady *with chipped legs.* (an actual newspaper ad)

MISPLACED: I was on my way to the doctor's *with rear end trouble* when my car's rear axle gave way, causing the accident. (from an actual insurance claim form)

MISPLACED: The accident was caused by a little guy in a small car *with a big mouth.*

The placement of one modifying word can change the meaning of a sentence. How do the following sentences differ?

In the poker game John almost won $500.

In the poker game John won almost $500.

Consider this gruesome, unintended meaning I once found in a paper:

MISPLACED: The police arrested a man in the Mt. Hope Cemetery who said he was digging up corpses trying to make some extra money.

CORRECTED: The police arrested a man digging up corpses in the Mt. Hope Cemetery; he said he was doing it to make some extra money.

▲ **PRACTICE 16-8:** Correct any sentence fragments, run-ons, or misplaced modifiers your professor marked on your last paper.

▲ **PRACTICE 16-9: Sentence Structure Exercise.** Correct any run-on sentences, sentence fragments, or misplaced modifiers in the following:

WHAT YOUR PROFESSOR'S OFFICE TELLS YOU

A Campus News Special Report
Angela Johnson, Social Editor

So you're thinking about visiting your professor in his office? Cornering the lion in his den. As a veteran faculty-watcher, let me tip off incoming freshmen about what to expect.

Relax if you see family pictures on the professor's desk, a child's hand-made pencil holder or a finger painting means you're in real luck. You might even be offered a cup of coffee, this professor is a pussycat, no lion. With chubby, sticky cheeks, your professor loves children; how can you go wrong?

But covered with debris and centuries of dust, the professor in the messy office will be a trial. You won't be able to sit though, he'll have the chair stacked with old magazines and memos. Which he can't find time to read because he worries about the meaning of life and where his grade book is.

Professor Neat, is a steel trap. Beware! A polished desk, an empty wastebasket, and a coat hung on a hanger instead of flung over a chair are warning signs, you should enter with care. Because Professor Neat plans to vacuum clean your mind with ruthless efficiency.

AGREEMENT

"Agreement" means the parts of a sentence are in harmony so readers are not confused. Here are three kinds of agreement to strive for.

Tense

All verbs must agree in tense unless you clearly prepare a reader for a time shift. Generally speaking, if your essay starts in the past tense, it should use the past tense throughout. Stay in the present if you start there.

Jose *came* to my house and *asked* to use my encyclopedia.

Jose *comes* to my house and *asks* to use my encyclopedia.

Jose *came* to my house often, but now that he *has* his own encyclopedia, he *stays* away. ("Now" prepares us for time shift.)

WRONG: Jose *came* to my house and *asks* to use my encyclopedia.

Subject–Verb Agreement

Subjects and their verbs must agree, meaning singular subjects require singular verbs and plural subjects require plural verbs.

A *collective noun* is a subject that includes many individuals but is thought of as one unit (singular) for a verb.

The wolf pack devours deer. (singular)

Wolves devour deer. (plural)

The community is going bankrupt. (collective singular)

Many area businesses are going bankrupt. (plural)

The government decides who is drafted. (collective singular)

Bureaucrats decide who is drafted. (plural)

Everyone is writing a paper this week. (collective singular)

All students are writing papers this week. (plural)

Noun–Pronoun Agreement

Pronouns represent nouns and must therefore be of the same gender and number (singular or plural) as the nouns they represent.

Paul wants *his* paper typed.

The dog doesn't care if *its* paper is typed.

Everyone wants *her* hair short these days.

WRONG: Everyone wants their papers typed. (his/her/one's)

WRONG: A paper should show their writer's style. (its)

▲ **PRACTIVE 16-10: Agreement Exercise.** Correct the agreement of tense, subject–verb, and noun–pronoun in the following:

CATCH THE VIRUS!

Consider a career in computer technology. They're not as hard to learn as everyone in society think they are. Anyone with an education in computers have hundreds of jobs waiting for them at graduation. Computers won't "byte" even though it has a mouse. And the terminology that seems so hard at first will get easier. A class of students learn the basic commands in one week and moved on to word processing one's papers during the first month. Get online today!

 ## SPELLING

I am a bad speller. I *need* a dictionary so I don't look stupid. For the past 35 years I have had to say to myself, "i" before "e" except after "c" everytime I've spelled "believe" or "receive." (But this does not apply to "foreign" or "neighbor.") Spelling just doesn't "come" to some people, and I expect I'll always rely on a dictionary more than most people do.

For the same reason people judge others based on looks or clothes, readers judge ideas and writing skills partly by the surface appearance of the paper. Fair or not, it's done. So the final task before typing any paper is to check the spelling of all words you're not 100 percent certain. It'll be worth the two minutes it takes. If you simply can't find a word, look up a synonym in a dictionary or thesaurus and your word may appear in the definition.

By the way, don't rely on your word processor's spell-checker to catch more than 75 percent of your misspellings. "My hat was a white pail" looks just fine to most computers, even though you meant, "My cat has a white tail."

Numbers

Spell out numbers under ten and spell out all numbers (even those under ten) that start sentences. Numbers over ten can be written as numerals. *But* if you compare numbers, both numbers must be in the same format.

- At the conference, five women arrived late.
- Twenty-five men left before noon.
- We saw 15 people leave after lunch.
- By the end of the day, 8 of 42 people remained.

DICTIONARY OF USAGE

The 25 Most Commonly Misused Words in English

advice, advise

Advice is a noun, meaning "guidance."

His father's advice was to study liberal arts.

Advise is a verb, meaning "counsel" or "give advice to."

His father advised him to study liberal arts.

affect, effect

Affect is a verb that means "influence."

The president's budget cuts affected public television.

Effect may be either a noun or verb, although it is used as a noun about 99 percent of the time. As a verb, it means "accomplish."

The president's public television cuts effected a $2 million savings nationwide.

As a noun, *effect* means "impact" or "result."

The cuts have had two effects locally: longer auctions and longer membership drives.

all right

"Alright" is not standard English.

a lot

This is the only way it appears; don't use "alot" in such sentences as this: "Don't make a lot of spelling mistakes."

The word "allot" is a verb, meaning to "distribute shares."

among, between

Between is used with two items or persons.

After graduating, he had to choose between a career in business and working for his father.

Among is used with three or more items.

> After graduating, he had to choose among a career in business, working for his father, or continuing for a master's degree.

amount, number

Amount is used with uncountable things.

> An amazing amount of work goes into completing a college course.

Number is used with countable things.

> What number of hours do you study for an average college course?

Amount applies to sand, weight, and volumes. But if you count the grains of sand in your navel someday, it will be a number, not an amount.

Number applies to people, years, and dollars.

beside, besides

Beside means "next to."

> My husband stands beside me.

Besides means either "in addition to" or "also."

> He does the laundry and babysits. Besides, he listens to my complaints.

etc.

Try to avoid *etc.* It sounds lazy. If you do use it, don't write "and *etc.*" *Etc.* means "and others."

farther, further

Farther means "a greater distance," and should be used only to refer to space and time.

> If I have to travel any farther between classes, I'm going to wear roller skates to school.

Further means "more" or "besides." It's used with ideas or abstractions.

> Our professor is always saying, "Let's go into that further." And after we exhaust the topic, he always seems to say, "further, we should consider . . ."

few, little

Few is used with countable items.

> Few students know this college was once a prison farm.

Little is used with uncountable items.

> Some would say how little the place has changed.

good, well

Good is an adjective and should always modify a noun, never a verb.

> Her essay made several good proposals.

> **Wrong:** She runs good. She feels good. She talks good.

Well is an adverb and should modify a verb.

She runs well, feels well, and talks well.

its, it's

Its is the possessive of "it"; it's means "it is."

It's a shame a deer can't shoot back at its hunters.

lie, lay

To lie means "to recline" and should be used if the reclining object or person can be thought of as doing it under its own power.

He lies down. The dog lies in the shade.

To lay means "to put in place" and should be used if another person or force puts the object in that position.

Dad lays the baby in the crib. I lay the book on the table.

Lie and lay are complicated because they're irregular verbs and the past tense of lie is the same as the present tense of lay.

Lie	Lay
I lie down. (today)	I lay it down. (today)
I lay down. (yesterday)	I laid it down. (yesterday)
I have lain down.	I have laid it down.
I am lying down.	I am laying it down.
I was lying down.	I was laying it down.

mad, angry

Mad means "insane." A person can be mad, but not "mad at" you. Use "angry."

might of

"Might of," "could of," "would of," "should of," and "must of" do not exist as English verbs. "Of" should be the helping verb "have."

Inez should have used "have" when she wrote the note to her teacher that said: "I must of got a hundred on the test—I studied all afternoon."

We may confuse this because the contraction "might've" (might have) sounds like the incorrect form.

prejudice

This requires a "d" ending when used with a helper verb—"is," "was," "are," or "were."

Dorothy is prejudiced.

raise, rise

Similar to the difference between lay and lie. You raise an object or person, but you rise yourself.

Bill raised his fist when he won the 100-yard dash.

Peter had to rise from where he'd fallen on the track to see his opponent celebrate.

than, then

Than is comparative.

Alaska has fewer people than Rhode Island.

Then refers to time.

Then we drove home.

that, which, and who

Who should be used to refer to people. *That* and *which* are used to refer to things or ideas.

Amy, *who* led the team to the state finals, broke her ankle in the final minutes of the regular-season game, an accident *that* cost the team its playoff game.

WRONG: The man that lives next door is bald.

there, they're, their

There refers to a place, *they're* is a contraction for "they are," and *their* is the possessive of "they."

They're going to take *their* tennis game over *there* on court three.

to, too

If you mean "very" or "also," use "too." Hint: The extra "o" suggests excess.

It's too hot to go anywhere; it's humid too.

try to

People often say "try and" when they mean *try to*.

We'll try to start the engine.

WRONG: Lets' try and go to the party.

unique

Unique means one of a kind, not just unusual.

Moe is unique if he has antennae and speaks Martian.

very, so

Avoid using either of these to intensify description. Usually, you can find a better word altogether, and most of the time just leaving out the *very* or *so* makes the description stronger.

WEAK: The very strong wind blew Paul across the courtyard.

BETTER: The strong wind blew Paul across the courtyard.

BEST: The howling gust blew Paul across the courtyard.

your, you're

Misusing these is a professional embarrassment. *Your* is possessive; *you're* is the contraction for "you are."

You're going to get in trouble if you misuse *your* words, but *you're* going to be a star if *your* writing is correct as well as lively.

▲ **PRACTICE 16-11: Word Usage Exercise.** Correct any errors of usage and spelling:

```
              ATTENTION!! JOB OPENING!!

COMMUNICATION MANAGER FOR SMALL COMPANY

   Young company desperatly requires writing advise. We do al-
right with manufacturing, but our lack of a communications man-
ager has begun to effect sales alot.
   If your graduating and are a very, very good writer, forward
you're  résumé to us by June 15. Depending on the total amount
recieved, we will notify applicants of interviews by July 1.
Applicants that are successful should of written reports, let-
ters, etc.
   We'll look farther into the qualifications of the best three
applicants at the interview. Their going to lie down ten rules
for good writing and than demonstrate what affect each rule
will have on business communications. The person we hire should
speak good and be ambitious. The best between the three final-
ists can start immediately. We need all the help we can get.
CONTACT: Personel Department
              Wordsmith Sign Company
```

▲ **PRACTICE 16-12: Summary Exercise.** For each of the following, write a sentence that:

1. Starts with "because," "since," or "if."
2. Has a "however" in the middle.
3. Contains two sentences joined with an "and."
4. Uses a colon.
5. Includes a quotation.
6. Includes a complete date and complete address.
7. Uses a singular possessive.
8. Uses a plural possessive.
9. Contains an interrupter phrase.
10. Has a dash.
11. Is followed by a legitimate sentence fragment.
12. Includes two words in the usage section that you have had trouble with.
13. Includes a semicolon.
14. Includes two words you frequently misspell.

▲ **PRACTICE 16-13: Summary Exercise.** Correct any errors in punctuation, sentence structure, spelling, or usage in the following:

December 3, 2000

Wade Biggs
Personnel Director
Fudge Motors, Inc.
Detroit, Michigan 11391

Dear Mr. Biggs,

Attached to this letter you will find my résumé. Which lists my employment and academic background. I hope your still considering me for the job in the swedish division of the company.

I used to make alot of errors in English but I received some good advise from one of my prof's at college, and now I write good. My prof told me the kind of affect bad grammar has on a potential employer who has hundreds of people to choose between. I know I'll go farther if I know how to use a semicolon; as in this sentence. Its important, to, knowing the difference among words like "amount" and "number." When you study wrighting since Third Grade as I have you soon learn to punctuate and use correct sentence structure. Although its hard sometimes if you hav'nt lain the rules down in front of yourself.

Commas for instance should mark two sentences connected with a conjunction. They also set off interrupters, these words block the flow of a sentence. Sitting like a frog flattened in the road, my prof told us to watch out for the sentence fragment. "Beware the galloping run-on he lectured us and shun the frivolous, comma." After I memorized these rules I knew I'd be an employee any company would of been proud to hire.

Sincerely,

Gustov Osterly

Gustov Osterly

▲ **PRACTICE 16-14:** Write a letter to the students who will take your writing course next term. Give them advice that will help them do well, and close by explaining two grammar or usage rules they must know. Give an illustration for each.

NOTE: Additional practices in mechanics are in *The Instructor's Manual.*

INDEX

A TROUBLESHOOTING GUIDE TO WRITING

Note: Many of these "problems" are normal procedure for most writers.

Problem	Possible Causes	Possible Cures	Chapter Reference
I don't know what to write about.	Unclear about assignment or purpose in writing.	Reread text. Reread assignment. Ask professor.	10–15
	Unclear about audience.	Visualize an audience and write to it.	1, 12 13, 14
I can't get started.	No ideas or vague ideas. Insufficient detail or visualization.	Brain teasers.	2–3
	Introduction jitters.	Start with main idea. Use intro brain teaser.	6
	Insecure about thinking. Fear of risk.	Overcome blocks and strive for honesty.	3 1
I start but then stall.	Ideas fuzzy or incomplete.	More brain teasers.	3
	Poor writing environment. Fear of messiness/risk.	Overcome these blocks.	6
I can't put my ideas or notes together.	You need a main point or heading for notes.	Work on thesis/outline.	5
I keep writing around the same idea—going nowhere.	Insufficient ideas/details.	More brain teasers.	2–3
	Redundancy.	Cut to essential idea.	7–8
I know what I want to say but not how to say it.	Word paralysis.	Freewrite, loop, or try oral composition. Talk to peers.	5–6